To Michael Boggs Matthews

Mike, you are a fantastic son as well as a great backpacking, swimming, and travel partner. In the last year you have accomplished more, through your own hard work, than most people do in a lifetime. As you turn 18 and graduate from high school, I am as proud of you as any father has ever been.

Dad

About the Author

Marty Matthews has used computers for over 40 years, from some of the early mainframe computers to recent personal computers. He has done this as a programmer, systems analyst, manager, vice president, and president of a software firm. As a result, he has first-hand knowledge of not only how to program and use a computer, but also how to make the best use of the information a computer can produce.

Twenty-five years ago Marty wrote his first computer book on how to buy mini-computers. Over 20 years ago Marty and his wife Carole began writing books as a major part of their occupation. They have written over 60 books, including ones on desktop publishing, web publishing, Microsoft Office, and Microsoft operating systems from MS-DOS through Windows Server 2003. Recent books published by **McGraw-Hill**/Osborne include *Windows Server 2003: A Beginner's* Guide, *Windows XP Professional: A Beginner's* Guide, *FrontPage 2003: The Complete Reference*, and *Windows 2000: A Beginner's Guide.*

Marty, Carole, and their son live on an island in Puget Sound where, on the rare moments when they can look up from their computers, they look west across seven miles of water and the main shipping channel to the snow-capped Olympic Mountains.

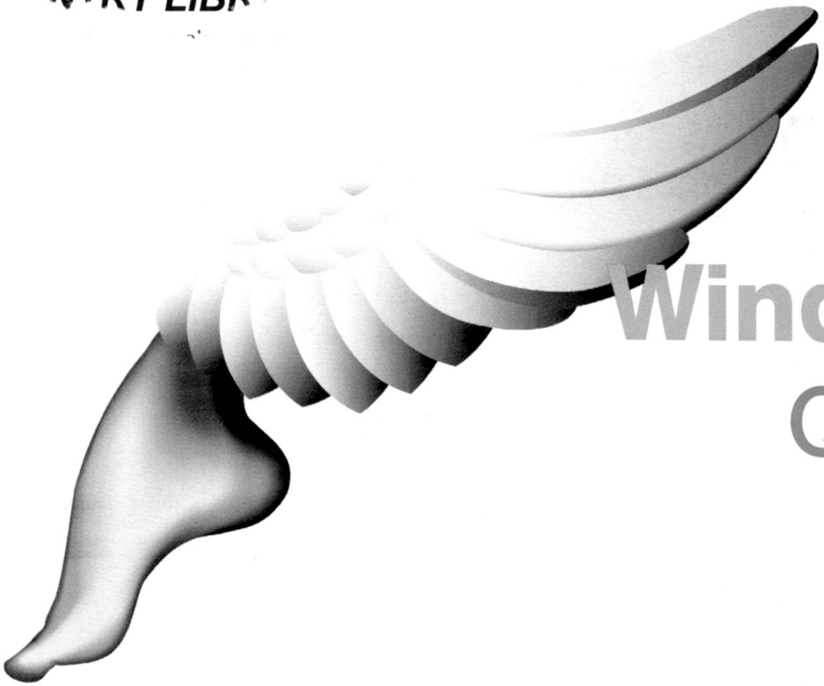

Windows® XP QuickSteps

MARTY MATTHEWS

McGraw-Hill/Osborne
New York Chicago San Francisco
Lisbon London Madrid Mexico City
Milan New Delhi San Juan
Seoul Singapore Sydney Toronto

McGraw-Hill/Osborne
2100 Powell Street, 10th Floor
Emeryville, California 94608
U.S.A.

To arrange bulk purchase discounts for sales promotions, premiums, or fund-raisers, please contact McGraw-Hill/Osborne at the above address. For information on translations or book distributors outside the U.S.A., please see the International Contact Information page immediately following the index of this book.

This book was composed with Adobe® InDesign®

Information has been obtained by McGraw-Hill/Osborne from sources believed to be reliable. However, because of the possibility of human or mechanical error by our sources, McGraw-Hill/Osborne, or others, McGraw-Hill/Osborne does not guarantee the accuracy, adequacy, or completeness of any information and is not responsible for any errors or omissions or the results obtained from use of such information.

WINDOWS® XP QUICKSTEPS

10 11 12 QPD/QPD 01987

ISBN 978-007-223218-9
MHID 007-223218-8

PUBLISHER / Brandon A. Nordin

VICE PRESIDENT AND ASSOCIATE PUBLISHER / Scott Rogers

ACQUISITIONS EDITOR / Roger Stewart

ACQUISITIONS COORDINATOR / Jessica Wilson

TECHNICAL EDITOR / John Cronan

COPY EDITORS / Chara Curtis, Harriet O'Neal

PROOFREADERS / Chara Curtis, Kellen Diamanti, Harriet O'Neal

INDEXER / Kellen Diamanti

COMPUTER DESIGNERS / Bailey Cunningham, Keith Eyer

ILLUSTRATORS / Kathleen Edwards, Pattie Lee

SERIES DESIGN / Bailey Cunningham

COVER DESIGN / Pattie Lee

Contents at a Glance

1 2 3 4 5 6 7 8 9 10

Contents

1

2

5

6

9

10

Acknowledgments

Although this book has only one name on the cover, it was really produced by a fantastic team of truly talented people. This team, which had just been formed, immediately pulled together to produce a really great book series in an incredibly short period of time. They did this by putting in endless hours, working selflessly with each other, and applying a great amount of skill.

John Cronan, technical editor, corrected many errors, added many tips and notes, and greatly improved the book. John is also a good friend and an author in his own right. Thanks John!

Bailey Cunningham, series designer and layout artist, provided equal parts of tremendous skill and endless patience to produce a beautiful book. Thanks Bailey!

Chara Curtis, copy editor for half the chapters and proof reader for the other half, added to the readability and understandability of the book while always having a smile in her voice. Thanks Chara!

Kellen Diamanti, indexer and proof reader, who just made it happen with very little direction and who is a delight to work with. Thanks Kellen!

Keith Eyer, layout artist and prepress expert jumped in and filled a desperate need and worked many late night and weekend hours to assure that this book series was shipped to the printer on time. Thanks Keith!

Harriet O'Neal, copy editor for half the chapters and proof reader for the other half, brought great knowledge of the English language and skill at editing to materially improve the book while listening to my considerations. Thanks Harriet!

Roger Stewart, Editorial Director at Osborne, believed in us against substantial odds to sell the series, and continued to stand behind us throughout the production process. Thanks Roger!

David Zielonka, Managing Editor at Osborne, provided a constant stream of production tips and support to the point that he personally reshot two chapters of screen shots in this book. Thanks David!

Carole Matthews, is not only my partner in this venture, but also my life partner for 32 years, provided the necessary support without which this book would not have been possible. Thanks my love!

Introduction

QuickSteps books are recipe books for computer users. They answer the question "How do I…?" by providing quick sets of steps to accomplish the most common tasks in a particular program. The sets of steps are the central focus of the book. QuickSteps sidebars show you how to quickly do many small functions or tasks that support primary funcitons. Notes, Tips, and Cautions augment the steps, yet they are presented in such a manner as to not interrupt the flow of the steps. The brief introductions are minimal rather than narrative, and numerous illustrations and figures, many with callouts, support the steps.

QuickSteps books are organized by function and the tasks needed to perform that function. Each function is a chapter. Each task, or "How To," contains the steps needed for accomplishing the function along with relevant Notes, Tips, Cautions, and screenshots. Tasks will be easy to find through:

- The Table of Contents, which lists the functional areas (chapters) and tasks in the order they are presented
- A How-To list of tasks on the opening page of each chapter
- The index with its alphabetical list of terms used in describing the functions and tasks
- Color-coded tabs for each chapter or functional area with an index to the tabs just before the Table of Contents

Conventions Used in this Book

Windows XP QuickSteps uses several conventions designed to make the book easier for you to follow. Among these are:

- A in the Table of Contents or the How To list in each chapter references a QuickSteps sidebar in a chapter.
- **Bold type** is used for words on the screen that you are to do something with, such as click **Save As** or open **File**.
- *Italic type* is used for a word or phrase that is being defined or otherwise deserves special emphasis.
- Underlined type is used for text that you are to type from the keyboard
- SMALL CAPITAL LETTERS are used for keys on the keyboard such as **ENTER** and **SHIFT**.
- When you are expected to enter a command, you are told to press the key(s). If you are to enter text or numbers, you are told to type them.
- When you are to open a menu, such as the Start menu or the File menu, you are told to "open **Start**" or "open **File**."

How to...

Chapter 1
Stepping into Windows XP

Windows XP is an *operating system.* Operating systems perform *the* central role in managing what a computer does and how it is done. An operating system provides the interface between you and the computer hardware: it lets you store a file, print a document, connect to the Internet, or transfer information over a local area network without knowing anything about how the hardware works.

This chapter explains how to start and/or log on to Windows XP; how to use its screens, windows, menus, and dialog boxes; and how to shut it down. You will see how to get help and discover some ways to have fun with Windows.

Start Windows

To start Windows, you need to turn on the computer. Sometimes that is all you need to do. If, when you turn on the computer you get a screen similar to Figure 1-1 (on a Dell computer), then you have started Windows. In many cases, in addition to turning on the machine, you also need to log on, as explained on page three. Also, the first time you start a new computer, you will be asked to activate and register it.

NOTE

The desktop on your screen is probably different from the one shown in Figure 1-1. Each manufacturer has its own default desktop, and if you upgrade to Windows XP, you will see still a different one.

Figure 1-1: When you start Windows XP, your screen should look something like this

NOTE

If you are logging on to a domain (see Chapter 9), you will be asked to press **CTRL+ALT+DEL** all together. Do so, then enter your user name and password, and press **ENTER** or click **OK**.

ACTIVATE AND REGISTER WINDOWS

If you purchase a new computer with Windows XP already installed or if you upgrade to Windows XP from an older version of Windows, you will be told that you have 30 days to activate Windows. You can do so by clicking the icon next to the message or the icon the message points to. You do not have to register your name and address, but if you want support from either Microsoft or your computer manufacturer, you need to register.

1. Click the **Activate Windows Now** message or icon. (See "Use the Mouse" later in this chapter for how to click.)
2. Choose between activation over the Internet or over the telephone, and click **Next**.
3. Choose if you want to register with Microsoft or the computer manufacturer.
4. If you choose to register, enter your name and address, and click **Next**. Windows will then connect to Microsoft over the Internet, activate your installation, and if you chose, register your installation.
5. When you are told the process was successful, click **OK**.

Figure 1-2: If you get this log on screen, select a user, and enter a password if you need to

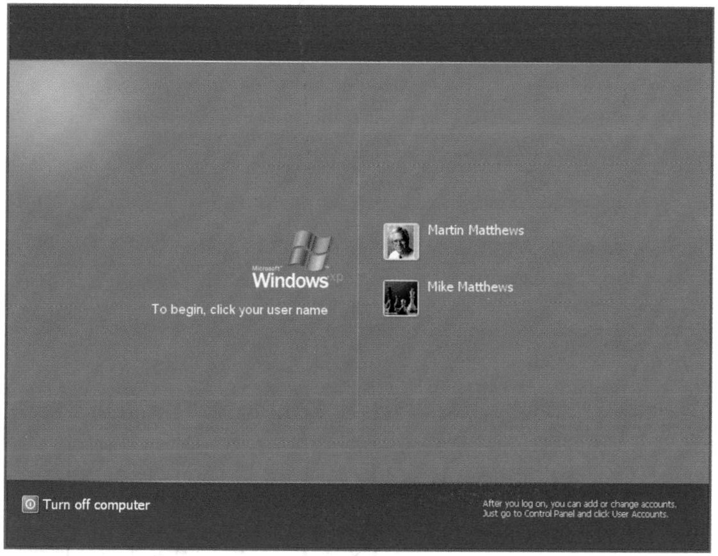

To activate over the telephone:

1. Select your location, which will give you one or more telephone numbers to dial.
2. On the screen you will be given an installation ID number that you must either give to the service representative on the telephone or punch in on your telephone keypad.
3. The service representative or an automated voice response will give you a confirmation number that you must enter in your computer to complete the activation process.

QUICKSTEPS

USING THE MOUSE

HIGHLIGHT AN OBJECT ON THE SCREEN

Highlight an *object* (a button, an icon, a border) on the Screen by pointing to it. *Point* at an object on the screen by moving the mouse until the tip of the pointer is on top of the object.

SELECT AN OBJECT ON THE SCREEN

Select an object on the screen by clicking it. *Click* means to point at an object you want to select and quickly press and release the left mouse button.

OPEN OR START AN OBJECT

Open an object or start a program by double-clicking it. *Double-click* means to point at an object you want to select and press and release the left mouse button twice in rapid succession.

OPEN A CONTEXT MENU FOR AN OBJECT

Open a context menu, which allows you to do things to an object, by right-clicking it. *Right-click* means to point at an object you want to select and quickly press and release the right mouse button.

MOVE AN OBJECT ON THE SCREEN

Move an object on the screen by dragging it. *Drag* means to point at an object you want to move, then press and hold the left mouse button while moving the mouse. You will drag the object as you move the mouse. When the object is where you want it, release the mouse button.

Log on to Windows

If, when you start Windows, you get the Log On screen shown in Figure 1-2, click your name and, if requested, enter your password. Windows will open. If a systems administrator installed your system, he or she should have given you your user name and password. If you installed the system, then you may not have set up users yet. Setting up users is discussed in Chapter 8.

Use the Mouse

A *mouse* is any pointing device–including trackballs, pointing sticks, and graphic tablets–with two or more buttons. This book assumes a two-button mouse. Moving the mouse moves the pointer on the screen. You *select* an object on the screen by moving the pointer so that it is on top of the object and then pressing the left button on the mouse.

You may control the mouse by either your left or right hand. Therefore, the buttons may be switched. (See Chapter 2 to switch the buttons.) This book assumes the right hand controls the mouse and the left mouse button is "*the* mouse button." The right button is always called the "right mouse button." If you switch the buttons, you must change your interpretation of these phrases.

Use the Screen

The Windows XP screen can hold windows and other objects. In its simplest form, shown in Figure 1-1, you see a background scene, a bar at the bottom, the Start button on the left, the time on the right, and the Recycle Bin above the time.

The parts of a screen are: the *desktop*, which takes most of the screen, the *Start button* in the lower-left, the *taskbar* across the bottom, the *notification area* in the lower-right, *desktop icons*, which can be anywhere on the desktop, and the *mouse pointer*, which can be anywhere on the screen.

QUICKSTEPS

USING THE NOTIFICATION AREA

The *notification area* on the right of the taskbar contains the icons of special programs as well as the time of day.

OPEN A PROGRAM

Click the program icon.

SEE THE DAY AND DATE

Point to the time.

SET THE TIME AND DATE

Double-click the time.

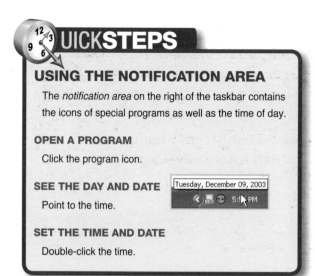

USE THE DESKTOP

The *desktop* is the entire screen except for the bar at the bottom. Windows, dialog boxes, and icons, such as the Recycle Bin, are displayed on the desktop. You can store *shortcuts*, which are icons for your favorite programs, on the desktop (see Chapter 2). You can drag windows, dialog boxes, and icons around the desktop. Double-click an icon on the desktop to open it.

USE THE START BUTTON

The *Start button* on the left of the taskbar, when clicked, opens the Start menu–the primary access to the programs, utilities, and settings that are available in Windows.

USE THE TASKBAR

The *taskbar* at the bottom of the screen contains the active *tasks*, which are icons and titles of the programs that are running on the computer or folders that are open. The taskbar also holds the Start button on the left and the Notification area on the right. Click a program on the taskbar to open it.

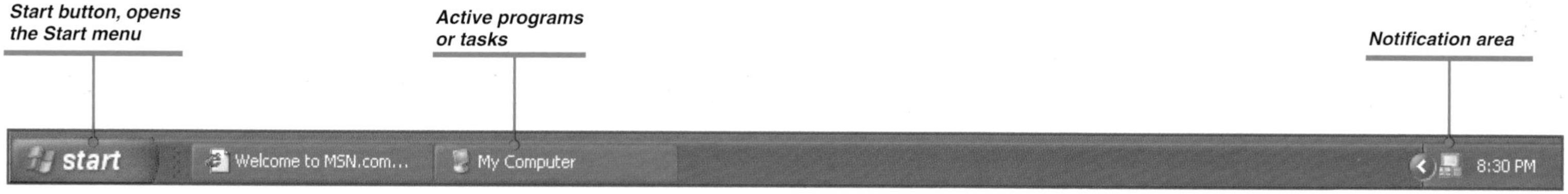

NOTE

Your taskbar may have an additional object, not shown above, between the Start button and the program tasks. This is called the Quick Launch toolbar and is described in Chapter 2.

USE A DESKTOP ICON

A *desktop icon* represents a program or folder that can be started or opened and moved about. The Recycle Bin is a desktop icon for a folder that contains all of the files that have been deleted since the Recycle Bin was last emptied. Double-click a desktop icon to open it.

USE THE MOUSE POINTER

The *mouse pointer*, or simply the *pointer*, shows where the mouse is pointing. Move the mouse to move the pointer.

> **NOTE**
>
> The two steps describing how to open the Start menu can be replaced with the two words "click **Start**." You can also open the Start menu by pressing the Windows flag key on your keyboard, if you have that key, or by pressing both the CTRL and ESC keys together (press and hold CTRL while pressing ESC; written CTRL+ESC). In the rest of this book, you will see the phrase "open **Start**." This means open the Start menu using any technique you

Open the Start Menu

To open the Start menu:

1. Point at the **Start** button by moving the pointer so that it is over the Start button. You will see that the button changes color. When this happens, the button is said to be selected or *highlighted.*
2. Press and release the left mouse button (given that your mouse buttons have not been switched) while the pointer is on the Start button. The Start menu will open, as you can see in Figure 1-3.

Use the Start Menu

The Start menu contains icons for programs and folders, plus access to control functions and other menus, as shown in Figure 1-3. The most important menu access is All Programs, which opens a subsidiary menu of programs. Log Off and Turn Off Computer are important control functions discussed later in this chapter. All other objects on the menu are icons for folders and programs. The five or six lower icons on the left change to reflect the programs you used most recently and will be different from those shown here.

> **NOTE**
>
> If you do not have the Internet programs on the Start menu, you do not have an Internet connection. See Chapter 4 to set one up.

The remaining icons in the Start menu fall into three categories: Internet programs, file-related folders and programs, and system management programs.

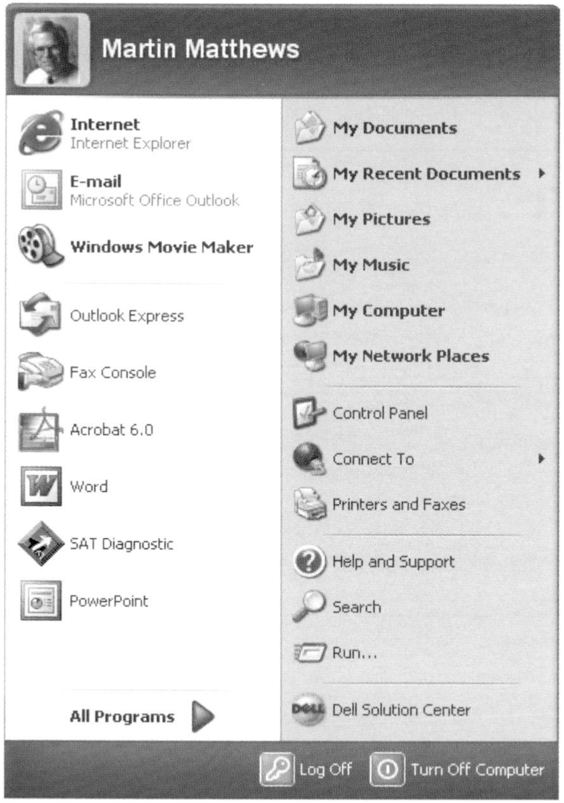

Figure 1-3: The Start menu provides access to the programs, utilities, and settings in Windows

NOTE

If you are using Windows XP Home Edition, you will not see Printers And Faxes, but you can add it, as discussed in Chapter 2.

START INTERNET PROGRAMS

Click either of the two icons on the top-left to start programs that use the Internet. The Internet Explorer lets you browse the World Wide Web, while Outlook (or Outlook Express) opens an e-mail program to send and receive messages. These programs are described in Chapter 4.

OPEN FILE-RELATED FOLDERS

Click any of the four to six icons on the top-right in Figure 1-3 to access files and folders. These icons start the Windows Explorer program and display the item identified by the icon. Windows Explorer will be discussed both later in this chapter and again in Chapter 3.

OPEN SYSTEM MANAGEMENT PROGRAMS

Click any of the remaining icons in the bottom-right of the Start menu to help you manage your computer and use its resources. The function of each is as follows:

- **Control Panel** provides access to many of the settings that govern how Windows and the computer operate. This allows you to customize much of Windows and to locate and cure problems. The Control Panel is discussed primarily in Chapter 2.

- **Connect To** allows you to set up and manage connections to your local area network and to the Internet. Connect To is discussed in chapters 4 and 9. (You may not have a Connect To if you don't have a dial-up connection.)

- **Printers And Faxes** allows you to set up and control how these devices operate and are shared with others. Printers are discussed further in Chapter 6.

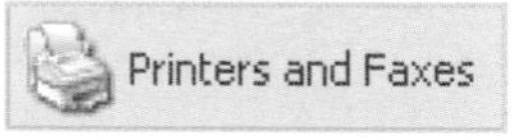

QUICKSTEPS

STARTING A PROGRAM

The method for starting a program depends on where the program icon is located. Here are the alternatives:

ON THE DESKTOP

Double-click the program icon, or "shortcut," on the desktop.

ON THE START MENU

Click the program icon on the **Start Menu**.

IN THE NOTIFICATION AREA

Click the program icon in the notification area.

ON THE ALL PROGRAMS MENU

1. Open **Start**.
2. Select **All Programs**.
3. Open the appropriate folder or folders
4. Click the program icon, as shown in Figure 1-4.

IN THE RUN COMMAND

1. Open **Start** and select **Run**.
2. Type the path and program name, and press **ENTER** or click **OK**.

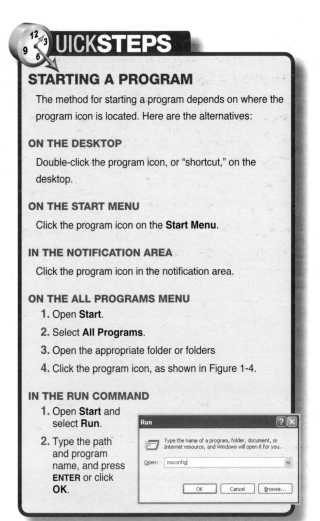

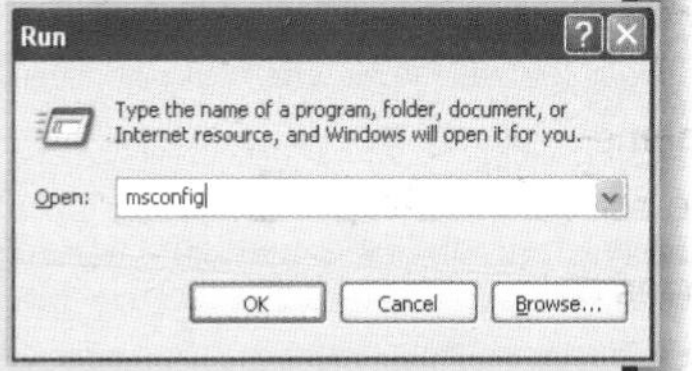

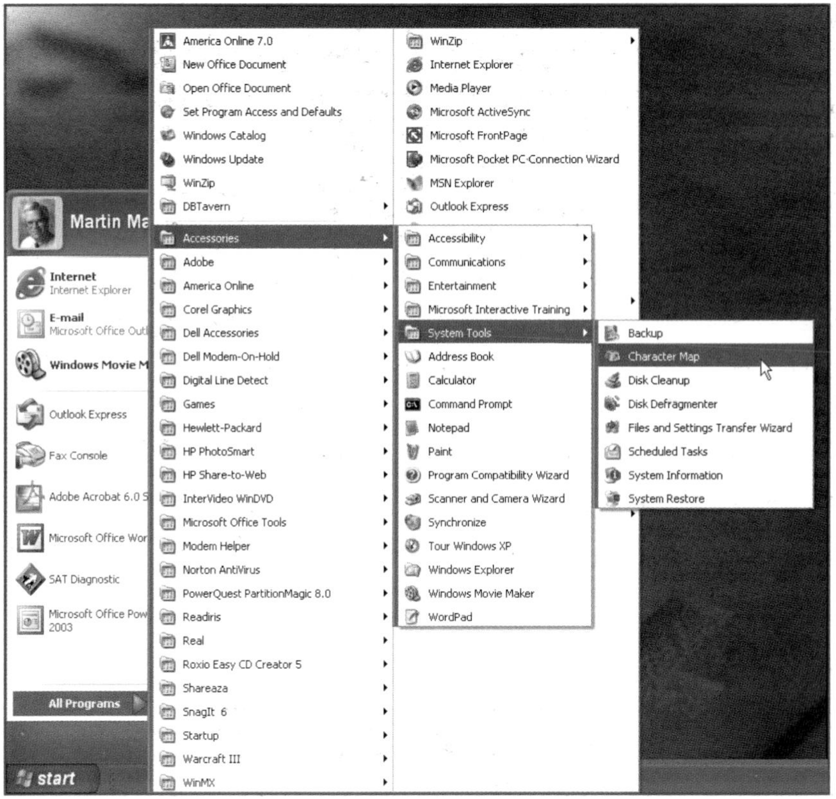

Figure 1-4: All Programs on the Start menu may lead you through several folders to find the program you want

TIP

When you move the pointer to an option on the Start menu, the option changes color and becomes selected.

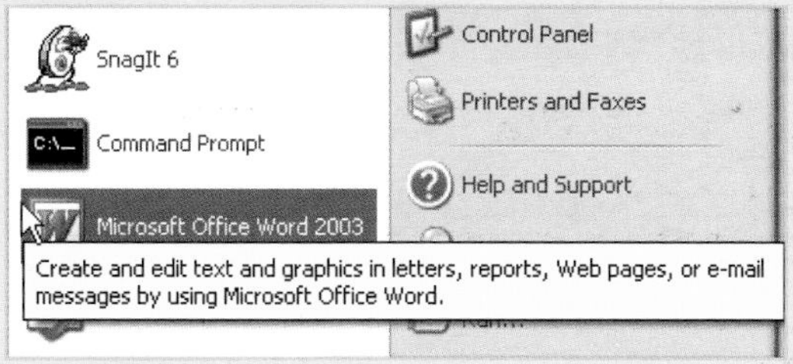

If you don't immediately click, a little message box, or *screen tip*, will appear. It gives you information about the option you selected.

TIP

In Chapter 3 you will see how to start programs with the Windows Explorer.

- **Help And Support** opens a window from which you can search for information on how to use Windows XP. It includes a tutorial and a troubleshooting guide. Help is discussed in more detail later in this chapter.

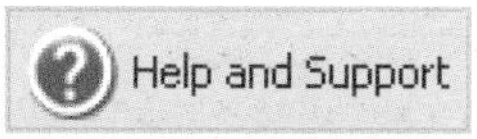

- **Search** lets you search for files, folders, computers, people, and information on your computer, on your local area network (LAN), and on the Internet. You can read more about Search in Chapter 3.

- **Run** lets you type a command that opens a folder or starts a program. Run is principally used to diagnose and cure problems.

- Your computer's manufacturer may have added an icon, as mine did, that connects you to its Internet help center.

Use a Window

When you start a program or open a folder, the program or folder appears in a "window" on your screen, as does the My Computer window in Figure 1-5.

A window has a number of features that are shown in Figure 1-5 and referred to in the balance of this book.

- The **title bar** contains the name of the program or folder in the window and is used to drag the window around the screen.
- The **Control Menu** icon opens the Control or System menu, which allows you to move, size, and close the window.
- The **menu bar** contains the menus that are available in the window.
- The **toolbar** contains tools related to the contents of the window. Click on a tool to use it. The toolbar is optional.
- The **address bar** contains the path to reach the window's contents. An address can be typed in the address bar. See Chapter 3. The address bar is optional.

QUICKSTEPS

USING A TASKS PANE

A tasks pane, such as the one in Figure 1-5, is used as an alternative to menus by placing some menu options in the tasks pane.

USE A TASKS PANE

Click an object in the detail pane to use its options in the tasks pane.

SELECT A TASKS PANE OPTION

Click the option.

CLOSE OR OPEN A TASKS PANE SECTION

Click the chevron on the upper-right of the tasks pane.

SWITCH THE TASKS PANE AND THE FOLDERS PANE

If the tasks pane is open, click **Folders** in the toolbar.

–Or–

If the Folders pane is open (see Chapter 3), click the **Close** button in the upper-left of the pane.

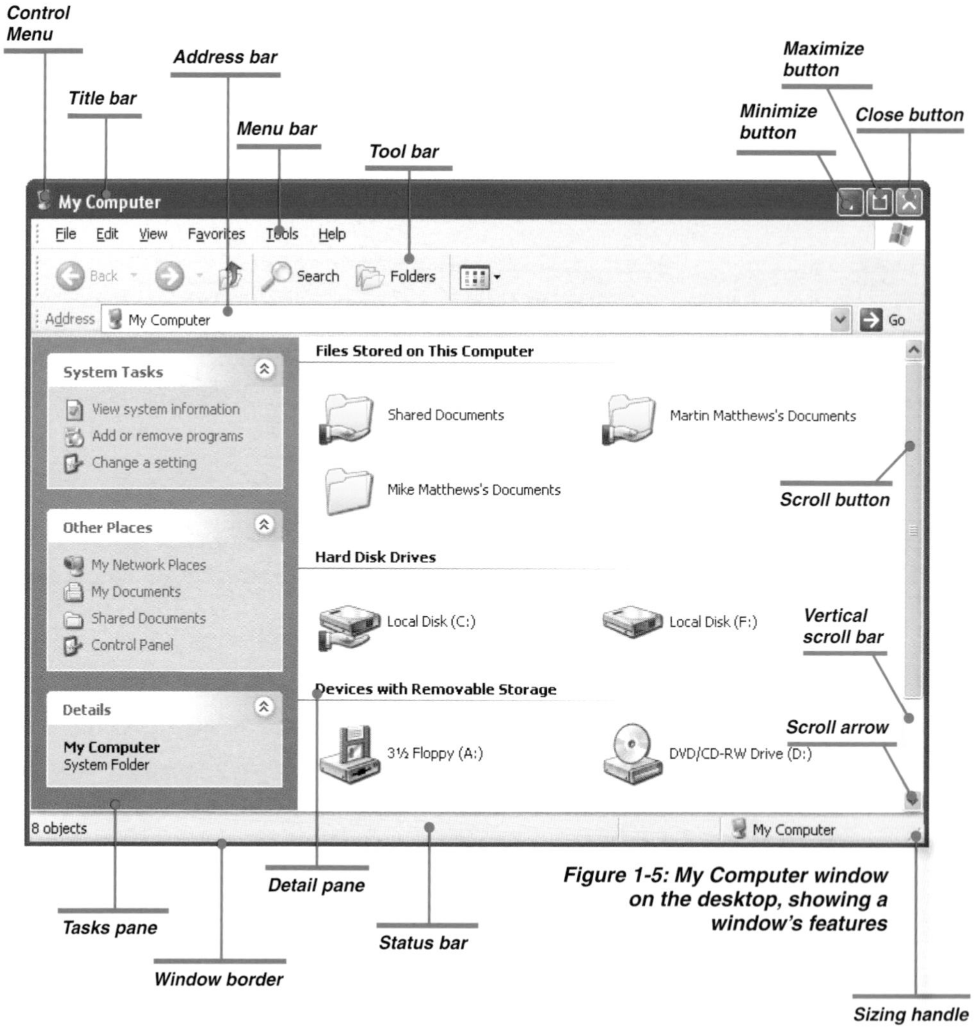

Figure 1-5: My Computer window on the desktop, showing a window's features

TIP

Double-clicking a window title bar toggles between maximizing and restoring a window to its previous size. This is much easier than clicking the maximize and restore buttons (the restore button is what the maximize button becomes when the screen is maximized).

NOTE

All windows have a title bar with a control menu icon; a title; and the minimize, maximize, and close buttons. All windows also have a border and sizing handle, both of which can be used to change the size of the window. *Almost* all windows have a menu bar. Other features are optional.

- The **tasks pane** contains a list of tasks that can be performed on the selected item in the detail pane. Tasks panes are discussed in the QuickSteps on the opposite page. The tasks pane is optional.
- The **window border** separates the window from the desktop and can be used to size the window horizontally or vertically by dragging either the vertical or horizontal border.
- The **detail pane** displays the principal object of the window, such as files, folders, programs, documents, or images.
- The **status bar** provides messages and information about what is displayed or selected in the window. The status bar is optional.
- The **sizing handle** allows a window to be sized diagonally, increasing or decreasing its height and width when you drag this handle.
- The **vertical scroll** bar allows you to move the contents of the pane vertically within the window so that you can see information that wasn't displayed.
- **Scroll arrows** move the window contents in small increments in the direction of the arrow.
- The **scroll bar** itself moves the contents in large increments.
- The **scroll button** can be dragged in either direction to move the contents in that direction.
- The **minimize button** decreases the size of the window so that you see it only as a task on the taskbar.
- The **maximize button** increases the size of the window so that it fills the screen.
- The **close button** shuts down and closes the program in the window.

1 2 3 4 5 6 7 8 9 10

TIP

There are several ways to distinguish a dialog box from a window. The purpose of a window is to display information, while the purpose of a dialog box is to gather information. Dialog boxes cannot be sized and do not have a control menu icon, a menu bar, or minimize and maximize buttons.

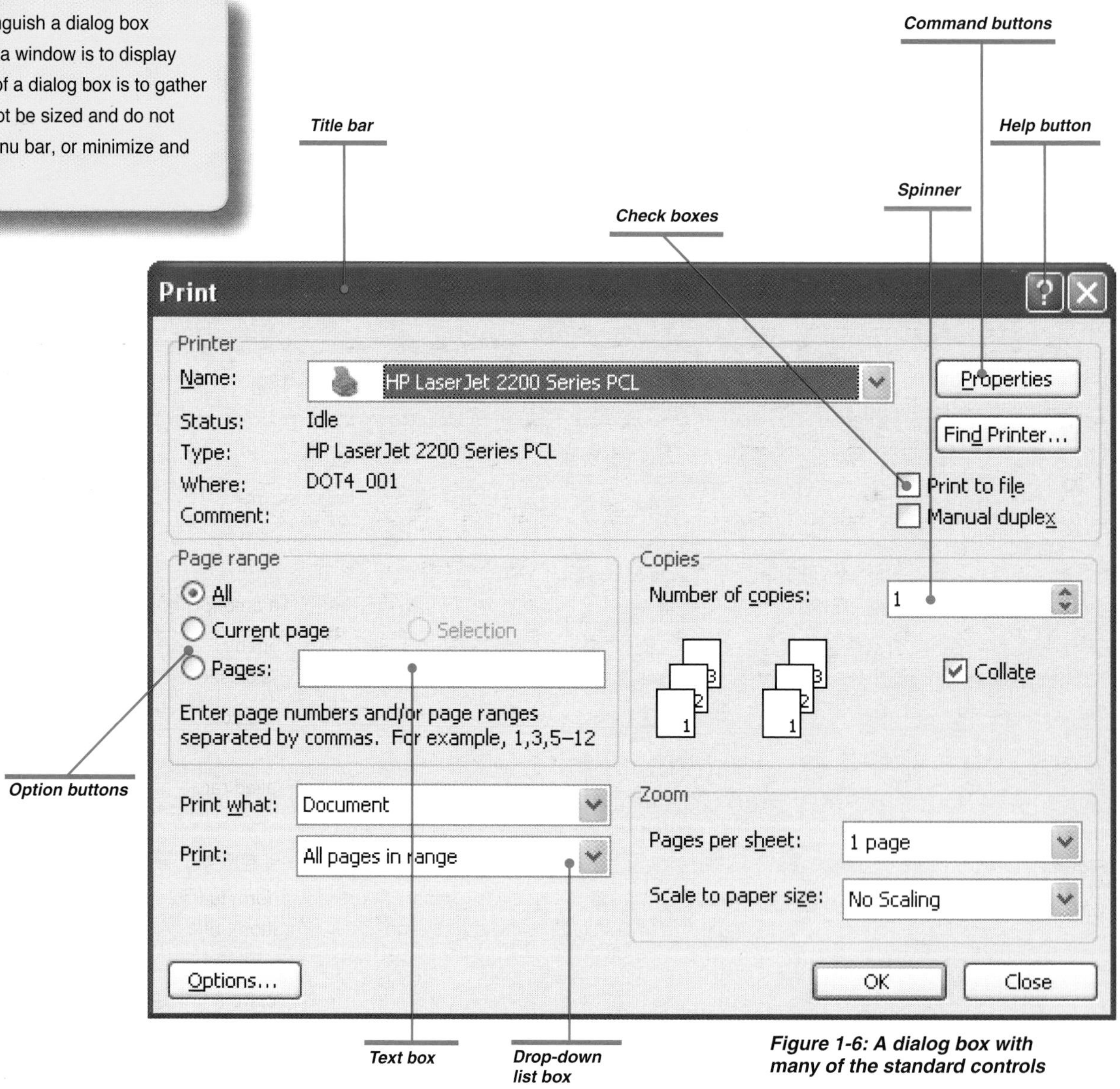

Figure 1-6: A dialog box with many of the standard controls

Use a Menu

A menu provides a way of selecting an action, such as Search, on an object, such as a folder. To use a menu in an open window:

1. Click the menu name in the menu bar.
2. Move the pointer to the desired option.
3. Click the desired option.

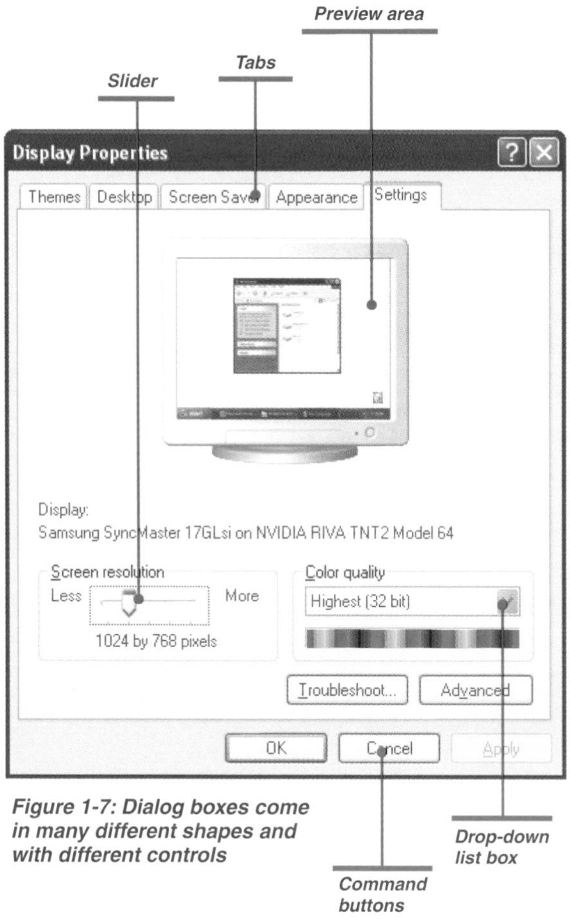

Figure 1-7: Dialog boxes come in many different shapes and with different controls

Use a Dialog Box

Dialog boxes gather information. A *dialog box* uses a common set of features called "*controls*" to accomplish its purpose. Figures 1-6 and 1-7 show two frequently used dialog boxes with many of the controls often seen.

The common controls in dialog boxes are used in these ways:

- The **title bar** contains the name of the dialog box and is used to drag the box around the desktop.
- **Tabs** let you select from among several pages in a dialog box.
- A **drop-down list box** opens a list from which you can choose one item that will be displayed when the list is closed.
- A **list box** (not shown) lets you select one or more items from a list; it may include a scroll bar.
- **Option buttons**, also called radio buttons, let you select one among mutually exclusive options.
- A **text box** lets you enter and edit text.
- **Command buttons** perform functions such as closing the dialog box and accepting the changes (the OK button), or closing the dialog box and ignoring the changes (the Cancel button).
- A **spinner** lets you select from a sequential series of numbers.

- A **slider** lets you select from several values.
- **Check boxes** let you turn features on or off.
- The **Help button** changes the pointer to a question mark. Click the question mark on a feature if you want to learn more about it.

You will have a great many opportunities to use dialog boxes, and for the most part, you can try dialog boxes and see what happens; if you don't like the outcome, you can come back and reverse the setting.

NOTE

On laptop, notebook, and some desktop computers, the Hibernate option may be replaced with Stand By. Stand By does everything Hibernate does but puts the computer into a special low-power state, which conserves power and preserves the battery, and allows you to quickly restart. On these computers, if you want to go into true hibernation, hold down **SHIFT** while clicking **Stand By**.

Leave Windows

You can leave Windows in three ways depending on what you want to do:

LOG OFF

Log off means to close the active programs and network connections and to close your user account but leave the computer running. To log off:

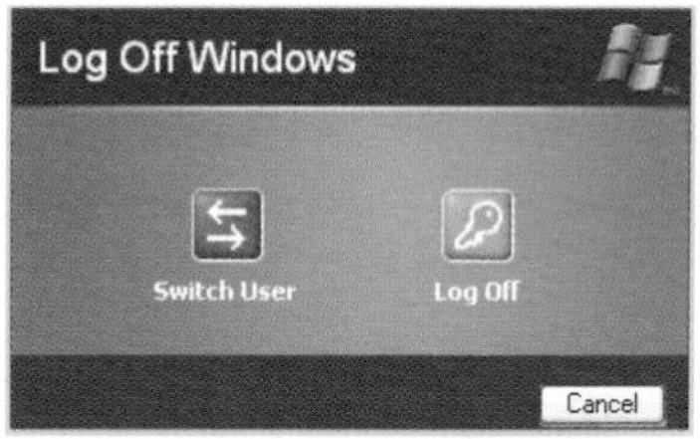

1. Open **Start** and click **Log Off**.
2. In the Log Off Windows dialog box, click **Log Off**.

SWITCH USERS

Switch users means to leave the active programs and network connections active and keep your user account active while you let another user use the computer. To switch users:

1. Open **Start** and click **Log Off**.
2. In the Log Off Windows dialog box, click **Switch User**.

SHUT DOWN

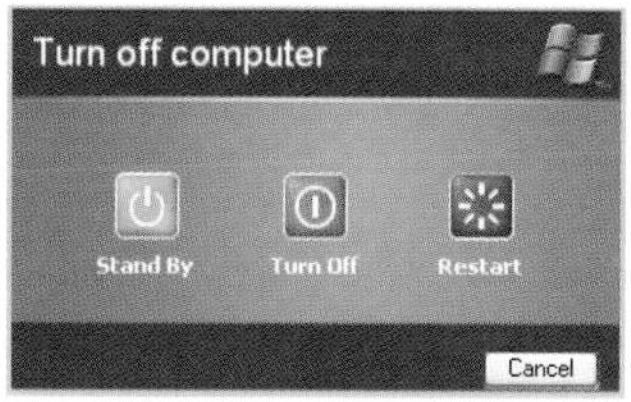

Shutting down means to log off all users and shut down the computer. To shut down:

1. Open **Start**.
2. Click **Turn Off Computer**.
3. In the Turn Off Computer dialog box, click one of these choices:
   - **Turn Off** shuts down Windows gracefully so that no information is lost and then turns off the computer (if it is done automatically) or tells you when it is safe for you to turn it off.
   - **Restart** shuts down Windows gracefully so that no information is lost and then restarts the computer. This is usually done when there is a problem that restarting Windows will fix or to complete setting up some programs.
   - **Hibernate** saves the current state of the computer, including the open programs and files and the active network connections, and then shuts down the computer. When you start up the computer at a later time, you will resume work with exactly the same programs, files, and network connections that you had open when you shut down.

Get Help

Windows XP Help provides both built-in documentation and online assistance that you can use to learn how to work with Windows. To use Help to start a program:

1. Open **Start** and click **Help And Support**. The Help And Support Center window, like the one in Figure 1-8, will open.
2. Choose **Windows Basic** under Help Topics, select **Core Windows Tasks**, and then click **Working With Programs**. A list of tasks for working with programs will be displayed.
3. Click **Start A Program**. Steps and notes related to starting a program will be displayed.
4. Click **Close** to close the Help And Support Center.

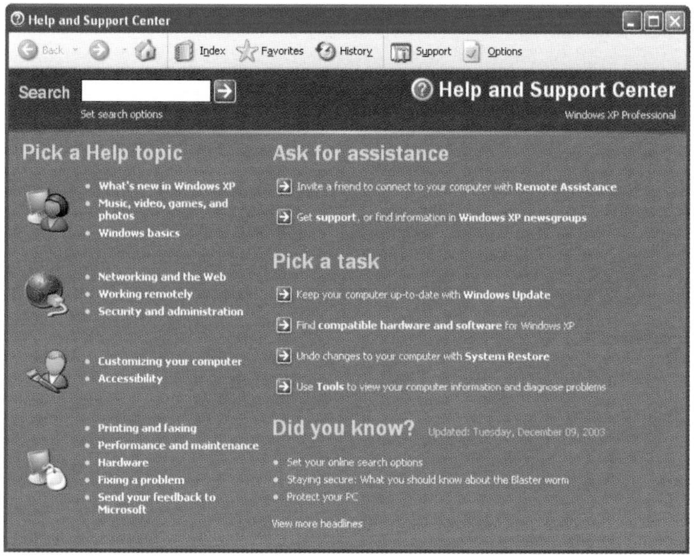

Figure 1-8: Windows XP Help And Support Center window

QUICKSTEPS

HAVING FUN WITH WINDOWS

Windows XP has a number of games besides FreeCell. Here is how to play three more:

PLAY HEARTS

Hearts is a card game that can be played by as many as four people on the network.

1. Open **Start**, select **All Programs**, choose Games, and click **Hearts**. The game board will appear.
2. Enter your name, and click **OK**. By default you will get three simulated opponents.

The objective is to have the lowest score by *not* taking tricks with hearts or the Queen of Spades in them *unless* you can take all such tricks. You take a trick by playing the highest card in the suite led for that trick. You begin the game by passing three cards from your hand to another player. You want to pass your highest hearts and spades. The person with the two of clubs leads. You must follow suite if you can. If you can't, you may throw away your high hearts or spades or any other card. Whoever takes a trick plays the first card for the next trick. Play continues until all cards have been played. At the end of a game, one point is assessed for each heart in the tricks you took plus 13 for the Queen of Spades. If you get all the hearts plus the Queen of Spades, you get zero points, and all other players get 26 points.

Continued...

Play FreeCell

FreeCell is an addictive solitaire card game. To start playing:

1. Open **Start**, select **All Programs**, choose **Games**, and click **FreeCell**. The game board will open.
2. Open **Game**, and then click **New Game**. A deck of cards will be spread out.

   The objective is to get the complete set of cards in each of the four suites in order from ace to king in the home cells in the upper-right. You may temporarily place up to four cards in the free cells in the upper-left. You may also temporarily place a card on the next highest card of the opposite color in the stacks at the bottom.
3. To move a card, click it, and then click where you want it to go. If it is not a legal move, you will be told that. If you get an empty column at the bottom, you can build your own sequence in it.

   The secret is to think several moves in the future and never fill up the free cells without having a way to empty them. The game is lost if you have no moves left and haven't moved all the cards to the home cells. Figure 1-9 shows a game that I have played for a few minutes and that is all but won. I have only to move the cards to the home cells. When all your cards are in order, they will be moved to the home cells automatically, and you will be told you won.
4. When you are done playing, click **Close** and then **Yes** to "resign" from the game if you did not finish it.

HAVING FUN WITH WINDOWS
(Continued)

PLAY MINESWEEPER

Minesweeper is a game of chance in which you try to accumulate points by not encountering mines.

1. Open **Start**; click **All Programs**.
2. Choose **Games**, and click **Minesweeper**. The game board will appear.

   The object is to find the mines hidden in the squares without clicking one. Click a square. You will see a number or a mine. The number tells you how many mines are contained in the eight surrounding squares. Mark the suspected mines with the right mouse button. Clicking a mine ends the game.
3. To restart the game, click the smiley-face reset button.

PLAY SOLITAIRE

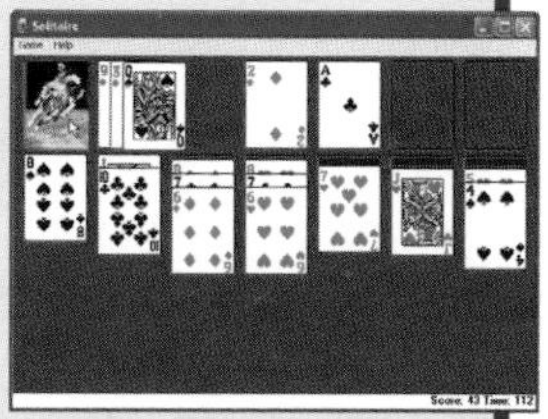

Solitaire is a game of chance and strategy. The object of the game is to end up with the deck of cards arranged sequentially in suites from the ace up to the king.

1. Open **Start**, select **All Programs**, choose **Games**, and click **Solitaire**. The game board will display.

   You will see a row of seven stacks of cards; all are face down except the top card. In the upper-left of the board is another down-turned stack of cards, which you can click. In the upper-right are four empty cells where you will place the suites, beginning with the aces.
2. Start a new game by opening **Game** and clicking **Deal**.

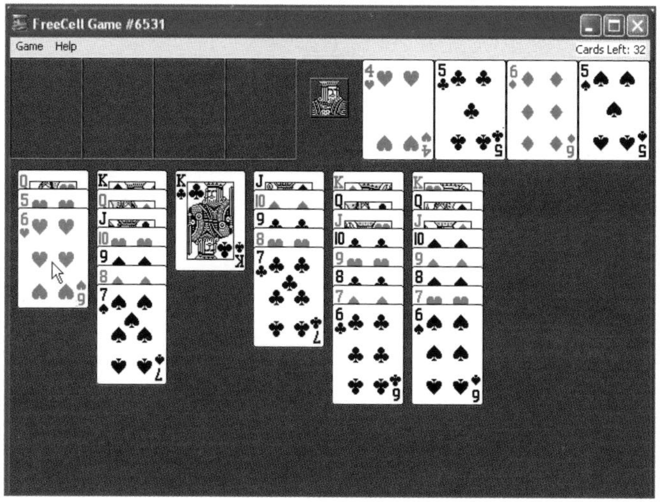

Figure 1-9: A FreeCell game about to be won

1 2 3 4 5 6 7 8 9 10

How to...

Chapter 2
Customizing Windows XP

Windows XP has many features that can be customized. You can keep the default Windows XP setup; or you can change the display, Start menu, taskbar, and sounds, or rearrange the desktop, and enable accessibility options.

Change the Look of Windows XP

A flexible and important area is how Windows looks. Here you'll see how to change the screen's look, including the desktop, the menu, and the taskbar.

Open Display Properties

Much of what you see on the Windows XP screen is controlled by the Display Properties dialog box. Open it to make many of the changes in this chapter.

1. With Windows XP running and displayed on your computer, right-click a blank area of the desktop. The desktop *context*, or *control, menu* will open.
2. Click **Properties**. The Display Properties dialog box will open, as shown in Figure 2-1.

Figure 2-1: Display Properties lets you change the appearance of Windows XP

Pick a New Screen Saver

When the computer is left on but not in use, the unchanging image on the screen can be burned into the face of a cathode-ray tube (CRT) monitor (the newer, thin, flat-screen monitors are not affected by this). To prevent this damage, you can choose to use a *screen saver*, which constantly changes the image on screen when the computer is not in use. Windows XP provides a number of alternative screen savers you can use.

1. Open **Display Properties**.
2. Click the **Screen Saver** tab, and open the **Screen Saver** drop-down list.
3. Click a screen saver option to see it previewed in the dialog box. See Figure 2-2.
4. Click **Preview** to see the screen saver on your full screen. Press **ESC** to return to the dialog box.
5. Click the up or down arrow on the **Wait** spinner to set the time to wait before enabling the screen saver.
6. When you have the screen saver you want, click **Settings**, if it is enabled, to see what settings are available for your screen saver.
7. When you are ready, click **OK** to close the dialog box.

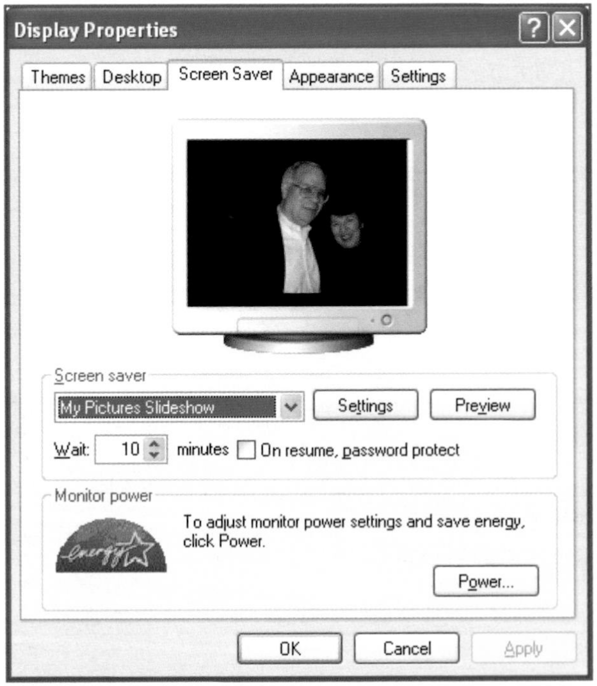

Figure 2-2: You can use your own pictures in the My Picture Show screen saver

TIP

Additional themes are available in Microsoft Plus! for Windows XP. This can be ordered online from Microsoft by clicking **More Themes Online** from the Theme drop-down list box.

QUICKSTEPS

CHANGING THE DESKTOP

You can quickly change the desktop with a theme, a background, or a color–all from the Display Properties dialog box.

SELECT A THEME

A *theme* controls not only the look of Windows but also the sounds, icons, and other elements.

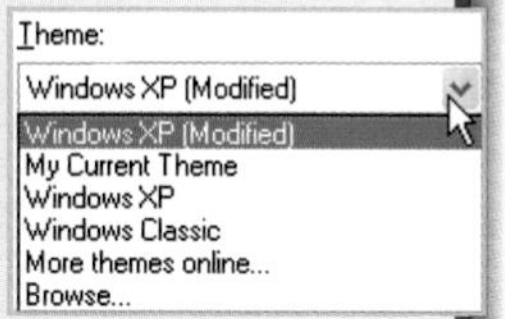

1. In the Display Properties dialog box, click the **Themes** tab if it is not already displayed.
2. Open the Theme drop-down list, and click the desired theme. See Tip on page 20.

CHOOSE A BACKGROUND IMAGE

The primary image that you see on the desktop is the *background*. Some manufacturers display one of their own; others use the Windows XP default. You can change either of these.

1. In the Display Properties dialog box, click the **Desktop** tab to display it.
2. Scroll the **Background** list, and click the background you want to use.

PICK A BACKGROUND COLOR

In place of a background image you can use a solid color.

1. In the Display Properties dialog box, click the **Desktop** tab if it is not already displayed.
2. Select **None** for the **Background**, open the **Color** drop-down list, and click the background color you want to use.

Continued...

Alter the Appearance of Objects

You can alter the appearance of windows, icons, and dialog boxes, changing their shapes and colors as well as the font used in those objects.

1. Open **Display Properties**.
2. Click the **Appearance** tab, and open the **Windows And Buttons** drop-down list.
3. Choose **Windows Classic Style**, the look of Windows 98; or choose **Windows XP Style**, a newer look, shown in Figure 2-3.
4. Open the **Color Scheme** drop-down list, and choose the color that is best.
5. Click **Effects** to open the Effects dialog box, select the options that are correct for you, click **OK** to close the Effects dialog box.

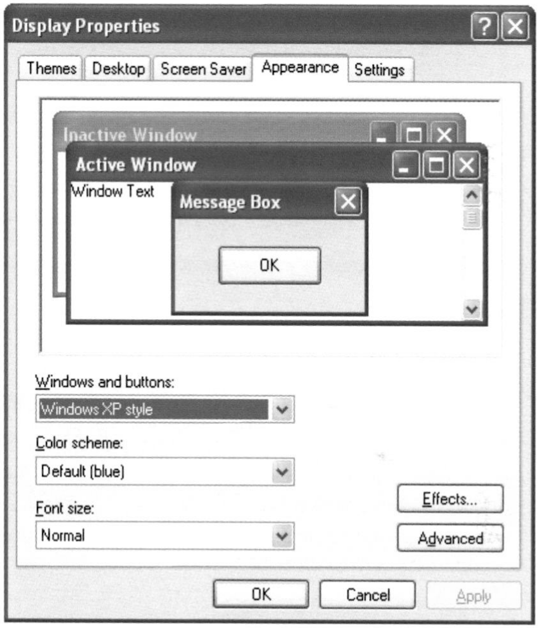

Figure 2-3: Look at possible changes in Display Properties Appearance tab without affecting the actual screen

6. Click **Advanced** to open the Advanced Appearance dialog box, select an object whose color and/or font you want to change, make those changes, and click **OK**.
7. When you are ready, click **OK** to close the Display Properties dialog box.

CHANGING THE DESKTOP *(continued)*

CREATE A THEME

When you have set up the Windows XP Display features the way you want them, you can save those settings as a theme of your own and transfer them to another computer.

1. In the Display Properties dialog box, click the **Themes** tab to display it.
2. Click **Save As**, type the filename you want to use, select the folder you want to store the file in, and click **Save**.

NOTE

You can make changes within a dialog box and see the changes in the preview area, as shown in Figure 2-4. If you don't like the changes, select a different scheme or click **Cancel**, and your actual screen is not changed.

TIP

The screen saver, My Pictures Slideshow, displays the pictures you have placed in the \My Documents\My Pictures\ folder.

NOTE

The command buttons (Troubleshoot and Advanced) at the bottom of the Settings tab lead you through a question-and-answer trouble-shooting session and provide access to settings that are specific to your display hardware.

Change the Resolution and Color

Depending on your computer and monitor, you can display Windows XP with various resolutions and color quality. You can select the resolution and color in the Settings tab of the Display Properties dialog box.

1. Open **Display Properties**.
2. Click the **Settings** tab; slide the **Screen Resolution** for a higher (to the right) or lower (to the left) resolution. (You can try this, and if you don't like it, come back and change it.)
3. Open the **Color Quality** drop-down list, and choose the color quality you want.
4. Click **OK** to close the Display Properties dialog box.

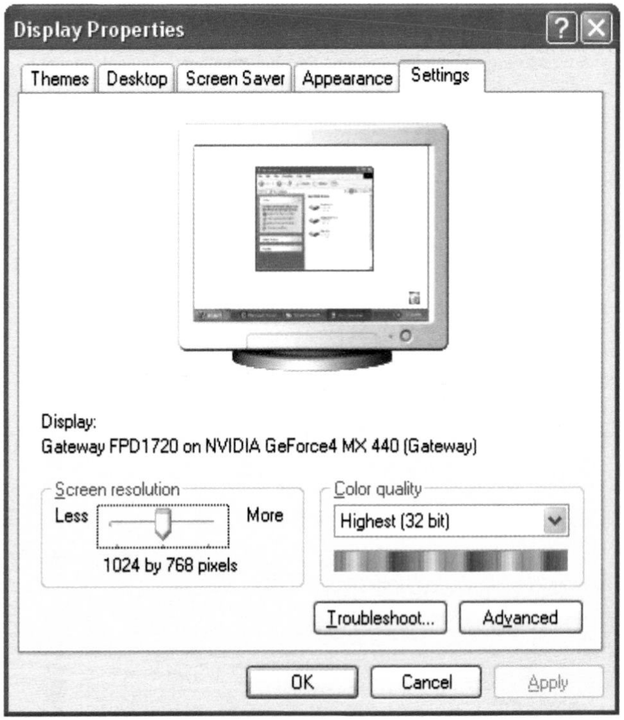

Figure 2-4: Increasing the resolution lets you see more on the screen, but what you see is smaller

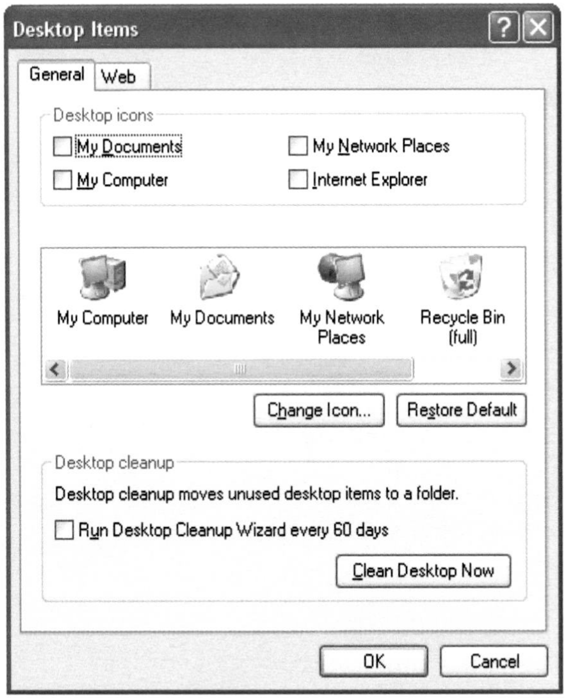

Figure 2-5: You can add and customize the Windows program icons on the desktop

NOTE

If you are using a notebook computer or a flat-panel display, to smooth the edges of screen fonts, you want to select ClearType in the Effect dialog box by opening **Display Properties Appearance** tab and clicking **Effects**.

Add Windows Program Icons

When you first install and start up Windows XP, normally the only icon on the desktop is the Recycle Bin, although some computer manufacturers may have additional icons. The purpose of having program icons on the desktop, called *shortcuts*, is to be able to easily start the programs by double-clicking their icons. To add and customize Windows program icons, such as Windows Explorer and Internet Explorer, to the desktop:

1. Right-click a blank area of the desktop, and click **Properties** to open the Display Properties dialog box.
2. Click the **Desktop** tab, and click the **Customize Desktop** button to open the Desktop Items dialog box, shown in Figure 2-5.
3. In **Desktop Icons**, select one to four icons that you want to have on the desktop. My choice is to have icons for My Computer and Internet Explorer. You can access the other two from My Computer.
4. To customize a Windows program icon, select the icon and click **Change Icon**. A dialog box of alternative icons will open.
5. Select the alternative you want, and click **OK**.
6. When you are satisfied with the Windows program icons you have selected and/or changed, click **OK**.
7. Click **OK** again to close the Display Properties dialog box.

Rearrange Desktop Icons

When you have the icons that you want on the desktop, they may be a mess. You can drag the icons to where you want them, or let Windows do it.

QUICKSTEPS

ADDING OTHER PROGRAM ICONS

The method for adding other program icons, or shortcuts, to the desktop depends on where the icons are.

ICONS ON THE START MENU

Open the **Start** menu, and drag the icon to the desktop.

ICONS ON THE PROGRAM MENU

1. Open the **Start** menu, and choose **All Programs**.
2. Point to the icon, hold down the right mouse button, and drag the icon to desktop. (This is called *right-drag*.)
3. Click **Copy Here**.

ICONS ON OTHER MENUS

1. Open the **Start** menu, select **All Programs**, and choose the subsidiary menu.
2. Point to the icon, hold down the right mouse button, and drag the icon to desktop.
3. Click **Copy Here**.

ICONS NOT ON A MENU

1. Open the **Start** menu, and click **My Computer**.
2. In My Computer, click **Folders** in the toolbar.
3. In the Folders pane, open the drive and folder(s) needed to locate the program.
4. Right-drag the program icon to the desktop, and click **Create Shortcut Here**.

TIP

The Recycle Bin cannot be renamed.

LET WINDOWS ALIGN ICONS

When you drag the icons where you want them, it may be hard to align them, so let Windows do that:

1. Drag the icons close to where you want them.
2. Right-click a blank area of the desktop, and select **Arrange Icons By**.
3. Click **Align To Grid**. Your icons will jump to an invisible grid and be aligned. Mine looked like this:

LET WINDOWS ARRANGE ICONS

1. Right-click a blank area of the desktop, and select **Arrange Icons By**.
2. Choose **Name**. The icons will be placed in a column alphabetically except that the *system* icons (My Computer, Recycle Bin, Internet Explorer, My Documents, and My Network Places) will be at the top.

Rename Desktop Icons

When you drag icons from various locations, they may have the word "Shortcut" in their names, or they may have names that are not very meaningful to you. To rename desktop icons:

1. Right-click an icon name you want to change, and click **Rename**.
2. Type the new name you want to use, and press **ENTER**.

Change the Start Menu

The Start menu has several areas you can customize, including its overall look, the size of the icons, the number of programs on it, the programs to use for the Internet and for e-mail, and how the Start menu operates.

Figure 2-6: The customization of the Start menu starts with choosing its look

CHANGE THE LOOK OF THE START MENU

You have a choice between the "Classic," or Windows 98, look and the newer Windows XP look, which has more emphasis on using the Internet.

1. Right-click **Start**, and click **Properties** to open the Taskbar And Start Menu Properties dialog box. See Figure 2-6.
2. Click your choice of **Start Menu** or **Classic Start Menu**. Your choice will be displayed in the dialog box, and you can change it if you wish.
3. When you are done changing the Start menu, click **OK**.

CHANGE THE SIZE OF THE START MENU ICONS

Depending on your screen resolution and your eyesight, you may want to change the size of the icons on the Start menu. If you are using the Windows XP Start menu, you can do that. See Figure 2-7 for this and other changes.

1. Right-click **Start**, and click **Properties** to open the Taskbar And Start Menu Properties dialog box.
2. Click **Customize**. The Customize Start Menu dialog box will open.
3. Choose either **Large Icons** (the default) or **Small Icons**.

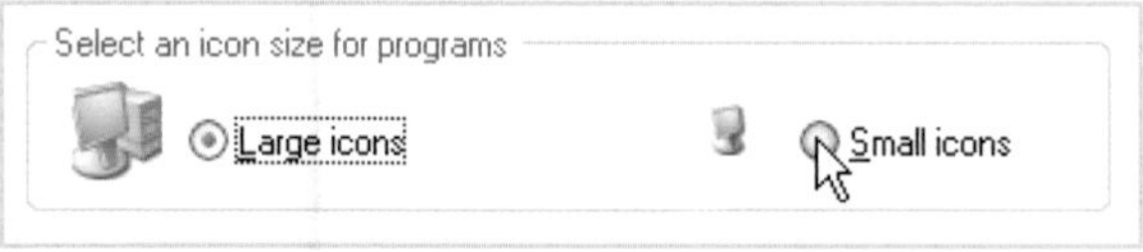

4. When you are done changing the Start menu, click **OK** twice.

NOTE

The changing of icon size only affects the icons on the left of the Start menu. The purpose of smaller icons is to list more programs.

CHANGE THE NUMBER OF PROGRAMS ON THE START MENU

On the lower-right side of the Start menu is a list of programs you have recently used (initially they are programs that Microsoft wants to promote). You can change the number of programs listed and erase the list.

1. Right-click **Start**, and click **Properties** to open the Taskbar And Start Menu Properties dialog box.

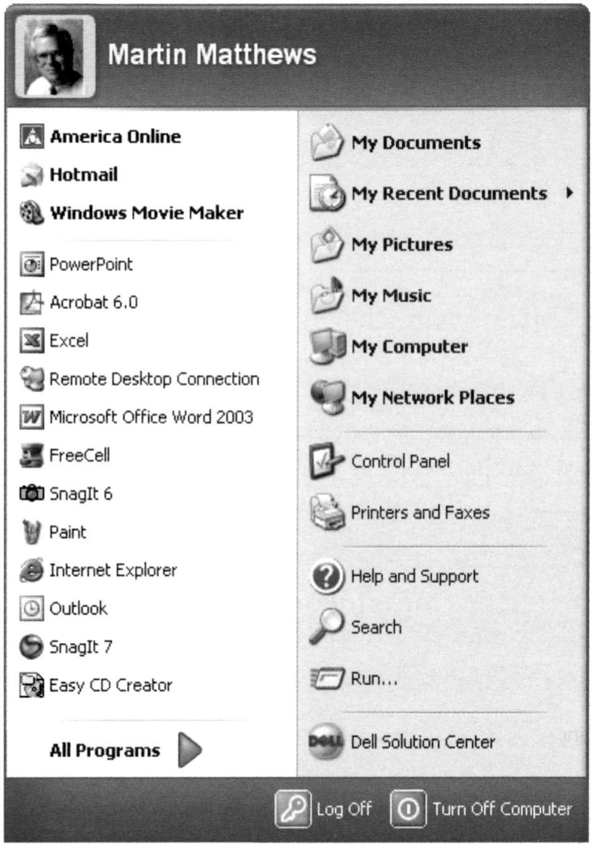

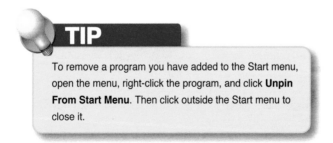

Figure 2-7: Start menu with many of the changes described here. Compare to Figure 1-3 in Chapter 1

TIP

To remove a program you have added to the Start menu, open the menu, right-click the program, and click **Unpin From Start Menu**. Then click outside the Start menu to close it.

2. Click **Customize**. The Customize Start Menu dialog box will open.
3. Click the up or down arrow on the spinner for the **Number Of Programs On Start Menu** to select the number of programs displayed.

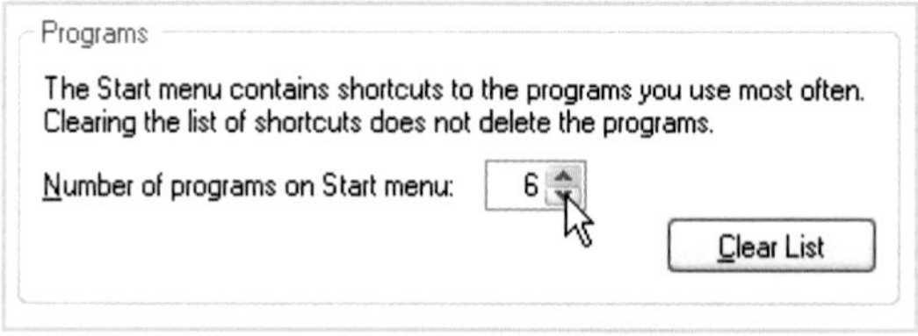

4. If you wish to erase the list and start over, click **Clear List**.
5. When you are done changing the Start menu, click **OK** twice.

CHANGE THE START MENU PROGRAMS USED FOR THE INTERNET

The Windows XP Start menu has spots for icons for an Internet browser (a program to access the World Wide Web) and an Internet e-mail program. Initially these icons open Internet Explorer and Outlook Express. However, you can change the programs opened, or you can turn off the icons.

1. Right-click **Start**, and click **Properties** to open the Taskbar And Start Menu Properties dialog box.
2. Click **Customize**. The Customize Start Menu dialog box will open.
3. If you want to change your Internet browser, open the **Internet** drop-down list, and select the browser you want to use.

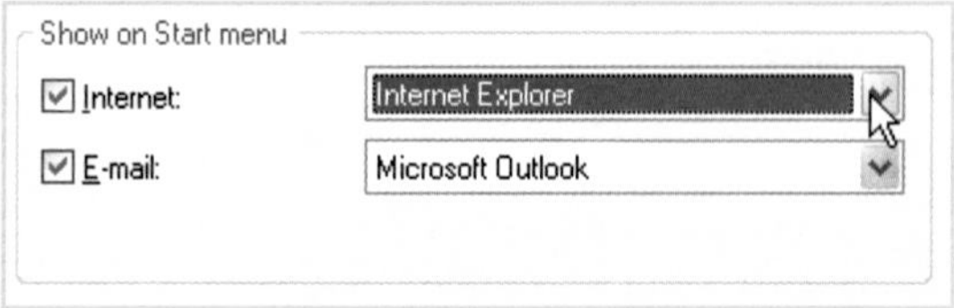

4. If you want to change your Internet mail program, open the **Internet** drop-down list, and select the program you want to use.

5. If you don't want to display either a browser or an e-mail program, click **Internet** and/or **E-Mail** to turn them off.

6. When you are done changing the Start menu, click **OK** twice.

CHANGE HOW THE START MENU OPERATES

Windows XP gives you considerable flexibility as to what is displayed on the right side of the menu and how those items work.

1. Right-click **Start**, and click **Properties** to open the Taskbar And Start Menu Properties dialog box.
2. Click **Customize**, and then click the **Advanced** tab. The Advanced tab of the Customize Start Menu dialog box will open. See Figure 2-8, which shows the default settings.
3. Select **Open Submenus When I Pause On Them With My Mouse** if you prefer that to actually clicking menu items.
4. Select **Highlight Newly Installed Programs** if you want to do that.
5. Select the **Start Menu Items** you want displayed on the right of the Start menu and how you want them to react when they are clicked.
6. Select List **My Most Recently Opened Documents** if you want such a list on the Start menu.
7. When you are done changing the Start menu, click **OK** twice.

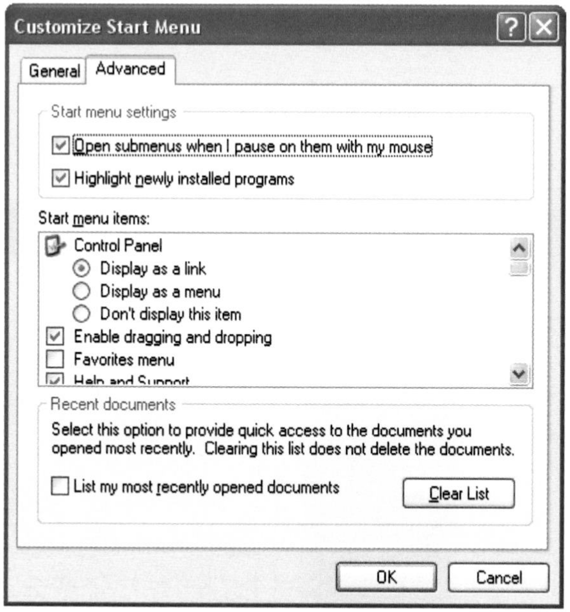

Figure 2-8: You can control what is displayed on the right side of the menu and how those items work

ADD PROGRAMS TO THE START MENU

You can add programs to the upper-left of the Start menu:

1. Open **Start**, select **All Programs**, and open the appropriate folders to display the program you want on the Start menu.
2. Right-click the program, and click **Pin To Start Menu**. The program will appear on the Start menu.
3. Click outside the Start menu to close it.

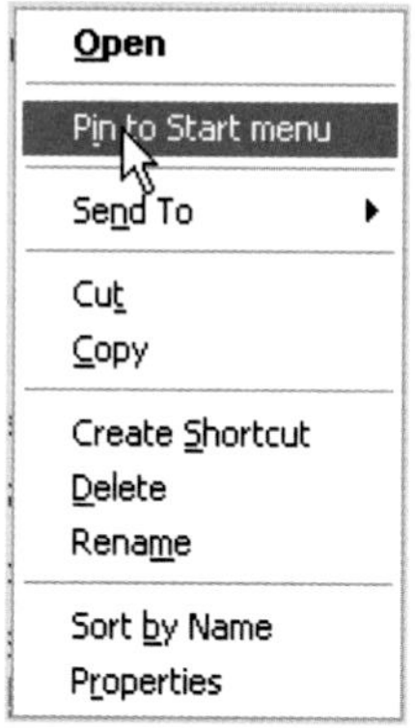

NOTE

In a dialog box you click a check box to select, or "check," it; you also click it to uncheck it. To make a clear distinction, we will use the term "select" to indicate that the check box should have a check mark in it.

1 2 3 4 5 6 7 8 9 10

Change the Taskbar

The taskbar at the bottom of the Windows XP screen has three standard areas: the Start button on the left, the task list in the middle, and the notification area on the right. In addition, there is an optional area called the Quick Launch toolbar. You can change the taskbar by moving and sizing it and by changing its properties.

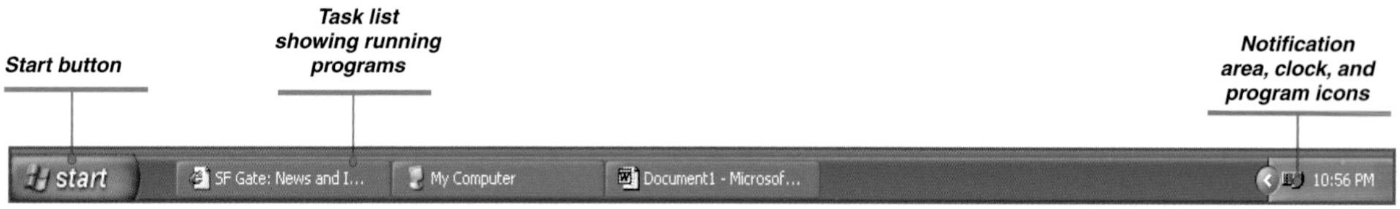

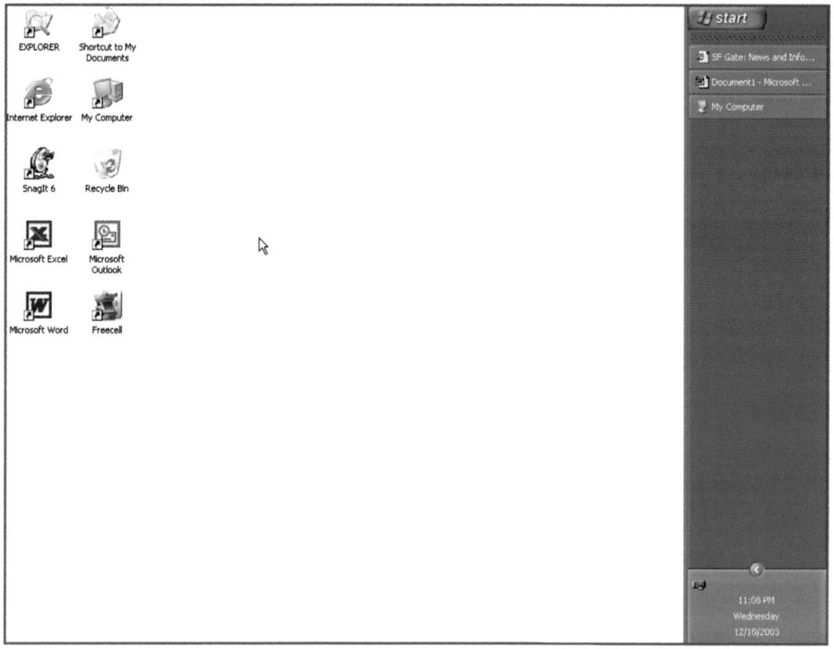

Figure 2-9: A taskbar can be moved to any of the four sides of the screen

MOVE AND SIZE THE TASKBAR

You can move the taskbar to any of the four sides of the screen. Do this by dragging any empty area of the taskbar to another edge. For example, Figure 2-9 shows the taskbar moved to the right edge.

You can size the taskbar by dragging the inner edge (top edge when the taskbar is on the bottom) in or out. Here is a taskbar at double its normal size:

Use the Quick Launch Toolbar

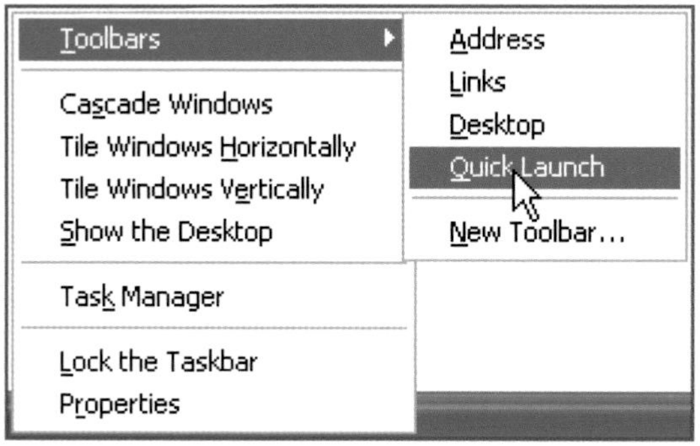

Although the QuickLaunch toolbar is turned off by default, when it is turned on it is placed next to the Start menu. It holds frequently used icons, and by clicking them you can easily start a program or open a folder.

TURN ON THE QUICK LAUNCH TOOLBAR

You can turn on the Quick Launch toolbar in the Taskbar And Start Menu Properties dialog box,

-Or-

Right-click a blank area of the taskbar, choose **Toolbars**, and click **Quick Launch**.

ADD PROGRAMS TO THE QUICK LAUNCH TOOLBAR

When you first turn on the Quick Launch toolbar, it has three icons, one each for Internet Explorer, Windows Media Player, and Show Desktop. (Show Desktop minimizes all the windows on the desktop so you can see the icons there.)

You can add program, file, and folder icons to the toolbar in all the ways you add them to the desktop, except that you drag the icons to the toolbar instead of to the desktop. See the QuickSteps "Adding Other Program Icons to the Desktop," found earlier in this chapter.

NOTE

The vertical column of dots on either side of the Quick Launch toolbar isn't available if "Lock The Taskbar" is enabled. Right-click the taskbar, and click **Lock The Taskbar** to unlock it (no check mark).

QUICKSTEPS

CHANGING TASKBAR PROPERTIES

OPEN TASKBAR PROPERTIES

Right-click an open area of the taskbar, and choose **Properties**. The Taskbar And Start Menu Properties dialog box opens with the Taskbar tab selected, as you can see in Figure 2-10.

LOCK THE TASKBAR

Locking the taskbar prevents it from being moved or resized. By default it is unlocked.

Click **Lock The Taskbar** to place a check mark there and lock the taskbar.

HIDE THE TASKBAR

Hiding the taskbar means that it is not displayed unless you move the mouse to the edge of the screen containing the taskbar. By default it is displayed.

Click **Auto-Hide The Taskbar** to place a check mark and hide the taskbar.

KEEP THE TASKBAR ON TOP

Keeping the taskbar on top means that it is always visible, nothing can cover it. By default it is kept on top.

Click **Keep The Taskbar On Top Of Other Windows** to remove the check mark and not keep the taskbar on top.

GROUP SIMILAR BUTTONS

Grouping similar items puts, for example, all Word documents in one icon or all Internet pages in one icon so they take less room on the taskbar. By default similar buttons are grouped.

Click **Group Similar Taskbar Buttons** to remove the check mark and disable this option.

Continued…

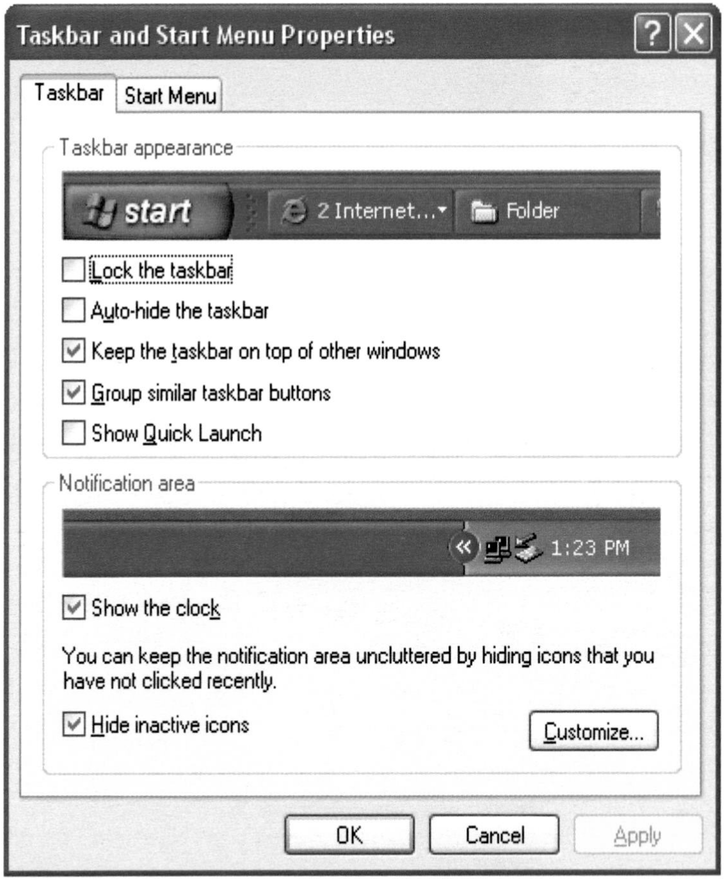

Figure 2-10: The Taskbar Properties dialog box sets how the taskbar looks and operates

CHANGING TASKBAR PROPERTIES

(Continued)

SHOW THE CLOCK

The clock in the notification area shows, at a minimum, the current time and can display the day and date. By default the clock is shown.

Click **Show The Clock** to remove the check mark and not display the clock.

HIDE INACTIVE ICONS

Hiding inactive icons removes icons that have not been recently used from the notification area. By default the inactive icons are hidden.

Click **Hide Inactive Icons** to remove the check mark and display the inactive icons.

CUSTOMIZE THE NOTIFICATION AREA

The notification area contains program icons put there by Windows or the program itself. It normally gets crowded. You can control which icons are displayed, hidden, or not there at all.

1. Click **Customize**. The Customize Notifications dialog box will open.
2. Click a program icon whose appearance you want to change.
3. Open the drop-down list that appears, and select the behavior you want.
4. When you have made the changes you want, click **OK**.

CLOSE TASKBAR PROPERTIES

After you've made any of these changes to the taskbar, click **OK** to enable them and close the Taskbar Properties dialog box.

REMOVE PROGRAMS FROM THE QUICK LAUNCH TOOLBAR

To remove a program icon from the Quick Launch toolbar, right-click the icon, choose **Delete**, and click **Delete Shortcut**.

Change How Windows XP Operates

How Windows XP operates is probably more important to you than how it looks. For that reason, Windows has a number of facilities to allow you to customize its operation.

Set and Use the Date and Time

The time in the lower-right corner of the screen may seem simple enough, but significant capability lies behind these simple numbers.

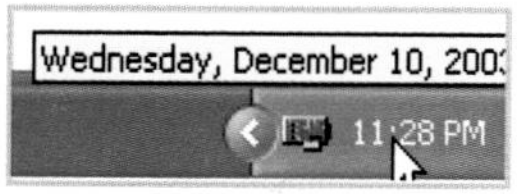

1. Move the mouse until your cursor is on the time in the notification area. The current day and date will appear.
2. Double-click the time. The Date And Time Properties dialog box will appear, as shown in Figure 2-11.
3. With the **Date & Time** tab selected, use the month drop-down list and the year spinner, click a day, or click an element of time (hour, minute, second), and use the spinner to set the selected time element.
4. Click the **Time Zone** tab, open the drop-down list box, and select your time zone.
5. Select **Automatically Adjust Clock For Daylight Saving Changes** if it isn't already checked and you want Windows to do that.
6. Click the **Internet Time** tab, select **Automatically Synchronize With An Internet Time Server** if it isn't already checked, select a time server, and click **Update Now**. Once turned on, Windows will check the time every seven days.
7. Click **OK** to close the Date And Time Properties dialog box.

QUICKSTEPS

REARRANGING THE QUICK LAUNCH TOOLBAR

The Quick Launch toolbar can be expanded to display more icons, moved around the taskbar, and "undocked" from the taskbar to become a floating, independent toolbar. Additionally, icons on the Quick Launch toolbar can be moved around and hidden.

SIZE THE QUICK LAUNCH TOOLBAR

Drag the vertical column of dots on the right of the toolbar to the right (to enlarge) or to the left (to reduce) the Quick Launch toolbar. As the toolbar is made smaller, icons may be hidden.

MOVE THE QUICK LAUNCH TOOLBAR

Drag the vertical column of dots on the left of the toolbar to move it to another location on the taskbar. To get around other icons on the taskbar, you may need to use a two-row taskbar or delete the other icons.

UNDOCK THE QUICK LAUNCH TOOLBAR

Drag the vertical column of dots on the left of the toolbar onto the desktop to make the Quick Launch toolbar a separate, floating toolbar. To reattach it, drag the toolbar back to the taskbar, placing where you want it.

MOVE ICONS WITHIN THE QUICK LAUNCH TOOLBAR

Drag the Quick Launch icons where you want them on the toolbar.

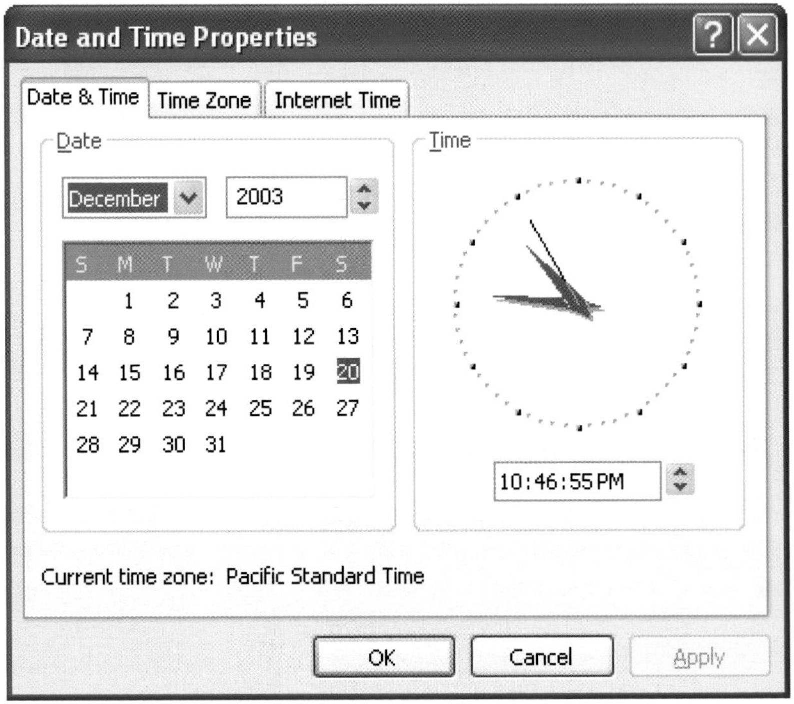

Figure 2-11: Setting the date and time can be automated using a government time server on the Internet

Use Accessibility Options

Accessibility Options provide alternatives to the normal way the mouse and keyboard are used as well as some settings that make the screen more readable. Accessibility Options are accessed from the Control Panel.

1. Open **Start** and click **Control Panel**.

2. In Category View, click **Accessibility Options**, and then click **Accessibility Options** again.
3. In Classic View, double-click **Accessibility Options**. In either view, the Accessibility Options dialog box will open, as you can see in Figure 2-12.
4. Select the options you want to use on the Keyboard, Sound, Display, and Mouse tabs (see Table 2-1). For the options you checked, click **Settings** to review and possibly change the specific settings of that option.
5. Click the **General** tab, to review and possibly change the settings that apply to all accessibility options.
6. When you have set up the accessibility options you want, click **OK**.

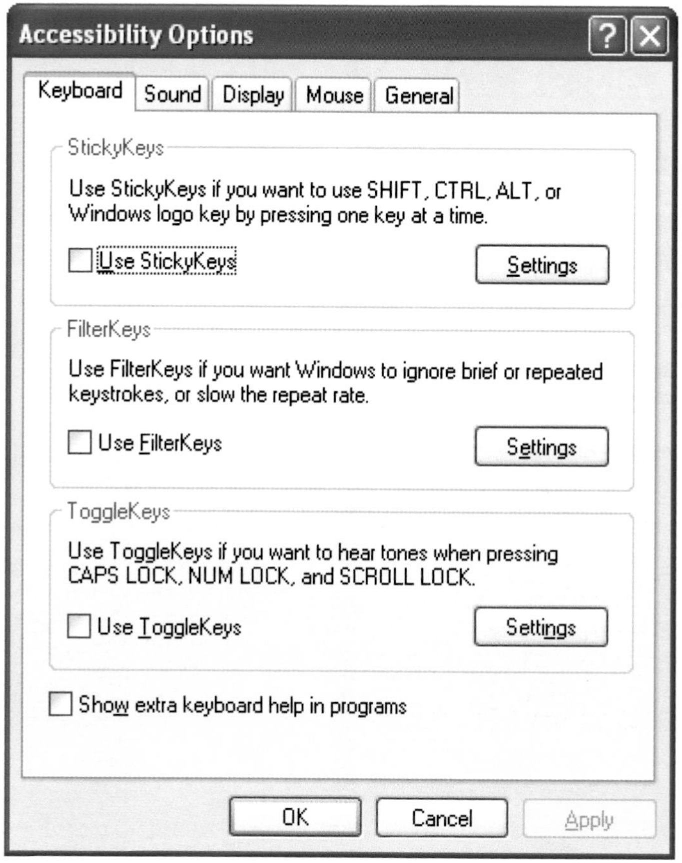

Figure 2-12: Accessibility Options let you access Windows XP and the programs that run under it in different ways

NOTE

Many of the Control Panel components are also available from other locations. For example, the Date And Time component opens the same dialog box as that which opened when you double-click the time in the taskbar.

QUICKSTEPS

USING THE CONTROL PANEL

The Control Panel is a facility for changing many of the functions available in Windows. The individual components of the Control Panel are discussed throughout this book (several in this chapter); this is an introduction to the Control Panel itself.

OPEN THE CONTROL PANEL

Open **Start** and click **Control Panel**. The Control Panel will open, as shown in Figure 2-13.

SWITCH THE CONTROL PANEL VIEW

The Control Panel has two configurations: the default Category View, shown in Figure 2-13, and Classic View, shown in Figure 2-14. Classic View has icons for all the Control Panel components in one window.

When in Category View, click **Switch To Classic View** in the task pane.

When in Classic View, click **Switch To Category View** in the task pane.

OPEN A CONTROL PANEL CATEGORY

Category View groups Control Panel components into categories that must be opened to see the individual components.

Click a category to open a pane, where you can select either a task you want to do or open a Control Panel component represented by an icon.

OPEN A CONTROL PANEL COMPONENT

In both Classic View and in the secondary window in Category View are icons for individual Control Panel components. To open a component:

Double-click (in Classic View) or click (in Category View) the component's icon.

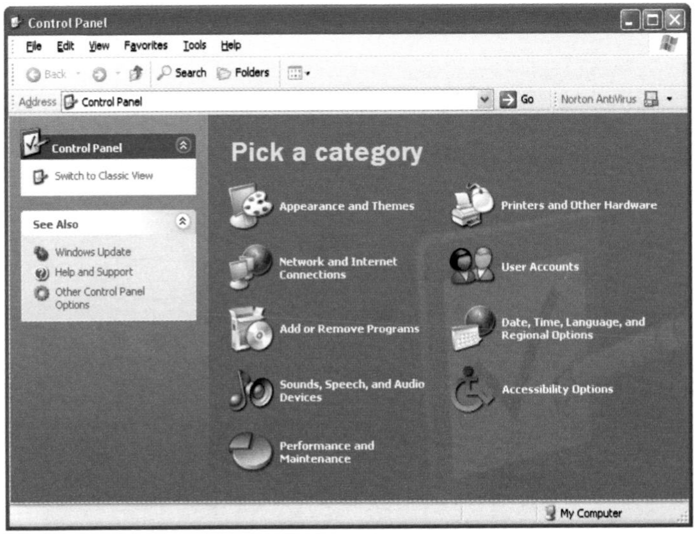

Figure 2-13: The Control Panel's Category View groups components into categories

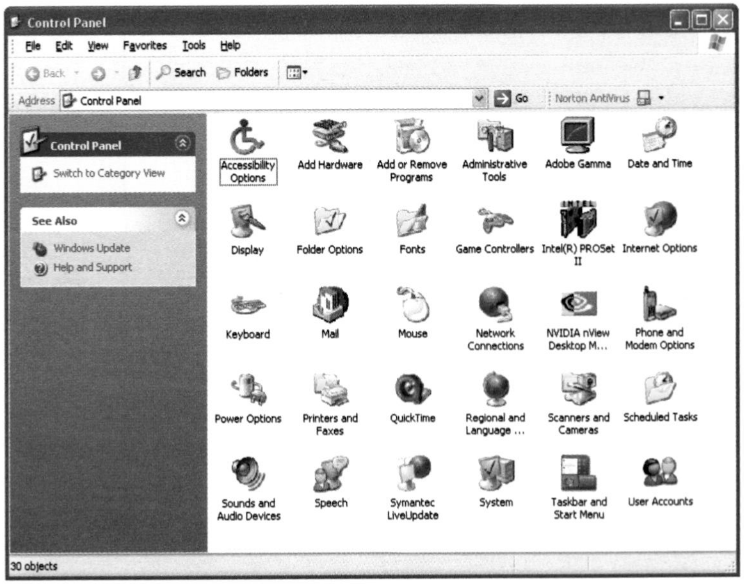

Figure 2-14: The Control Panel's Classic View shows all the components in the Control Panel

TABLE 2-1: ACCESSIBILITY OPTIONS

TAB	OPTION	DESCRIPTION	TURN ON OR OFF
Keyboard	StickyKeys	Simulates pressing a pair of keys, such as **CTRL+A**, by pressing one key at a time. The keys **SHIFT**, **CTRL**, and **ALT** "stick" down until a second key is pressed. This is interpreted as two keys pressed together.	Press either **SHIFT** key five times in succession.
Keyboard	FilterKeys	Enables you to press a key twice in rapid succession and have it interpreted as a single keystroke; also slows down the rate at which the key is repeated if it is held down.	Hold down the right **SHIFT** key for eight seconds.
Keyboard	ToggleKeys	Plays a tone when **CAPS LOCK**, **NUM LOCK**, or **SCROLL LOCK** is pressed.	Hold down **NUM LOCK** for five seconds.
Sound	SoundSentry	Displays a visual indicator when the computer makes a sound. The indicator can be a flashing, active, caption bar; a flashing, active window; or a flashing desktop.	Open **Accessibility Options**, and click **Use SoundSentry** in the Sound tab.
Sound	ShowSounds	Tells compatible programs to display captions when sound and speech are used.	Open **Accessibility Options**, and click **Use ShowSounds** in the Sound tab.
Display	High Contrast	Uses high-contrast colors and special fonts to make the screen easy to use.	Press together left **SHIFT**, left **ALT**, and **PRINT SCREEN**.
Display	Cursor Options	Enables you to change the cursor blink rate and the width of the cursor to make it easier to see.	Open **Accessibility Options**, and set the **Blink Rate** and **Width** in the Display tab.
Mouse	MouseKeys	Enables you to use the numeric keypad instead of the mouse to move the pointer on the screen.	Press together left **SHIFT**, left **ALT**, and **NUM LOCK**.

Customize the Mouse

The mouse lets you interact with the screen and point at, select, and drag objects. You also can start and stop programs and close Windows. While you can use Windows without a mouse, it is much more difficult, making it important that the mouse operates in the most comfortable way possible. Change the way the mouse works through the Control Panel Mouse component:

> **NOTE**
>
> If you have purchased a mouse separately from your computer and have installed its software (such as IntelliPoint), your tabs will probably be different and its features may not be as described here.

1. Open **Start** and click **Control Panel**.
2. In Category View, click **Printers And Other Hardware**, and then click **Mouse**.
3. In Classic View, double-click **Mouse**. In either view the Mouse Properties dialog box will open, as you can see in Figure 2-15.
4. Double-click the folder in the middle-right of the **Buttons** tab. If the folder opens, your double-click speed is OK. If not, adjust the **Speed** slider until the folder opens when you double-click on it.
5. Select the options you want to use on the **Buttons** and **Pointer Options** tabs. Check marks indicate the options you want.
6. Open the **Pointers** tab. If you want to change it, select a different scheme.
7. When you have set up the mouse the way you want, click **OK**.

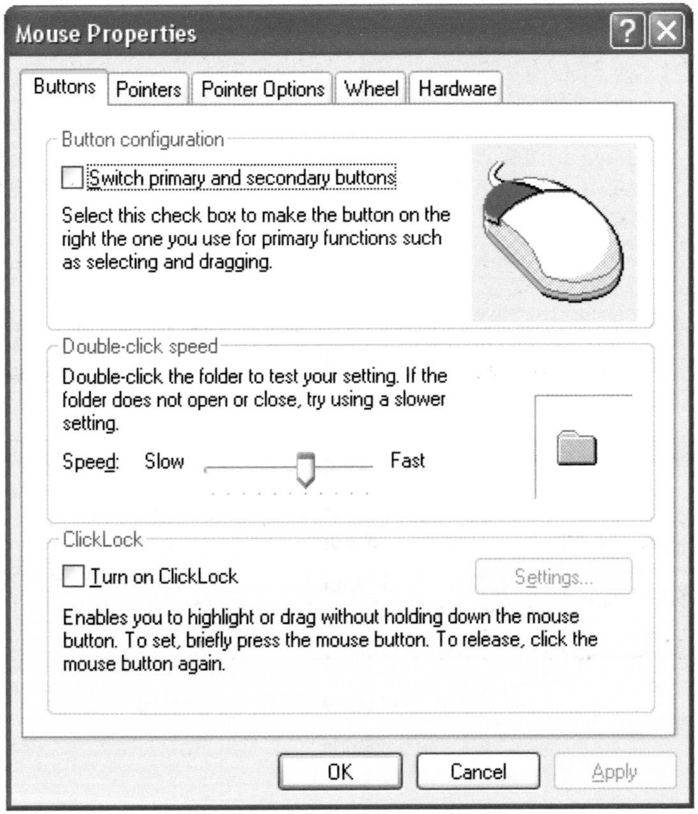

Figure 2-15: The mouse is the primary way you communicate with Windows XP

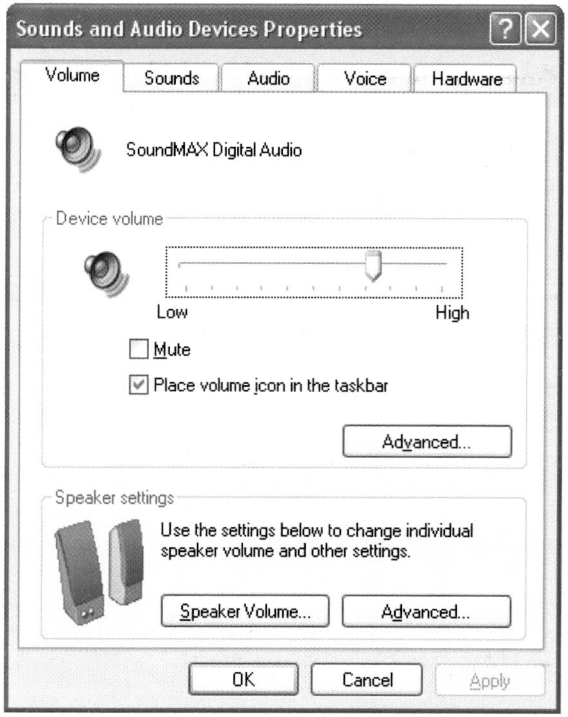

Figure 2-16: Windows XP has extensive audio capability including up to seven-speaker surround sound; set this up in the Sounds and Audio Devices Properties dialog box, click Advanced and then open Speaker Setup

Customize the Keyboard

Windows requires a keyboard for textual communications. You can change the length of the delay before a key that is held down is repeated and the rate at which the key is repeated.

1. Open **Start** and click **Control Panel**.
2. In Category View, click **Printers And Other Hardware**, and then click **Keyboard**.
3. In Classic View, double-click **Keyboard**. In either view the Keyboard Properties dialog box will open.
4. Point in the test area in the middle of the dialog box, and press a key to see how long you wait before the key is repeated and how the repeated character appears.
5. Drag **Repeat Delay** in the direction desired, and then test the repetition again.
6. Drag **Repeat Rate** in the direction desired, and then test the repetition again.
7. Drag **Cursor Blink Rate** in the direction desired.
8. When you have set up the keyboard the way you want, click **OK**.

Change Sounds

Windows XP uses sound to alert and entertain you. Through the Control Panel's Sounds And Audio Devices component you can select the sound scheme you want. See Figure 2-16.

1. Open **Start** and click **Control Panel**.
2. In Category View, click **Sounds, Speech, And Audio Devices**, and then click **Sounds And Audio Devices**.
3. In Classic View, double-click **Sounds And Audio Devices**. In either view, the Sounds And Audio Devices Properties dialog box will open.
4. Drag **Device Volume** in the direction desired.
5. Click the **Sounds** tab, and if you want to change it, select a different sound scheme.
6. When you have set up the sounds the way you want, click **OK**.

Change Regional Settings

Windows XP lets you determine how numbers, dates, currency, and time are displayed and used, as well as the languages that will be used. Choosing a primary language and locale sets all the other settings. You can customize these options through Regional And Language Options.

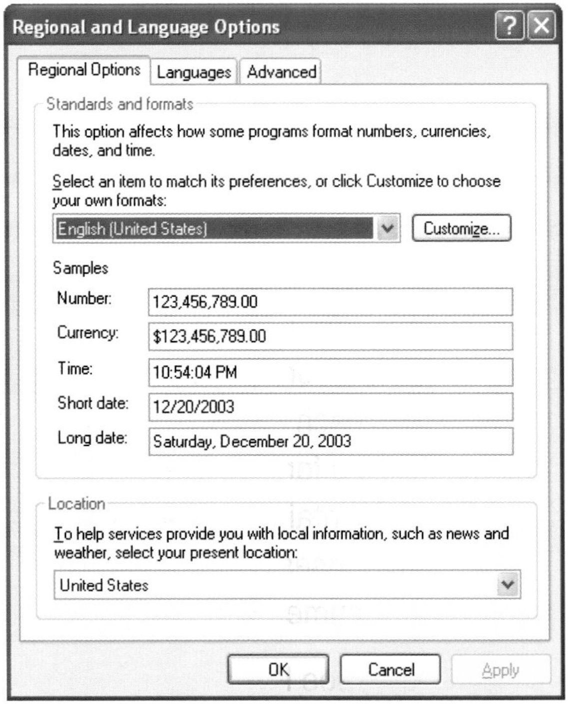

Figure 2-17: Regional and Language Options allow Windows XP to operate almost anywhere in the world

1. Open **Start** and click **Control Panel**.
2. In Category View, click **Date, Time, Language, And Regional Options**; and then click **Regional And Language Options**.
3. In Classic View, double-click **Regional And Language Options**. In either view, the Regional And Language Options dialog box will open, as you can see in Figure 2-17.
4. Select the primary language and region in which the computer will be used. This changes the standards and formats.
5. Customize these settings by clicking **Customize;** going into the individual tabs for numbers, currency, time, and date; and setting how you want items displayed.
6. Open the **Languages** tab, and select the secondary languages in which you will be typing and how you want to switch between them.
7. When you have set up the regional settings the way you want, click **OK**.

How to...

- *Display Files and Folders*
- *Changing Windows Explorer Views*
- *Identify Disk Storage Devices*
- *Select and Open Folders*
- *Create New Folders*
- *Renaming and Deleting*
- *Customize Explorer*
- *Change Folder Options*
- *Select Multiple Files and Folders*
- *Copying and Moving*
- *Use the Recycle Bin*
- *Create Shortcuts*
- *Search for Files and Folders*
- *Create Files*
- *Encrypt Files and Folders*
- *Compress Files and Folders*
- *Change Other Attributes*
- *Zipping Files and Folders*
- *Back Up Files and Folders*
- *Managing Disks*
- *Write Files and Folders to a CD*

Chapter 3
Storing Information

The information on your computer—documents, e-mail, photographs, music, and programs—are stored in *files*. So that your files are organized and more easily found, they are kept in *folders*, and folders can be placed in other folders for further segmentation. For example, a folder labeled "My Trips" contains folders for each year, 2003 and 2004. The 2003 folder contains folders for Yellowstone and Disneyland. The Yellowstone folder contains a folder of pictures, notes, sound recordings, and expenses. Such a set of files and folders is shown in the My Documents folder in Figure 3-1.

In this chapter you'll see how to create, use, and manage files and folders like these. (In this chapter the term "objects" refers to any mix of files, folders, and disk drives.)

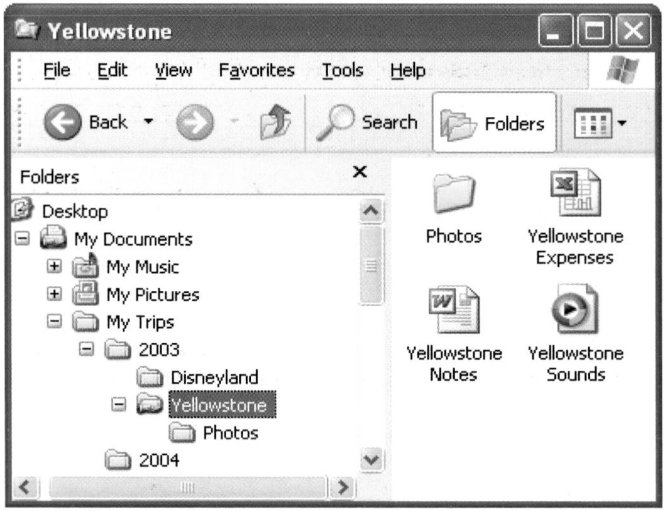

Figure 3-1: Windows Explorer in Folders view showing files in folders within other folders

Display Files and Folders

The tool that Windows XP provides to display and work with files and folders is *Windows Explorer* (called "Explorer" from here on). It has two views: the *Folders view*, shown in Figure 3-1, and the *Tasks view*, shown in Figure 3-2.

To open Explorer in Tasks view you must choose what you want it to display from among the choices on the right of the Start menu.

1. Start your computer if it's not running and log on to Windows XP if necessary.
2. Click **Start**. The Start menu will open and you'll see these choices in the upper right of the menu:

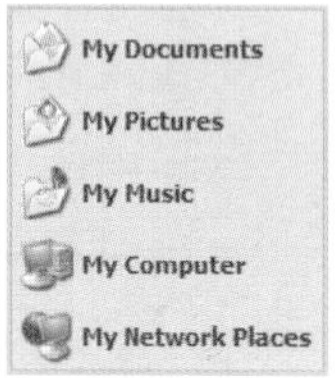

3. Click **My Computer**. Explorer will open in Tasks view, as shown in Figure 3-2. Your view will be different, with a different number of drives and different names for your documents.

Close and reopen an area of the Tasks pane by clicking here

Double-clicking an object on the right of Explorer opens it so that you can see and work with its contents

Tasks pane, allows you to perform tasks on displayed objects and to go to other places

Details provides information about the object you have selected

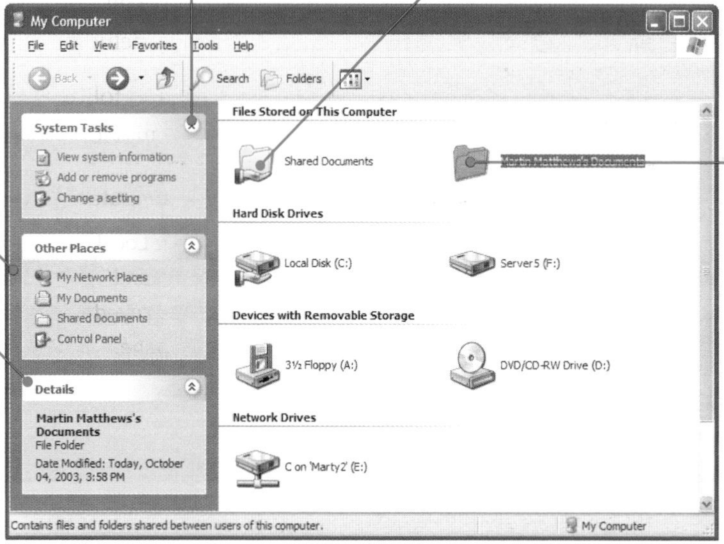

Clicking an object on the right of Explorer selects it and gives you information about it in the Tasks pane Details

Figure 3-2: Windows Explorer in Tasks view

QUICKSTEPS

CHANGING WINDOWS EXPLORER VIEWS

CHANGE FROM TASKS TO FOLDERS VIEW

When in Tasks view, to switch to Folders View click the **Folders** button on the toolbar.

CHANGE FROM FOLDERS TO TASKS VIEW

When in Folders view, to switch to Tasks view, either:

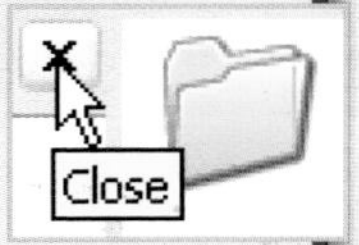

Click the **Folders** button on the toolbar.

–Or–

Click the **Close** button in the Folders pane.

OPEN EXPLORER IN FOLDERS VIEW

From the Desktop, to open the Explorer, either:

Right-click **Start** and choose **Explore.**

–Or–

Press (Windows logo key)+E (both keys together).

NOTE

My Computer is one particular view of Explorer that opens to show all of the storage devices on the computer.

Identify Disk Storage Devices

Files and folders are held on various physical storage devices called *disk drives*. You will have some, but not necessarily all, of the following:

- Primary floppy disk, labeled "A:"
- Secondary floppy disk, labeled "B:"
- Primary hard disk, labeled "C:"
- Primary CD or DVD Drive, labeled "D:"
- Other disk drives, labeled "E:" and on

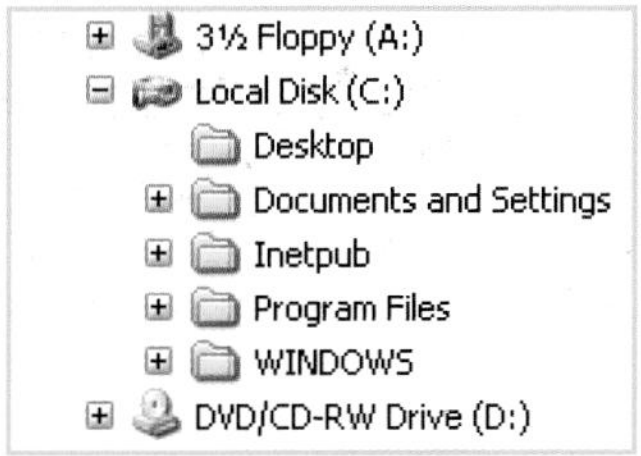

Your primary floppy drive is always labeled "A:" Your primary hard disk is always labeled "C:". Other drives have flexible labeling. Often the CD or DVD drive will be drive "D:".

Select and Open Folders

When you open Explorer in Tasks view with My Computer you see the disk drives on your computer as well as two folders, *Shared Documents* and *My Documents* (which may also include your name, as you saw in Figure 3-2).

To work with these drives and folders you must select them, and to see their contents you must open them. Here's how to do that:

1. Open **Start** and click **My Computer** to open Explorer in Tasks view.
2. Click **Local Disk (C:)**. "Your Local Disk (C:)" will be highlighted and its characteristics will be displayed under Details in the Tasks pane.

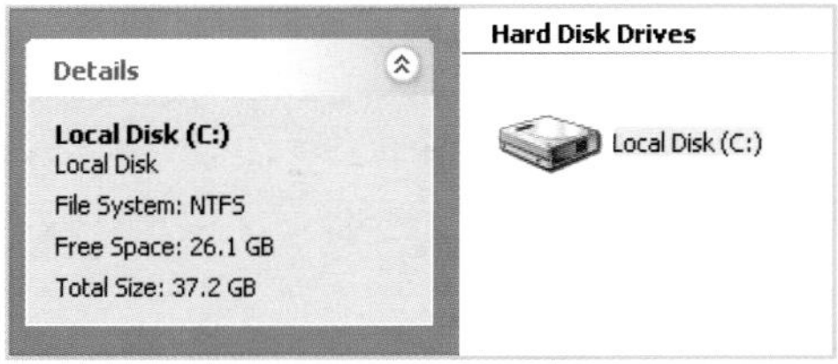

1 2 3 4 5 6 7 8 9 10

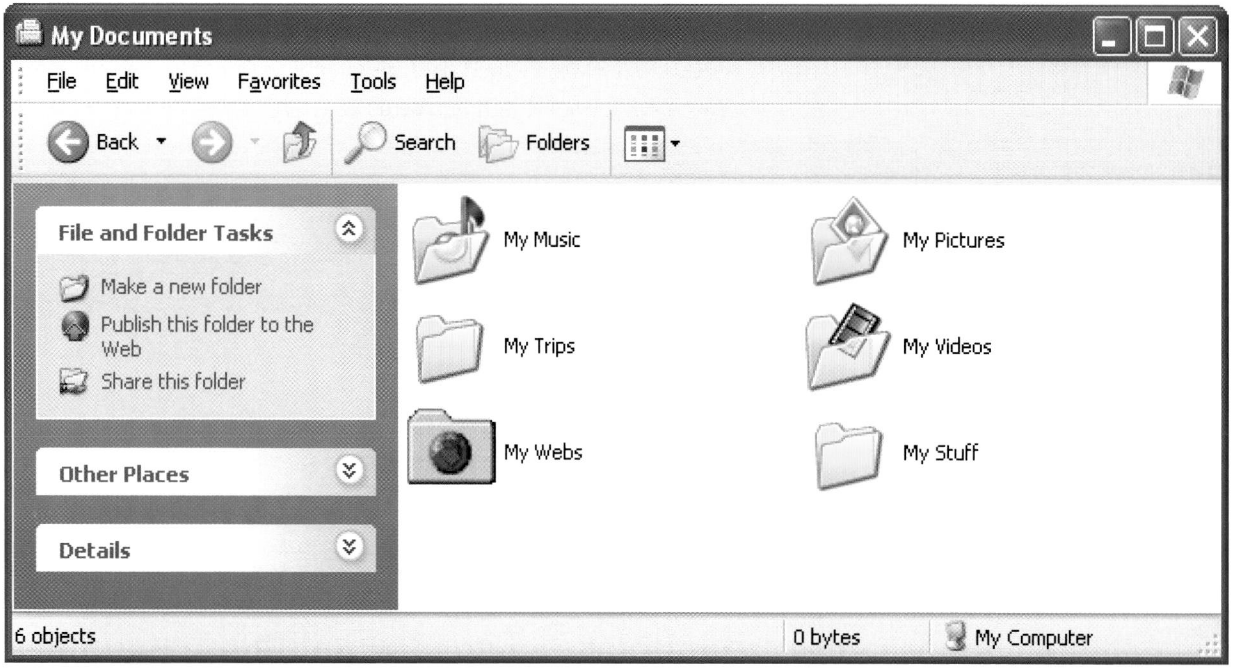

Figure 3-3: The contents of My Documents within My Computer

3. Double-click **My Documents** (or the folder with your name and Documents). The contents of Explorer will change to show the files and folders in My Documents. At a minimum this is My Music and My Pictures. You will probably have others as well, as shown in Figure 3-3.
4. Keep double-clicking each folder to open it until you see the contents you are looking for.

QUICKSTEPS

RENAMING AND DELETING FILES AND FOLDERS

RENAME A FILE OR FOLDER

With the file or folder in view but not selected, to rename it:

Slowly click the name twice, type the new name, and press **ENTER.**

–Or–

Right-click the name, choose **Rename**, type the new name, and press **ENTER**.

DELETE A FILE OR FOLDER

With the file or folder in view, to delete it:

Click the icon to select it, press **DELETE**, and click **Yes** to confirm the deletion.

–Or–

Right-click the icon, choose **Delete**, and click **Yes** to confirm the deletion.

RECOVER A DELETED FILE OR FOLDER

To recover a file or folder that has been deleted:

Open Explorer's **Edit** menu and choose **Undo Delete.**

–Or–

Double-click the **Recycle Bin** on the desktop to open it, right-click the file or folder icon, and choose **Restore.**

PERMANENTLY DELETE A FILE OR FOLDER

If you're sure you want to permanently delete a file or folder, either:

Click the icon to select it, press and hold **SHIFT** while pressing **DELETE**, and click **Yes** to confirm the deletion.

–Or–

Double-click the **Recycle Bin** to open it, right-click the icon, choose **Delete**, and click **Yes** to confirm the deletion.

Create New Folders

While you could store all your files within one of the ready-made folders in Windows XP—such as My Documents, My Music, and My Pictures—you will probably want to make your files easier to find by creating several subsidiary folders.

For example, to create the My Trips folder discussed earlier:

1. Open **Explorer** in Tasks view to display My Documents as described immediately above. Make sure nothing is selected.
2. Click **Make A New Folder** at the top of the Tasks pane. A new folder will appear with its name highlighted.
3. Type the name of the folder, such as My Trips, and press **ENTER**. Double-click your new folder to open it.

As an alternative to using the Tasks pane, right-click the open area in the right, or *detail pane*, of Explorer. Choose **New** and click **Folder** (as shown in Figure 3-4). Type a name for the folder and press **ENTER**.

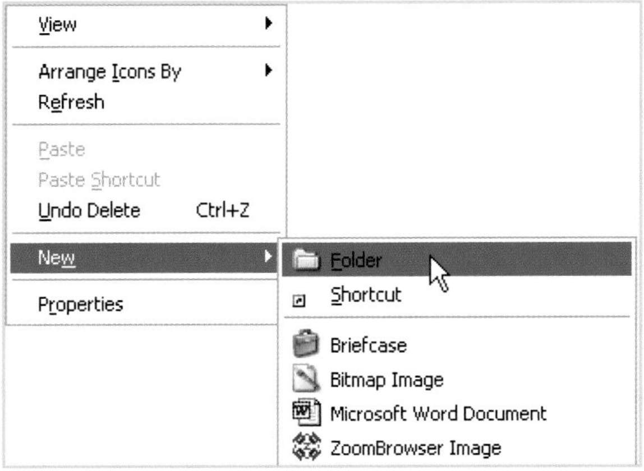

Figure 3-4: Creating a new folder by right-clicking in the Detail pane

Customize Explorer

You can customize how Explorer looks and which features are available with Explorer's View menu.

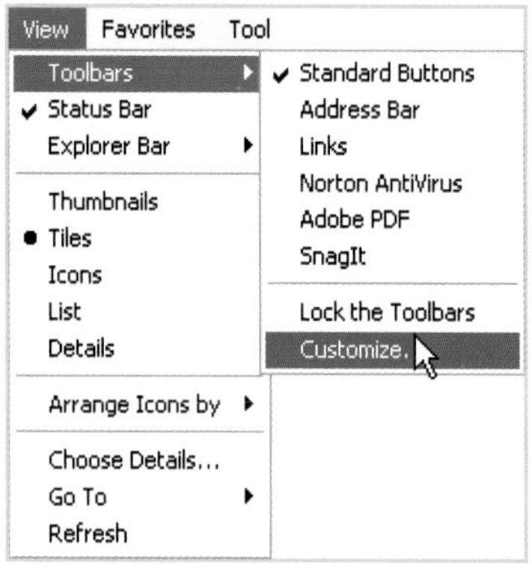

1. Open **Start**, click **My Computer**, and click the **Folders** button to display the Folders pane.
2. Click the **View** menu and point at **Toolbars**. Standard Buttons and, possibly, Lock the Toolbars are selected, while Address Bar and Links (Internet browser-related options) are not.
3. Click **Customize** to open the Customize Toolbar dialog box. Here you can change the tools on the toolbar to fit your preferences by selecting an icon on the left and clicking Add, or by selecting an icon on the right and clicking **Remove**. Click **Close**.
4. Reopen the **View** menu and click **Status Bar**. This turns on an information bar at the bottom of the window, as you can see in Figure 3-5.

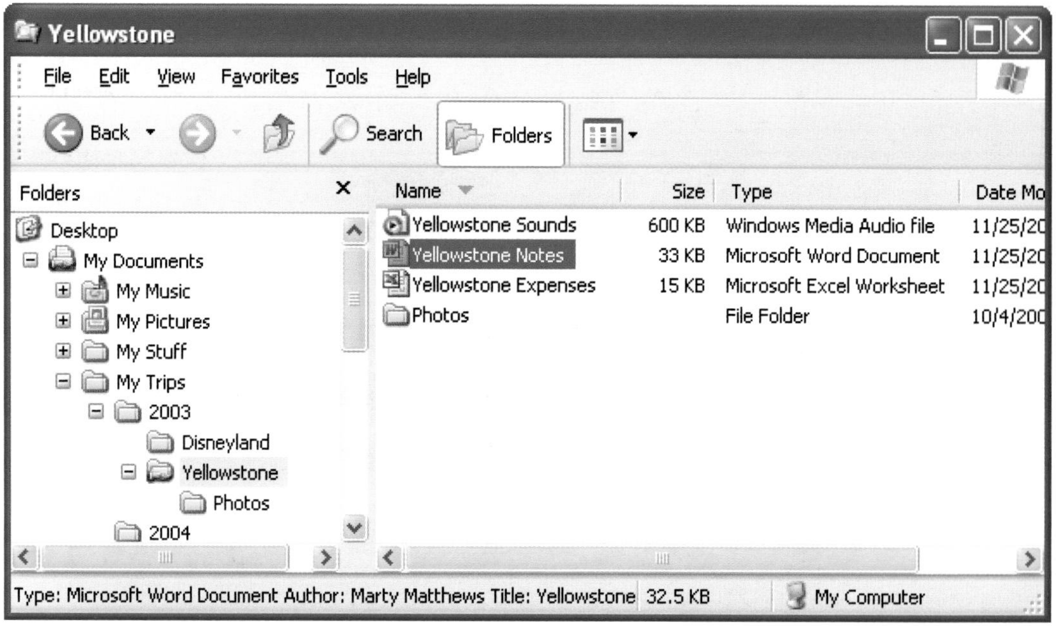

Figure 3-5: Windows Explorer in Folders view with files in Detail view and the status bar displayed

5. Reopen the **View** menu and click several display types to see your options: Thumbnails, Tiles, Icons, List, and Details. Leave the window in Details display, which is shown in Figure 3-5. (You can also switch the display with the Views button on the toolbar.)

6. Reopen the **View** menu and point at **Arrange Icons By**. This determines how the files and folders are laid out on the screen (how they are sorted).
7. If necessary, reopen the **View** menu and click **Choose Details**. This determines the information that is shown in the Details display. Click **Cancel**.
8. If necessary, reopen the **View** menu and point at **Go To**. This determines what Explorer displays next. Many of these options are available either on the left of the Explorer toolbar (shown next) or in the Folders pane.

Change Folder Options

The Folder Options dialog box provides many options to make Explorer look and behave differently. To open Folder Options:

1. Open **Explorer** in either Folders or Tasks pane view.
2. Open **Tools** and click **Folder Options**. The Folder Options dialog box will open with the General tab, as shown in Figure 3-6. This allows you to:
   - Not display the tasks pane, as was true in earlier Windows versions.
   - Open a new window for each folder you open.
   - Use a single-click in place of a double-click to open a window and determine whether or not to permanently underline an icon title as in an Internet browser.

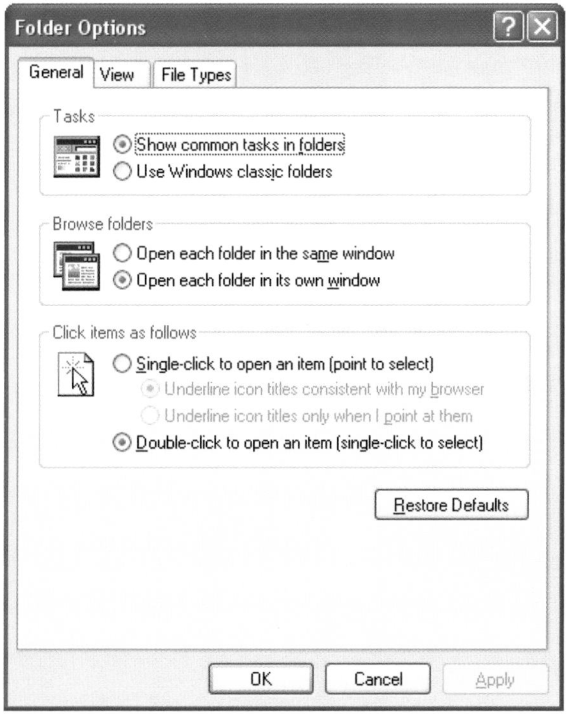

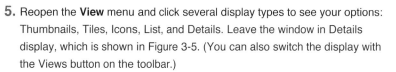

Figure 3-6: Folder Options, General tab

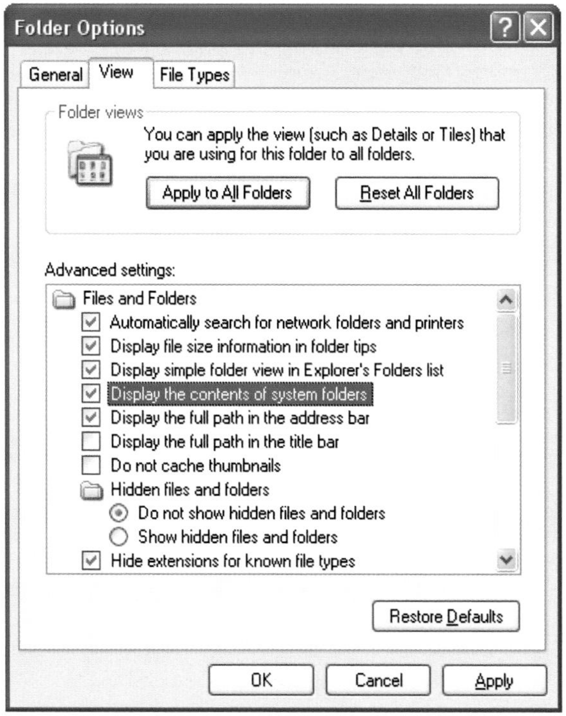

Figure 3-7: Folder Options, View tab

3. Click the **View** tab, as shown in Figure 3-7. This gives you a number of options that determine what is displayed for the current folder and allow you to apply these changes to all folders. The defaults generally work for most people. Advanced users may want to:
   - Display the contents of system folders.
   - Show hidden files and folders.
   - Not hide extensions for known file types.
   - Not hide protected operating system files.
4. Click the **File Types** tab. This shows all of the file types that are registered on your computer. The types vary, depending on the programs that are installed. File registration associates a file type with a program that can open, edit, and print it. It also provides an icon, a title, and a file extension that is used with each file type.
5. Scroll the list of **Registered File Types** until you see one you are familiar with, such as "DOC" files for Microsoft Word. In the lower part of the dialog you will see a description of the associations for this type, like this:

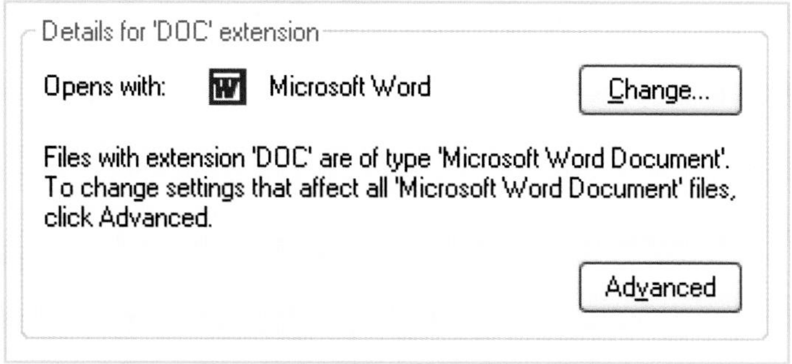

6. When you are ready, click **Close** to close the Folder Options dialog box.

Select Multiple Files and Folders

Often you will want to do one or more operations—such as copy, move, or delete—on several files and/or folders at the same time. To select several files or folders:

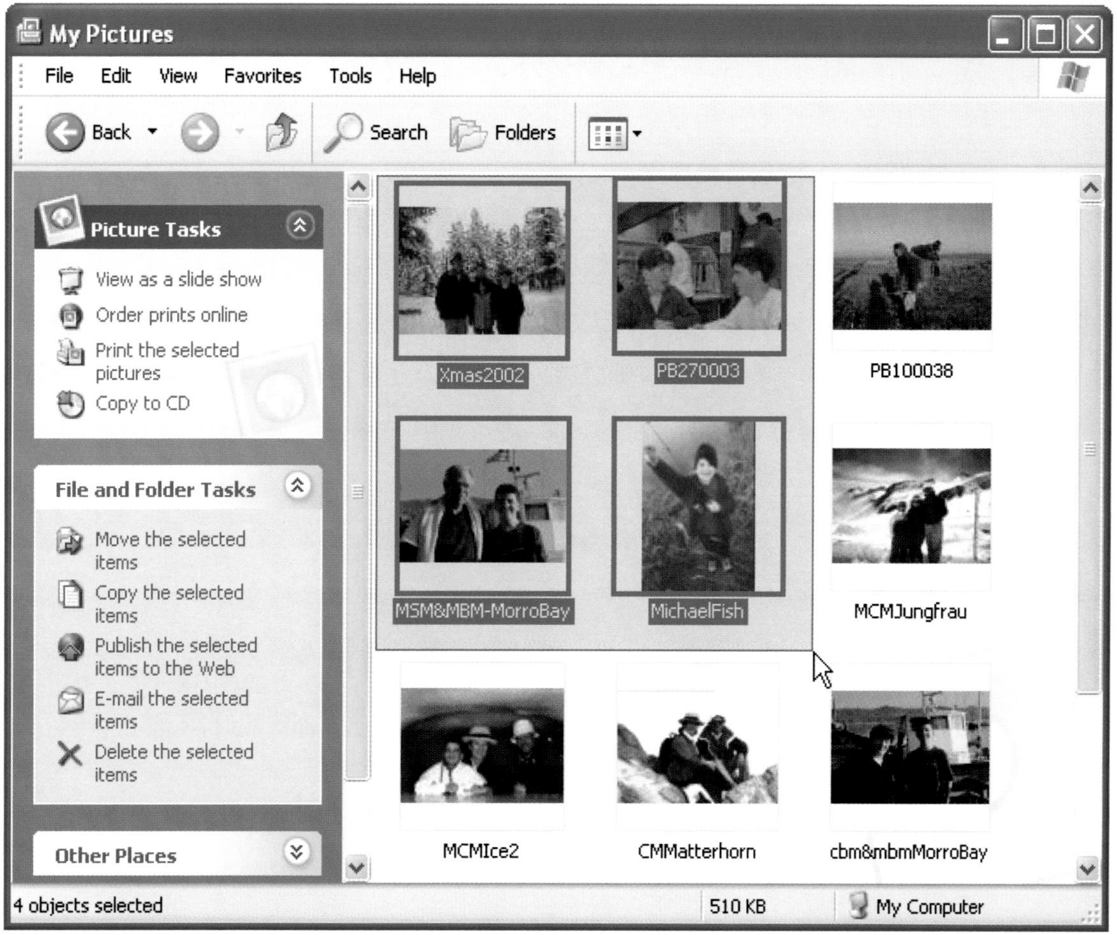

Figure 3-8: Selecting several files and/or folders

Move the mouse pointer to the upper-left, just outside of the top and left-most object. Then drag the mouse to the lower-right, just outside of the bottom and right-most object, creating a band around the objects, as shown in Figure 3-8.

–Or–

Click the first object, and press and hold **CTRL** while clicking the remaining objects if the objects are not contiguous. If the objects are contiguous, click the first object, press and hold **SHIFT,** and click the last object.

QUICKSTEPS

COPYING AND MOVING FILES AND FOLDERS

Copying and moving files and folder are similar actions and can be done with the mouse alone, with the mouse and a menu, with the keyboard, and with the mouse and the tasks pane.

COPY WITH THE MOUSE

To copy with the mouse, press and hold **CTRL** while dragging any file or folder from one folder to another on the same disk drive, or drag a file or folder from one disk drive to another.

MOVE NON-PROGRAM FILES ON THE SAME DISK WITH THE MOUSE

Move non-program files from one folder to another on the same disk with the mouse by dragging the file or folder.

MOVE NON-PROGRAM FILES TO ANOTHER DISK WITH THE MOUSE

Move non-program files to another disk by pressing and holding **SHIFT** while dragging them.

MOVE PROGRAM FILES WITH THE MOUSE

Move program files to another folder or disk by pressing and holding **SHIFT** while dragging them.

COPY AND MOVE WITH THE MOUSE AND A MENU

To copy and move with a mouse and a menu, press and hold the right-mouse button while dragging the file or folder. When you release the right-mouse button, a context menu opens and allows you to choose whether to copy, move, or create a shortcut (see "Create Shortcuts" later in this chapter).

Continued…

Figure 3-9: Determining where to move a file

COPYING AND MOVING FILES AND FOLDERS *(continued)*

COPYING AND MOVING WITH THE MOUSE AND THE TASKS PANE

If you select a file or folder by clicking it or by moving the current selection with the arrow keys, the Files And Folder Tasks list appears in the tasks pane.

When you select **Move This File** or **Copy This File**, a Move Items or Copy Items dialog box appears (see Figure 3-9), where you can select the destination.

1. Open the series of disks and folders by clicking them as needed to display the folder you want to copy or move the file or folder to.
2. Click **Copy** or **Move**.

COPY AND MOVE WITH THE KEYBOARD

Copying and moving using the keyboard is done with three sets of keys:

- **CTRL+C**, "Copy," copies the selected item to the Windows Clipboard
- **CTRL+X**, "Cut," copies the selected item to the Windows Clipboard and deletes it from the original location.
- **CTRL+V**, "Paste," copies the current contents of the Windows Clipboard to the currently open folder and to any additional folders you want to copy to by opening them and pressing **CTRL+V**.

To copy a file from one folder to another using the keyboard:

1. In Explorer, open the disk and folder containing the file to be copied.
2. Select the file and press **CTRL+C** to copy the file to the Clipboard.
3. Open the disk and folder that is to be the destination of the copy.
4. Press **CTRL+V** to paste the file into the destination folder.

Use the Recycle Bin

If you do a normal delete from Explorer or the desktop, the item or items deleted will go into the Recycle Bin. Should you change your mind about the deletion, you can reclaim an item from the Recycle Bin as explained in the QuickSteps "Renaming and Deleting Files and Folders" earlier in this chapter.

The Recycle Bin is a special folder that can contain both files and folders. You can open it and see its contents as you would any other folder, by double-clicking its desktop icon. Figure 3-10 shows my Recycle Bin after I've deleted a number of files. What makes the Recycle Bin special are the two special tasks in the Tasks pane:

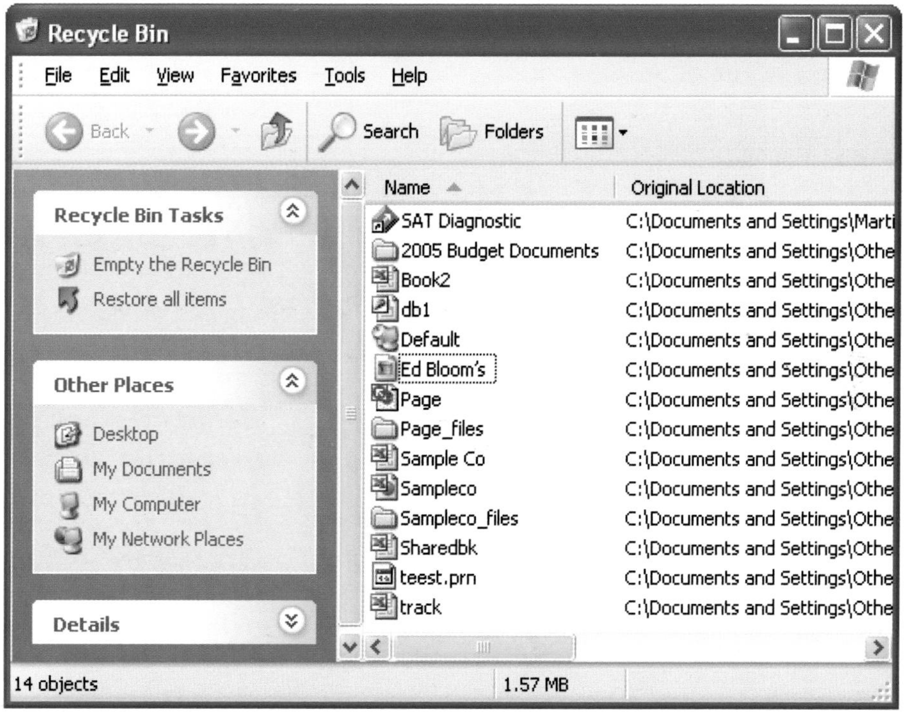

Figure 3-10: The Recycle Bin is a special folder whose contents can be permanently emptied or restored to their original locations

- **Empty the Recycle Bin**, which permanently removes all of the contents of the Recycle Bin
- **Restore All Items**, which returns all the contents to their original folders, in effect "undeleting" all of the contents

Obviously, there is a limit to how much the Recycle Bin should hold. You can limit the amount of space it takes so that it doesn't take over your hard disk. That and other settings are made in the Recycle Bin's Properties dialog box.

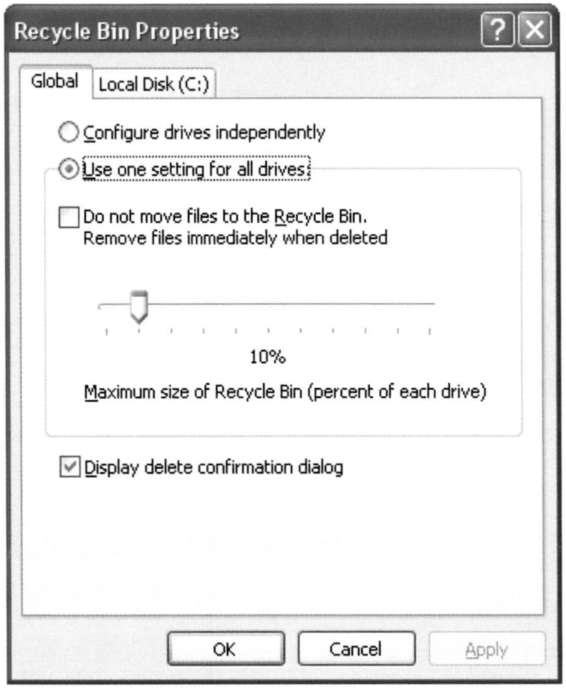

Figure 3-11: The amount of space used by the Recycle Bin can be set independently for each drive or set to allocate the same amount for all drives

1. Right-click the **Recycle Bin** on the desktop and click **Properties**. The Recycle Bin Properties dialog box will open, as you can see in Figure 3-11.
2. If you have multiple hard disks and want to independently set the amount of Recycle Bin space on each, click **Configure Drives Independently**. Otherwise, keep the default setting and use the slider to set the percentage of the drive used.
3. If you don't want to use the Recycle Bin, click **Do Not Move Files To The Recycle Bin**. (This is strongly discouraged.)
4. If you don't need to see the deletion confirmation message, click that check box to deselect it.
5. When you are ready, click **OK** to close the dialog box.

Create Shortcuts

Shortcuts allow you to quickly access files from places other than where the files are stored. For example, you can start a program from the desktop even though the actual program file is stored in some other folder. To create a shortcut:

Drag a program file (one with an .exe extension) to a different folder (as from a folder to the desktop).

–Or–

Press and hold the right mouse button while dragging any file or folder to a different folder, and then choose **Create Shortcuts Here**.

Search for Files and Folders

With large and, possibly, several hard disks, it is often difficult to find files and folders on a system. Explorer's Search serves that purpose.

1. Open **Explorer** and click **Search** on the toolbar.
2. Click **All Files And Folders**. The search criteria pane opens.
3. Enter all or part of the filename or a word or phrase in the file, and select where to look for the file or folder
4. If needed, enter information about when the file or folder was created, what its size is, and set any desired advanced option.

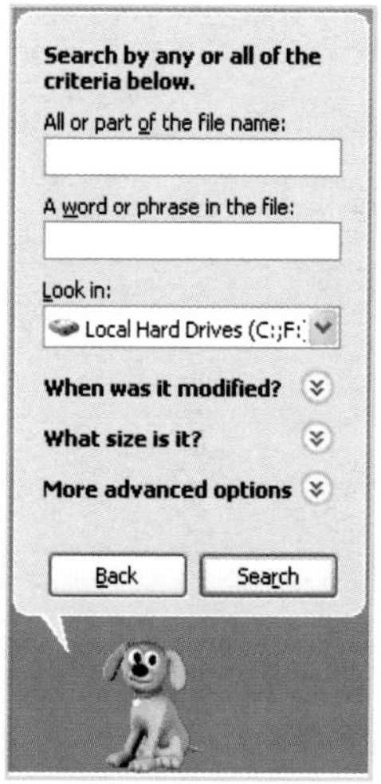

5. Click **Search**. The search will begin. Files and folders that match the criteria are found and listed in the detail (right) pane of Explorer, as shown in Figure 3-12.
6. If you see too many files, you can refine the search, narrowing the criteria to get only the results you want.
7. When you are done, close Explorer.

NOTE

You can tell if an object is a shortcut in two possible ways: "Shortcut" is in its title (unless you've renamed it), and an upward pointing arrow is in the lower-left of the icon, like this:

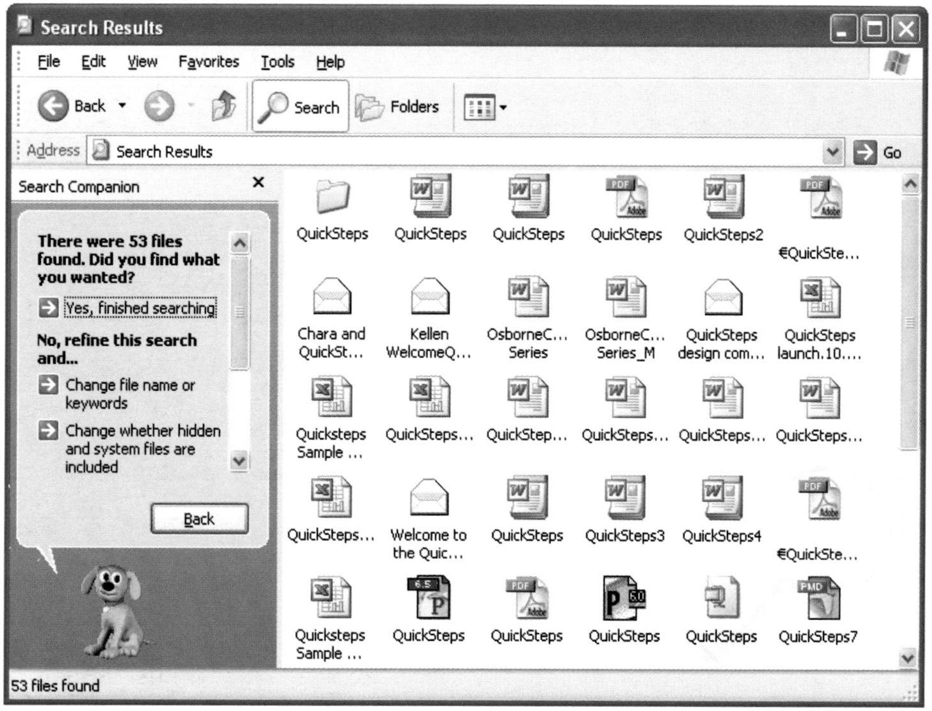

Figure 3-12: Search criteria may need to be refined to give you only the files you are looking for

1 2 3 4 5 6 7 8 9 10

Create Files

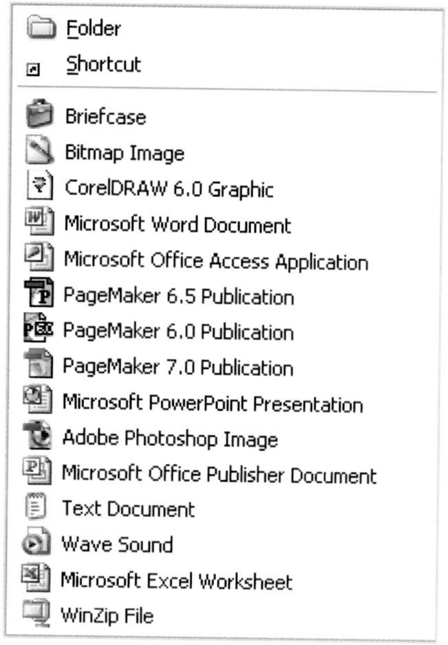

Files are usually created by applications or by copying existing files; however Windows has an additional file creation capability that creates an empty file and opens the application to allow work on the file.

1. Open **Explorer** and open the folder in which you want to create the new file.
2. Right-click a blank area of the detail or right pane of Explorer and choose **New**. A menu of all the file types that can be created by the registered applications on your computer will appear.
3. Click the file type you want to create.

NOTE

You can let someone else use an encrypted file by giving them your logon username and password. In addition, in many organizations an administrator will have the ability to decrypt files so that information cannot be lost through encryption.

Encrypt Files and Folders

Windows XP Professional, but not XP Home, has the ability to encrypt files and folders so they cannot be read without the key to decrypt them. The key is attached to the person who performed the encryption. When she or he logs on to the computer, the files can be used as if they were not encrypted. If someone else logs on, the files cannot be accessed. Even if someone takes the disk to another computer, all that will be displayed is gibberish. To encrypt a file or folder:

1. Open **Start**, select **My Computer**, and click **Folders** in the toolbar.
2. In the folders tree on the left, open the drive and folders necessary to display the files or folders you want to encrypt on the right.

3. Right-click the file or folder and choose **Properties**. In the General tab, click **Advanced**. The Advanced Attributes dialog box opens.

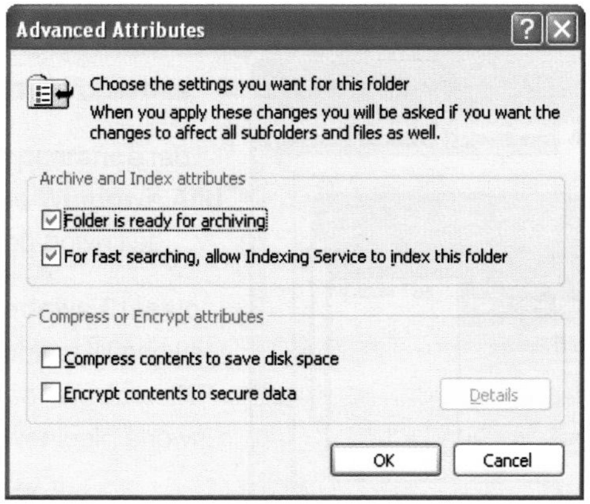

TIP

It is recommended that folders rather than files be the encrypting container because many applications save temporary and secondary files during execution.

4. Click **Encrypt Contents To Secure Data**.
5. Click **OK** twice. If you are encrypting a file, you may get an Encryption Warning that the file is not in an encrypted folder, which means that when you edit the file, temporary or backup files might be created that are not encrypted.

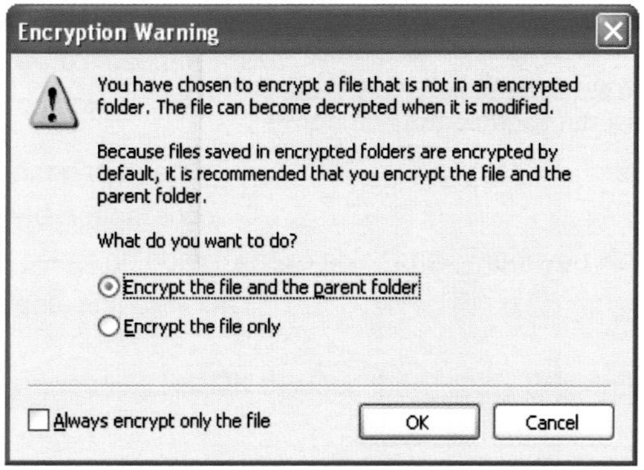

6. Choose whether you want to encrypt only the file or both the file and the folder that contains it. Click **OK**. The title under the file or folder icon turns a color, normally green.

1 2 3 4 5 6 7 8 9 10

> **NOTE**
>
> A file or folder that has been compressed cannot also be encrypted.

> **CAUTION**
>
> Since Read-only and Hidden files or folders can be easily changed by anyone who knows about them, they are not intended to be used as significant security measures.

Compress Files and Folders

You can reduce the amount of disk space a file or folder takes by compressing it. This is often useful when sending files or folders via e-mail.

1. Open **Explorer** in Folders view.
2. In the folders tree on the left, open the disk and folders necessary to display the files or folders you want to compress on the right.
3. Right-click the file or folder and choose **Properties**. In the General tab, click **Advanced**. The Advanced Attributes dialog box opens.
4. Click **Compress Contents To Save Disk Space**, and click **OK** twice. The title under the file or folder icon turns a color, normally blue.

Change Other Attributes

Encryption and Compression, described above, are two of five or six file or folder attributes (encryption is not available in Windows XP Home). The others are shown in Table 3-1.

TABLE 3-1: FILE AND FOLDER ADDITIONAL ATTRIBUTES

ATTRIBUTE	DESCRIPTION
Read-Only	The file or folder cannot be changed.
Hidden	The file or folder cannot be seen unless Show Hidden Files And Folders is selected in the Folder Options View tab.
File or Folder Is Ready For Archiving	This serves as a flag to backup programs that the file or folder is ready to be backed up.
Allow Indexing	This allows the Windows Indexing Service to index the file or folder so that searching for the file can be done quickly. (See Chapter 5 for how to use the Indexing Service.)

QUICKSTEPS

ZIPPING FILES AND FOLDERS

Windows XP has a new way to compress files and folders called "zipping." *Zipped* files have the extension .zip and are compatible with programs like WinZip. Zipped files take less room on a disk, and are transmitted over the Internet faster.

CREATE A ZIPPED FOLDER

You can create a new zipped folder and drag files to it.

1. Open **Start** and click **My Computer**. Click **Folders**.
2. Open the drive and folders to the reach the location you want for the zipped folder.
3. Right-click in a blank area of the right pane, select **New,** and click **Compressed (Zipped) Folder**. The zipped folder will appear.
4. Drag files and folder into the zipped folder to compress them.

SEND A FILE OR FOLDER TO A ZIPPED FOLDER

1. In Explorer, right-click a file or folder you want zipped.
2. Select **Send To** and click **Compressed (Zipped) Folder**. A new zipped folder will appear and will contain the original file or folder, now compressed.

EXTRACT ZIPPED FILES AND FOLDERS

To unzip a file or folder, simply drag it out of the zipped folder, or you can extract all of a zipped folder's contents.

1. Right-click a zipped folder and click **Extract All**. The Extraction Wizard will open.
2. Click **Next**, enter or browse to the location of where you want the extracted files and folders, and click **Next**.
3. When the files are extracted, click **Finish**. Close Explorer when you are ready.

To set the additional attributes:

1. Open **Explorer** in Folders view.
2. In the folders tree on the left, open the drive and folders necessary to display the files or folders whose attributes you want to set on the right.
3. Right-click the file or folder and choose **Properties**. In the General tab you can set **Read-Only** and **Hidden**. Do that if you wish and click **OK**.
4. If you want to set archiving or indexing, click **Advanced**. The Advanced Attributes dialog box opens.
5. Click the attribute you want to set, and click **OK** twice.

Back Up Files and Folders

Backing up copies important files and folders on your disk and writes them on another device, such as a recordable CD or a Zip drive. To start Backup:

Open **Start**, select **All Programs**, choose first **Accessorie**s, then **System Tools**, and finally click **Backup.**

–Or–

Open Expl**orer** in Folders view, right-click a disk drive to backup, and click **Properties**. Click the **Tool**s tab, and click **Backup Now**.

In either case, the Backup Or Restore Wizard opens. You are now ready to:

1. Click **Next**, choose **Back Up Files And Settings**, and click **Next** again.
2. Choose to back up just your documents and settings, everybody's documents and settings, all information on the computer, or data of your choice (due to limited time and backup space, the latter choice is often the best). Click **Next**.
3. If you select to choose what to back up, the dialog box shown in Figure 3-13 opens.
4. Select the folders and files to back up. Click **Next** and choose the backup type and the media to use. Depending on the media you are using, you may be asked to name the file. Then click **Save**.

5. Confirm the drive and backup name. If needed click **Next** and put the back up media in its drive. Then click **Finish**. The Backup Progress dialog box will open and show you the status, as you can see in Figure 3-14.
6. When the backup is complete, click **Close** and close any remaining dialog boxes.

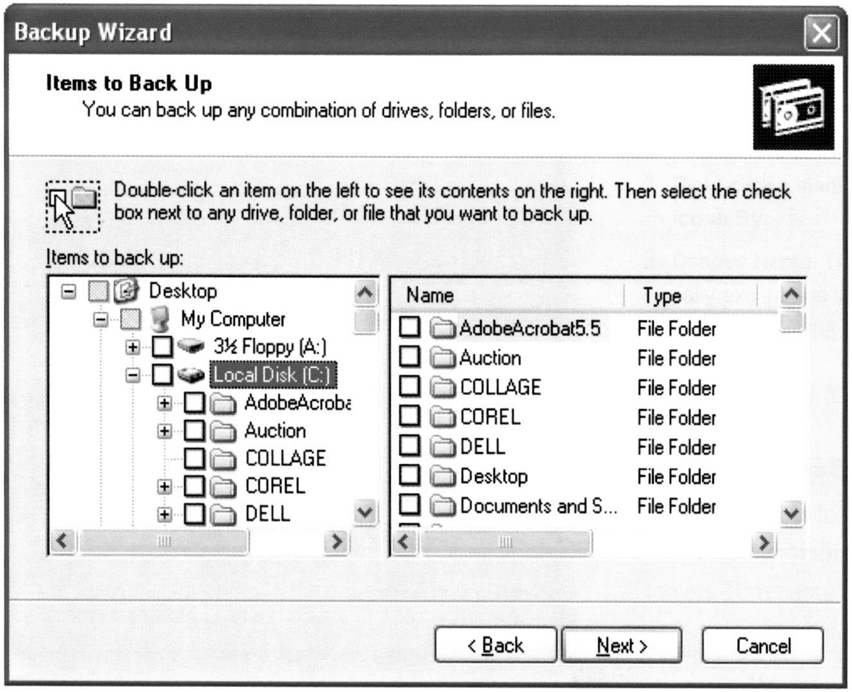

Figure 3-13: Selecting files and folders to back up

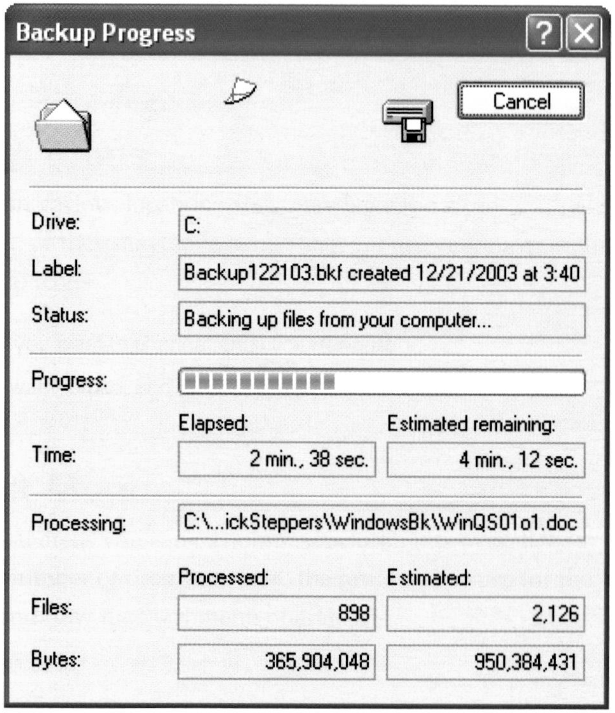

Figure 3-14: Carrying out a backup

QUICKSTEPS

MANAGING DISKS

Windows provides three tools to help manage the files and folders stored on hard disks.

CLEANUP A DISK

Disk Cleanup helps you get rid of old files on your hard disk. Windows looks through your hard disk for types of files that can be deleted and lists them, as shown in Figure 3-15. You can then select the types of files you want to delete.

1. Open **Explorer**, right-click a disk drive, and click **Properties**.
2. Click **Disk Cleanup**. Windows will calculate how much space you could save.

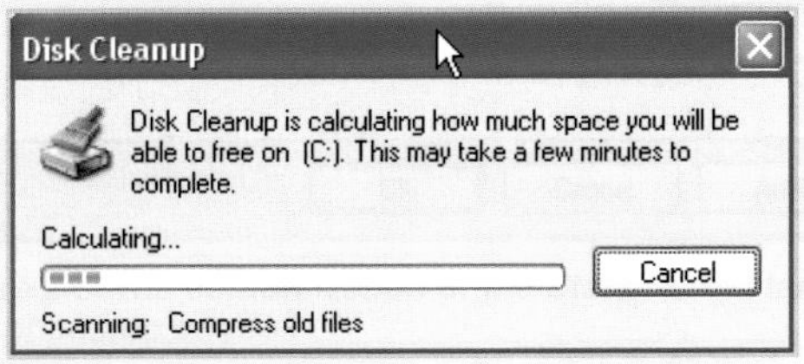

3. Select the types of files to delete, click **OK** to delete them, and close the Properties dialog box.

CHECK FOR ERRORS

Error Checking tries to read and write on your disk, without losing information, to determine if bad areas exist. If it finds a bad area, that area is flagged so that the system will not use it. Error Checking automatically fixes file system errors and attempts recovery of bad sectors.

1. Open **Explorer**, right-click a disk drive, and click **Properties**.

Continued...

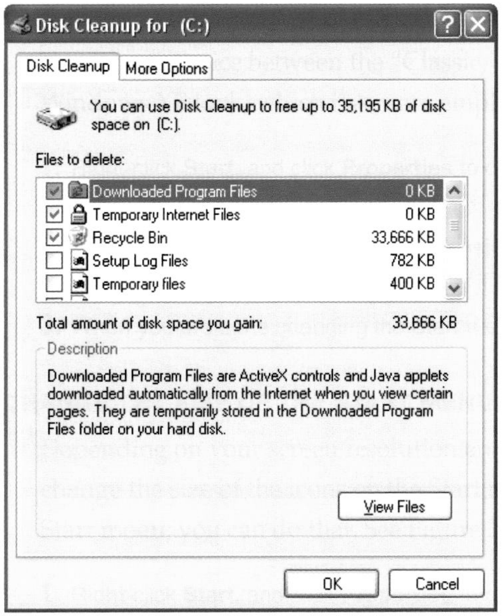

Figure 3-15: Selecting the types of files to delete with Disk Cleanup

Figure 3-16: Defragmenting brings pieces of a file together in one contiguous area

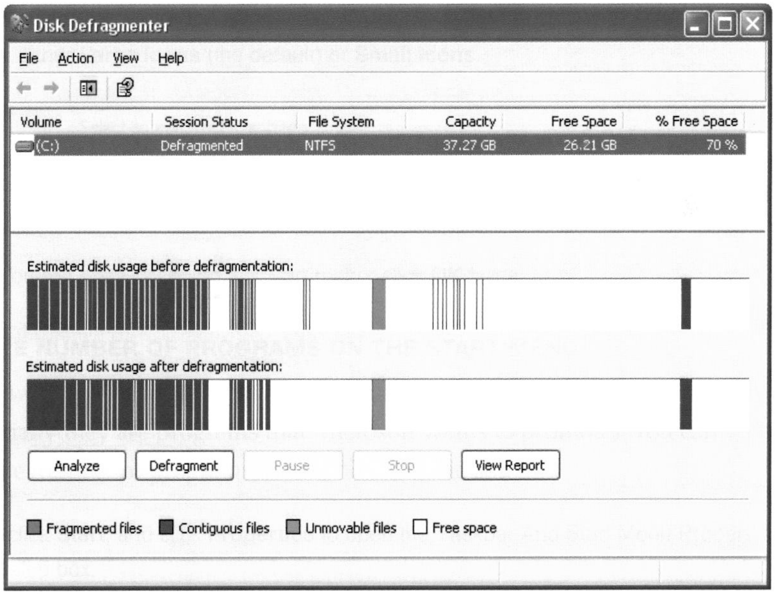

MANAGING DISKS *(continued)*

2. Click the **Tools** tab, and click **Check Now**. Select whether you want to automatically fix errors and attempt recovery of bad sectors, and click **Start**. You may be told you have to restart Windows to do error checking. If so, close any open applications, click **Yes**, and restart your computer. Error checking will automatically begin when Windows restarts.

You will be shown the status of the error checking and told of any problems that cannot be fixed. When Error Checking is complete, your computer will be restarted.

DEFRAGMENT A DISK

When files are stored on a hard disk they are broken into pieces (or *fragments*) and individually written to the disk. As the disk fills, the fragments are spread over the disk as space allows. To read a file that has been fragmented requires extra disk activity and slows access. To fix this, Windows has a defragmentation process that rewrites the contents of a disk, placing all of the pieces of a file in one contiguous area.

1. Open **Explorer**, right-click a disk drive, and click **Properties**.
2. Click the **Tools** tab, and click **Defragment Now**. The Disk Defragmenter will open. Click **Analyze** and you will be told if your disk needs to be defragmented.
3. To go ahead, click **Defragment**. You will be shown the process graphically as it proceeds. When it is done, you will see how well it did, as shown in Figure 3-16. Some fragments may remain.

Write Files and Folders to a CD

Windows XP allows you to copy ("burn," or record) files to a writable or rewritable CD. You must have a CD-R or CD-RW drive and blank media.

1. Place a blank recordable disk (or disc) in the drive. You will be asked if you want to open the writable CD folder using Windows Explorer, do nothing, or start some other CD writing software.
2. Choose **Open A Writable CD Folder Using Windows Explorer** and click **OK**. An Explorer window will open for the CD drive.
3. Create any new folders you want on the CD in the CD drive window. Then open another Windows Explorer window, locate the files and folders you want on the CD, and drag them to the CD drive window.
4. When all the files and folders are the way you want, such as in Figure 3-17, click **Write These Files To CD** in the tasks pane. The CD Writing Wizard will open.
5. Enter a CD name and click **Next**. When the process is complete, click **Finish**.

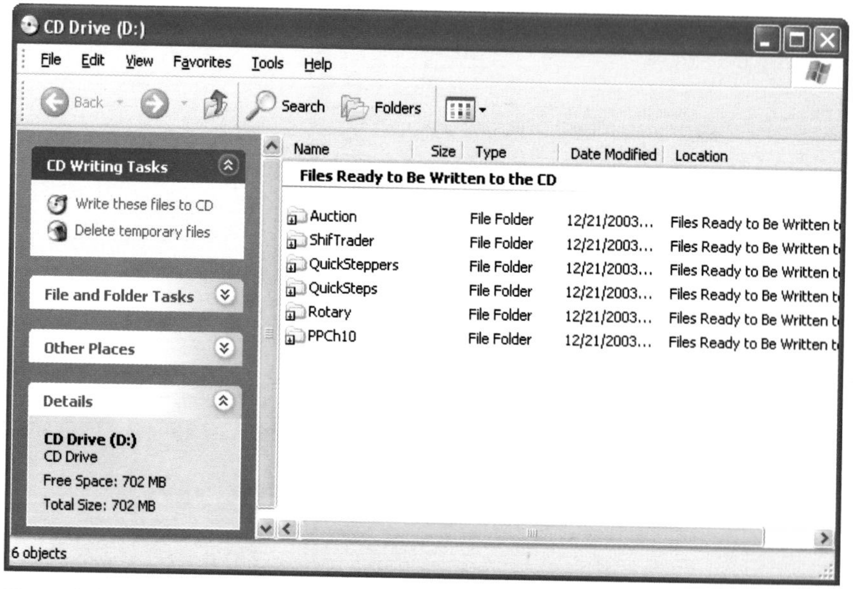

Figure 3-17: Files and folder ready to be written to a CD

How to...

Chapter 4
Using the Internet

The Internet provides a major means for world-wide communications between both individuals and organizations, as well as a major means for locating and sharing information. For many, having access to the Internet is the primary reason for having a computer. To use the Internet, you must have a connection to it, either a dial-up connection or a broadband connection. You then can send and receive e-mail, access the World Wide Web, and use Instant Messaging.

Connect to the Internet

You can connect to the Internet using a telephone line, a cable TV cable, or a satellite link. With a telephone line, you can connect with either a *dial-up* connection or a *DSL* (digital subscriber line) connection (see comparison in Table 4-1). DSL, cable TV, and satellite connections are called *broadband* connections because of their higher (than dial-up) speed and common set up (see comparison in Table 4-2). You must have access to at least one of these forms of communication in order to connect to the Internet. You must also set up the Internet connection itself.

1 2 3 4 5 6 7 8 9 10

TABLE 4-1: ***Comparison of Dial-Up and DSL Connections***

FEATURE	DIAL-UP	DSL
Cost	Average $20/month	Average $40/ month
Speed	Up to 48 Kbps* download**, 33 Kbps upload	Most common: 768 Kbps download, 128 Kbs upload
Connection	Dial up each time	Always connected
Use of line	Ties up line, may want a second line	Line can be used for voice and FAX while connected to the Internet

** Kbps is Kilobits (thousands of bits, 1 or 0) per second.*
*** Download is receiving information from the Internet on your computer.*

TABLE 4-2: ***Representative Speeds, Costs, and Reliability for Internet Connections***

SERVICE	DOWNLOAD SPEED	UPLOAD SPEED	MONTHLY COST	RELIABILITY
Dial-Up	48 Kbps	33.6 Kbps	$20	Fair
DSL	768 Kbps	128 Kbps	$40	Good
Cable Internet	1 Mbps	500 Kbps	$40	Good
Satellite Internet	1 Mbps	150 Kbps	$60	Fair

Set Up Communications

Communications is the physical link between your computer and the Internet. To set up communications, you must first choose between a dial-up and broadband connection. For a dial-up connection, you must first set up a modem.

INSTALL A MODEM

If a modem came with your computer or if one was already installed when you upgraded to Windows XP, your modem was probably automatically installed and you don't need to do anything more. In that case, or if you are unsure, skip to "Set Up a Dial-Up Connection." Otherwise, if you need to install a modem:

1. Make sure a modem is either physically installed in your computer or, if you have an external modem, that it is connected to your computer, plugged in, and turned on.
2. Open **Start** and click **Control Panel**.
3. In Category view, click **Printers And Other Hardware** and then click **Phone And Modem Options**.

   –Or–

   In Classic view, double-click **Phone And Modem Options**. The Phone And Modem Options dialog box will open.
4. Click the **Modems** tab. If it shows Unknown Modem, select that and click **Remove**. If it shows a likely modem, as shown next, your modem is installed and you can skip to "Set Up a Dial-Up Connection."

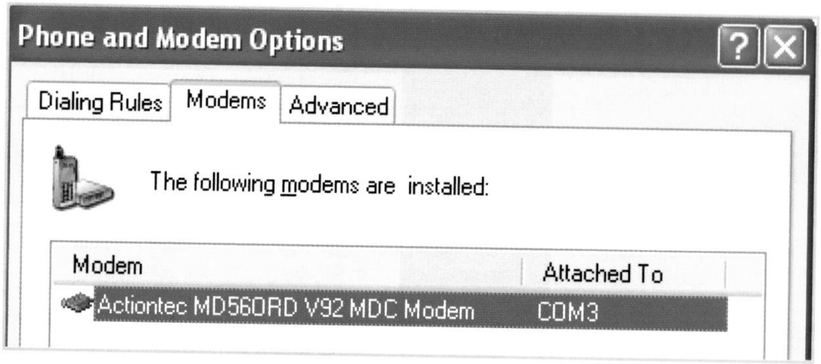

TIP

To test your modem, open the Modems tab of the Phone and Modem Options dialog box, select your modem and click **Properties**. Click the **Diagnostics** tab and click **Query Modem**. If your modem is working, you should get a set of command responses as shown in Figure 4-1.

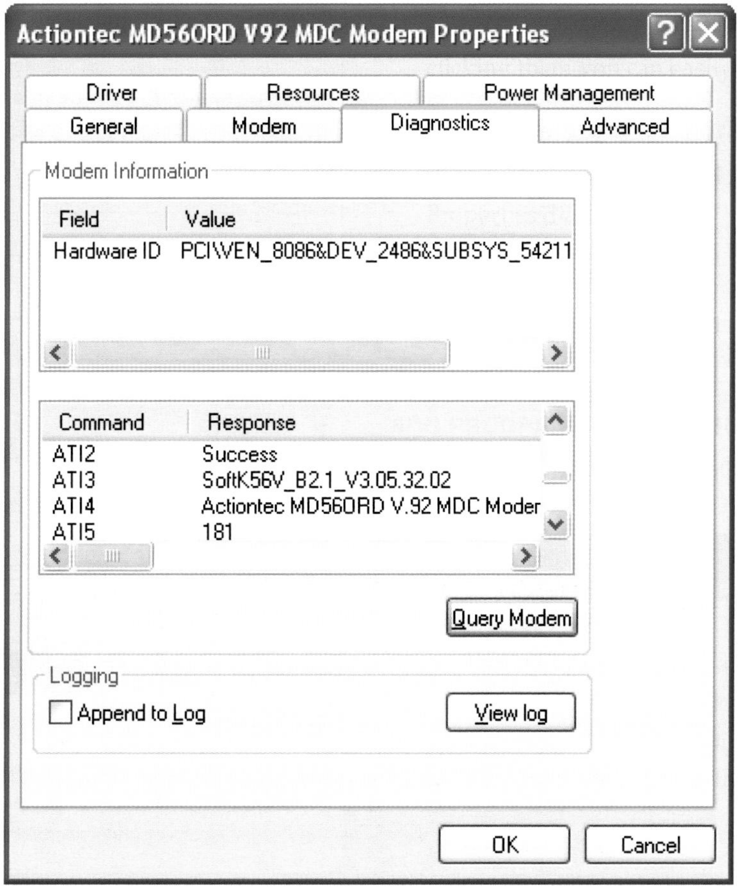

Figure 4-1: Commands and responses showing communication with a modem

5. Click **Add** to open the Add Hardware Wizard and click **Next**. If only the correct modem is displayed, skip the next step. If several modems are shown and one is correct and the rest are not, uncheck the incorrect ones and skip the next step. If an incorrect modem or Unknown Modem is shown, select it and click **Change**. If no modem is found, click **Next**.
6. If you have an installation disk for your modem that is correct for Windows XP, click **Have Disk**, insert the disk, select the drive, click **OK**, select the manufacturer and model, and click **OK**. If you don't have a disk, under Manufacturer select **Standard Modem Types** and under Model select the speed of your modem, then click **Next**.
7. Select the COM (communications) port to which the modem is connected (with an external modem you can look to see where it is plugged in, with an internal modem you have to know how it was installed) and click **Next**. Finally, you are told that your modem has been installed successfully. Click **Finish** to close the Add Hardware Wizard and then close the Phone And Modem Options dialog box.

SET UP A DIAL-UP CONNECTION

With a modem installed and working, you can set up a *dial-up connection* that uses the modem to dial and connect to another computer at the other end of a phone line.

1. If your Control Panel isn't open, click **Start** and then click **Control Panel**. If your Control Panel is already open, click **Back**.

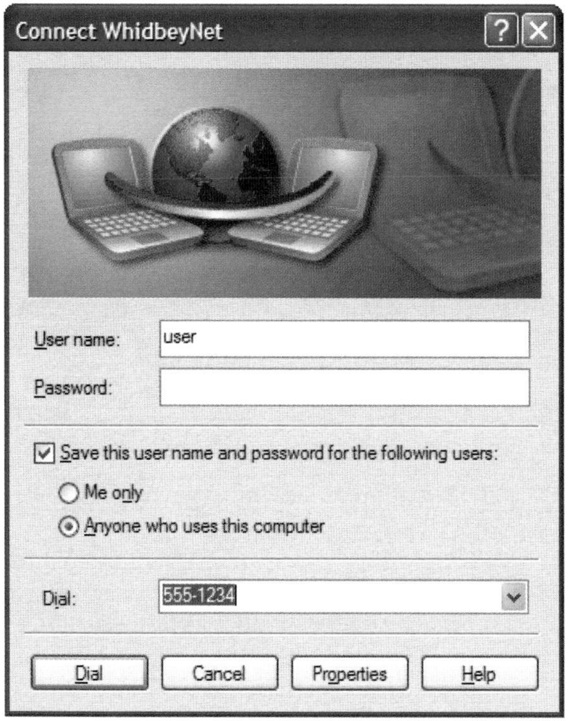

Figure 4-2: A dial-up connection requires a user name, password, and phone number

2. In Category view, click **Network And Internet Connections**, and click **Network Connections**.

   -Or-

   In Classic view, double-click **Network Connections**.

   In either case, click **Create A New Connection**. The New Connection Wizard will open. Click **Next**.
3. Select **Connect To The Internet** and click **Nex**t. Choose **Set Up My Connection Manually** (see "Configure an Internet Connection" for other options) and click **Next**. Select **Connect Using A Dial-Up Modem**, and again click **Next**.
4. Enter a name (it can be anything) for your connection and click **Next**. Enter the phone number to dial. Click **Next**.
5. Enter the user name and password (twice) given to you by your Internet Service Provider (ISP). (See the Note in this chapter on what you need to connect to the Internet.)
6. Choose whether anyone else can use this user name and password, whether this is the default Internet connection, and whether you want the Internet firewall turned on. There is no right or wrong answer on the first two questions. The firewall is a good idea for security. When you are ready, click **Next**.
7. You are told you have successfully set up a dial-up connection. If you would like a shortcut on the desktop so that you can quickly open this connection, click the check box and then click **Finish**. An icon will appear in the Network Connections window, and the Connect dialog box opens, as you can see in Figure 4-2.
8. Confirm the phone number you need to dial, your user name, and, if you wish, change your password. Click **Dial**. You should hear your modem dialing and going through the *handshaking* (beeps and pinging sounds) with the modem on the other end. When the connection is made, you will see a message out of the notification area.

9. To disconnect, right-click the connection icon in the notification area and click **Disconnect**.

> **NOTE**
>
> Sometimes a DSL or TV cable connecting device is called a "modem," but it is not an analog-to-digital converter, which is the major point of a **mo**dulator-**dem**odulator. Therefore, that term is not used for those services in this book.

SET UP A BROADBAND CONNECTION

A broadband connection—made with a DSL phone line, a TV cable, or a satellite connection—is normally made with a device that connects to your local area network (LAN) and allows several computers on the network to use the connection. (See Chapter 9 to set up a network.) With a network set up, your computer connected to the network, and a broadband service connected to the network, your computer is connected to the broadband service. There is nothing else you need to do to set up a broadband connection.

Configure an Internet Connection

In the process of establishing either a dial-up connection or a broadband connection, you may have also configured an Internet connection. The easiest way to check that is to try to connect to the Internet by opening **Start** and clicking **Internet**. If an Internet web page is displayed, like the MSN page shown in Figure 4-3, then you are connected and you need do no more. If you did not connect to the Internet and you know that your dial-up or broadband and network connections are all working properly, you need to configure your Internet connection.

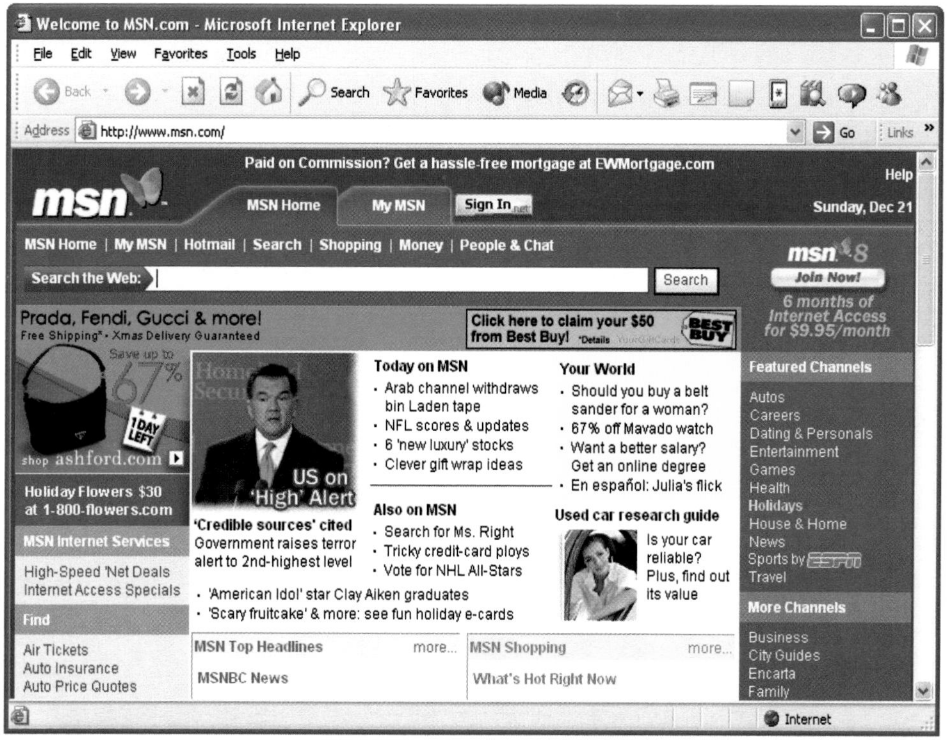

Figure 4-3: The easiest way to see if you have an Internet connection is to try to connect

NOTE

For the sake of writing convenience and because Windows XP comes with Internet Explorer, I am going to assume you are using Internet Explorer to access the Internet.

TIP

If you think your modem has been set up properly yet you are not getting connected when you open Internet Explorer, look at the Internet Options in Internet Explorer by opening the **Tools** menu, choosing **Internet Options**, and clicking the **Connections** tab. See if you have a dial-up connection specified and that it dials the connection. If not, make the necessary corrections.

1. If Internet Explorer did not connect to the Internet and the New Connection Wizard did not open, you can start the New Connection Wizard by opening **Start** and choosing **All Programs**, selecting **Accessories**, choosing **Communications**, and clicking **New Connection Wizard**.
2. Click **Next**, accept the default **Connect To The Internet**, and click **Next** again. If you have an ISP you want to use and they have given you a CD, click that option. If you have an ISP without a CD, click **Set Up My Connection Manually**. If you don't have an ISP, click **Choose From A List Of Internet Service Providers (ISPs)**. Whether using the CD choice or choosing from a list, follow the instructions on the screen to complete the set up. If you use the manual choice, follow on with these steps.
3. Choose how you want to connect to the Internet, as shown in Figure 4-4. If you will use a modem, leave the default choice of the first option. If you will use a broadband connection (such as DSL or a cable connection), determine if you have to sign on. If so, select the second choice; otherwise, select the third choice. In any case, once you have made your choice, click **Next**. If you made the third choice (Always On), click **Finish** and skip to Step 6.
4. Enter the name of your Internet service provider, which will be the name of this connection, and click **Next**. If necessary, enter the phone number of the data connection to your ISP and click **Next**.
5. Enter the user name and password (twice) given to you by your ISP, choose the options that are correct for you and the computer you are using, and click **Next**. You are shown a summary of the connection you want to make. If it is not correct, click **Back** and make the necessary corrections. When it is correct, click **Finish**.
6. Once more, open **Start** and click **Internet**. If asked, click **Connect** and then **Dial**. If you still do not connect to the Internet, you may need to re-install your modem, in which case you should go to "Install a Modem" earlier in this chapter. If you are using a broadband connection, you may need to go to Chapter 9 and look at potential network problems.

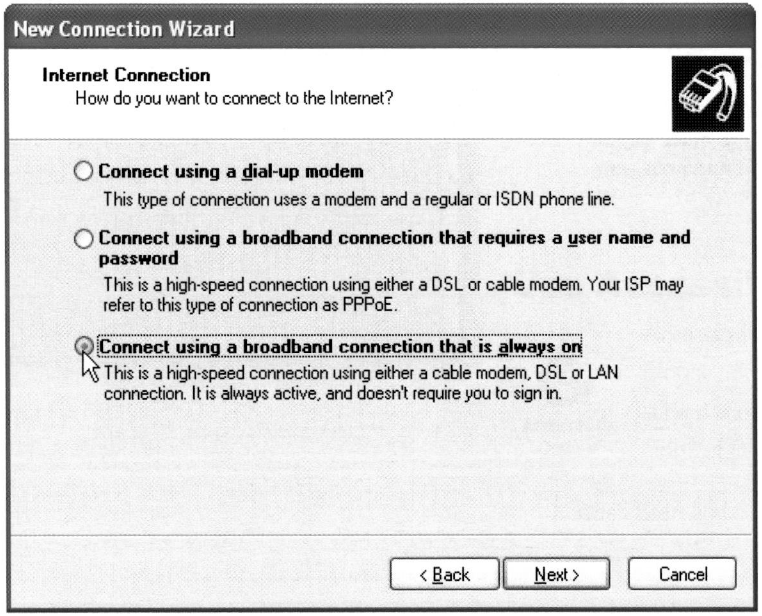

Figure 4-4: Most broadband connections are always on and don't require a user name and password

NOTE

To connect to the Internet, you need to have an existing account with an Internet service provider (ISP) and you need to know your ISP's phone number for your modem to dial. You also must have the user name and password for your account. If you want to use Internet mail, you need to know your e-mail address, the type of mail server (POP3, IMAP, or HTTP), the names of the incoming and outgoing mail servers, and the name and password for the mail account. This information is provided by your ISP when you establish your account.

TIP

If you are using the Quick Launch toolbar (see Chapter 2), you can quickly launch Internet Explorer by clicking its icon in the Quick Launch toolbar.

Use the World Wide Web

The *World Wide Web* (or just the *Web*) is the sum of all the web sites in the world—examples of which are CNN, EBay, and MSN (which was shown in Figure 4-3 above). The World Wide Web is what you can access with a *web browser,* such as Internet Explorer which comes with Windows XP.

Search the Internet

You can search the Internet in two ways: by using the search facility built into the Internet Explorer and by using an independent search facility on the Web.

SEARCH FROM THE INTERNET EXPLORER

To use the Internet Explorer's search facility:

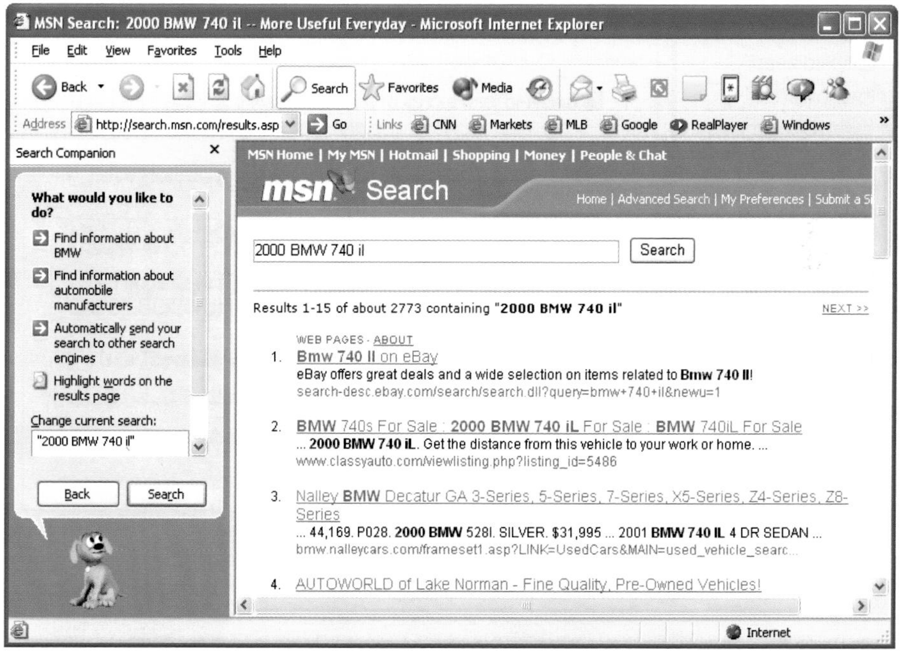

Figure 4-5: The results of a search using the Internet Explorer Search Companion

QUICKSTEPS

BROWSING THE INTERNET

Browsing the Internet uses a browser, like Internet Explorer, to go from one web site to another to see the sites' contents. You can browse to a site by directly entering a site address, by navigating to a site from another site, or by using the browser controls. First, of course, you have to start the browser.

STARTING A BROWSER

Most likely your Internet browser is Internet Explorer. In any case, to start your default browser open **Start** and click **Internet**.

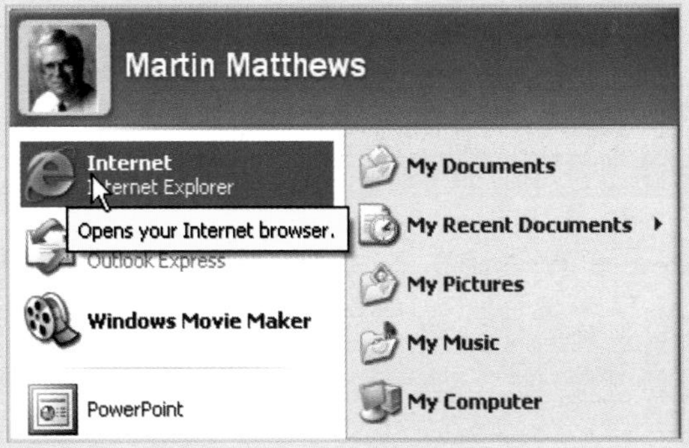

ENTER A SITE DIRECTLY

To go directly to a site:

1. Start your browser and drag over the existing address, or URL (uniform resource locator), in the address text box.
2. Type the address of the site you want to open and either click **OK** next to the address box or press **ENTER**.

Continued...

1. Open **Start** and click **Internet** to open Internet Explorer.
2. Click **Search** on the toolbar to open the Search Companion.

3. In the text box, type what you want to search for and click **Search**. The resulting web sites are shown in the right-hand pane of the Internet Explorer, as illustrated in Figure 4-5.
4. Click the link of your choice to go to that site.

SEARCH FROM AN INTERNET SITE

There are many independent Internet search sites. The most popular is Google.

1. Open **Start** and click **Internet** to open Internet Explorer.
2. Drag over the current address in the Address bar, type www.google.com, and either click **Go** or press **ENTER**.
3. In the text box, type what you want to search for and click **Google Search**. The resulting web sites are shown in a full web page, as illustrated in Figure 4-6.
4. Click the link of your choice to go to that site.

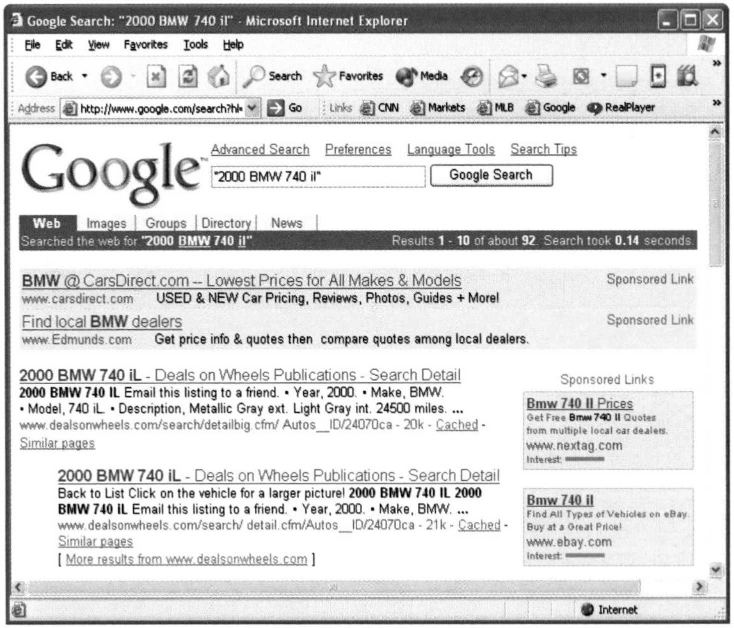

***Figure 4-6:* The results of a search using Google**

BROWSING THE INTERNET *(Continued)*

USE SITE NAVIGATION

Site navigating means to use a combination of links and menus on one web page to locate and open another web page, either in the same site or in another site.

- **Links** are words, phrases, sentences, or graphics that always have an open hand when the mouse pointer is moved to them and, when clicked, take you to another page. They are often underlined—if not initially, then when you move the mouse pointer to them.
- **Menus** contain one or a few words, in either a horizontal or vertical list, that always have an open hand when the mouse pointer is moved to them and, when clicked, take you to another page.

USE BROWSER NAVIGATION

Browser navigation means using the controls within your browser to go to another web page. Internet Explorer has two controls not discussed elsewhere that are used for navigation:

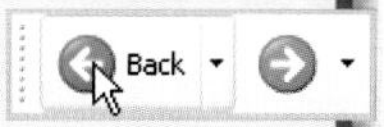

- **Back and Forward** buttons take you to the next or previous page in the stack of pages you have viewed most recently.
- **Links** bar takes you one of several sites when you click its icon or name in the links bar.

TIP

When you enter search criteria, place quotation marks around it to get only results that satisfy your full criteria.

Keep a Favorite Site

Sometimes you visit a site that you would like to return to quickly or often. Internet Explorer has a memory bank called Favorite Sites to which you can save sites for easy retrieval.

SAVE A FAVORITE SITE

To add a site to Favorite Sites:

1. Open **Start** and click **Internet** to open Internet Explorer.
2. Open the web page you want in your favorites list and make sure its correct address or URL is in the Address bar.
3. Open **Favorites** on the menu bar and click **Add To Favorites**.
4. Adjust the name as needed in the text box (you may want to type in a name you will readily associate with that site) and click **OK**.

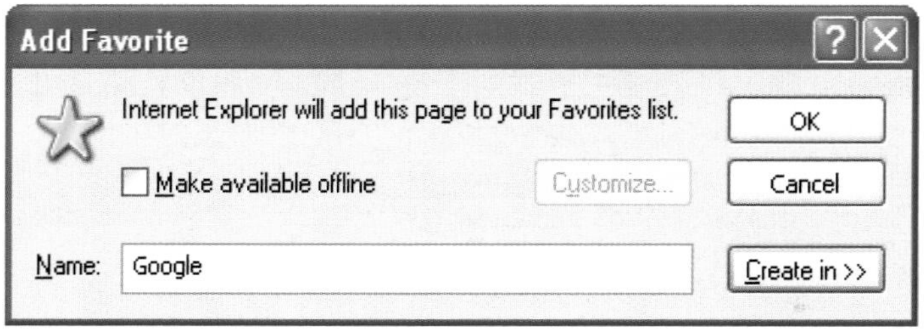

OPEN A FAVORITE SITE

To open a Favorite Site you have saved:

1. Open **Start** and click **Internet** to open Internet Explorer.
2. Open the **Favorites** menu or click **Favorites** on the toolbar and click the site you want.

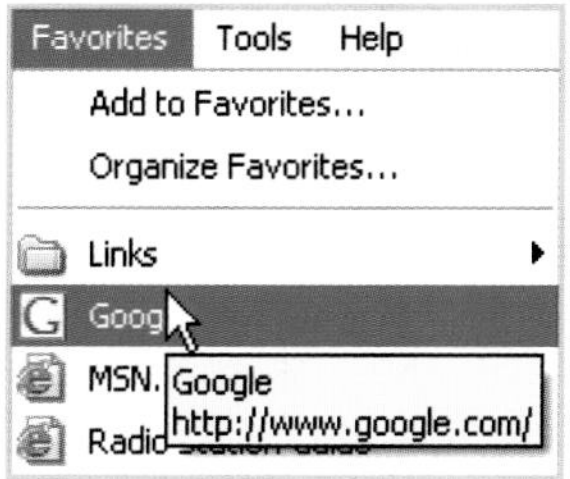

QUICKSTEPS

ORGANIZING FAVORITE SITES

You will probably find that you have a number of favorite sites, and it is hard to find them. Internet Explorer provides three ways to organize your favorite sites.

DRAG FAVORITES ON LIST

The items on your Favorites list are in the order you added them unless you drag them to a new location.

1. Open **Start** and click **Internet** to open Internet Explorer.
2. Open **Favorites**, locate the site you want to position, and drag it to the location in the list where you want it.

PUT FAVORITES IN FOLDERS

Internet Explorer comes with several default folders. You can also add folders and you can put sites in a folder:

1. Open **Start** and click **Internet** to open Internet Explorer.
2. Open the web page you want in your favorites list and make sure its correct address or URL is in the Address bar.
3. Open **Favorites** on the menu bar and click **Add To Favorites**.
4. Adjust the name as needed in the text box, click **Create In**, select the folder to use, and click **OK**.

CREATE NEW FOLDERS

To create your own folders within Favorites:

1. Open **Start** and click **Internet** to open Internet Explorer.
2. Open **Favorites**, click **Organize Favorites**, click **Create Folder**, type the name of the folder and press ENTER.
3. Drag the site links to the new folder and then click **Close**.

Use the Links Bar

The links bar allows you to store and, with one click, access sites you frequently use—for example, news or sports sites you go to every day.

ADD A SITE TO THE LINKS BAR

To add a site to your links bar:

1. Open **Start** and click **Internet** to open Internet Explorer.
2. Directly enter or browse to the site you want to add to your links bar.
3. Drag the icon on the left of the address text box to the location in the links bar where you want to place the link.

OPEN A LINK

To open a link, simply:

1. Open **Start** and click **Internet** to open Internet Explorer.
2. On the links bar, click the link you want to open.

Change Your Home Page

When you first start Internet Explorer, a given web page is automatically opened. This page is called your "home page." (You can also go to this page by clicking the Home page icon.) To change your home page:

1. Open **Start** and click **Internet** to open Internet Explorer.
2. Directly enter or browse to the site you want as your home page.
3. Open **Tools** and click **Internet Options.**

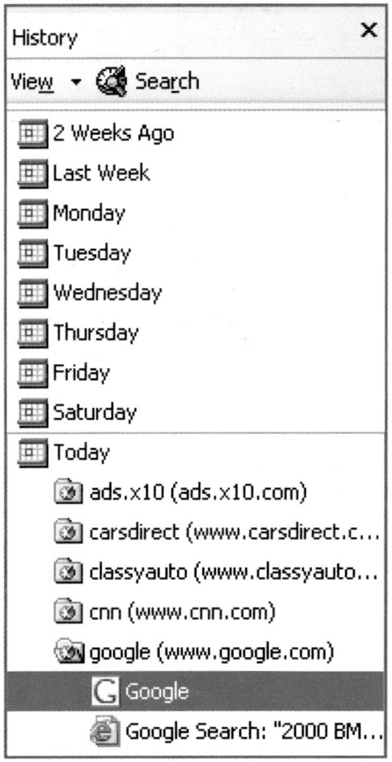

Figure 4-7: History allows you to find a site that you visited in the recent past

4. In the **General** tab, under Home Page, click **Use Current**. The web page currently being displayed will become your new home page.
5. Close Internet Options.

Access Web History

The Internet Explorer keeps a history of the web sites you visit, and you can use that history to return to a site. You can set the length of time to keep sites in that history, and you can clear your history.

USE WEB HISTORY

To use web History:

1. Open **Start** and click **Internet** to open Internet Explorer.
2. Click **History** on the tool bar to open the History pane.
3. Click the day, web site, and page you want to open, as shown in Figure 4-7.

SET AND CLEAR HISTORY

You can set the length of time to keep your Internet history and you can clear this history.

1. Open **Start** and click **Internet** to open Internet Explorer.
2. Open **Tools** and click **Internet Options.**
3. In the General tab use the days spinner to set the number of days to keep history and/or click **Clear History** to do that.

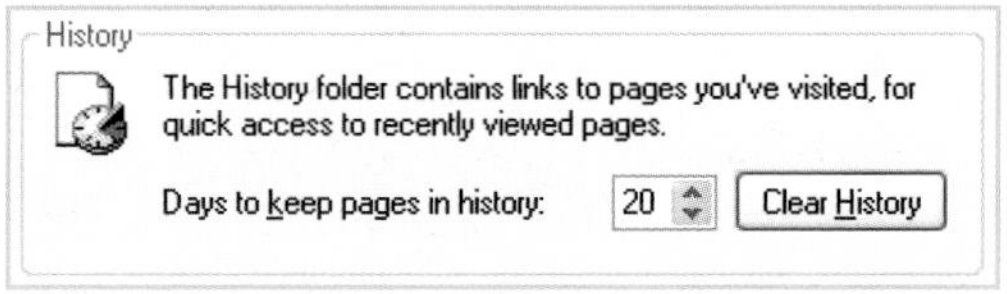

QUICKSTEPS

CONTROLLING INTERNET SECURITY

Internet Explorer allows you to control three aspects of Internet security. You may categorize sites by the degree to which you trust them, determine how you want to handle *cookies* placed on your computer by web sites, and set and use ratings to control the content of web sites that can be viewed. These controls are found in the Internet Options dialog box:

1. Open **Start** and click **Internet** to open Internet Explorer.
2. Open **Tools** and click **Internet Options**.

CATEGORIZE WEB SITES

Internet Explorer allows you to categorize web sites into zones: Internet (sites that are not classified in one of the other ways), Local Intranet, Trusted Sites, and Restricted Sites (as shown in Figure 4-8).

From the Internet Options dialog box:

1. Click the **Security** tab. Click the **Internet** zone. Note its definition.
2. Click **Custom Level**. Select the elements in this zone that you want to disable, enable, or prompt you before using. Alternatively, select a level of security you want for this zone and click **Reset**. Click **OK** when you are finished.
3. Click each of the other zones where you can identify either groups or individual sites you want in that zone.

HANDLE COOKIES

Cookies are small pieces of data that web sites store on your computer so they can remind themselves who you are. These can save you from having to constantly enter your name and ID. Cookies can also be dangerous,

Continued...

Copy Internet Information

You occasionally find something on the Internet that you want to copy— a picture, some text, or a web page.

COPY A PICTURE FROM THE INTERNET

To copy a picture from an Internet web page to a folder on your hard disk:

1. Open Internet Explorer and locate the web page containing the picture you want.
2. Right-click the picture and click **Save Picture As...** Locate the folder in which you want to save the picture, and click **Save**.
3. Close Internet Explorer if you are ready.

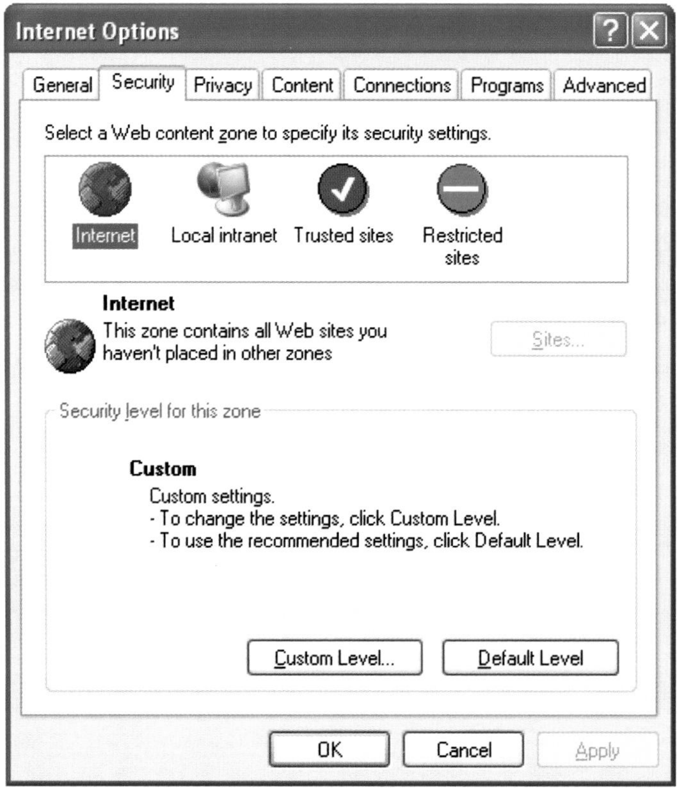

Figure 4-8: Internet Explorer allows you to categorize web sites into zones and determine what can be done within those zones

CONTROLLING INTERNET SECURITY *(Continued)*

letting people into your computer where they can potentially do damage.

Internet Explorer lets you determine the types and sources of cookies you will allow and what those cookies can do on your computer (see Figure 4-9).

From the Internet Options dialog box:

1. Click the **Privacy** tab. Select a privacy setting by dragging the slider up or down.
2. Click **Advanced** to open the Advanced Privacy Settings dialog. If you wish, click **Override Automatic Cookie Handling** and select the settings you want to use.
3. Click **OK** to return to the Internet Options dialog box.

CONTROL CONTENT

You can control the content that will be displayed by Internet Explorer.

From the Internet Options dialog box:

1. Click the **Content** tab. Click **Enable** to open the Content Advisor dialog box, shown in Figure 4-10.
2. Individually select each of the four categories and drag the slider to the level you want to allow.
3. Click **OK** to close the Content Advisor.

When you are ready, click **OK** to close Internet Options.

COPY TEXT FROM THE INTERNET

To copy text from a web page to a Microsoft Word document:

1. Open Internet Explorer and locate the web page containing the text you want.
2. Drag across the text, then right-click that selection and choose **Copy**.
3. Open Microsoft Word and the document (or new document) in which you want to paste the text. Right-click where you want the text and choose **Paste**.
4. Close Internet Explorer if you are ready.

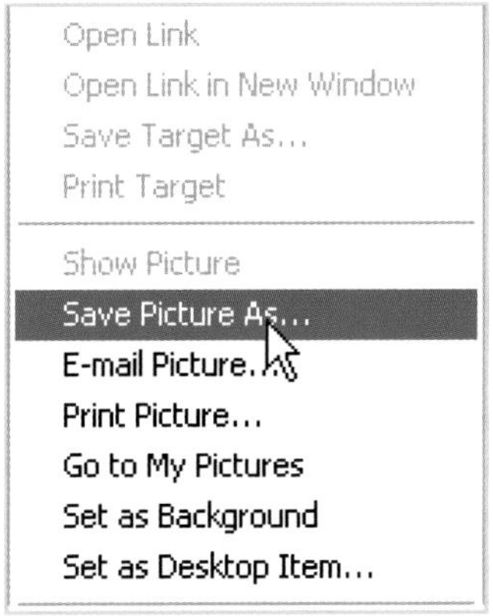

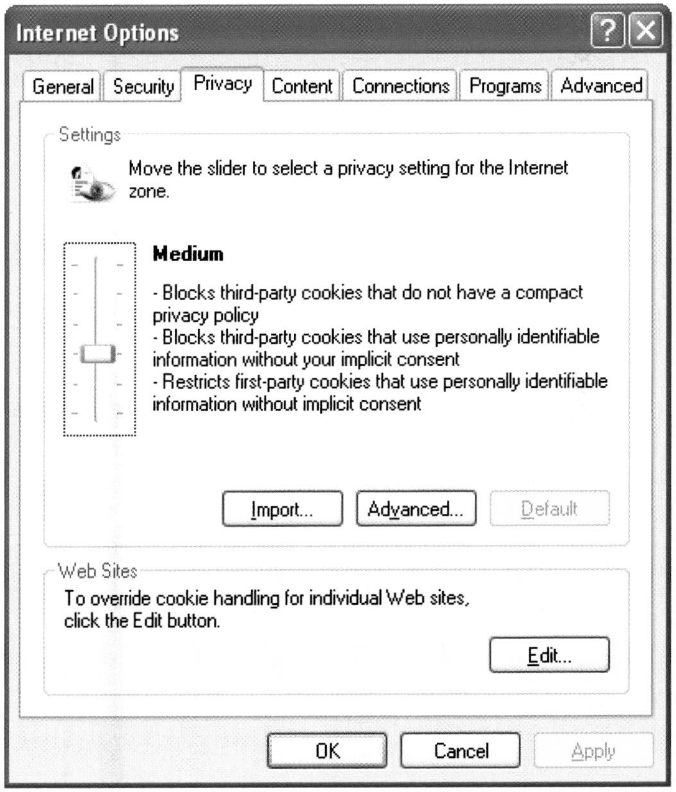

Figure 4-9: Determine how you will handle cookies that web sites want to leave on your computer

CAUTION

Material you copy from the Internet is normally protected by copyright; therefore, what you can do with it is limited. Basically, you can store it on your hard disk and refer to it. You cannot put it on your own web site, sell it, copy it for distribution, or use it for a commercial purpose without the permission of the owner.

NOTE

Chapter 7 discusses working with audio and video in depth.

COPY A WEB PAGE FROM THE INTERNET

To make a copy of a web page and store it on your hard disk:

1. Open Internet Explorer and locate the web page you want to copy.
2. Open **File** and click **Save As**. In the Save Web Page dialog box, select the folder in which to save the page, enter the file name you want to use, and click **Save**.
3. Close the Internet Explorer if you are ready.

Play Internet Audio and Video

You can play audio and video from the Internet with the Media button in Internet Explorer, directly from a link on a web page, and with the Media Player.

Figure 4-10: You can set the level of content allowed in five categories

NOTE

To successfully play audio and video from the Internet you should have a broadband connection.

USE INTERNET EXPLORER'S MEDIA BUTTON

The Media button opens the Media pane with WindowsMedia.com.

1. Open **Internet Explorer** and click **Media** on the toolbar. The Media pane opens, as shown in Figure 4-11.
2. Select from currently featured pieces ("Today"), Music, Movies, or Radio, and then select the piece you want to listen to or watch. The first time you do this you will get a message asking if you want to play the link in Internet Explorer or in its own window so you can continue to browse the Web as you watch or listen.
3. When you are done, close the Media pane and Internet Explorer.

Figure 4-11: The Media button opens the Media pane from where you can select audio and video pieces to play

PLAY DIRECTLY FROM A WEB PAGE

Many web pages have links to audio and video files, such as those shown in the lower right of the CNN page in Figure 4-12. To play these files, simply click the links. If you have several audio players installed (for example Windows Media Player and Real Player), you will be asked which one you want to use. Make that choice and the player will open to play the requested piece.

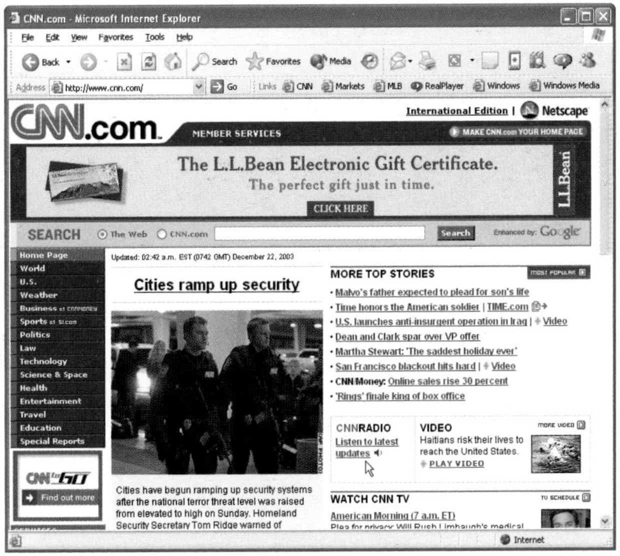

Figure 4-12: Play an audio or video link on a web page by clicking it

TIP

To search for a radio station, enter its call letters in the Search text box and press **ENTER**.

PLAY WITH MEDIA PLAYER

The Windows Media Player is a separate program that comes with Windows XP. With it you can locate radio stations and other audio and video sources on the Internet. (The Windows Media Player is discussed more fully in Chapter 7.)

1. Open **Start**, select **All Programs**, and click **Windows Media Player**.
2. Click **Media Guide** on the left to see a featured set of movie trailers and audio presentations you can select by clicking them, as shown in Figure 4-13.
3. Alternatively, click **Radio Tuner** to see a list of featured stations you can click and be able to search for others.
4. Click **Close** when you are done with the Media Player.

Figure 4-13: Many different audio and video programs are available in Media Player

Use Internet E-Mail

Windows XP includes Outlook Express, shown in Figure 4-14, that allows you to send and receive e-mail and to participate in newsgroups.

Establish an E-Mail Account

To send and receive mail you must have an e-mail account with an Internet Service Provider (ISP) and that account must be set up in Outlook Express. The section, "Configure an Internet Connection" earlier in this chapter, discussed setting up an account with an ISP and noted that for e-mail you need:

- Your e-mail address
- The type of mail server the ISP uses (POP3, IMAP, or HTTP)
- The names of the incoming and outgoing mail servers
- The name and password for your mail account

With an Internet connection established and with the above information, you may set up an account in Outlook Express.

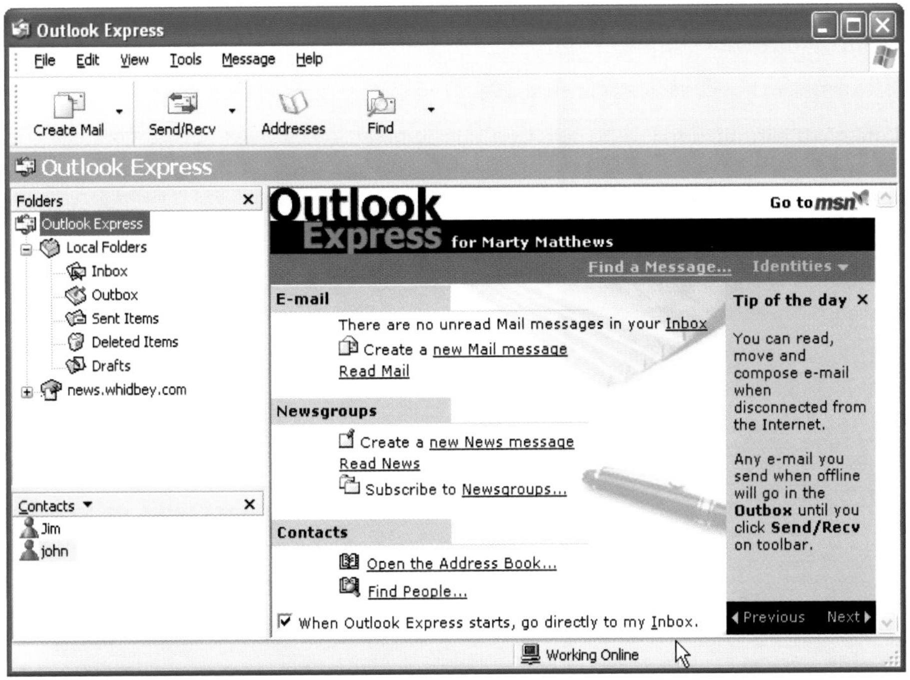

Figure 4-14: Outlook Express provides access to e-mail and newsgroups

1. Open **Start** and click **E-mail**. (This assumes that Outlook Express is your default e-mail application. If it isn't, open **Start**, select **All Programs**, and click **Outlook Express**.) If Outlook Express has not been previously set up, the Internet Connection Wizard will open; if it doesn't, go to the earlier section, "Configure an Internet Connection," and open it.
2. Enter the name you want people to see when they get your e-mail and click **Next**.
3. Enter your e-mail address and click **Next**.
4. Select the type of mail server used by your ISP, enter the names of your ISP's incoming and outgoing mail servers, and click **Next**.
5. Enter your account name and your password and whether you want Windows to remember your password so you don't have to enter it each time you sign on to the mail server.
6. When you have completed these steps click **Next**, and then click **Finish**.

Use the next two sections, "Create and Send E-Mail" and "Receive and Reply to E-Mail," to test your setup.

Create and Send E-Mail

To create and send an e-mail message:

1. Open **Outlook Express** and click **Create Mail** on the toolbar. The New Message window will open, similar to the one in Figure 4-15.

1 2 3 4 5 6 7 8 9 10

TIP

To be able to quickly start Outlook Express, open Start and drag the Outlook Express icon to the Quick Launch toolbar (see Chapter 2).

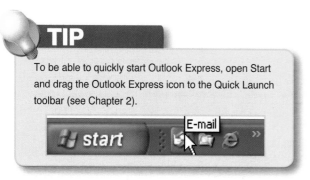

2. Start to enter a name in the **To** text box. If the name is in your address book (see the QuickSteps "Using the Address Book" in this chapter) it will be automatically completed if you press **ENTER**. If the name is not automatically completed, finish typing a full e-mail address (such as **billg@microsoft.com**).
3. If you want more than one addressee, place a semi-colon (;) after the first addressee and then type a second one as in Step 2.
4. If you want to differentiate the addressees to whom the message is principally being sent from those for whom it is just information, press **TAB** and put the second or subsequent addressees in the **Cc** text box as you did in the **To** text box.
5. Press **TAB,** enter a subject for the message, press **TAB** again, and type your message.
6. When you have completed your message, click **Send**. If you are ready, close Outlook Express.

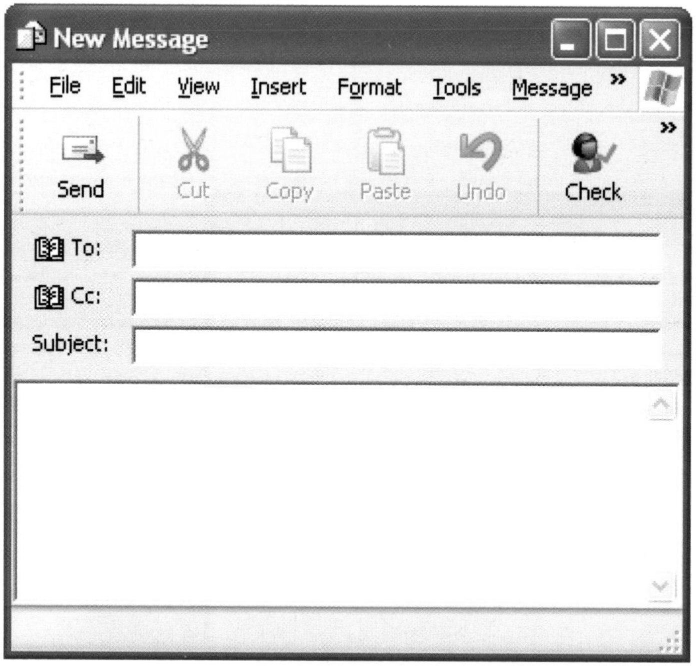

Figure 4-15: Sending e-mail messages is an easy and fast way to communicate

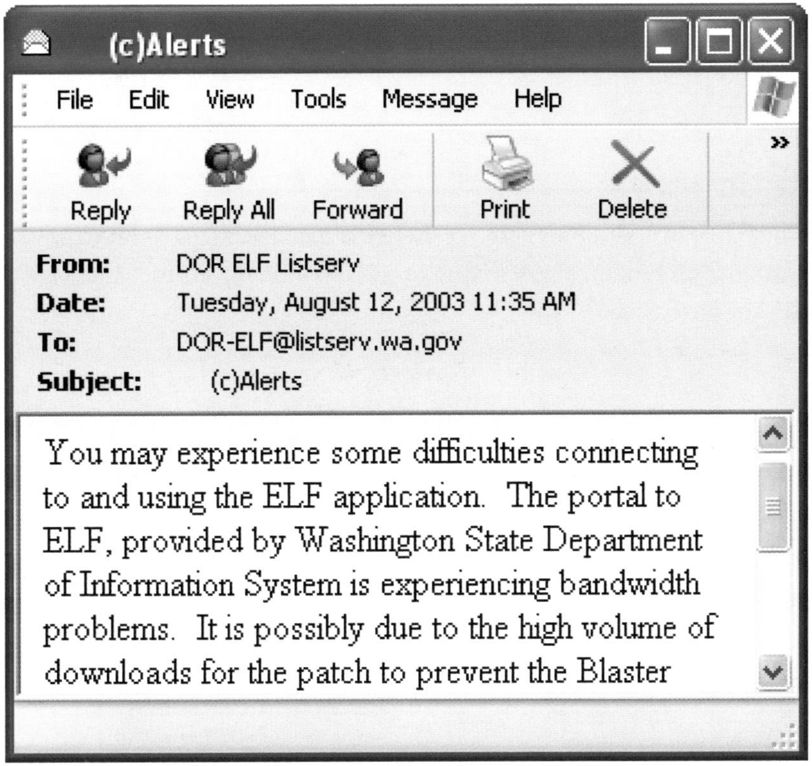

Figure 4-16: Work with a message you have received by opening it in its own window

Receive E-Mail

Depending on how Outlook Express is set up, it may automatically receive any e-mail you have when you are connected to your ISP. If not, or if you need to dial your ISP, click **Send/Recv**. In any case, the mail you receive will go into your Inbox. To open and read your mail:

1. Open **Outlook Express** and click **Inbox** in the Folders list to open your Inbox, which contains all of the messages you receive and haven't deleted.
2. Click a message in the Inbox to read it in the Preview pane at the bottom of the window, or double-click a message to open the message in its own window, as shown in Figure 4-16.
3. Print or delete a message in either the Inbox or its own windows by clicking the appropriate button on the toolbar. Close Outlook Express if you are finished with it.

Respond to E-Mail

You may respond to messages you receive in three ways by first clicking the message in your Inbox and then:

- Click **Reply** to return a message to just the person who sent the original message.

  –Or–

- Click **Reply All** to return a message to all the people who were addressees (both To and Cc) in the original message.

  –Or–

- Click **Forward** to relay a message to people not shown as addressees on the original message.

TIP

Normally, the contents of your Inbox are sorted by date, the most recent message at the top. You can sort on any of the columns by clicking the column heading, as shown in Figure 4-17. The first time you click, the column is sorted alphabetically, the second time it is sorted in inverse alphabetical order.

TIP

While you can have several e-mail addresses in a single contact's Properties dialog box, there is not an easy way to select any but the default address. A better solution is to have several contacts with the same name but different e-mail addresses. That way, when you send an e-mail to that person you will be asked which address you want to use.

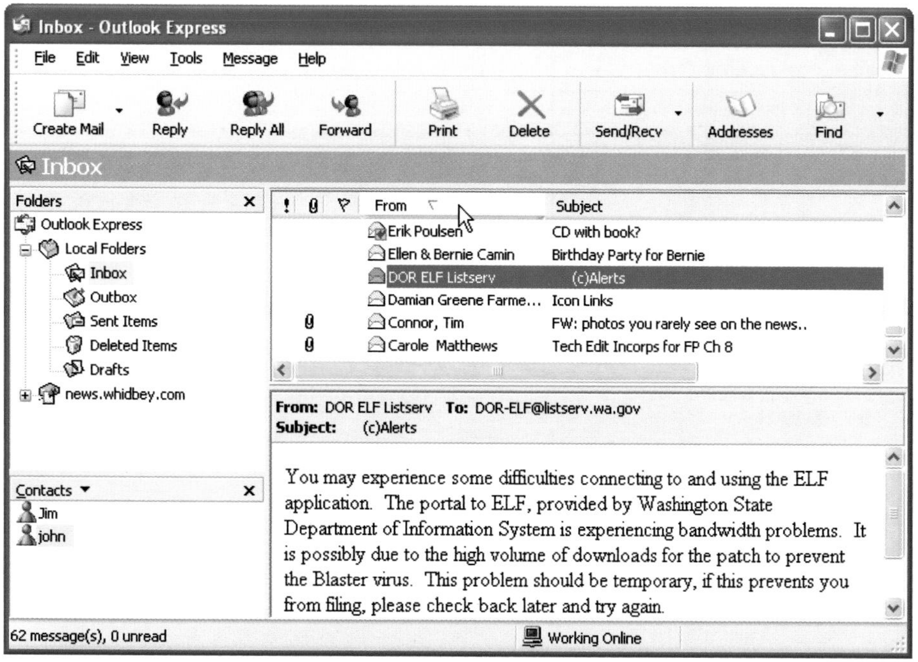

In all three cases a window very similar to the New Message window opens and allows you to add or change addressees and the subject, and add a message.

Use Stationery

If you would like to add some character to your e-mail messages, you can send them with a background image. You can do this individually for each message or for all your messages.

APPLY STATIONERY TO INDIVIDUAL MESSAGES

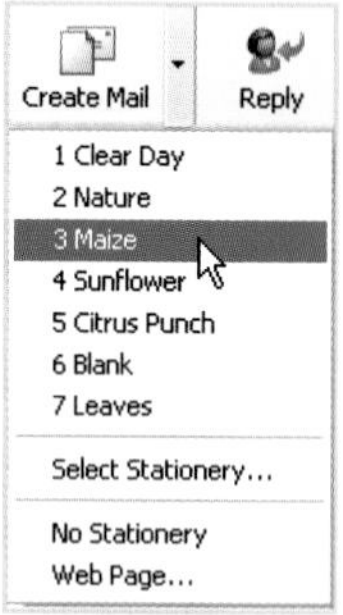

1. Open **Outlook Express** and click the **Create Mail down arrow** on the toolbar.
2. Choose one of the seven preselected backgrounds or click **Select Stationery** for additional options, select one, and then click **OK**. The New Message window will open.
3. Address, enter, and send the message as you otherwise would, and then close Outlook Express.

Figure 4-17: Sort messages in the Inbox by who sent them or their subject, as well as by the date they were sent

QUICKSTEPS

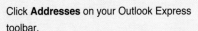

USING THE ADDRESS BOOK

The Address Book, shown in Figure 4-18, allows you to collect addresses and other information about the people with whom you correspond or otherwise interact.

OPEN THE ADDRESS BOOK

To open the Address Book:

Click **Addresses** on your Outlook Express toolbar.

ADD A NEW ADDRESS

To add a new address to the Address Book:

1. Click **New** on the toolbar and click **New Contact**. The contact's Properties dialog box opens.
2. Enter as much of the information as you have or want. For e-mail, you need a name and an e-mail address. You can have several e-mail addresses for each contact. For each, type it in the E-Mail Address text box and click **Add**.
3. When you are ready, click **OK** to close the Properties dialog box.

ADD A GROUP OF ADDRESSES

To add a group of addresses that you want to send a single message to:

1. Click **New** on the toolbar and click **New Group**. The group's Properties dialog box opens.
2. Enter the group name and click **Select Members**. The Select Group Members dialog box opens and allows you to find and select contacts who are currently in the Address Book. Alternatively, you can create a new contact and have it added to the group.
3. When you are ready, click **OK** twice, first to close the Select Group Members box and next to close the Properties dialog box. Click **Close** to close the Address Book.

APPLY STATIONERY TO ALL MESSAGES

1. Open **Outlook Express**, open **Tools**, and click **Options**.
2. Click the **Compose** tab and under Stationery click **Mail**.
3. Click **Select**, select the stationery that you want to apply to all your e-mail, click **OK**, and then close Outlook Express.

Apply Formatting

The simplest messages are sent in plain text without any formatting. These messages take the least bandwidth and are the easiest to receive. If you wish, you can send messages with formatting using HTML, the Internet's Hypertext Markup Language with which many web sites have been created. You can do this for an individual message and for all messages.

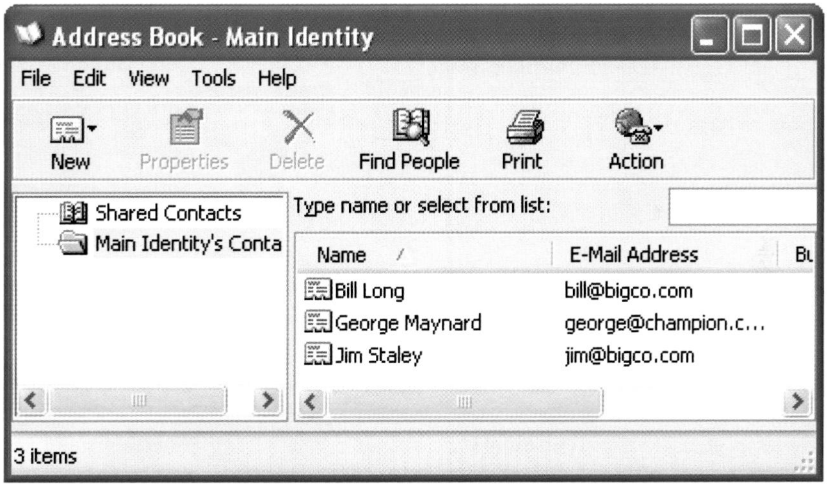

Figure 4-18: The Address Book provides a place to store information about the people you correspond with

1 2 3 4 5 6 7 8 9 10

TIP

If you see an e-mail address in an e-mail message that you want in your address book, right-click the address and choose **Add To Address Book**. This creates a new contact and opens its properties dialog box for you to make changes and add other information.

CAUTION

Not all e-mail programs can properly receive HTML messages, resulting in messages that are not very readable. However, most programs put out in the last five years can handle HTML.

APPLY FORMATTING TO INDIVIDUAL MESSAGES

1. Open **Outlook Express** and click the **Create Mail** button on the toolbar.
2. Open **Format** and click **Rich Text (HTML)**.
3. Address, enter, and send the message as you otherwise would, and then close Outlook Express.

APPLY FORMATTING TO ALL MESSAGES

1. Open **Outlook Express**, open **Tools**, and click **Options**.
2. Click the **Send** tab, under **Mail Sending Format** click **HTML**.
3. Click **OK**, and then close Outlook Express.

SELECT A FONT AND A COLOR FOR ALL MESSAGES

To use a particular font and font color on all of your e-mail messages (you must send your mail using HTML in place of plain text—see "Apply Formatting to All Messages"):

1. Open **Outlook Express**, open **Tools**, and click **Options**.
2. Click the **Compose** tab. Under **Compose Font,** click **Font Settings** opposite Mail.
3. Select the font, style, size, effects, and color that you want to use (see Figure 4-19) with all your e-mail, then click **OK**, and then close Outlook Express.

ATTACH A SIGNATURE

To attach a closing on all of your e-mail messages:

1. Open **Outlook Express**, open **Tools**, and click **Options**.
2. Click the **Signatures** tab and click **New**. Under Edit Signature, enter the closing text you want to use, or click **File** and enter or browse to the path and file name you want for the closing.
3. Click **Add Signatures To All Outgoing Messages**, as shown in Figure 4-20, and click **OK**, and then close Outlook Express.

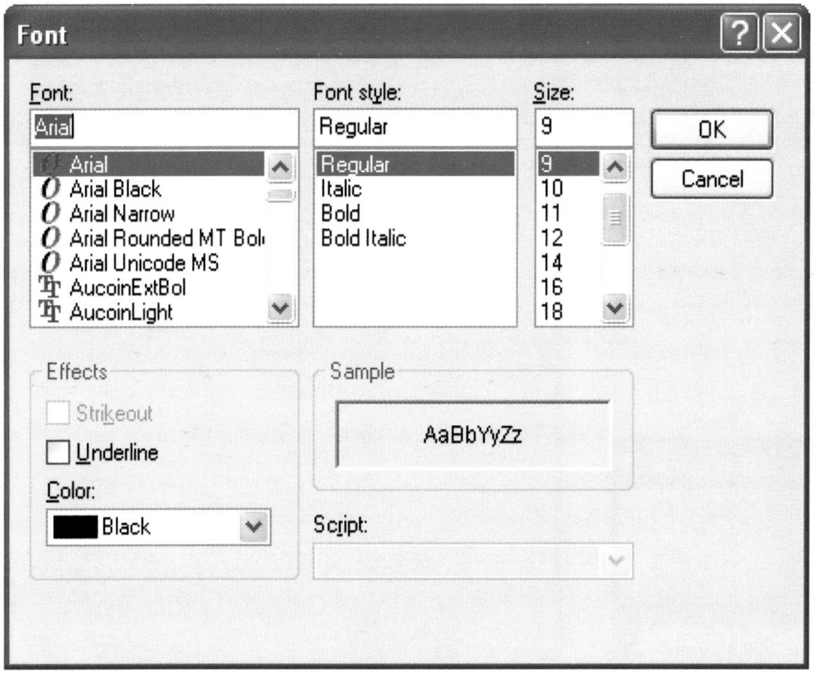

Figure 4-19: If you send your mail using HTML in place of plain text, you can apply fonts and color and do many other things not available with plain text

Attach Files to E-Mail

You can attach and send files, such as documents or images, with e-mail messages:

1. Open **Outlook Express** and click the **Create Mail** button on the toolbar.
2. Click **Attach** on the toolbar. Select the containing folder and name of the file you want to send, and click **Attach**.
3. Address, enter, and send the message as you normally would, and then close Outlook Express.

Participate in Newsgroups

Newsgroups are organized chains of messages on a particular subject. Newsgroups allow people to enter new messages and respond to previous ones. To participate in one or more newsgroups you need to set up a newsgroup account, then locate and open a particular newsgroup, and finally send and receive messages within the newsgroup.

SET UP A NEWSGROUP ACCOUNT

Setting up a new account for a newsgroup is similar to setting up the account for your e-mail. To set up a newsgroup account, you need the name of the news server and, possibly, an account name and password.

1. Open **Outlook Express**, open **Tools**, and choose **Accounts**.
2. Click **Add** and **News**. Enter the name you want displayed, and click **Next**. Enter your e-mail address if not already displayed, and click **Next**.
3. Enter the name of your news server. Your ISP or sponsoring organization will give you this. If you do not need to enter an account name and password, your ISP or sponsoring organization will tell you this and you can skip to step 5.

> **NOTE**
>
> If you have several e-mail accounts, you may click Advanced in the Signatures tab of the Options dialog box and select the account(s) with which to use a selected signature.

4. To enter an account name and password, click **My News Server Requires Me To Log On**, and click **Next**. Enter your account name and password, click **Remember Password** (if desired), and then, if necessary (your ISP or sponsor will tell you), click **Log On Using Secure Password Authentication (SPA)**.
5. Click **Next**, click **Finish**, click **Close**. A new folder will appear in the Folders pane of Outlook Express.
6. Click **Yes** to download the newsgroups from the news account you just set up. If necessary, click **Connect** to connect to the Internet. If all of your entries are okay, you will be connected. If your account name and password are in error, you are told so and given a chance to fix them. A list of newsgroups will be displayed, as shown in Figure 4-21.

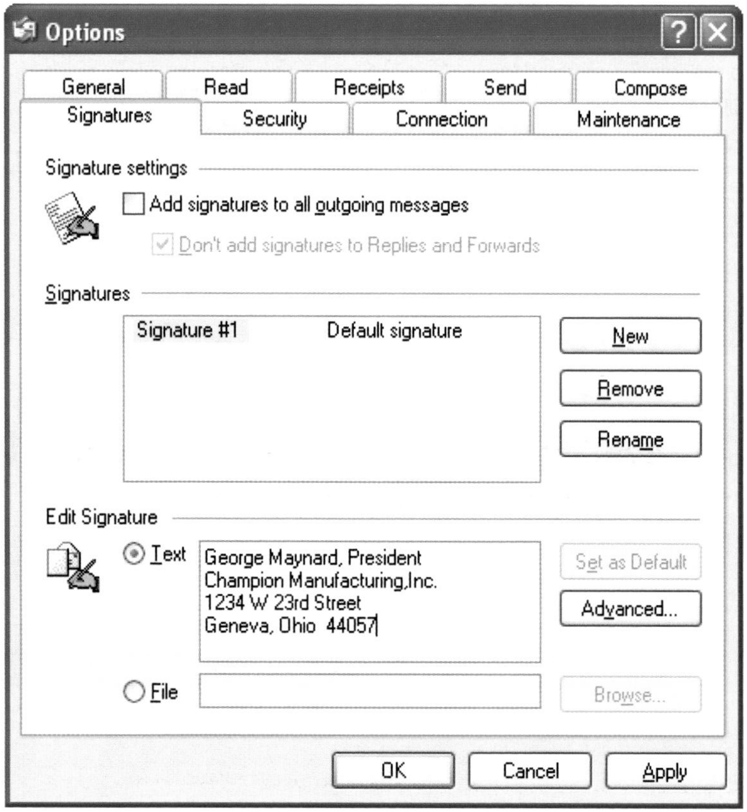

Figure 4-20: A "signature" in Outlook Express is really a closing

SUBSCRIBE TO A NEWSGROUP

Most general purpose news servers, such as those maintained by ISPs, have many newsgroups, probably only some of which might interest you. To subscribe (meaning read and reply to messages they contain) to those (if you have just come from setting up a newsgroup account skip to Step 2):

1. Open **Outlook Express** and click your news server in the Folders pane. If you have not subscribed to a newsgroup you will be asked if you want to. Click **Yes**. If you have subscribed to a newsgroup and want to subscribe to more, click **Newsgroups** in the right pane. In either case the Newsgroup Subscription dialog box will open.
2. To search for a particular newsgroup enter a keyword (such as "BMW") in the Display Newsgroups Which Contain text box and press **ENTER**.

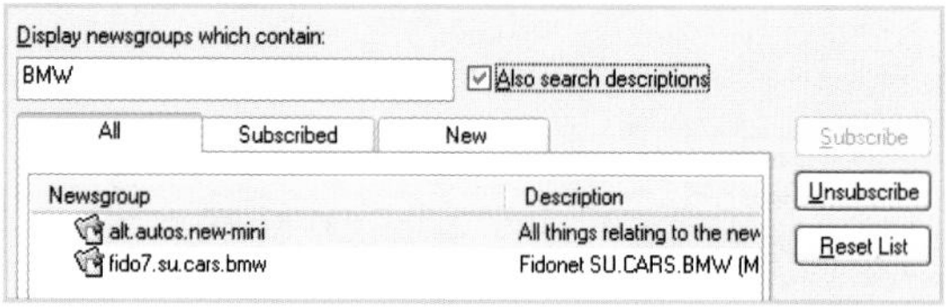

TIP

With a New Message window open, you can drag a file from the Windows Explorer or the Desktop to the message and it will automatically be attached and sent with the message.

3. Double-click the newsgroups to which you want to subscribe. After you have selected the newsgroups, click **OK**. You are returned to Outlook Express.

READ AND POST MESSAGES IN A NEWSGROUP

You can read and send newsgroup messages like e-mail messages, but with two differences. You can choose to reply to the newsgroup or to the individual, and a new message is called a New Post, as in posting to a bulletin board. If someone replies to this message, it gets added to the end of the original message, thereby creating a chain, or *thread*, of messages on a given subject.

1. Open **Outlook Express**, open your news server in the Folders pane, and click a newsgroup you want to open. A list of messages will be displayed.

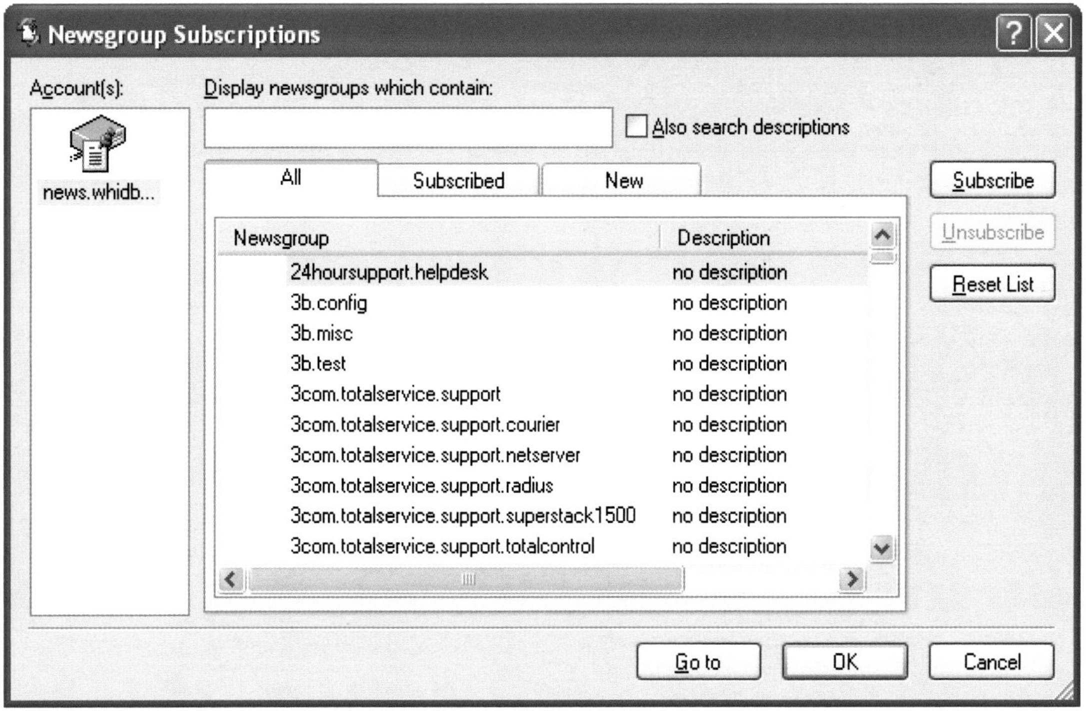

Figure 4-21: A list of newsgroups to which you can subscribe

1 2 3 4 5 6 7 8 9 10

2. Click one to have it shown in the bottom pane, as shown in Figure 4-22, or double-click to have a message opened in its own window.

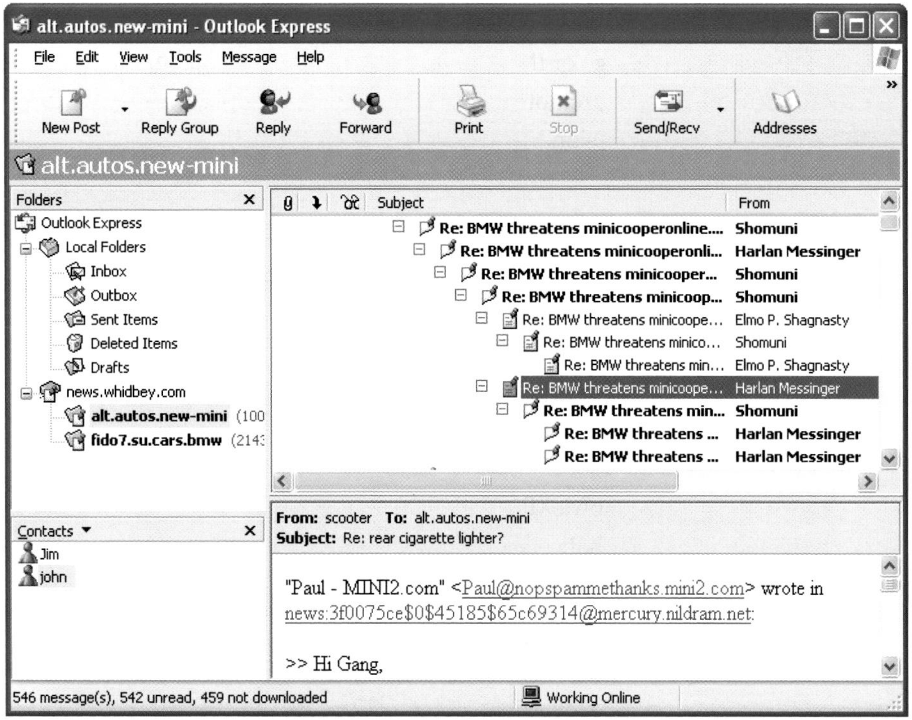

Figure 4-22: A newsgroup provides a thread on a given topic to which you can add your comments

3. To respond to a newsgroup message:

- Click **New Post** on the toolbar to create a public message that will begin a new thread.

–Or–

- Click **Reply Group** on the toolbar to create a public message in the thread you have selected.

–Or–

- Click **Reply** on the toolbar to create a private message to the person who wrote the message you have selected.

–Or–

- Click **Forward** on the toolbar to send a copy of the message you have selected to another individual.

4. Type and send the message as you would any e-mail message. When you are ready, close Outlook Express.

Use Windows Messenger

Windows Messenger allows you to instantly send and receive messages (or *chat*) with others who are online at the same time as you. (It is frequently called "Instant Messaging" or IM.) Windows Messenger can also handle teleconferencing, the live, remote interaction of several people complete with audio and video transmission.

Set Up Windows Messenger

Windows Messenger is installed automatically with Windows XP and automatically starts when you start Windows XP. Its use requires that you first have a Microsoft Passport or an MSN or Hotmail account. Then you are able to set up your contacts and personalize Messenger to your tastes.

ESTABLISH A PASSPORT

When you first use Windows XP you will be asked if you want to set up a .NET Passport account. To do that:

1. If you canceled out of the .NET Passport question, you can start the .NET Passport Wizard after the fact by clicking the **Windows Messenger** icon in the notification area or by opening **Start**, choosing **All Programs**, and clicking **Windows Messenger**.
2. From Windows Messenger click **Click Here To Sign In.** The .NET Passport Wizard will open. Click **Next**. If you already have an e-mail account, click **Yes**; otherwise, go to the discussion earlier in this chapter, "Establish an E-Mail Account," and complete that first.
3. If you already have a Passport, click **Yes I Want To Sign In With My Passport** and click **Next**. Skip to Step 5.
4. Without a passport click **No** and click **Next** twice. The .NET Passport registration will open in your browser. Enter the information requested, click **I Agree**, and when you are told you have successfully registered your e-mail address, close your browser. You will be returned to the .NET Passport Wizard. Click **Back**, click **Yes I Want To Sign In With My Passport**, and click **Next**.

NOTE

There is also MSN Messenger, which is just a little different from Windows Messenger, but the two can share messages between them, although voice and applications will depend on versions of both.

NOTE

Windows Messenger does not normally create a permanent record, unless you specifically save the exchange.

TIP

If you want to stop receiving comments from another person (for example, that person's remarks are getting offensive) click **Block**.

> **NOTE**
>
> There may be a newer version of Windows Messenger available through Windows Update, depending on the version of Windows XP that you have installed. If you get an Internet message from Microsoft to this effect, go ahead and download the update.

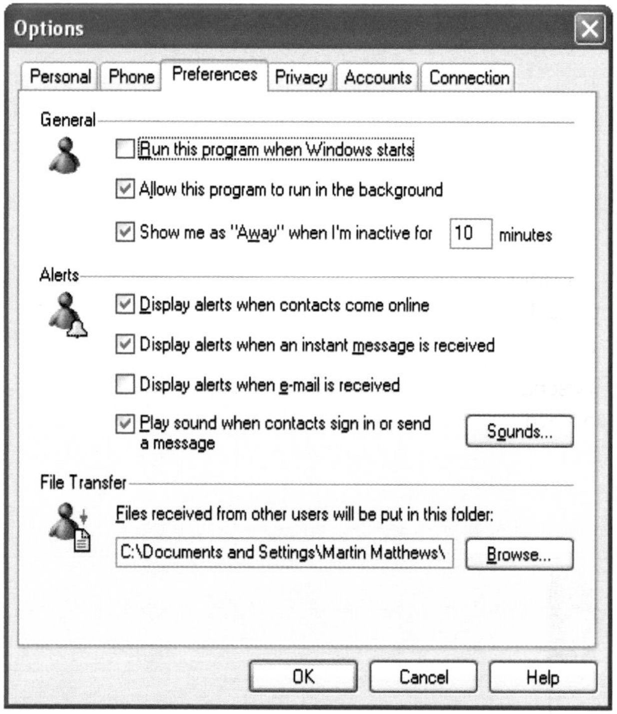

Figure 4-24: Setting Windows Messenger preferences

5. Enter your e-mail address and your .NET Passport password, then click **Next**. Click **Finish** to close the wizard. Windows Messenger will open, as you can see in Figure 4-23.

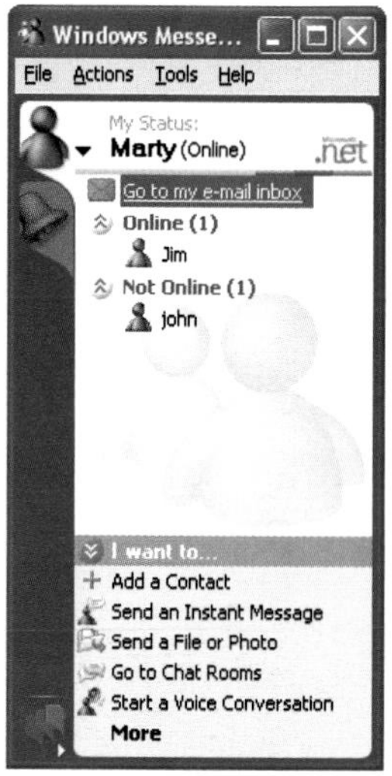

Figure 4-23: Windows Messenger ready for use

ADDING CONTACTS TO MESSENGER

To use Windows Messenger you must enter contacts whom you want to "talk" to:

1. If Windows Messenger is not already open, double-click its icon in the notification area. If the icon isn't there, open **Start**, choose **All Programs**, and click **Windows Messenger**.
2. Click **Add A Contact** in the tasks pane at the bottom on the Windows Messenger window. If you know your contact's e-mail address, click **By E-mail Address Or Sign-in Name** and click **Next**. Enter the e-mail address and click **Next**. Depending on the person's status, different things can occur:
   - If the person has a Passport account, you will be told you were successful in establishing the contact.
   - If the person is logged on to Windows Messenger, you will be told you can chat with that contact.
   - If the person isn't logged on, you will be told you can send an e-mail message asking your contact to sign on.
   - If the person doesn't have a Passport account, you will be told you can send an e-mail message telling your contact about Passport and how to install it.
3. In any of the preceding cases, click **Next**, enter your own message to add to the canned message, and click **Finish** to close the Add A Contact wizard.
4. If you want, click **Search For A Contact**, and click **Next**. Enter the information as best you can, and click **Next**. If there is more than one person who fits your criteria, select the correct one and click **Next**. You are told the person was found, but you cannot immediately add him or her to your contact list due to the privacy policy. You can send the person an e-mail message by clicking **Next**, entering your message, and clicking **Finish** to close the Add A Contact Wizard.

QUICKSTEPS

USING WINDOWS MESSENGER

Using Windows Messenger is very simple: double-click a contact who is online and the Conversation window will open. Most additional functions start by initiating a conversation and then starting the additional function. For example, if you want to use a whiteboard after starting a normal Windows Messenger conversation, simply click **Start Whiteboard**. The other parties will have to agree, but that is all there is to it.

SEND A MESSAGE

With the Conversation window open (done by double-clicking a contact), send a message by typing it in the bottom pane and clicking **Send** or pressing **ENTER**. Change the font and/or add one of the smiley faces or objects to express emotions.

RECEIVE A MESSAGE

With a conversation in process, a received message simply appears in the Conversation window, as you can see in Figure 4-25. If someone sends you an instant message without a conversation open, you will get a little pop-up message from your notification area. Double-click this message to open a Conversation window with the sender.

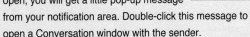

SEND ATTACHMENTS

If you want to attach a file to the message, click **Send File Or Photo** in the right pane of the Conversation window. Select the document to send, and click **Send**. This illustration shows a conversation that includes the transfer of a file.

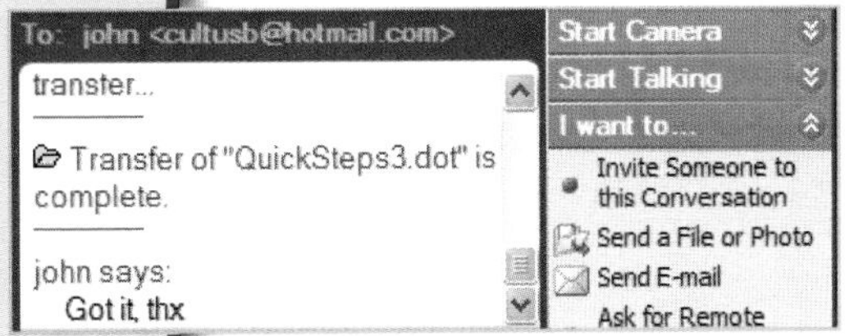

Continued...

5. When you are done adding contacts and want to leave Windows Messenger, click **Close**. You will be told that Windows Messenger is still running.

As you are successful in adding contacts, these people will be notified with a message.

PERSONALIZE MESSENGER

There are a number of ways to personalize Windows Messenger.

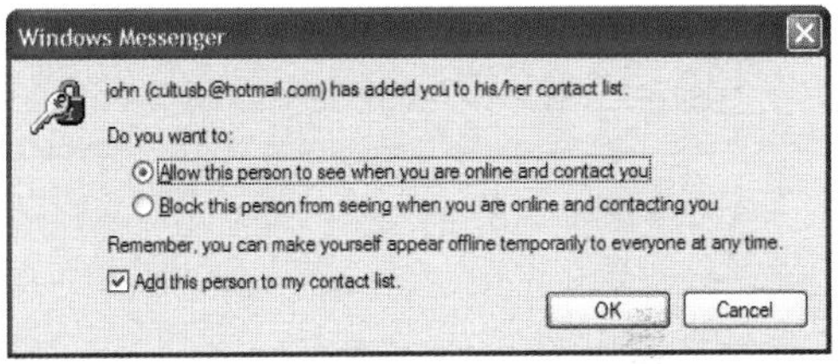

1. Open **Windows Messenger**, open **Tools**, and choose **Options**. Click the **Personal** tab, enter the name you want to use and click **Change Font** to determine the font to use for instant messaging.
2. Click the **Phone** tab if you want people to know one or more of your phone numbers, and enter the numbers.
3. Click the **Preferences** tab, shown in Figure 4-24, and set the options that are best for you.
4. Click the **Privacy** tab and place your contacts on either the Allow or Block lists. To move a contact from one column to the other, select that contact and click **Allow** or **Block**.
5. When you have personalized Windows Messenger the way you want, click **OK**. If you want to leave Windows Messenger, click **Close**.

USING WINDOWS MESSENGER

(Continued)

USE AUDIO AND VIDEO

If you have a sound board with speakers and a microphone, you can hold an audio conversation, literally talking over the Internet as you would over a phone, by clicking **Start Talking**. If it is the first time this feature has been used, follow the instructions in the wizard that opens. (If you don't have a broadband connection, the audio will not be very satisfactory.)

If you have a video camera set up, you can send real-time pictures over Windows Messenger by clicking **Start Camera**. Here broadband is almost mandatory.

SHARE AN APPLICATION OR A WHITEBOARD

You can share an application among two or more people by clicking **Start Application Sharing**. For example, say you and several associates are working on the budget. You could load the budget into Excel (only one person needs a copy of Excel) and then share the application during a conversation on the budget.

A built-in feature for application sharing is a whiteboard, which is started by clicking **Start Whiteboard**. Here all the parties to a conversation can use a drawing application as they are holding a conversation.

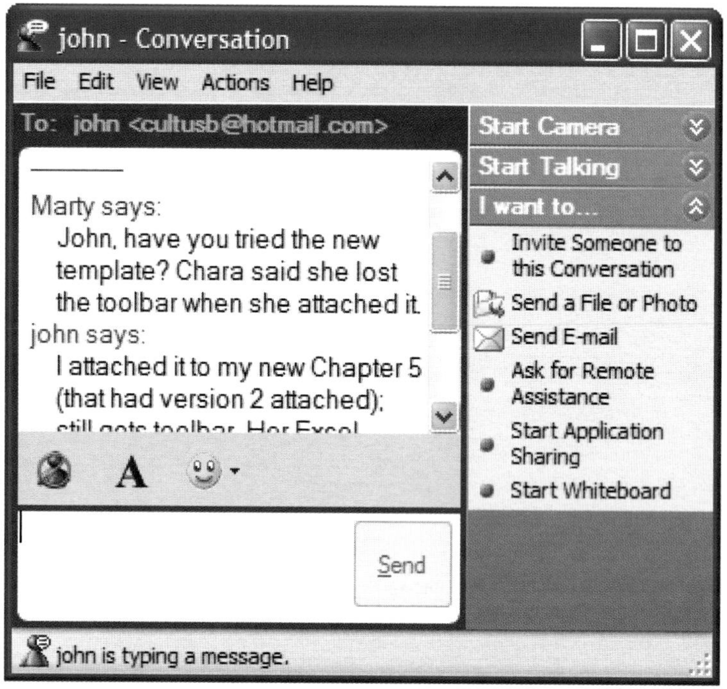

Figure 4-25: When a conversation is in process you can see who said what in the Conversation window

TIP

Files you receive through Windows Messenger are stored in My Documents\My Received Files. You can quickly open them by opening the Conversation **File** menu and choosing **Open Received Files**.

How to...

Chapter 5 Managing Windows XP

Running programs is one of Windows XP's major functions. Managing Windows XP entails setting up the starting and stopping of programs in a number of different ways. Managing also includes the maintenance and enhancement of Windows XP and the setting up of remote assistance so you can have someone help you from a distance.

Start and Stop Programs

Previous chapters have discussed starting programs from the Start menu, through All Programs, through a shortcut on the desktop, and by locating the program with Windows Explorer. All of these methods of starting a program require a direct action by you. Windows also provides several ways to automatically start programs and to monitor and manage them while they are running.

Start Programs Automatically

Sometimes you will want to start a program automatically and have it run in the background every time you start the computer. For example, you might automatically run an antivirus program or, as I do, a screen capture program (SnagIt), used to capture the figures and illustrations you see here. To automatically start a program, open a folder, or open a file in a program:

Figure 5-1: Programs in the Startup folder are automatically started when you start the computer

1. Open **Start**, choose **All Programs**, right-click **Startup**, and click **Open All Users**. The Startup folder will open, as you can see in Figure 5-1.
2. Open **Windows Explorer**, and position the window so you can see both it and the Startup window on the desktop at the same time.
3. Open the folders needed to display the program file you want to automatically start, or the folder or disk drive you want to automatically open, or the file you want to automatically start in its program.
4. Press and hold the right mouse button while dragging (right-drag) the program file, the folder, or the file to the open Startup folder. When you reach the Startup folder, click **Create Shortcuts Here**.
5. Close the Startup folder and Windows Explorer. The next time you start your computer, the action you want will take place.

NOTE

Some programs, including Norton AntiVirus, automatically start when the computer is started without being in Startup. You can see these programs and manage them using MSConfig, discussed later in this chapter.

Start Programs Minimized

Sometimes when you start programs automatically, you want them to run in the background, or minimized. To do that:

1. Open **Start**, choose **All Programs**, right-click **Startup**, and click **Open All Users** to open the Startup folder.

2. Right-click the program you want minimized, and choose **Properties**. Click the **Shortcut** tab.
3. Open the **Run** drop-down box, and click **Minimized**, as shown in Figure 5-2.
4. Click **OK** to close the Properties dialog box, and then close the **Startup** folder.

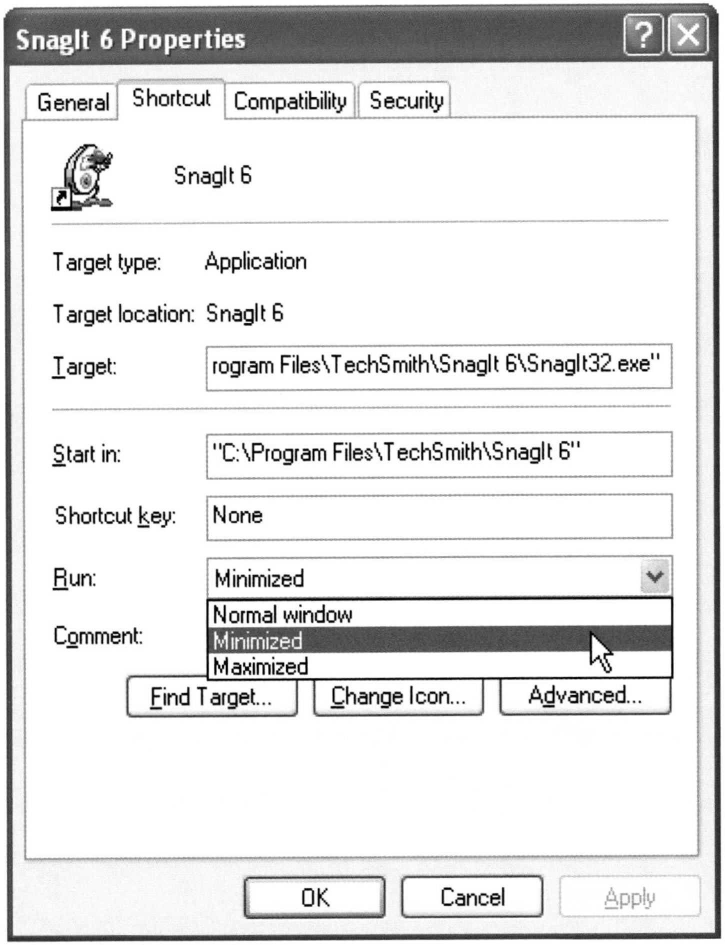

Figure 5-2: Minimizing a program, when it has automatically started, lets it run in the background

Schedule Programs

You can schedule a program, such as Backup or the Defragmenter, to run automatically using Windows XP's Task Scheduler. For a program to run automatically, you may need to specify how the program is to run, using command-line parameters. See how to use Help in Step 2 of "Start Older Programs" later in this chapter to learn what parameters are available for the program you want to run.

1. Open **Start**, select **All Programs**, choose **Accessories,** select **System Tools**, and click **Scheduled Tasks**.
2. Double-click **Add Scheduled Task** in the detail pane. The Scheduled Task Wizard opens. Click **Next**. A list of applications opens.
3. Select the application (for example, Backup) you want to run. Click **Next**. Enter a name for the task and specify its frequency. Click **Next**.
4. Specify the time of day the task is to run; whether it is to run every day, only weekdays, or every so many days; and when it is to start.Click **Next**.

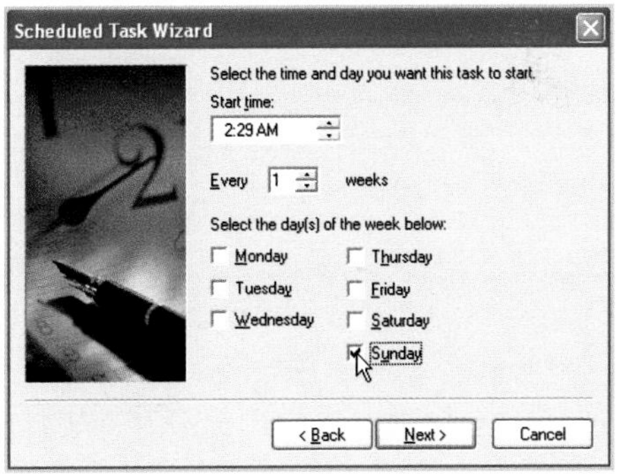

1 2 3 4 5 6 7 8 9 10

NOTE

As the scheduled task exists in Figure 5-3, it will only start the backup program; it won't do a backup. You must do that using command-line parameters.

TIP

If you select a task in the Scheduled Tasks window, you get a tasks pane in which you can Rename, Move, Copy, and Delete scheduled tasks.

5. Enter the user name and password of the person or administrator who is responsible for running this task and who has the appropriate permissions to run it (see Chapter 8). Click **Next**.
6. Click **Open Advanced Properties For This Task When I Click Finish**, and click **Finish**. The Task Properties dialog box will open, as shown in Figure 5-3.
7. In the Run text box and after the program name, type a space, and then enter the command-line parameters needed to run the program.
8. Click the **Schedule** tab and review the schedule you have already established. Click the **Settings** tab and change any settings that apply to the program you want to run.
9. When you are done scheduling the task, click **OK**. You should see the program in the Scheduled Tasks window, similar to Figure 5-4. Close the Scheduled Tasks window.

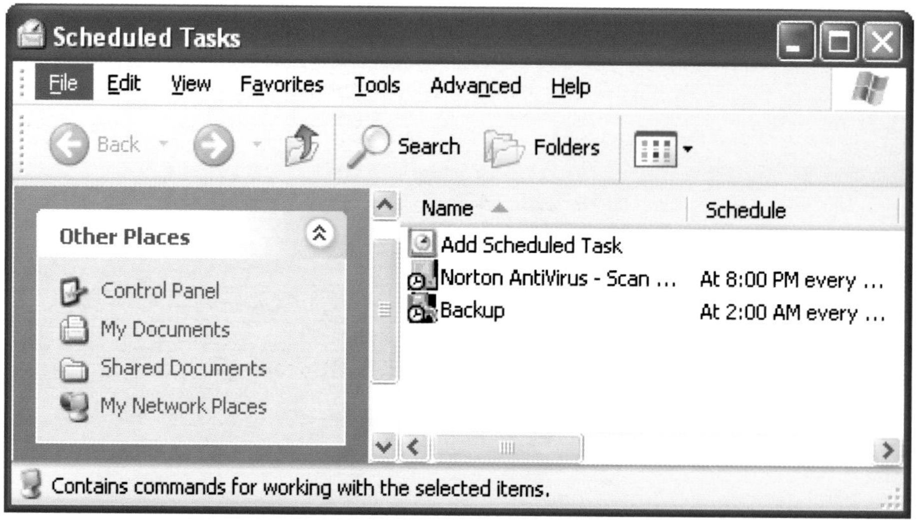

Figure 5-4: Remove and manage scheduled tasks by right-clicking the tasks and choosing Properties in the Scheduled Tasks window

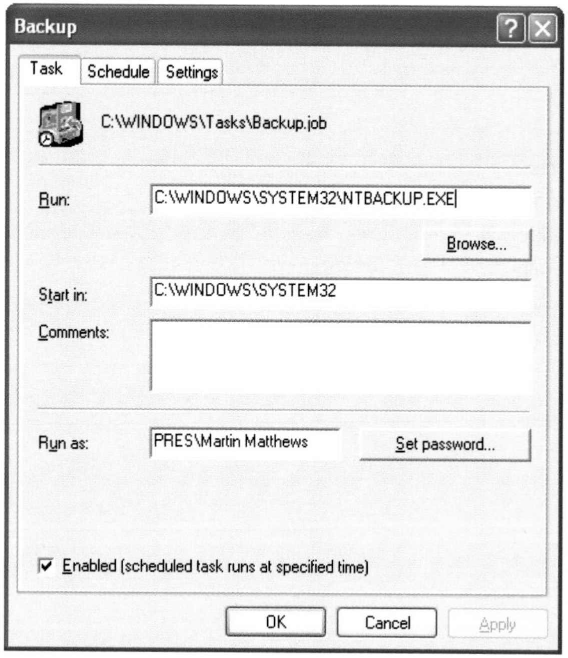

Figure 5-3: Program command-line parameters must be entered in the Run text box to have the program run unattended

QUICKSTEPS

SWITCHING PROGRAMS

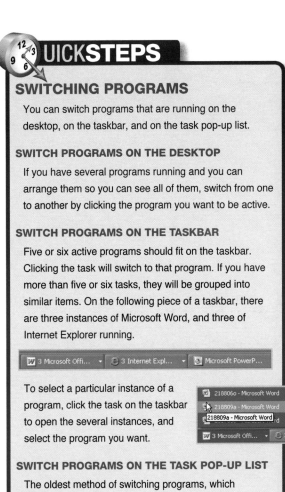

You can switch programs that are running on the desktop, on the taskbar, and on the task pop-up list.

SWITCH PROGRAMS ON THE DESKTOP

If you have several programs running and you can arrange them so you can see all of them, switch from one to another by clicking the program you want to be active.

SWITCH PROGRAMS ON THE TASKBAR

Five or six active programs should fit on the taskbar. Clicking the task will switch to that program. If you have more than five or six tasks, they will be grouped into similar items. On the following piece of a taskbar, there are three instances of Microsoft Word, and three of Internet Explorer running.

To select a particular instance of a program, click the task on the taskbar to open the several instances, and select the program you want.

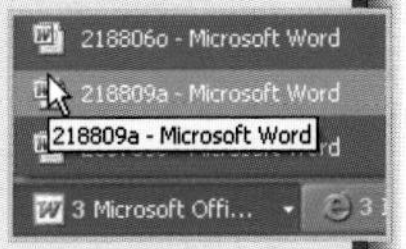

SWITCH PROGRAMS ON THE TASK POP-UP LIST

The oldest method of switching programs, which predates Windows 95 and the taskbar, is using the task pop-up list.

1. Press **ALT+TAB** and hold down **ALT**. The task pop-up list will appear.
2. While continuing to hold **ALT**, press **TAB** to select the program you want.

Control with the Task Manager

The Windows Task Manager, shown in Figure 5-5, performs a number of functions; most importantly, it allows you to see what programs and processes (individual threads of a program) are running and to unequivocally stop both. A cool page of real-time graphs and tables also shows you what is happening at any second on your computer, as you can see in Figure 5-6. To start and use the Task manager:

1. Press **CTRL+ALT+DELETE**. Alternatively, you can right-click a blank area of the taskbar and choose **Task Manager**.
2. Click the **Applications** tab. You'll see a list of the programs you are running, as shown in Figure 5-5.
3. Select a program in the list. Click **End Task** to stop the program, or click **Switch To** to activate that program.
4. Click **New Task** to open the Run command, where you can enter a program you want to start. See "Start a Program in Run," next.
5. Click the **Processes** tab. Here you see a list of all the processes that are currently running and their CPU and memory usage. Most of these processes are parts of Windows.
6. Click the **Performance** tab. This tab graphically shows the CPU memory usage (see Figure 5-6), while the Networking tab shows the computer's use of the network. The Users tab shows the users that are logged on to the computer, and it allows you to disconnect them if they are coming in over the network or to log them off if they are directly logged on.
7. When you are ready, close the Windows Task Manager.

QUICKSTEPS

STOPPING PROGRAMS

Stopping a program may be simply closing it or a desperate attempt to keep a program from harming your data or other programs.

USE THE CLOSE BUTTON

One of the easiest ways to close a program is to click the Close button on the upper-right of all windows.

USE EXIT FROM A MENU

Almost all programs have an Exit command on the menu on the far left of the menu bar; often this is the File menu. Open this menu and click **Exit**.

CLOSE FROM THE TASKBAR

Right-click a task on the taskbar, and click **Close.**

CLOSE FROM THE KEYBOARD

Press **ALT+F4.**

If none of these options work, see "Control with the Task Manager."

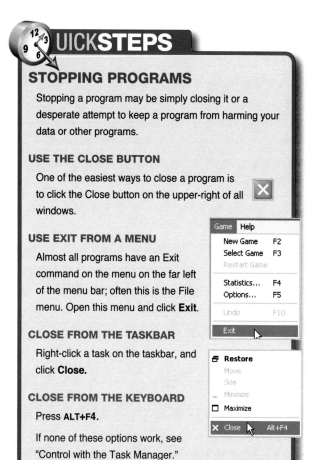

Figure 5-5: The Task Manager shows you what programs are running and allows you to stop them

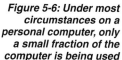

TIP

If you don't want tasks grouped on the taskbar, right-click an empty area of the task bar, choose **Properties**, and click to deselect **Group Similar Taskbar Buttons**. Close the Properties dialog box.

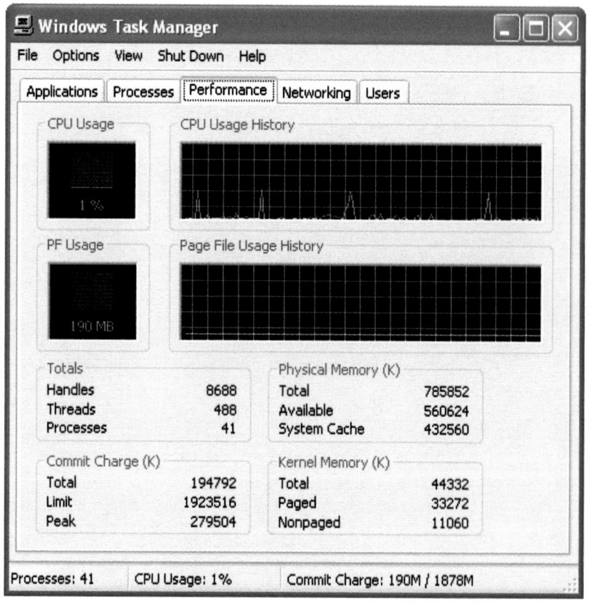

Figure 5-6: Under most circumstances on a personal computer, only a small fraction of the computer is being used

Start a Program in Run

The Start menu has an option called "Run" that opens the Run dialog box. From this dialog box, you can start most programs if you know the path of the program, its name, and don't mind typing all that information.

1. Open **Start** and click **Run**. The Run dialog box will open.
2. Type the path and file name of the program you want to run, and press **ENTER**.

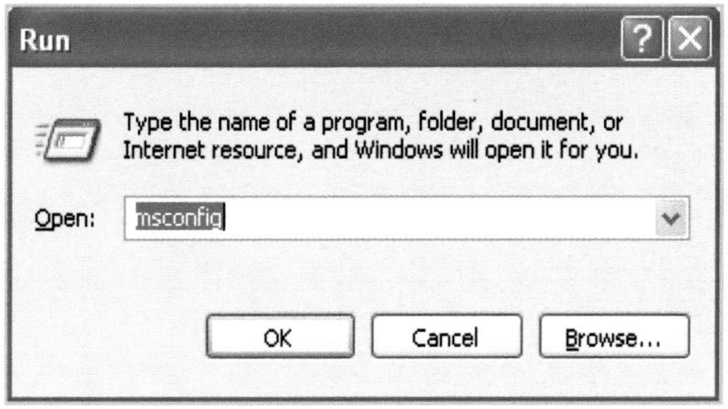

CAUTION

It is generally not a good idea to end a process. Instead, stop the program in the Applications tab that is generating the processes.

NOTE

Programs that are part of Windows or in the root directory (C:\) do not require you to type the path. See "Control Automatic Programs" later in this chapter.

Start Older Programs

While you can start most programs from the desktop or Start menu, older, less sophisticated programs (often called "16-bit programs"), especially games, require that they be run in their own isolated window named Command Prompt (also called a DOS, or Disk Operating System, window). Here you can type DOS commands at the flashing underscore, which is the *command prompt*.

1. Open **Start**, select **All Programs**, choose **Accessories**, and click **Command Prompt**. The Command Prompt window will open.
2. Type help and press **ENTER**. A list of commands that can be used at the command

prompt will be displayed, as shown in Figure 5-7.

3. To run a program on a floppy disk in the A:\ drive, type a:\, press **ENTER**, type dir, press **ENTER** to see the name of the program, type the name of the program, and press **ENTER**. The program should run, although not all will run in Windows XP.
4. When you are done with the Command Prompt window, type exit and press **ENTER**.

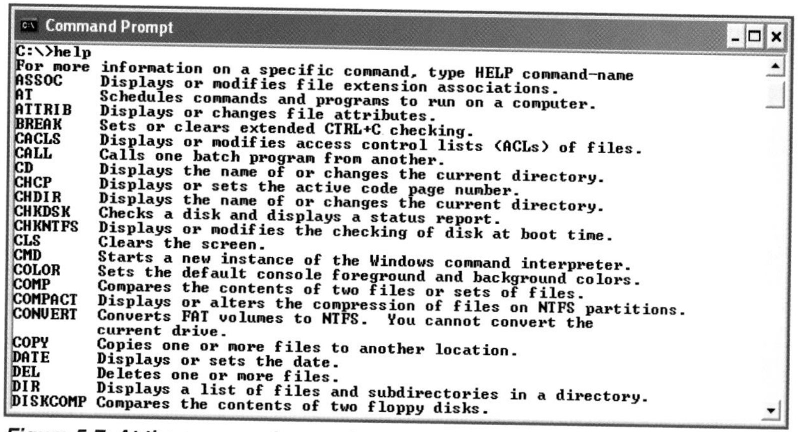

Figure 5-7: At the command prompt you can type DOS commands, which Windows will execute

Control Automatic Programs

Sometimes when you install a program, it sets up itself or other programs to run in perpetuity, even if that is not what you had in mind. Many of these programs are not started from the Startup folder. To control these programs and prevent them from running, Windows XP has a program named MSConfig, and the easiest way to start it is in the Run dialog box.

1. Open **Start** and click **Run**. The Run dialog box will open.
2. Type msconfig and press **ENTER**. The System Configuration Utility dialog box opens.
3. Click the **Startup** tab. Here you will see all of the programs that start when Windows starts, as you can see in Figure 5-8.
4. Click to deselect the program(s), to not start them, the next time Windows starts. Click **OK** to close the System Configuration Utility. Click

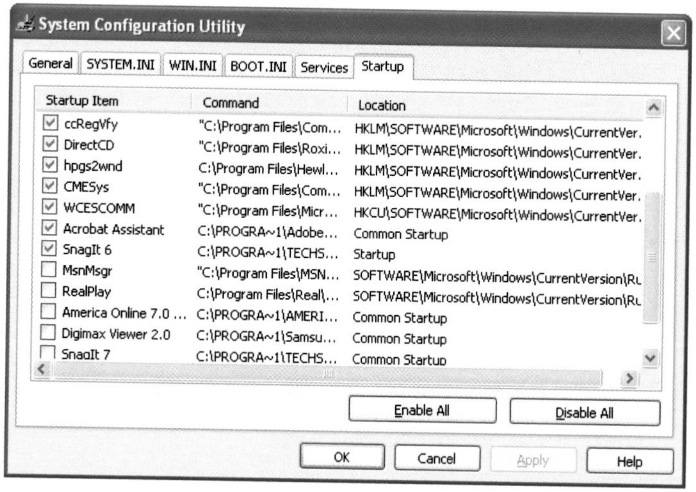

Figure 5-8: In the System Configuration Utility (MSConfig), you can see and stop from running all of the programs that Windows starts

CAUTION

Unless you are trying to diagnose a problem and have considerable experience doing that, you normally do not want to change the settings in the System Configuration Utility.

NOTE

While the Indexing Service speeds up searches, the index processing, which is ongoing, takes a considerable amount of computer resources. Normally, the indexing only takes place while the computer is otherwise idle, but if you have a limited-resource machine and/or you are doing a resource-intensive task, you may want to temporarily suspend indexing.

Restart to restart your computer and reflect the changes you have made.

5. Click **OK** when you are told that you have used the System Configuration Utility to make changes to the way Windows starts. The System Configuration Utility dialog box will open once more. Click **Close**. If you don't want to see the message or have MSConfig open automatically when you start Windows, click **Don't Show This Message Or Launch The System Configuration Utility When Windows Starts**.

Start Indexing Service

Windows has an Indexing Service that, if you let it run, will substantially speed up your searches for files and folders.

1. Open **Windows Explorer**, and click **Search** to open the Search Companion.

Figure 5-9: The Indexing Service uses idle time to index your files and folders

2. Click **Change Preferences**, and then click **With Indexing Service**. The Indexing Service dialog box opens.
3. Click **Yes, Enable Indexing Service**, as shown in Figure 5-9; and then click **OK**.
4. Close the **Search Companion**, and close **Windows Explorer**.

1 2 3 4 5 6 7 8 9 10

QUICKSTEPS

RUNNING ACCESSORY PROGRAMS

Windows XP comes with a number of accessory programs (see Figure 5-10). Access these by opening **Start**, selecting **All Programs**, choosing **Accessories**, and, if needed, clicking **System Tools**. Many of these programs are discussed elsewhere in this book, but Calculator, Character Map, Notepad, and Paint will be looked at here.

CALCULATOR

The Calculator has two views: one shows a standard desktop calculator; the other, a comprehensive scientific one, shown in Figure 5-11. To switch from one view to the other, open **View** and choose the other view. To use a calculator, click the numbers on the screen or type them on the keyboard.

CHARACTER MAP

The Character Map gives you a way to select the many special characters available in the Windows XP character sets but not on a normal keyboard (see Figure 5-12).

1. Select the font you want for the special character.
2. Double-click the character to copy it to the Clipboard.
3. In the program where you want the character, select **Paste**.

Continued...

Maintain Windows XP

Windows XP maintenance consists of periodic updates for fixes and new features, restoring Windows when hardware or other software damages it, getting information about it, and installing new hardware and software.

Update Windows XP

Periodically you are reminded to "Stay current with automatic updates" in a little balloon in the lower-right of your screen.

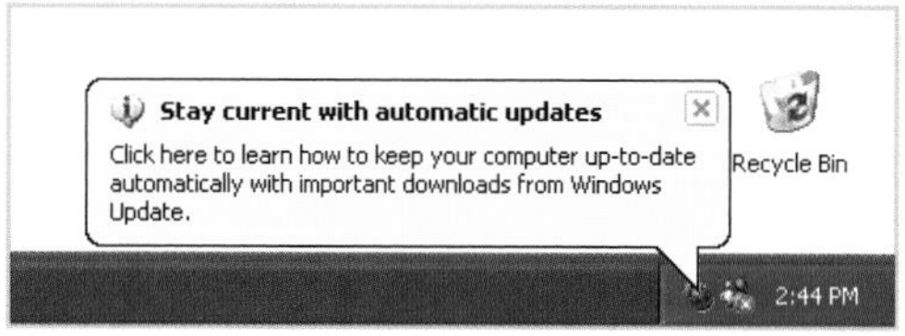

If you turn on Automatic Updates, on a periodic basis Window will automatically determine if any updates are available, download the updates (which come from Microsoft) over the Internet, and install them.

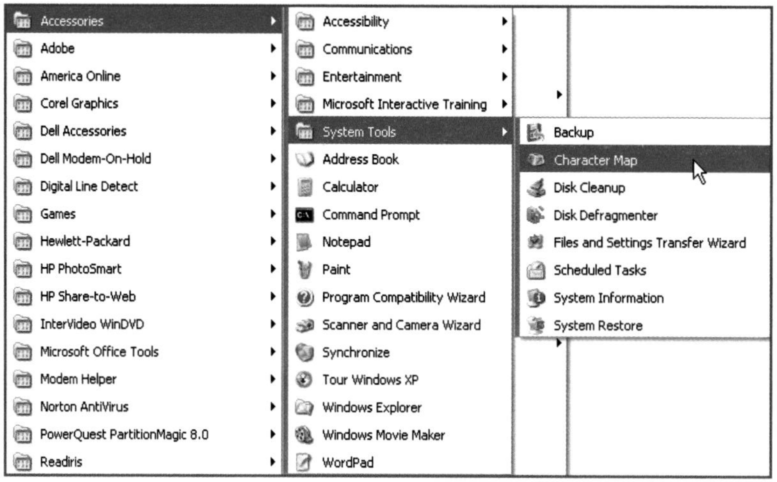

Figure 5-10: Windows XP's accessory programs are available on the Accessories and System Tools menus

RUNNING ACCESSORY PROGRAMS *(Continued)*

NOTEPAD

Notepad is a simple text editor you can use to look at and create unformatted .txt files. If you double-click a text file in Windows Explorer, Notepad will probably open and display the file. If a line of text is too long to display, open **Format** and click **Word Wrap**. To create a file, simply start typing in the Notepad window. Before printing a file, open **File**, click **Page Setup**, and select the paper orientation, margins, header, and footer.

PAINT

Paint lets you open, create, and simply edit bitmap image files in .bmp, .gif, .ico, .jpg, .png, and .tif formats. Several drawing tools and many colors are available to create simple drawings and illustrations.

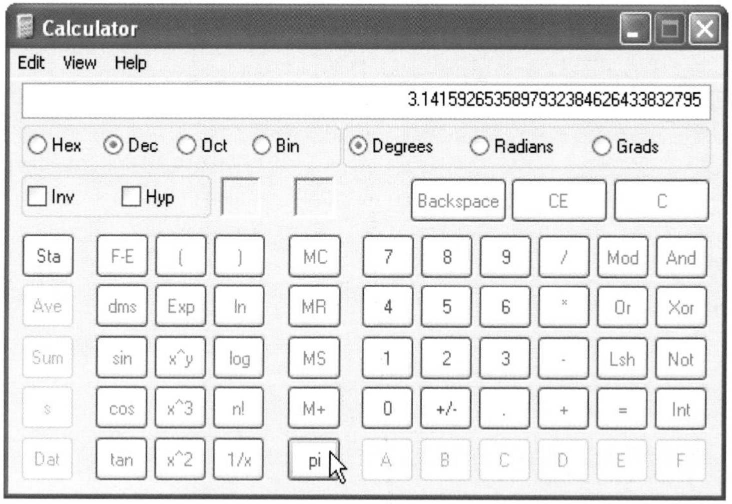

Figure 5-11: The Scientific view of the Calculator provides a number of advanced functions

Figure 5-12: Most special characters in European-based languages are available from the Character Map

TURN ON AUTOMATIC UPDATES

1. Click the **Stay Current With Automatic Updates** balloon to open the Automatic Updates Setup Wizard. Follow its instructions to turn on Automatic Updates.

   –Or–

   If the Automatic Updates balloon is not available, open **Start**, click **Control Panel**, and in Classic view, double-click **System**. Click the **Automatic Updates** tab, shown in Figure 5-13.

2. Determine the amount of automation you want, and click one of the three choices.
   - The first choice automatically determines if there are updates that are needed, then asks your permission before downloading and requests permission again before installing them.
   - The second choice, which is the default, automatically determines if there are updates and automatically downloads them. It then asks you before installing them.
   - The third choice does everything automatically on a schedule you determine.

3. Click **OK** when you are finished.

Figure 5-13: Automatic Updates determines which updates you need and can automatically download and install them

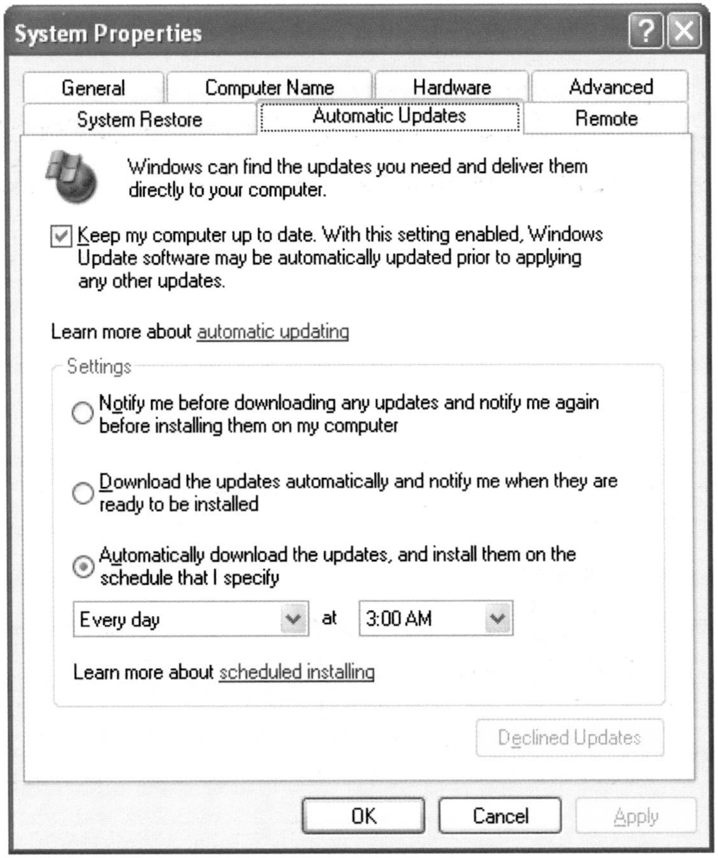

APPLY AUTOMATIC UPDATES

If you choose either the first or second option, you will get a notice when updates are ready to download and/or install.

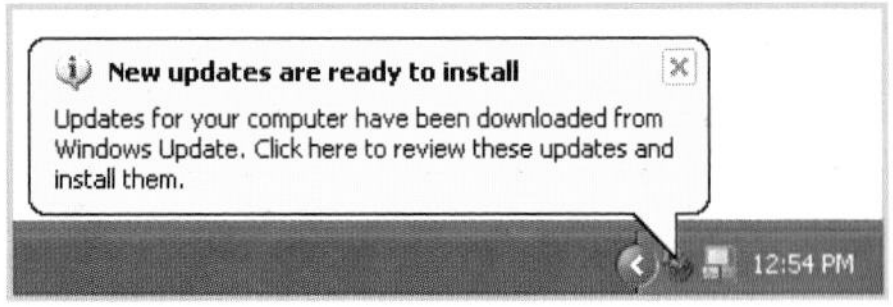

When you click the icon pointed to, the Automatic Updates dialog box opens. If you click Details, you will see the specific updates being proposed, along with a description of each. You can choose to download and/or install each update by clicking the check box. When you are ready, click either **Download** or **Install,** or delay the download and/or installation by clicking **Remind Me Later** and specifying a time.

Restore Windows XP

System Restore keeps track of the changes you make to your system, including the software you install and the settings you make. If a hardware change, a software installation, or something else causes the system not to run properly, you can use System Restore to return the system to the way it was.

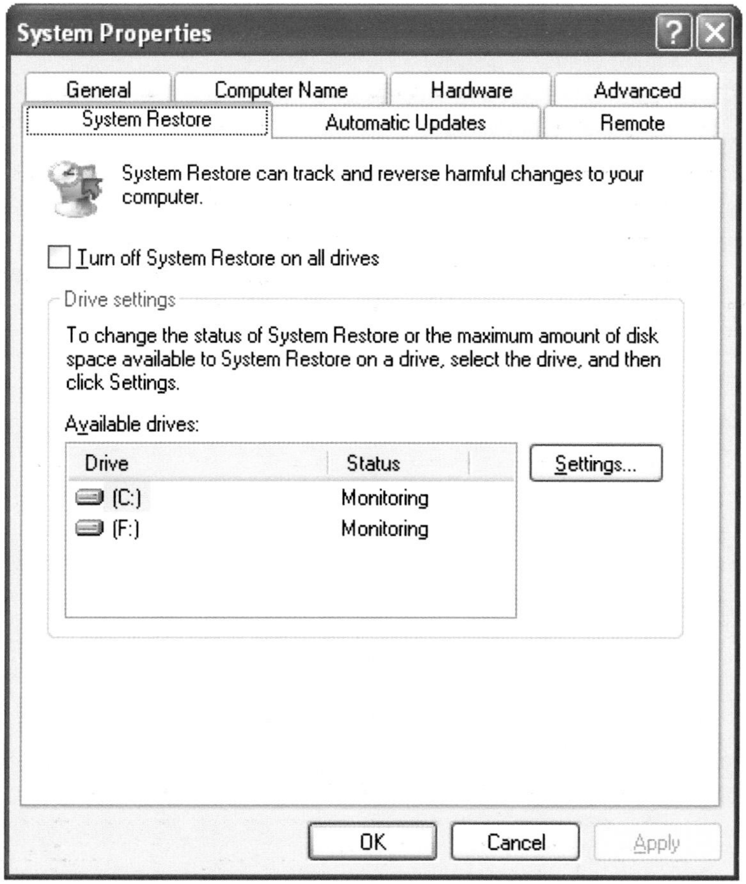

Figure 5-14: System Restore returns the system system settings to those of a previous time when it was operating normally

SET UP SYSTEM RESTORE

In a default install of Windows XP, System Restore is automatically installed. If you have at least 200MB of free disk space after installing Windows XP, System Restore will be turned on and the first restore point will be set. If System Restore is not enabled, you can turn it on and set a restore point:

1. Open **Start**, click **Control Panel**, and in Classic view, double-click **System**. In the System Properties dialog box, click the **System Restore** tab. The System Restore page will appear, as you can see in Figure 5-14.
2. If System Restore is turned off, a check mark will be in the check box. Click the check box to turn it on.
3. If you have only one hard-disk drive, you directly drag the slider to decrease the amount of disk space used by System Restore. If you have multiple drives, you click the drive you want, and then click **Settings**. On the System Drive (generally drive C), you can only adjust the disk-space usage. On a second or higher drive, you can turn off the System Restore's usage of that drive as well as adjust the amount of disk space used.
4. If you have multiple disk drives, when you have adjusted the settings for a given drive, click **OK**. When you have adjusted the settings for all the drives on the system, click **OK**.

> **NOTE**
>
> System Restore does not restore or make any changes to data files, only to system and application program files. Data files must be backed up, using either the Windows XP or a third-party backup program, and then restored from a backup.

CREATE RESTORE POINTS

A restore point is an identifiable point in time when you know your system was working correctly. If you save your computer's settings at that point, you can then use those settings to restore your computer to that point. To create a restore point:

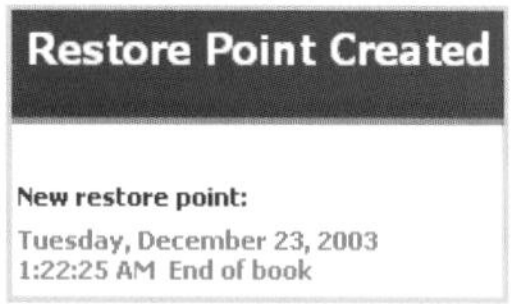

1. Open **Start**, select **All Programs**, choose **Accessories** and then, **System Tools**, and click **System Restore**. The System Restore window opens, as shown in Figure 5-15.
2. Click **Create A Restore Point**, and click **Next**. Enter a name for the restore point (the date and time are automatically added, and you cannot change the name once you create it).
3. Click **Create**. You will be told when the restore point is created. Click **Close**.

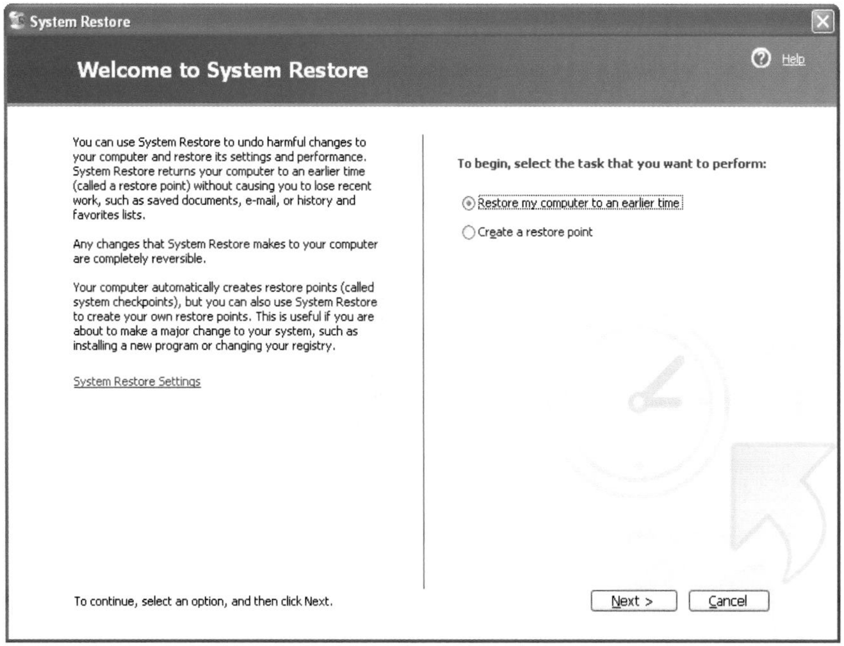

Figure 5-15: Use the System Restore window to set a restore point or to do a restore

NOTE

The percentage of disk space used by System Restore depends on the size of the disk. With a relatively small disk (under 500 MB), it could use a large percentage. With a disk above 500 MB, the percentage is reduced to 12 percent.

RUN SYSTEM RESTORE FROM WINDOWS

If you can start and operate Windows normally, try to execute the following steps. If you can't make it through these steps without Windows crashing, go to the next section.

1. Open **Start**, select **All Programs**, choose **Accessories** and then **System Tools**, and click **System Restore**. The window you saw in Figure 5-15 opens.
2. Accept the default, **Restore My Computer To An Earlier Time**, and click **Next**. The Select A Restore Point window will open, as shown in Figure 5-16.
3. Select a date in bold print from the calendar on the left. You can change the month by clicking either < or >. When you have selected a date, click a restore point from the list on the right, and click **Next**.
4. A confirmation window opens, telling you that Windows will be restarted and that you should save documents and shut down programs. Click **Next**. Your system will be restarted. As it restarts, you are told you can choose another restore point or undo the restoration. Click **OK**.

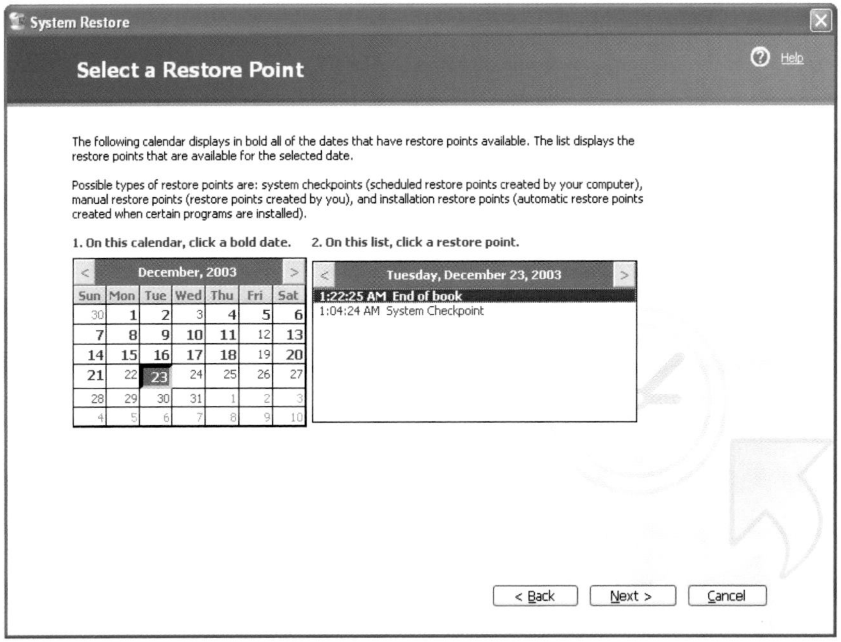

Figure 5-16: You can do a system restore at any of the restore points on the computer and return all of the Windows settings and registry to that time

1 2 3 4 5 6 7 8 9 10

NOTE

You may or may not have the mouse working. The instructions here assume you don't.

TIP

If you are on a shared computer, you must log on as the Administrator, with a password, in order to run System Restore.

Run System Restore from Safe Mode

Safe Mode means running Windows with the fewest possible drivers and accessories. The reason for this is to allow you to fix whatever is preventing it from running normally. You can start System Restore in Safe Mode.

1. If your computer is turned on, turn it off, and make sure it is fully powered down. Let it sit for at least two full minutes. This allows all of the components to fully discharge and will give you a clean restart.
2. After your computer has sat for at least two minutes without power, turn the computer on. As soon as the memory check is complete, press and hold the **F8** function key. After a moment, the Windows Advanced Options Menu will appear.
3. If necessary, press **HOME** or use the **UP ARROW** key to go to the top choice, **Safe Mode**, and then press **ENTER**. If the Operating System menu appears, make sure that Microsoft Windows XP is chosen and press **ENTER** again. You will see many lines of information appear about the drivers that are being loaded, and then Windows will begin loading in Safe Mode.
4. If you are asked to, press **CTRL+ALT+DELETE**, enter your password, and press **ENTER**. Press **ENTER** to acknowledge you are starting in Safe Mode.
5. Press **CTRL+ESC** to open the Start menu, use the arrow keys to select **All Programs**, press **ENTER**, select **Accessories**, press **ENTER**, select **System Tools**, press **ENTER**, finally select **System Restore**, and press **ENTER**. The System Restore window will open, as you saw earlier.
6. Make sure that **Restore My Computer To An Earlier Time** is selected; if not, use the arrow keys to select it, then press **ALT+N** to go to the next page.
7. Use the arrow keys to select the restore date you want to use, press **TAB** to go to the list of restore points, and use the arrow keys to select the restore point you want to use. Press **ENTER**. Then press **ALT+N** to begin the restore.
8. Confirm that no programs are running. If any are, press **ALT+TAB** to get the list of open programs. Then use the arrow keys to select the open program (do not select System Restore), and press **ALT+F4** to close the program.
9. When you are ready, press **ALT+N** to begin the restoration. Several messages will appear telling you about the progress of the restoration, then Windows will restart. The System Restore window will appear, telling you that the restoration was successful. Click **OK**.

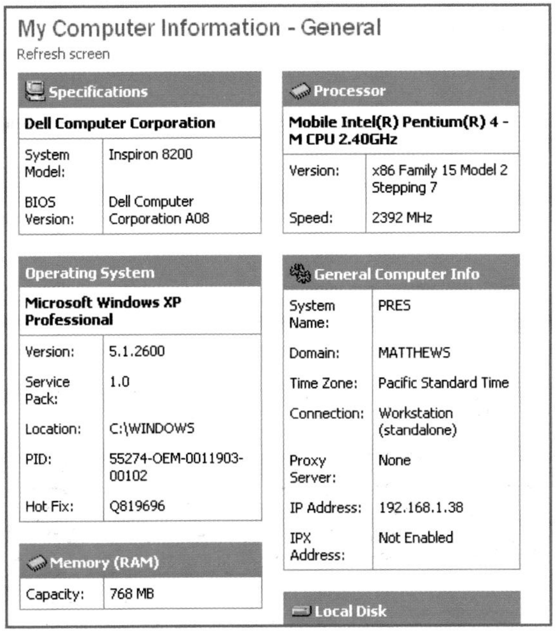

Figure 5-17: My Computer Information provides an overview of the computer and what is installed on it

Get System Information

When you are working on a computer problem, you, or possibly a technical-support person working with you, will want some information about your computer. The two primary sources of that information are My Computer Information and Advanced System Information. The easiest way to access these is to open **Start**, select **Help And Support**, click **Support** on the toolbar, and then, under See Also in the lower-left, click either **My Computer Information** or **Advanced System Information**.

MY COMPUTER INFORMATION

My Computer Information provides general system information as well as lists of the hardware and software installed and its status. Click **My Computer Information** to see the list of available topics. Then click any of these options to see further information. Figure 5-17 shows the general system information for a Dell laptop.

ADVANCED SYSTEM INFORMATION

Advanced System Information provides detailed system information and lets you look at services that are running, at group policy settings, and at the error log. Click **Advanced System Information** to see the list of available topics, then click any of the topics to see more information. Figure 5-18 shows the summary-level information that is available.

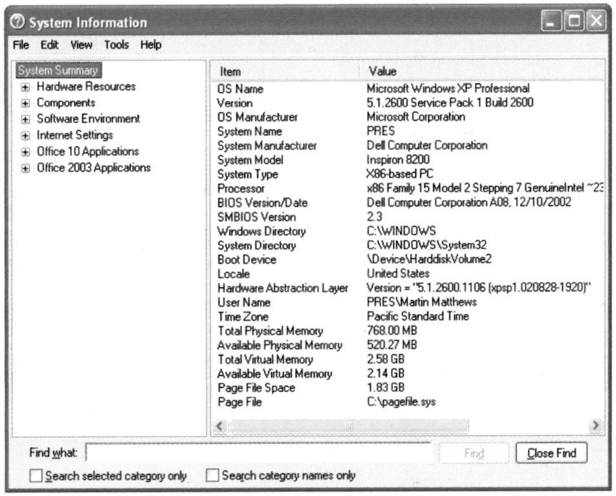

Figure 5-18: Advanced System Information provides a great depth of information useful in troubleshooting

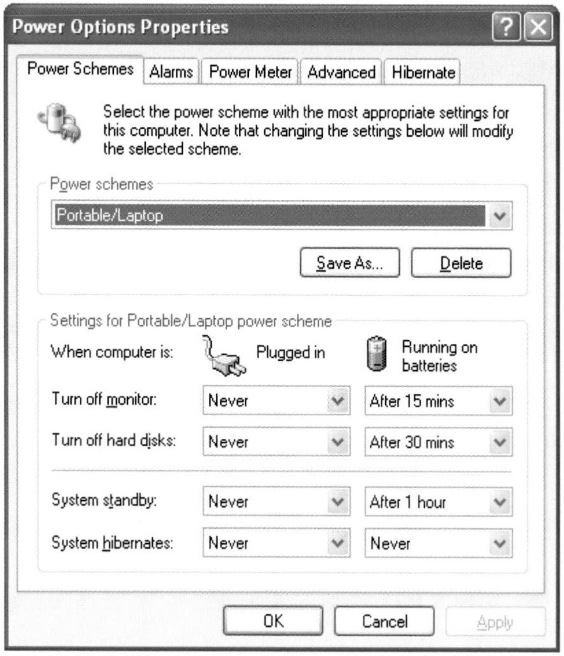

Figure 5-19: The Windows XP power options available on a laptop or notebook computer

Set Power Options

Setting power options is important on laptop and notebook computers that run at least some of the time on batteries. It can also be useful on desktop computers to conserve power. The Windows XP Power Options provide a number of settings that allow you to manage your computer's use of power.

1. Open **Start**, select **Control Panel**, and in Classic View, double-click **Power Options**. If you are using a laptop or notebook computer, your power options will look like those in Figure 5-19. If you are using a desktop computer, your settings will look like those in Figure 5-20.
2. Open the **Power Schemes** drop-down list, and if appropriate, select a scheme that is better for you. Each scheme has a number of settings. If you change settings, you can use **Save As** to name and save your particular configuration of settings.
3. Click each of the tabs that you see, and look at the settings available to you. These settings are also affected by the power scheme you are using. The three possible power modes—stand by, hibernate, and shut down—are explained in Table 5-1.
4. When you are ready, click **OK** to accept the changes you have made to your Power Options.

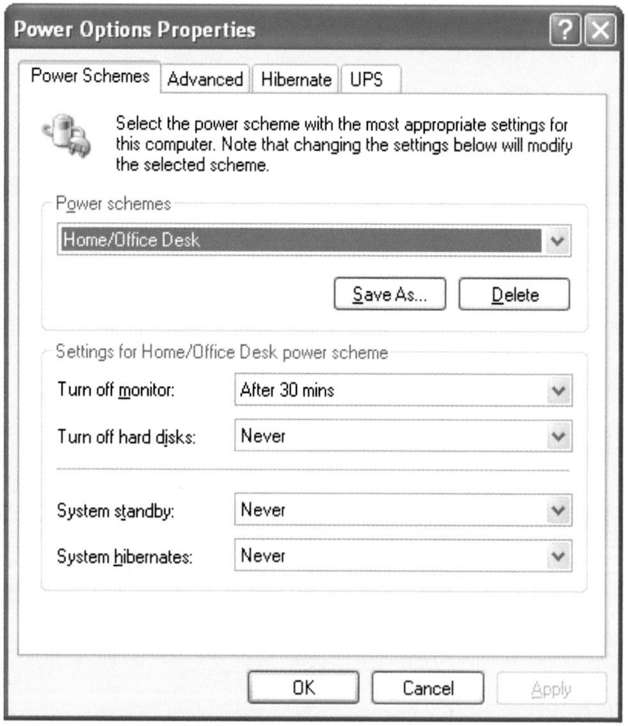

Figure 5-20: The Windows XP power options available on a desktop computer

NOTE

If a desktop computer has Hibernate selected (in the Hibernate tab), more drop-down lists may appear at the bottom of the Power Schemes tab of the Power Options Properties dialog box.

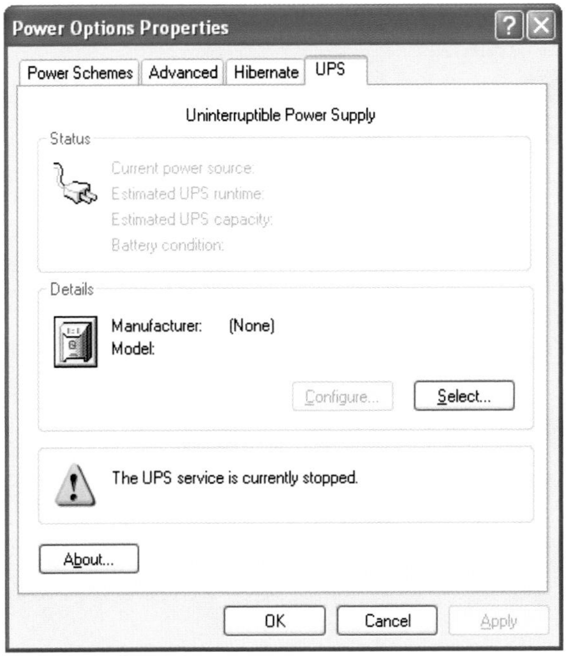

Figure 5-21: If you have a UPS, you can connect it to either a serial or USB port and control it through the Power Options Properties dialog box

TABLE 5-1: WINDOWS XP POWER MODES

POWER MODE	DESCRIPTION
Stand By	Turns off the monitor, hard disk, and various parts of the computer but leaves memory running. When you start up, you quickly return to the exact position where you were when you went into stand by/hybernation.
Hibernate	Saves everything about your current session to disk, then turns off all power. The process of shutting down and then restarting takes longer, but when you restart, you will be returned to the exact position where you went into hibernation.
Shut Down	Saves all current files, closes all current programs, and then removes all power from the system. When you restart the system, you must also restart any programs that were running and reopen any files that were open.

USE AN UNINTERRUPTIBLE POWER SUPPLY

With a desktop computer, you can use an uninterruptible power supply, or UPS. Your computer power cord plugs into the UPS, which in turn plugs into a wall outlet. The UPS has batteries that will supply power to the computer for a short time (from 5 to 30 minutes), enough to get you through brief power interruptions or allow you to gracefully shut down on longer ones. Some UPSs have either a serial or USB (universal serial bus) connection to your computer that gives your computer information and will even shut down your computer. This is controlled in the UPS tab of the Power Options Properties dialog box, shown in Figure 5-21.

1 2 3 4 5 6 7 8 9 10

NOTE

In medium to larger organizations, application software might be available over the LAN (local area network) on a server. Generally, it is better to download the software and then do the installation from your computer than to do the installation over the network.

TIP

If you are having trouble installing a program for no discernable reason, make sure you are logged on with administrative permissions. Some programs or installation situations require these permissions, and without them the program just refuses to install.

TIP

Unless you are specifically told otherwise, always save a downloaded file to your hard disk and then start it by double-clicking. That way, if there is a problem, you can restart it without having to download it a second time.

Add and Remove Software

Today, almost all application and utility software comes in one of two ways: on a CD or downloaded from the Internet.

INSTALL SOFTWARE FROM A CD

If you get software on a CD and your computer is less than six years old, all you need to do is put the CD in the drive, wait for the install program to automatically load, and follow the displayed instructions, which are normally very few. When the installation is complete, you probably need to acknowledge that by clicking **OK** or **Finish**. Then remove the CD from its drive. That is all there is to it.

INSTALL SOFTWARE FROM THE INTERNET

To download and install a program from the Internet:

1. Open **Start** and click **Internet**. In the Address bar, type the URL (uniform resource locator, also called address) for the source of the download. Press **ENTER**.
2. Locate the link for the download, and click it. A dialog box, shown in Figure 5-22, will open and ask if you want to run or save the program. Click **Save**. The Save As dialog box will open. The default location is the desktop, which is good–at least initially–because you must double-click the program to start it. With the desktop open, click **Save**.

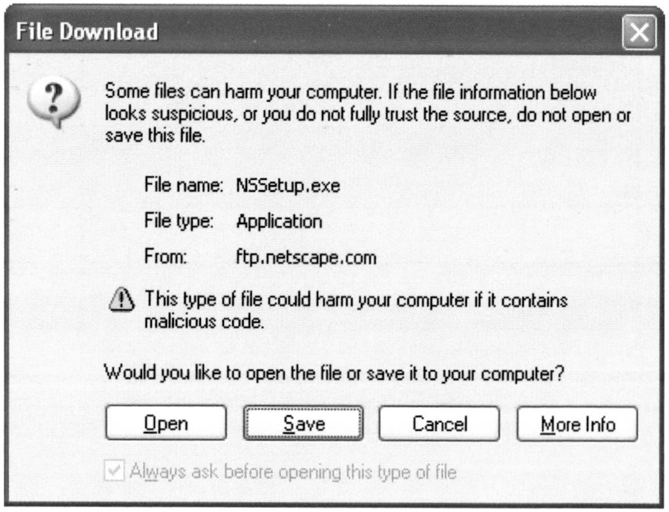
File Download
Some files can harm your computer. If the file information below looks suspicious, or you do not fully trust the source, do not open or save this file.
File name: NSSetup.exe
File type: Application
From: ftp.netscape.com
This type of file could harm your computer if it contains malicious code.
Would you like to open the file or save it to your computer?
Open
Save
Cancel
More Info
Always ask before opening this type of file

Figure 5-22: The File Download dialog box enables you to choose between saving and opening the downloaded file

3. When you are told the download is complete, click **Close**. If the program did not automatically install, double-click the program that is now on your desktop, and follow the instructions that are presented to you.
4. When the installation is complete, you may be notified, the program may be started, Windows Explorer may be opened to show where the program is installed, and/or one or more shortcuts may be left on the desktop.
5. Close the Explorer window and any other dialog boxes that are open.

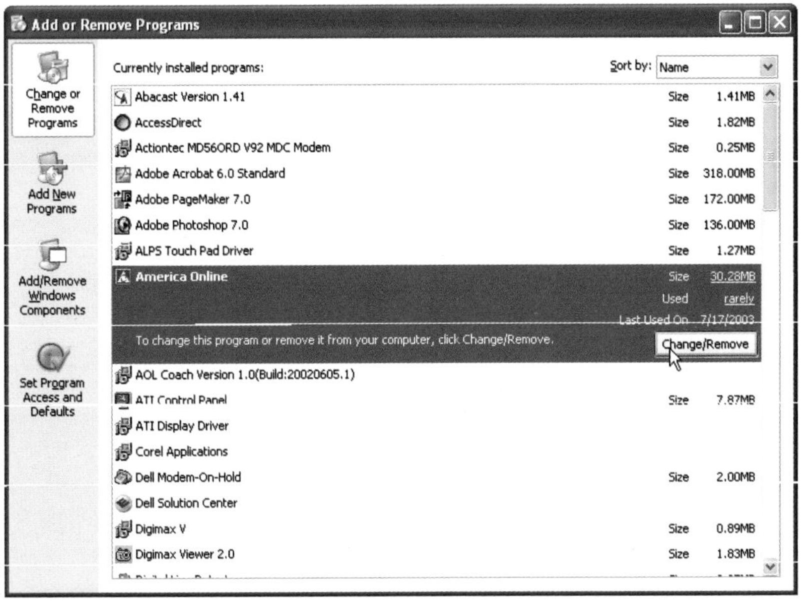

Figure 5-23: Programs are removed through the Add Or Remove Programs control panel

NOTE

The Change command or the change part of the Change/Remove command is used to install updates and patches to programs. It requires that you have either a CD with the changes or have downloaded them.

REMOVE SOFTWARE

There are at least two ways to get rid of a program you have installed and one way not to do it. You do not want to just delete the program files in Windows Explorer. That leaves files in other locations and all the settings in the registry. To correctly remove a program, you need to use either the uninstall program that comes with many programs or Windows XP's Add Or Remove Programs. To do the latter:

1. Open **Start**, click **Control Panel**, and in Classic view, double-click **Add Or Remove Programs**. The Add Or Remove Programs control panel will open, as you see in Figure 5-23.
2. Select the program you want to remove, and click **Remove** or **Change/Remove**. Click **Yes**, you are sure you want to remove it. The Remove Programs From Your Computer Wizard will start and display the progress.
3. When Uninstall has successfully completed, you will be told that. Click **OK**, close the Add Or Remove Programs window, and close the Control Panel.

Add Hardware

Most hardware today is *Plug and Play*. That means you can plug it in and immediately use it. When you first turn on the computer after installing the hardware, you often get a little balloon message telling you that you have new hardware. You usually need do nothing more; the installation will complete by itself. With other equipment, you must click the icon the balloon points to for the installation to proceed. In either case, you are told when it has successfully completed.

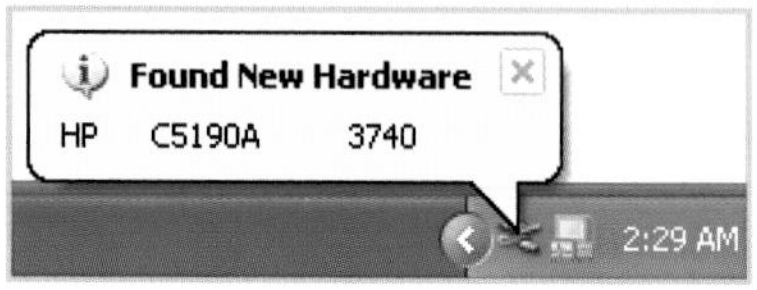

Problems may occur when you have older hardware, and the programs that run it, called *drivers*, are not included with Windows XP. Then you must locate the drivers. Here are some options for locating drivers:

- The **manufacturer** of the device is generally the best source, but as hardware gets older, manufacturers stop writing new drivers. The easiest way to look for manufacturer support is on the Internet. If you know the manufacturer's web site, you can enter it; or you may have to search for it. If you must search, start out by typing the manufacturer's name in Internet Explorer's Address bar. This uses MSN Search and gives you a list of sites.
- **Microsoft** has the most popular drivers for recent devices and, as a part of Windows Update (discussed earlier in this chapter), the ability to scan your system and see if it has any drivers to help you. The first step with Microsoft is to look at Windows Update by opening **Start**, selecting **All Programs**, and clicking **Windows Update**. Click **Scan For Updates**, and see if a driver for your device is found.
- **Third-party** sources can be found using search engines like Google (http://www.google.com) and searching on **device drivers**. You should find a number of sources, as you can see in Figure 5-24. Some of these sources charge you for the driver; others are free. Make sure the driver will work with Windows XP.

Figure 5-24: Many device drivers can be found by searching the Internet, although you may have to pay for them

Use Remote Assistance

Remote Assistance allows you to invite someone to remotely look at your computer, control it for purposes of assisting you, and chat with you. The other person must be using either Windows XP or Windows Server 2003, and both of you must have Passport accounts and Windows Messenger to chat. To use Remote Assistance you must set it up.

SET UP REMOTE ASSISTANCE

Remote Assistance is set up through the Control Panel:

1. Open **Start**, click **Control Panel**, and in Classic view, double-click **System**.
2. Click the **Remote** tab, make sure **Allow Remote Assistance Invitations To Be Sent From This Computer** is checked, and click **Advanced**.
3. Determine if you want a person to control your computer, and check the **Remote Control** check box accordingly. Leave the 30-day default for the time an invitation for remote assistance is to remain open.

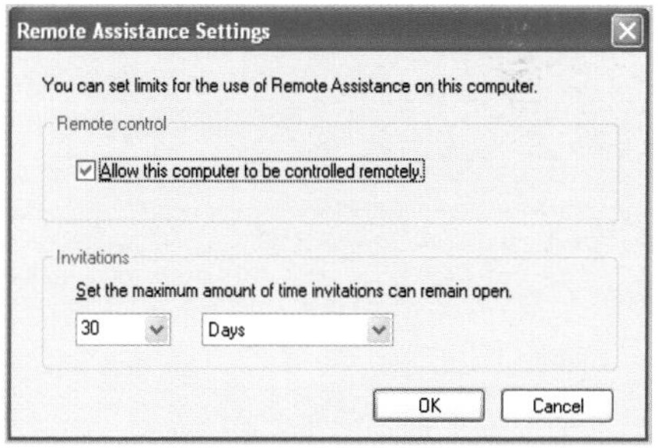

4. Click **OK** twice to close the two open dialog boxes, and then close the Control Panel.

REQUEST REMOTE ASSISTANCE

For remote assistance, first find someone willing to provide it and request the assistance via e-mail or Windows Messenger. Then, to begin a Remote Assistance session:

1. Open **Start**, select **All Programs**, and click **Remote Assistance**. The Help And Support Center opens.

Figure 5-25: You can use either e-mail or Windows Messenger to request Remote Assistance

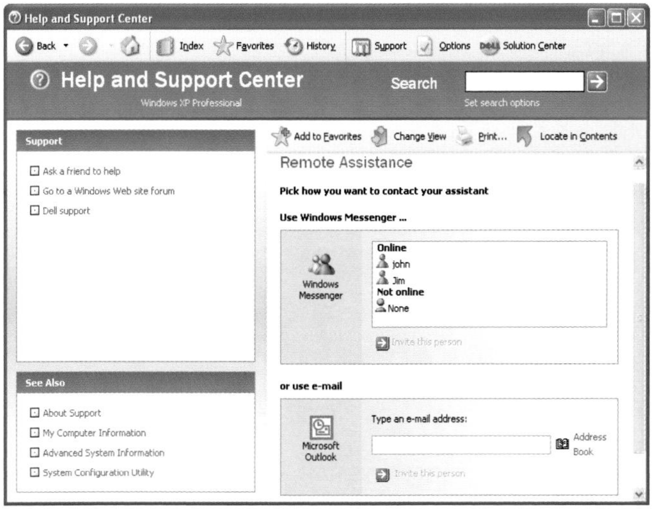

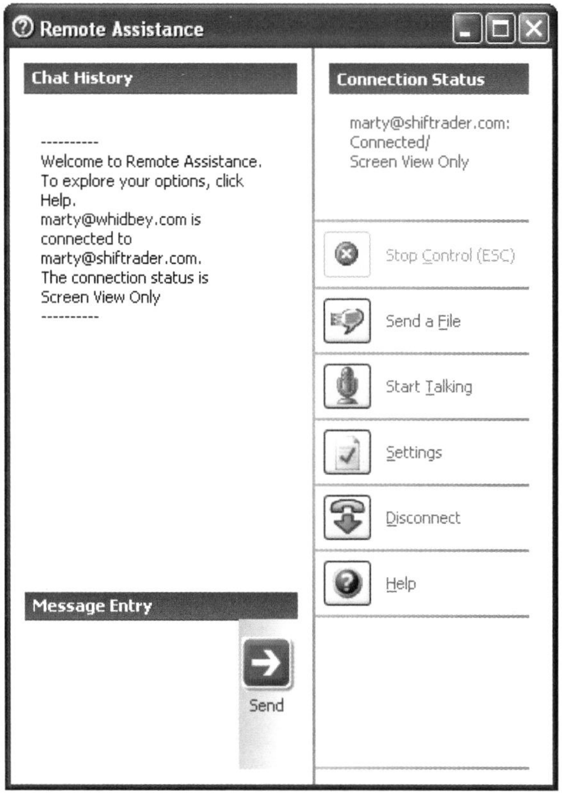

Figure 5-26: If remote assistance is not going the way you want, click Disconnect

2. Click **Invite Someone To Help You**. You can use Windows Messenger or either Outlook Express or Microsoft Outlook, as in Figure 5-25. In Windows Messenger, select a person who is online, and click **Invite This Person**. A message tells you an invitation has been sent.

3. Upon acceptance of your invitation, you are asked to confirm it. Click **Yes**. The Remote Assistance window opens, as in Figure 5-26.
4. Type a message to the other person, who can see anything on your computer.
5. The other person can click **Take Control**, and you'll get a message asking if that is what you want. If you do, click **Yes**. If you become uncomfortable, you can click **Stop Control** or press **ESC** at any time.

6. To end the session, send a message to that effect, click **Disconnect**, and close both the Remote Assistance and the Help And Support Center windows.

PROVIDE REMOTE ASSISTANCE

If you want to provide remote assistance, you follow a simple set of steps:

1. Upon receiving a request for assistance, accept or decline by clicking the link or pressing **ALT+T** or **ALT+D**.

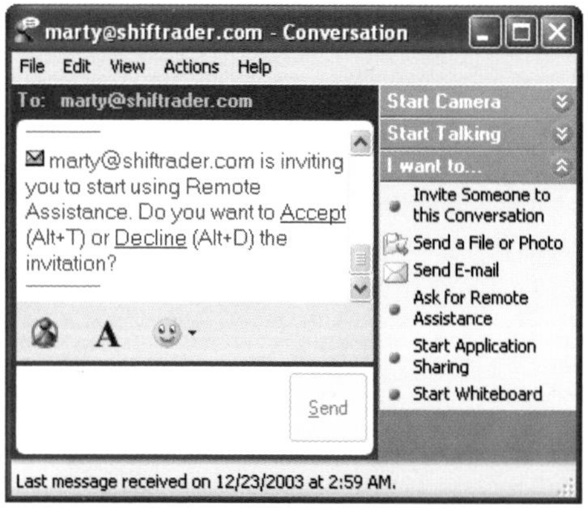

2. If you accept and the other person approves, you are shown their screen and can take control of their computer. You can view the screen actual size or scale it to fit on your screen, as shown in Figure 5-27.

3. To return sole control to the other person, click **Release Control** or press **ESC**. Click **Disconnect** to end the session, and click **Close** in both the Remote Assistance window and the Conversation dialog box.

NOTE

You are protected from misuse of Remote Assistance in four ways: without an invitation, the person giving assistance cannot come onto your computer; you can limit both the time the invitation remains open and the time the person can be on your computer; you can determine whether the person can control your computer or just look at it; you can click Stop Control, or press esc, or press any key sequence that includes esc, at any time, to immediately cut the other person off.

NOTE

With Remote Assistance, the other person can look at and control your computer only if you invite him. You can specify how long he has access; determine if he can only look or whether he also can control; and you can click the "Kill" button to instantly disconnect the other person.

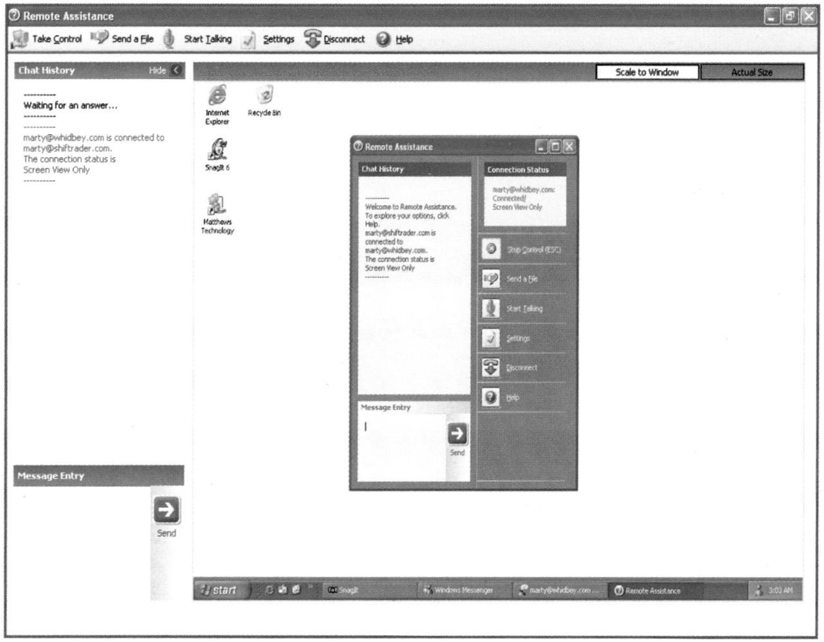

Figure 5-27: The remote screen is shown on the assistance provider's screen

1 2 3 4 5 6 7 8 9 10

How to...

Chapter 6 Working with Documents and Pictures

In this chapter you will discover the many aspects of creating documents and pictures and how to install and use printers with documents and pictures. You will also learn how to set up and use the Windows fax capability with documents and pictures.

Create Documents and Pictures

Creating documents and pictures is primarily done with programs outside of Windows XP, although Windows has simple programs to do it. Windows XP also has facilities to bring documents and pictures in from other computers, from the Internet, and from scanners and cameras.

QUICKSTEPS

ACQUIRING A DOCUMENT

The documents in your computer got there because they were either created with a program on your computer, they were brought to the computer on a disk, or they were downloaded from either a local area network (LAN) or the Internet.

CREATE A DOCUMENT WITH A PROGRAM

1. Start the program. For example, start Microsoft Word by opening **Start**, selecting **All Programs**, and clicking **Microsoft Word**.
2. Create the document using the facilities in the program. In Word, for example, type the document, and format it using Word's formatting tools.
3. Save the document by (again, in Word), opening **File**. Then choose **Save As**, select the disk drive and folder in which to store the document, enter a file name, and click **Save**, as shown in Figure 6-1. Close the program used to create the file.

BRING IN A DOCUMENT FROM A DISK

Use Windows Explorer to bring in a document from a disk or other removable storage device:

1. Open **Start** and click **My Computer**.
2. Double-click the drive in which you inserted the disk (this could be a floppy, CD, or other device), and double-click to open any necessary folders to locate the document file.
3. Click **Folders** on the toolbar. In the Folders pane, select the disk and display (but do not select or open) the folder(s) in which you want to store the file.
4. Drag the document file to the displayed folder, as illustrated in Figure 6-2. When you are done, close Windows Explorer.

Continued...

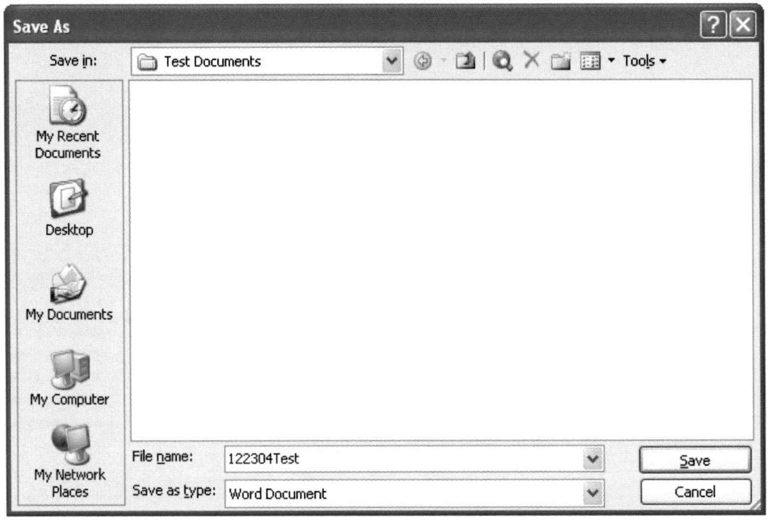

***Figure 6-1:** Most document creation programs let you choose where you want to save the files you create*

***Figure 6-2:** You can drag a document file from either a disk on your computer or from another computer on your network*

ACQUIRING A DOCUMENT *(Continued)*

DOWNLOAD A DOCUMENT ACROSS A NETWORK

Use Windows Explorer to bring in a document from another computer on your network:

1. Open **Start** and click **My Network Places**.
2. Double-click the *share* (folder on another computer that has been shared), and double-click to open any necessary subfolders to locate the document file.
3. Click **Folders** on the toolbar. In the Folders pane, select the disk and display (but do not select or open) the folder(s) on your computer in which you want to store the file.
4. Drag the document file to the displayed folder. When you are done, close Windows Explorer.

DOWNLOAD A DOCUMENT FROM THE INTERNET

Use your Internet browser to bring in a document from a site on the Internet:

1. Open **Start** and click **Internet**.
2. Type an address, search, or browse to a site and page from which you can download the document file.
3. Use the links and tools on the web site to select and begin the file download.
4. When asked, select the disk and open the folder(s) in which you want to store the file on your computer.
5. Complete the download. When you are done, close your browser.

Create a Picture

Pictures are really just documents that contains an image, and they can be created or brought into your computer in the same way as any other document (see the "Creating a Document" QuickSteps). For example, to create and save a picture in Paint:

1. Open **Start**, select **All Programs**, choose **Accessories**, and click **Paint**.
2. Create the picture using the tools in Paint. For example, select the **Pencil** tool, choose a color, and do the drawing.
3. Save the document by opening **File**. Then choose **Save As**, select the disk drive and folder in which to store the document, enter a file name, and click **Save**. Close Paint.

Install Cameras and Scanners

Installing cameras and scanners depends a lot on the device—whether it is Plug and Play (plug it in and it starts to function), what type of connection it has, and so on. Most recent cameras and scanners are Plug and Play devices. To use them:

1. Plug the device into the computer. If it is Plug and Play, the first time you plug it in you will get a message that new hardware has been found.

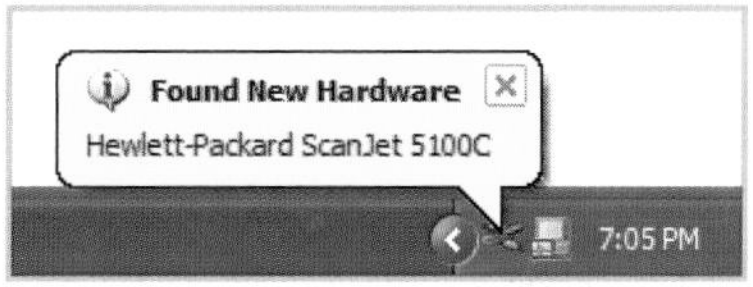

2. Open **Start**, click **Control Panel**, and, in Classic View, double-click **Scanners And Cameras**. If you see your device, installation is complete, as shown in Figure 6-3, and you can skip the remainder of these steps.
3. Click **Add An Imaging Device**. The Scanner And Camera Installation Wizard opens. Click **Next**.
4. If you have a disk that came with the device, place it in the drive, and click **Have Disk**. If a driver appears, complete the installation and close the Installation Wizard. If you cannot find the driver, cancel out of the Scanner And Camera Installation Wizard and use the manufacturer's installation program on the disk. If you don't have a disk, you can see if the Manufacturer and Model list in the wizard has a driver for your device.

Figure 6-3: Most recent Plug and Play cameras and scanners are automatically found and installed

Scan Pictures

Scanners allow you to take printed images and convert them to digital images on your computer. The scanner must first be installed, as described in "Install Cameras and Scanners" earlier in this chapter. To scan a picture:

1. Open **Start**, click **Control Panel**, and, in Classic View, double-click **Scanners And Cameras**.
2. Double-click your scanner. The Scanner And Camera Wizard opens. Click **Next**.
3. Choose your scanning preferences, as shown in Figure 6-4, and click **Next**. Type the group name, select the file format, and choose the location in which to store the picture. Click **Next** to start the scan.
4. After scanning, select what you want to do with the picture. Make that selection, click **Next**, and then click **Finish**.

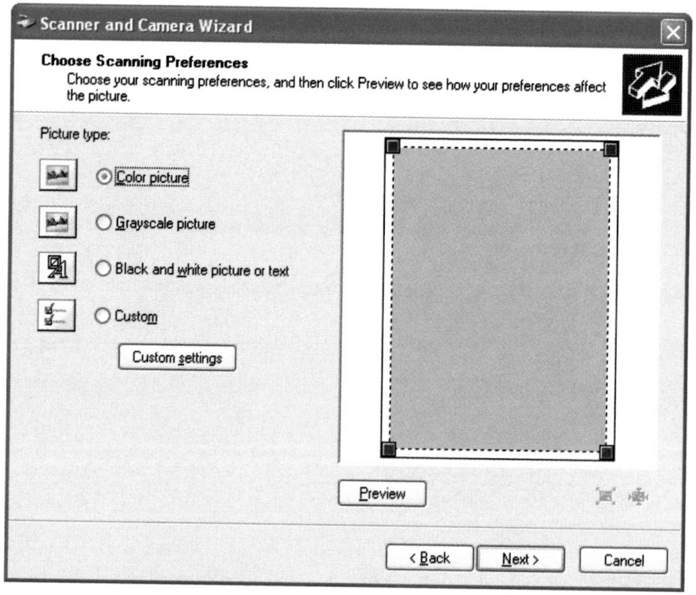

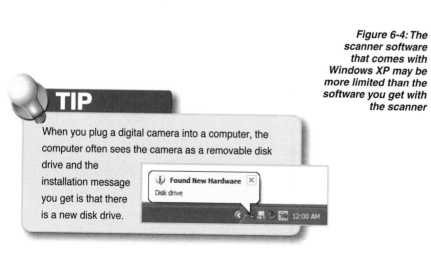

Figure 6-4: The scanner software that comes with Windows XP may be more limited than the software you get with the scanner

TIP

When you plug a digital camera into a computer, the computer often sees the camera as a removable disk drive and the installation message you get is that there is a new disk drive.

Transfer Camera Images

When most digital cameras are plugged into the computer and installed, the computer sees them as a removable disk drive. Therefore, to look at and transfer the images to your hard disk, you use Windows Explorer.

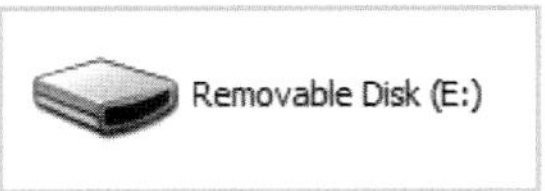

1. Open **Start**, click **My Computer**, and double-click **Removable Disk**. Images of your picture files should open. These images are still in your camera.
2. If your view does not show the pictures, open **View** and click **Thumbnails**. You should see small images of your pictures, as shown in Figure 6-5.
3. If the Folders pane is not open, click **Folders** to open it. In the Folders pane, display the drive and folders to where you want to transfer the pictures in your camera.
4. Hold down **CTRL** while clicking the thumbnail images that you want to store in the folder you just located.
5. Drag the photos to the folder you located. When you are done, close Windows Explorer.

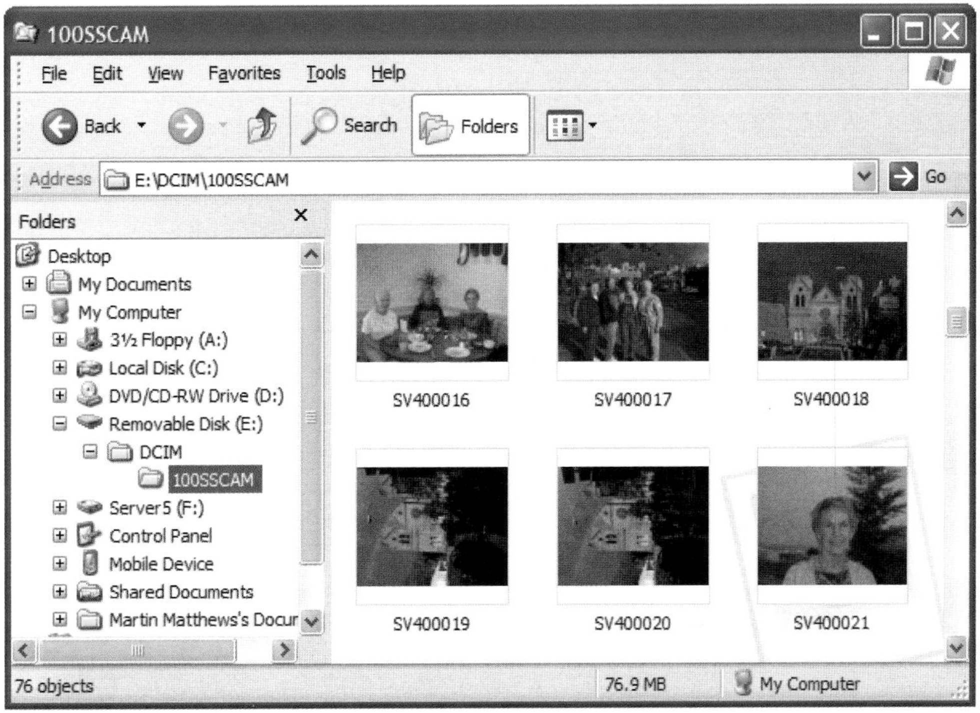

Figure 6-5: You can look at the photos in a recent digital camera by locating the "Removable Disk" in Windows Explorer

Figure 6-6: Use the Thumbnails View setting to get a quick glimpse of the pictures in a folder

View Pictures

Once you have brought pictures into your computer from a camera, a scanner, or an Internet download, you can look at them on your computer screen. Assuming that your pictures are stored in My Pictures:

1. Open **Start**, click **My Documents**, and double-click **My Pictures**. (If your pictures are not stored in My Pictures, click **Folders** and open the folders necessary to locate your pictures.)
2. If your view does not show the pictures, open **View** and click **Thumbnails**. You should see small images of your pictures, as shown in Figure 6-6.
3. To see an image enlarged, double-click its thumbnail. The image will open in Windows Picture And Fax Viewer, similar to Figure 6-7.
4. If you have several pictures you want to view, click the right and left arrows on the bottom-left of the window to sequentially go through them.
5. When you are done, close both the Windows Picture And Fax Viewer and the My Pictures window.

Figure 6-7: The Windows Picture And Fax Viewer offers a very good way to see a set of pictures on your computer

Print Documents and Pictures

It is important to be able to install and fully use printers so that you can transfer your digital documents to paper.

NOTE

Windows XP Professional has a Printers And Faxes option on the Start menu. In Windows XP Home, it isn't there, but it can be added through the Taskbar And Start Menu Properties dialog box, as discussed in Chapter 2. If Printers And Faxes is not on the Start menu, you can open it by first opening Control Panel and then, in Classic View, double-clicking Printers And Faxes.

Install a Printer

All printers are installed using the Printers And Faxes window. Because there are differences, look separately at installing local Plug and Play printers, local other printers, network printers, and selecting a default printer. Also, if you are installing a local printer, first consider the following checklist.

CHECKLIST PRIOR TO INSTALLING A PRINTER

A local printer is one that is attached to your computer with a cable or wireless connection. Make sure that your printer meets the following conditions *before* you begin to install.

NOTE

Some laptop computer and printer combinations are connected via an infrared beam or other wireless connection. In this case, "plugging the printer into the computer" means to establish that wireless connection.

- It is plugged into the correct port on your computer (see manufacturer's instructions).
- It is plugged into an electrical outlet.
- It has fresh ink, toner, or ribbon, which, along with the print heads, are properly installed.
- It has adequate paper.
- It is turned on.

INSTALL A LOCAL PLUG AND PLAY PRINTER

Installing Plug and Play printers is supposed to be pretty automatic, and for the most part, it is.

1. With your computer and printer turned off, plug them together. Then make sure the other points in the above checklist are satisfied.
2. Turn on your printer and your computer. Your computer should find and automatically install the new printer and give you a balloon message to that effect.

3. Open **Start** and click **Printers And Faxes** (in Windows XP Home, open **Control Panel** and then, in Classic View, double-click **Printers And Faxes).** The Printers And Faxes window should open and you should see your new printer. Select that printer and leave the mouse pointer there. You should see "Status: Ready," as shown in Figure 6-8. (If you don't see your printer, it was not installed. Go to the next section.)
4. Right-click the new printer, click **Properties**, and click **Print Test Page**. If your test page prints satisfactorily click **OK**; otherwise, click **Troubleshoot** and follow the suggestions.
5. When you are ready, close the printer properties dialog box and the Printers And Faxes window.

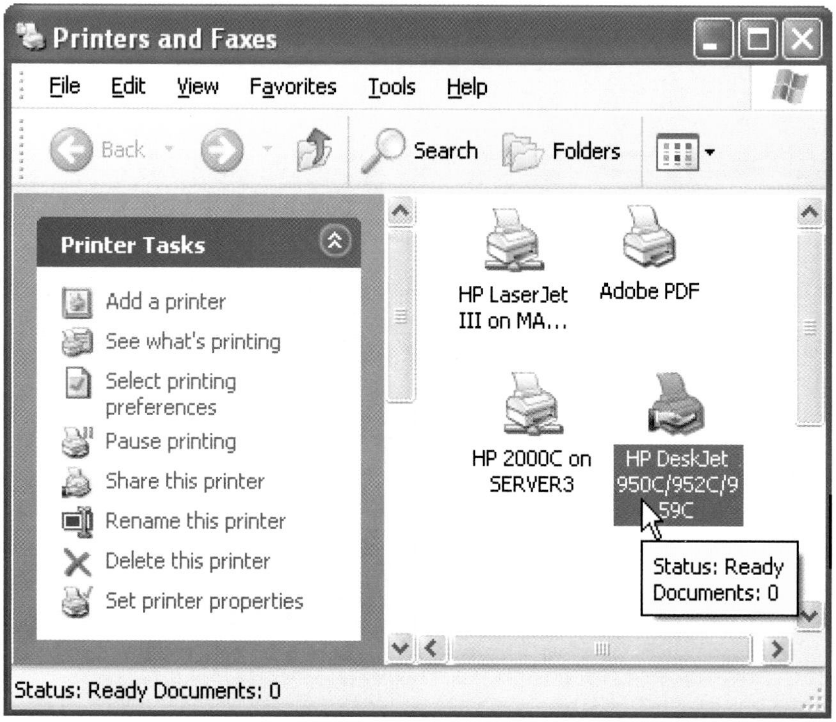

Figure 6-8: When you plug in a Plug and Play printer, it should be recognized by the computer and automatically installed

INSTALL A LOCAL OTHER PRINTER

If a printer isn't automatically installed in the process of using steps 1 through 3 above, you must go through a manual procedure.

1. If a CD came with your printer, providing it says that it is for Windows XP, place that CD in its drive and follow the on-screen instructions to install the printer. When this is complete, right-click the new printer in the Printers And Faxes window, click **Properties**, and click **Print Test Page**. A test page will be printed. Skip to Step 8.
2. Without a manufacturer's CD, open **Start**, click **Printers And Faxes** (in Windows XP Home, open **Control Panel**, and then, in Classic View, double-click **Printers And Faxes)**, and click **Add A Printer** in the tasks pane. Click **Next**.
3. Accept the default **Local Printer Attached To This Computer**, deselect **Automatically Detect And Install My Plug and Play Printer**, and click **Next**.
4. Select **Use The Following Port:**, open the drop-down list and select the correct port (on the newest printers it is probably USB 1, on the majority of other printers it is LPT1), and click **Next**.

Figure 6-9: Manually installing a printer requires that you know some facts about the printer, of which the most difficult is knowing what port is it plugged into

5. Select the manufacturer and model of the printer you want to install. If you can't find your printer, click **Windows Update** to download the latest printer drivers. Then, once more, search for the manufacturer and model. When you find the correct printer, click **Next**.
6. Confirm or change the printer name, and choose whether you want this printer to be your default printer. Click **Next**. If asked, determine if you want to share the printer, and, if so, enter the share name. Click **Next**.
7. Determine if you want to print a test page, and click **Next**. When the Add Printer Wizard is finished, you will get a summary of the selected settings, as shown in Figure 6-9. If there are any problems, click **Back** and correct them; otherwise, click **Finish**. Your printer will be installed, and a test page will be printed if you made that choice.
8. If your test page prints satisfactorily, click **OK**; otherwise, click **Troubleshoot** and follow the suggestions. When you are ready, close the printer properties dialog box (if it is open) and close the Printers And Faxes window.

TIP

If your printer was automatically installed, but a CD came with your printer and you wonder if you should install using the CD, the general answer is no. Most printer drivers in Windows XP originally came from the manufacturers and have been tested by Microsoft, so they should work well. Unless the printer came out after the release of Windows XP (October 2001), the driver in XP should be newer.

INSTALL A NETWORK PRINTER

Network printers are not directly connected to your computer but are available to you as a result of your computer's connection to a network and the fact that the printers have been shared. There are three types of network printers:

- Printers connected to someone else's computer, which they have shared
- Printers connected to a dedicated printer server, which have been shared
- Printers directly connected to a network (they, in effect, have a built-in computer)

The first two types of network printers are installed with the Network Printer option in the Add Printer Wizard and will be described here. The third option is installed (generally, automatically) with the Local Printer option.

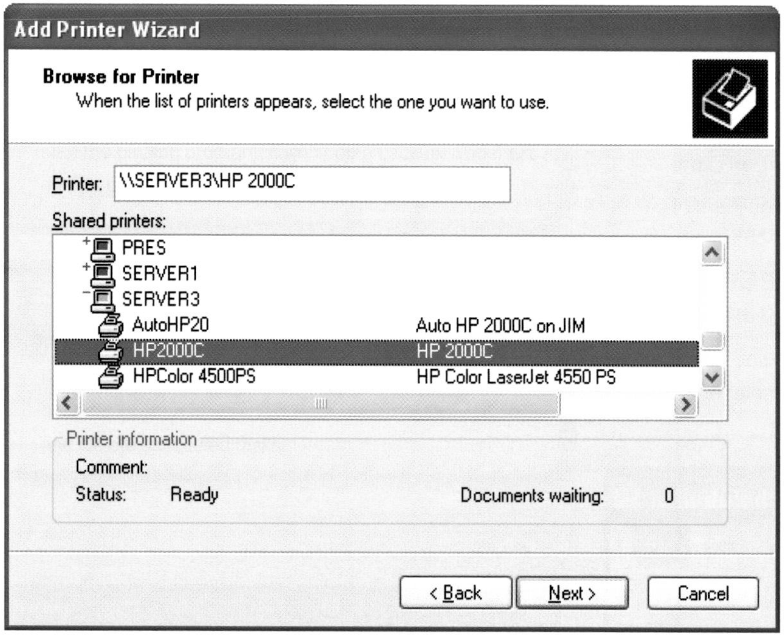

Figure 6-10: A printer on another computer must be shared by that computer before you can use it

1. Open **Start**, click **Printers And Faxes** (in Windows XP Home, open **Control Panel**, and then, in Classic View, double-click **Printers And Faxes)**, and click **Add A Printer** in the tasks pane. Click **Next**.
2. Select **A Network Printer** and click **Next**. Accept **Browse For A Printer** and click **Next**.
3. Scroll through the computer and printers on your network to locate the printer you want. Select that printer, as shown in Figure 6-10, and click **Next**. You are told you are about to connect to a printer on another computer and asked if you want to do that. Click **Yes**.
4. Select if you want to make this your default printer and click **Next**. You are shown a summary of your settings. Click **Finish**. Close the Printers And Faxes window.

IDENTIFY A DEFAULT PRINTER

With several printers, one must be identified as your default printer—the one that will be used for printing whenever you don't select another one. To change your default printer:

Open **Start**, click **Printers And Faxes** (in Windows XP Home open **Control Panel**, and then, in Classic View, double-click **Printers And Faxes)**, right-click the printer you want to be the default, and click **Set As Default Printer**. Close the Printers And Faxes window.

SHARE A PRINTER

If you have a printer attached to your computer and you want to let others use that printer, you can share it:

1. Open **Start** and click **Printers And Faxes** (in Windows XP Home open **Control Panel**, and then, in Classic View, double-click **Printers And Faxes)**.
2. Right-click the printer you want to share, and click **Sharing**. The printers Properties dialog box will open.
3. Choose **Share This Printer**, enter a share name, and click **OK.** Close the Printers And Faxes window.

QUICKSTEPS

PRINTING

Most printing is done from in a program. Use Microsoft Word, whose Print dialog is shown in Figure 6-11, as an example.

PRINT DOCUMENTS

To print:

Open **File** and choose **Print** to open the Print dialog box. Click **OK** to print using the defaults.

CHOOSE A PRINTER

To choose which printer you want to use:

Open **File** and choose **Print** to open the Print dialog box. Open the printer **Name** drop-down list and choose the printer you want.

DETERMINE SPECIFIC PAGES TO PRINT

In the Page Range section of the Print dialog box you can:

- Print all pages.
- Print only the current page.
- Print a series of individual pages and a range of pages by specifying the individual pages separated by commas, and specifying the range with a hyphen. For example: 4,6,8-10,12 will print pages 4,6,8,9,10,12.

NOTE

You can print just the even or odd pages by opening the **Print** drop-down list in the bottom left of the Print dialog box and making that selection

Print Pictures

Printing pictures from a program is exactly the same as described in the Printing QuickSteps. Additionally, Windows has a Photo Printing Wizard to print pictures from either the Windows Explorer or the Windows Picture And Fax Viewer.

1. Open **Start**, choose **My Pictures**, select the picture(s) to print, and click **Print This Picture** (if only one) or **Print These Pictures** (if several). The Photo Printing Wizard opens.
2. Click **Next**. Select or deselect pictures so that only the ones you want printed have check marks. Click **Next**.
3. Select the printer to use and click **Next**. Select the layout and the number of times to use each picture, click **Next**, and click **Finish**. The pictures will be printed.

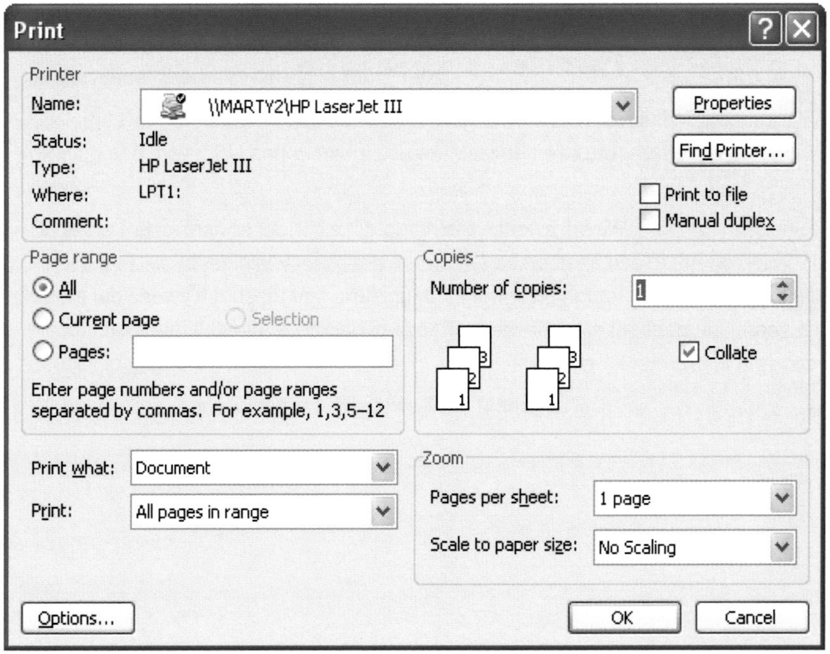

Figure 6-11: The Microsoft Word Print dialog box is similar to those in other programs

Print to a File

There are two primary reasons to print to a file: to have a file you can take to a remote printer, and to get information out of one program and into another. The first requires formatting the information for a printer and then sending it to a file. In the second, you must create a "printer" to produce unformatted generic text. Look first at creating a text file printer and then at how to print to a file.

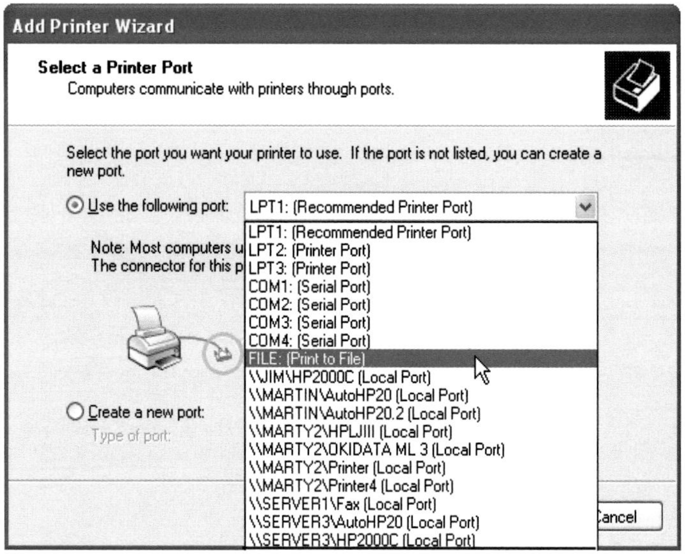

Figure 6-12: By printing to a file you can transfer information from one program to another when there is no other way to do it

CREATE A TEXT FILE PRINTER

1. Open **Start** and click **Printers And Faxes** (in Windows XP Home, open **Control Panel**, and then, in Classic View, double-click **Printers And Faxes)**.
2. Click **Add A Printer** and click **Next**. Select **Local Printer**, deselect **Automatically Detect And Install My Plug And Play Printer**, and click **Next**.
3. In the Select A Printer Port dialog box, open the **Use The Following Port** drop-down list and choose **File (Print To File) (see Figure 6-12)**. Click **Next**.
4. In the Install Printer Software dialog box, scroll down and choose **Generic** as the manufacturer, and **Generic / Text Only** printer. Click **Next**.
5. Enter a name you want for the printer and click **No** (you do not want to use it as your default). Click **Next**. If asked, determine if you want to share the printer; if so, enter the share name, and click **Next**.
6. Select **No** to printing a test page, click **Next**, and click **Finish**. A new icon will appear in your Printers And Faxes window. Close the Printers And Faxes window.

SELECT PRINT TO FILE

Whether you want to print to a file in order to print on an actual remote printer, or print to a file in order to create a text file, the steps are same once you have created a text file printer:

1. In the program in which you are working, open **File** and choose **Print**.
2. Select the ultimate printer or the generic text file printer, click **Print To File**, and click **OK**. Select the folder and file name to use and click **OK**.

Print Web Pages

Printing web pages is little different from printing in any other program.

1. Open **Start** and click **Internet** to open your browser (assumed to be Internet Explorer).
2. Browse to the page you want to print and click **Print** in the Standard toolbar, or open **File**, click **Print**, select the printer and other options, and again click **Print**.

3. Close your Internet browser.

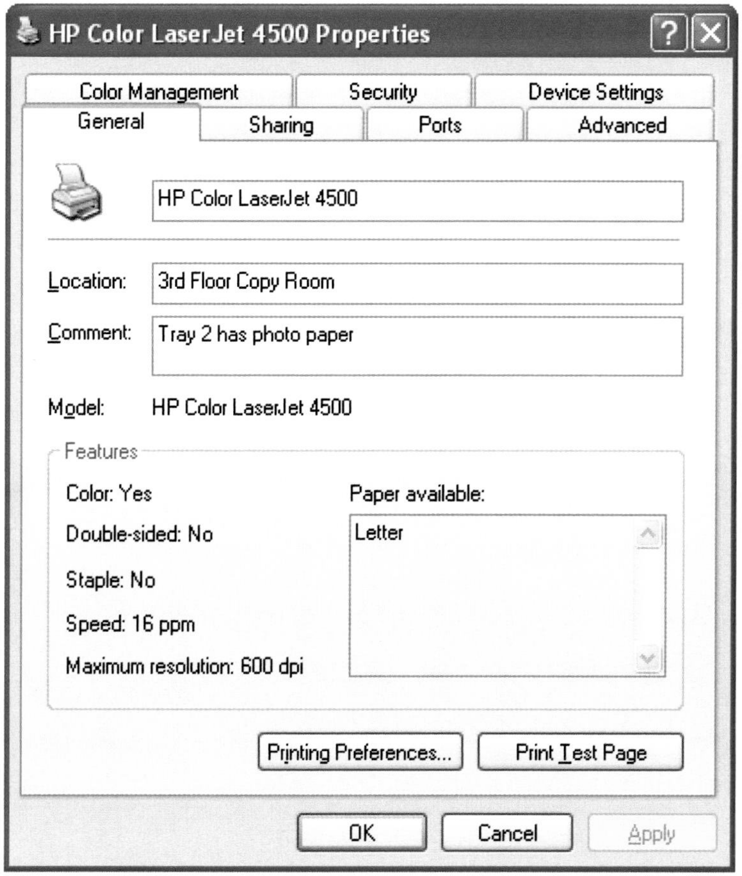

Configure a Printer

Configuration of a printer is usually done for special purposes and usually isn't required. Nevertheless, all configuration is done from the printer's Properties dialog box.

1. Open **Start** and click **Printers And Faxes** (in Windows XP Home, open **Control Panel** and then, in Classic View, double-click **Printers And Faxes**).
2. Right-click the printer you want to configure and click **Properties**. The printer's Properties dialog box will open.

On the General tab (shown in Figure 6-13), you can change the printer name, its location, and enter a comment. In the Ports tab, you can change the port used by the printer, configure ports, and set up printer pooling. In the Device Settings tab, you can set what is loaded in each paper tray, how to handle font substitution, and what printer options are available (your printer may be different). Though most printer configurations are self-explanatory, several items are worthy of further discussion and are discussed below.

Figure 6-13: Printers, while having many settings, are often run without ever changing the settings

1 2 3 4 5 6 7 8 9 10

TIP

If you have a program that automatically prints certain tasks, such as incoming orders, you might want to assign it a lower priority than a word processing task, such as a new proposal.

PRINTER POOLING

Printer pooling allows you to have two or more physical printing devices with the same print driver assigned to one printer. When print jobs are sent to the printer, Windows determines which of the physical devices is available and routes the job to that device.

1. In the Properties dialog box for the printer to which all work will be directed, click the **Ports** tab, and click **Enable Printer Pooling**.
2. Click each of the ports with a printing device that is to be in the pool. When all the ports are selected, click **OK** to close the Properties dialog box.
3. If the printer that contains the pool isn't already selected as the default printer, right-click the printer and choose **Set As Default Printer**.

PRINTER PRIORITY

Assigning several printers to one printing device allows you to have two or more settings used with one device. If you want to have two or more priorities automatically assigned to jobs going to a printer, create two or more printers that all point to the same printer port but that have different priorities. Then, have high-priority print jobs printed to a printer with a priority of 99, and low-priority jobs printed to a printer with a priority of 1.

1. Install all printers as previously described in "Install a Printer," all with the same port. Name each printer to indicate its priority, such as "High Priority Printer" and "Low Priority Printer."
2. In the Printers And Faxes window, right-click the high-priority printer and choose **Properties**.
3. Select the **Advanced** tab, enter a Priority of 99, and click **OK**.
4. Similarly, right-click the other printers, open their Properties dialog box, select the **Advanced** tab, and set the priority from 1 for the lowest priority to 98 for the second highest priority.

Jobs with the highest priority will print before jobs with a lower priority if they are in the *queue* (waiting to be printed) at the same time.

Figure 6-14: Setting the paper type and size in each paper tray

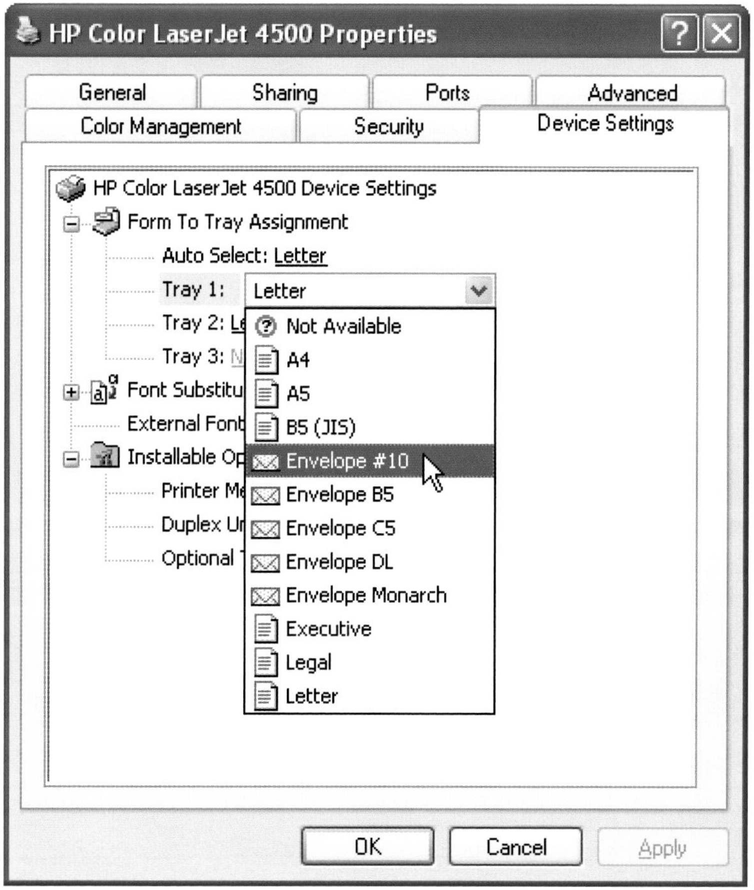

ASSIGN PAPER TRAYS

Some printers have more than one paper tray, and each tray can have different types or sizes of paper. If you assign types and sizes of paper to trays in the printer's Properties dialog box, and a user requests a type and size of paper when printing, Windows XP automatically designates the correct paper tray for the print job:

1. In the Properties dialog box for the printer whose trays you want to assign, select the **Device Settings** tab.
2. Open each tray and select the type and size of paper in that tray, similar to what you see in Figure 6-14.
3. When you have set the paper type and size in each tray, click **OK**.

SPOOL SETTINGS

The time it takes to print a document is normally longer than the time it takes to transfer the information to the printer. Printer spooling temporarily stores information on disk, allowing Windows to feed it to the printer as it can be handled. Under most circumstances, you want to use printer spooling and not tie up the program waiting for the printer. The printer Properties Advanced tab lets you choose to spool or not and gives you two options if you spool.

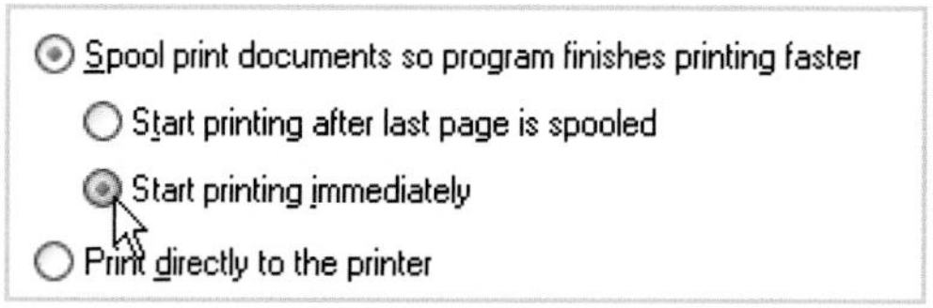

1 2 3 4 5 6 7 8 9 10

NOTE

The separation files work with HP and PostScript or compatible printers. They will not work with all printers.

TIP

If you know or have a guide to either the PCL or PostScript language (or both), you can open and modify these files (or copies of them) with any text editor, such as Notepad, to suite your particular purpose.

- **Start Printing After Last Page Is Spooled** waits to print until the last page is spooled, allowing the program to finish faster and the user to get back to the program faster, but it takes longer to finish printing.
- **Start Printing Immediately** allows printing to be done sooner, but the program will be tied up a little longer.

The default Start Printing Immediately provides a middle ground between getting the printing done and getting back to the program.

USE SEPARATOR PAGES

If you have several jobs on a printer, it might be helpful to have a separator page between them. A separator page can also be used to switch a printer between PostScript (a printer language) and PCL (Printer Control Language) on Hewlett-Packard (HP) and compatible printers. Four sample SEP separation files come with Windows XP and are installed in the \Windows\System32\ folder:

- **Pcl.sep** prints a separation page before the start of each print job on PCL-compatible printers. If the printer handles both PostScript and PCL, it will be switched to PCL.
- **Pscript.sep** does *not* print a separation page, but printers with both PostScript and PCL will be switched to PostScript.
- **Sysprint.sep** prints a separation page before the start of each print job on PostScript-compatible printers.
- **Sysprtj.sep** is the same as Sysprint.sep but in the Japanese language.

You can choose to have a separator page added at the beginning of each print job by clicking **Separator Page** on the Advanced tab of the Properties dialog box, clicking **Open**, browsing for and selecting the page you want, and clicking **OK** twice.

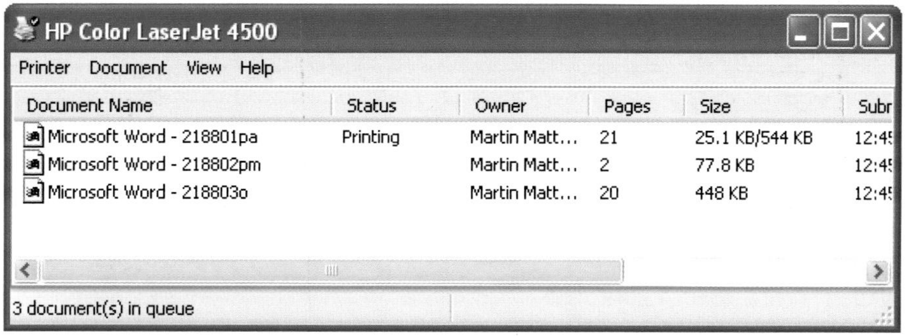

Figure 6-15: Controlling printing takes place in the printer's window and allows you to pause, resume, restart, and cancel printing

Control Printing

To control printing means to control the process as it is taking place with one print job or several in line. If several print jobs are spooled at close to the same time, they form a *print queue*, waiting for earlier jobs to finish. You may control printing in several ways, as described below. These tasks are handled in the printer's window, which is similar to Figure 6-15 and is opened by double-clicking the appropriate printer in the Printers And Faxes window or by clicking the printer icon in the notification area of the taskbar.

PAUSE, RESUME, AND RESTART PRINTING

While printing, a situation may occur (such as needing to change paper) where you want to pause and resume printing, either for one or for all documents.

- **Pause all documents**: In the printer's window open **Printer** and choose **Pause Printing**. "Paused" will appear in the title bar, and if you look in the Printer menu, you will see a check mark in front of Pause Printing.
- **Resume printing all documents**: In the printer's window open **Printer** and choose **Resume Printing**. "Paused" disappears from the title bar and the check mark disappears in the Pause Printing option in the Printer menu.
- **Pause a document**: In the printer's window, select the document or documents to pause, open **Document**, and choose **Pause**. "Paused" will appear in the Status column of the document(s) you selected.

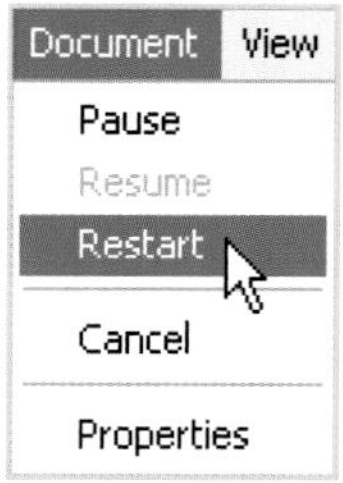

- **Resume printing a paused document where it left off**: In the printer's window, select the document, open **Document**, and choose **Resume**. "Printing" will appear in the Status column of the document selected.
- **Restart printing at the beginning of a document**: In the printer's window, select the document, open **Document**, and choose **Restart**. "Restarting" and then "Printing" will appear in the Status column.

1 2 3 4 5 6 7 8 9 10

NOTE

You cannot change the order in which documents are being printed by pausing the current document that is printing. You must either complete printing the current document or cancel it. You can, however, use Pause to get around intermediate documents that are not currently printing. For example, suppose you want to immediately print the third document in the queue, but the first document is currently printing. You must either let the first document finish printing or cancel it. You can then pause the second document before it starts printing, and the third document will begin printing when the first document is out of the way.

CANCEL PRINTING

Canceling printing can be done either at the printer level for all the jobs in the printer queue or at the document level for selected documents. A canceled job is deleted from the print queue and must be restarted by the original program.

- **Cancel a job**: In the printer's window, select the job or jobs that you want canceled. Open **Document** and choose **Cancel**. The job or jobs will disappear from the window and the queue.
- **Cancel all the jobs in the queue**: In the printer's window, open **Printer** and choose **Cancel All Documents**. You are asked whether you are sure you want to cancel all documents. Click **Yes**. All jobs will disappear from the queue and the printer window.

REDIRECT DOCUMENTS

If you have two printers with the same print driver, you can redirect all the print jobs that are in the queue for one printer to the other, where they will be printed without the user(s) having to resubmit them. You do this by changing the port to which the queue is directed.

1. In the printer's window, open **Printer**, choose **Properties**, and select the **Ports** tab.
2. If the second printer is in the list of ports, select it. Otherwise, click **Add Port** to open the Printer Ports dialog box. Choose **Local Port**, and click **New Port**, which opens the Port Name dialog box.
3. Enter the UNC (Uniform Naming Convention) name for the printer (for example, \\Server3\HPCLJ4500) and click **OK**.
4. Click **Close** and then click **OK**. The print queue will be redirected to the other printer.

CHANGE A DOCUMENT'S PROPERTIES

A document in a print queue has a Properties dialog box, shown in Figure 6-16, which is opened by right-clicking the document and selecting **Properties**. The General tab allows you to change a number of things:

- **Priority**: To change a document's default priority of 1, the lowest priority, so the document can be printed before another that hasn't started printing yet, set the document's priority in the document's Properties dialog box to anything higher than the other document by dragging the **Priority** slider to the right.
- **Who to Notify**: To change who is optionally notified of any special situations occurring during printing and when a document has finished printing, put the name of another person (the individual's user name on a shared computer or network) in the **Notify** text box of the document's Properties dialog box.
- **Set Print Time**: To change when a job is printed, open a document's Properties dialog box, select **Only From** at the bottom under Schedule, and then enter the time range within which you want the job printed. This allows you to print large jobs, which might otherwise clog the print queue, at a time when there is little or no load.

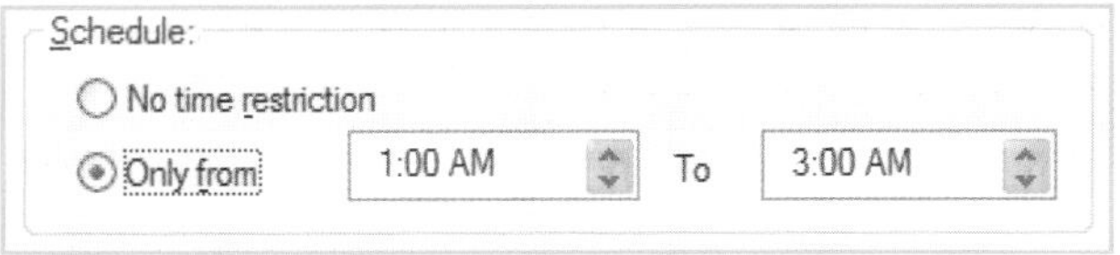

NOTE

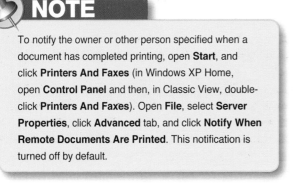

To notify the owner or other person specified when a document has completed printing, open **Start**, and click **Printers And Faxes** (in Windows XP Home, open **Control Panel** and then, in Classic View, double-click **Printers And Faxes**). Open **File**, select **Server Properties**, click **Advanced** tab, and click **Notify When Remote Documents Are Printed**. This notification is turned off by default.

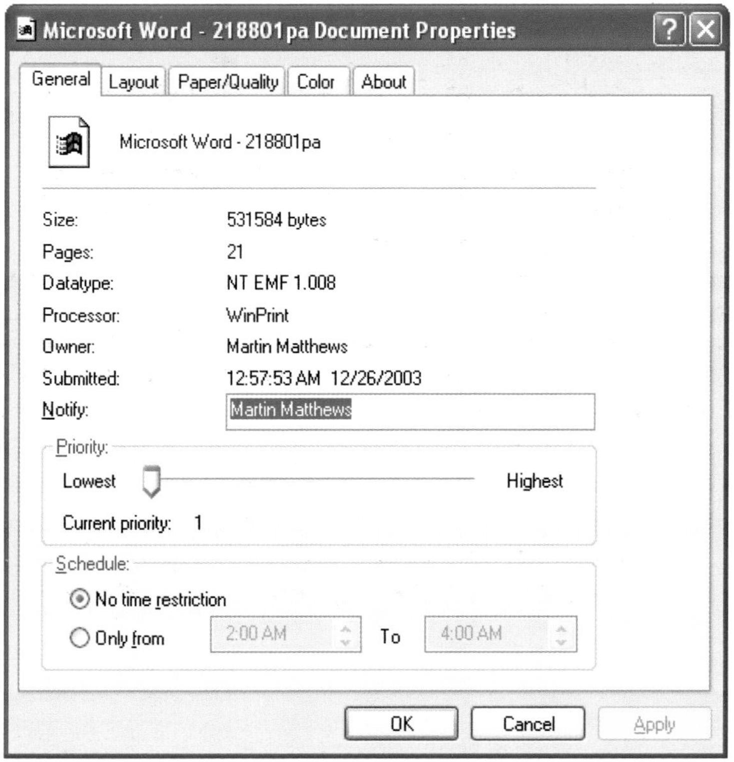

Figure 6-16: Setting the properties of a document in the print queue

1 2 3 4 5 6 7 8 9 10

QUICKSTEPS

HANDLING FONTS

A *font* is a set of characters with the same design, size, weight, and style. A font is a member of a *typeface* family, all with the same design. The font 12-point Arial bold italic is a member of the Arial typeface with a 12-point size, bold weight, and italic style. Windows XP comes with a number of fonts, shown in Figure 6-17.

ADD FONTS

To add fonts to those that are installed by Windows XP:

1. Open **Start**, click **Control Panel**, and, in Classic view, double-click **Fonts**. The Fonts window opens.
2. Open **File** and choose **Install New Font**. The Add Fonts dialog box opens, like the one in Figure 6-18.
3. Open a drive and folder that contains the fonts you want (this can be a floppy, a CD/DVD, or a network drive).
4. Select the fonts you want to install from the List Of Fonts, check the **Copy Fonts To Fonts Folder** check box, and then click **OK**. The new fonts appear in the Fonts window.

DELETE FONTS

Remove fonts simply by selecting them and pressing **DELETE** or by right-clicking the font(s) and choosing **DELETE**. In either case, you are asked whether you are sure. Click **Yes** if you are. The fonts will be placed in the Recycle Bin, and can be recovered.

USE FONTS

Fonts are used or specified from within a program. In Microsoft Word, for example, you can select a line of text and then open the Font drop-down list on the Formatting toolbar. Every program is a little different. One nice feature in recent versions of Word is that the list shows what the fonts look like.

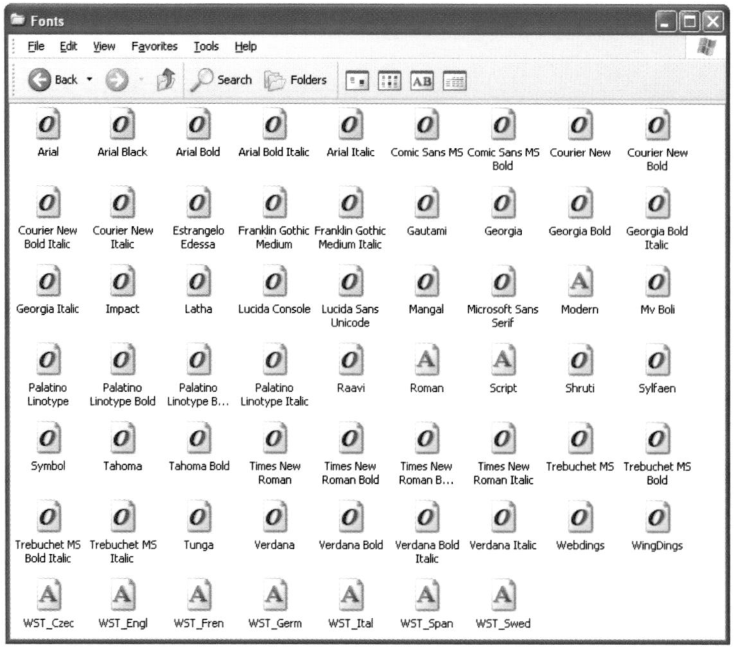

Figure 6-17: Windows XP comes with a number of fonts, but you can add others

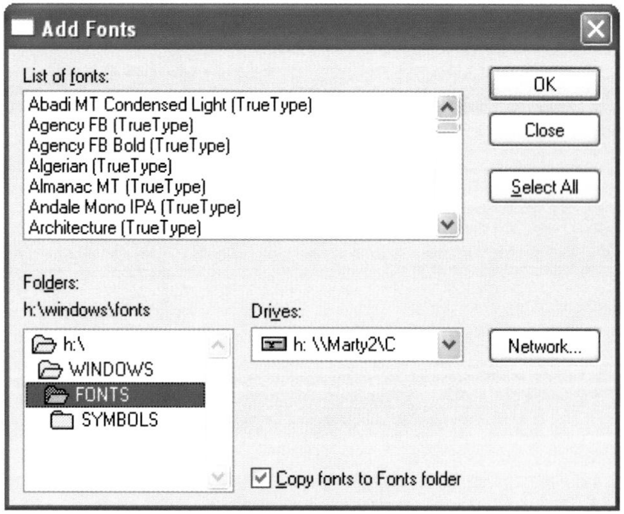

Figure 6-18: Adding fonts from another computer on the network

Fax Documents and Pictures

The capability to send and receive faxes is included in Windows XP as part of the printing function and allows a program, such as Microsoft Word, to "print" to a remote fax by specifying "fax" as a printer. There is also a Fax Console that lets you directly send and receive faxes as you would an e-mail message. This service requires that you have a fax modem in your computer and a phone line connected to it (see Chapter 5 on setting up and working with modems). This fax service is not fully installed by default when you install Windows XP, but you can easily do that.

TIP

To select several fonts in the Add Fonts dialog box, hold down **SHIFT** and click the first and last font to select several contiguous fonts, or hold down **CTRL** and click each font to select several fonts that are not contiguous.

Set Up Faxing

To set up faxing:

1. Open **Start** and click **Printers And Faxes** (in Windows XP Home, open **Control Panel** and then, in Classic View, double-click **Printers And Faxes)**.
2. Click **Set Up Faxing** in the tasks pane. If requested, insert your Windows XP CD and click **Exit** to close the introductory Windows XP window. When Setup is done, you are returned to the Printer And Faxes window, which has a new Send A Fax option and a fax "printer" icon.

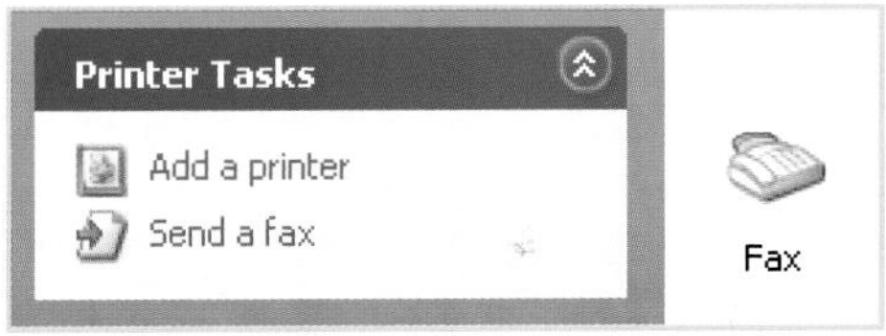

NOTE

In Windows XP Home Edition, you have to go through an extra step by clicking Install A Local Fax Printer.

Send a Fax

Sending a fax is as easy as printing plus answering a few questions:

1. Open a document in a program such as Microsoft Word. Open the **File** menu and choose **Print**. Open the printer **Name** drop-down list, choose **Fax**, and click **OK**. The Fax Configuration Wizard will open.
2. Click **Next**. Fill in the sender information, and then click **Next**. Select the modem to use and make sure send is enabled. Click **Next** again.

1 2 3 4 5 6 7 8 9 10

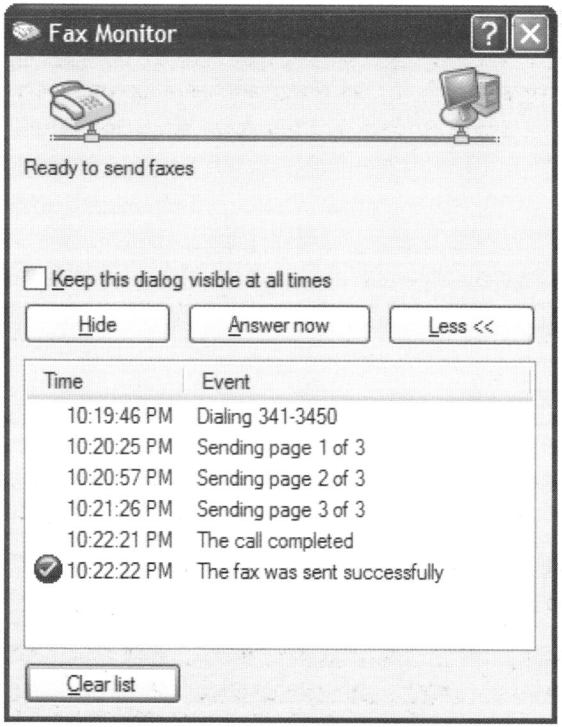

Figure 6-19: The Windows XP faxing capability allows you to "print" to it from any application

3. Enter your Transmitting Subscriber Identification (TSID—normally your fax number and company name, displayed at the top of the fax when you send it), and click **Next**.
4. Your configuration settings are displayed. If these are not correct, click **Back**, make the necessary corrections, and when you have the correct settings, click **Finish**. The Send Fax Wizard will open. Click **Next**.
5. Enter the Recipient Information and click **Next**. If you want to send a cover page, click **Select A Cover Page Template...**, fill in the information you want on the cover page, and click **Next**.
6. Enter when you want to send the fax, set its priority, and click **Next**. You are shown the settings you have made. Use **Back** to make any corrections and then click **Finish**. The Fax Monitor will open, and if you click **More**, you will see the progress of faxing: Dialing, Sending, Completed, as shown in Figure 6-19.

Receive a Fax

You receive faxes using the Fax Console, which is opened from the Start menu.

1. Open **Start**, select **All Programs**, choose **Accessories**, select **Communications**, choose **Fax**, and click **Fax Console**.

   –Or–

   Double-click the fax "printer" in the Printers And Faxes window.
2. Open **Tools** and click **Configure Fax**. Click **Next**. Skip Sender Information and click **Next**. Select the modem to use, click **Enable Receive**, and choose whether you want manual or automatic answer. Click **Next**.
3. Skip the Transmitting Subscriber Identification (TSID), click **Next**, enter your Called Subscriber Identification (CSID—normally your fax number and company name, sent back to the caller when you receive a fax), and click **Next**.
4. Choose whether to immediately print an incoming fax, to store it in a separate folder, or to do both. If you want to print a fax, specify on which printer, and if you want to store it in a folder, specify the path to the folder (an incoming fax is automatically stored in the Inbox folder, so the folder you specify would be storing a second copy). Click **Next**.
5. Your configuration settings are displayed and you are asked if these are correct. If they are not, click **Back** and make the necessary corrections. When you have the correct settings, click **Finish**.

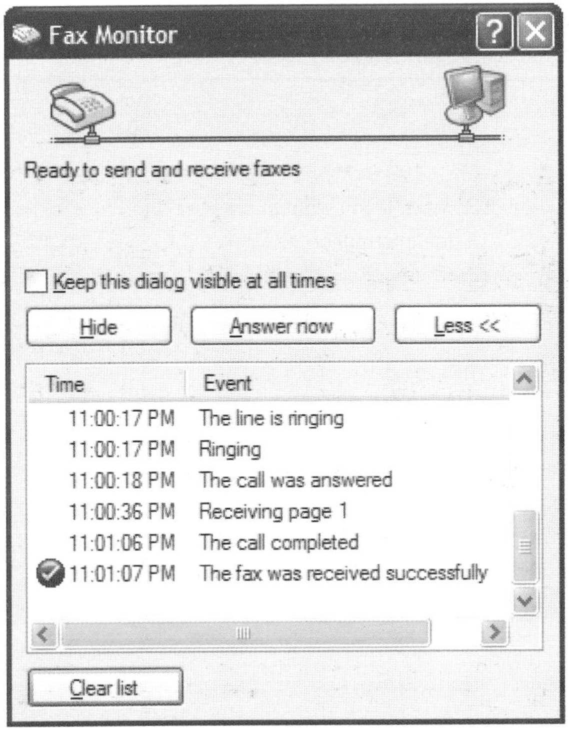

Figure 6-20: The Fax Monitor provides a log of what is happening during a fax transmission

6. If you chose Manual Answer Mode in the Fax Configuration Wizard (Step 2), you must wait until you hear the phone ring with the fax message and then click the **Receive Now** button on the toolbar or open **File** and choose **Receive A Fax Now**.

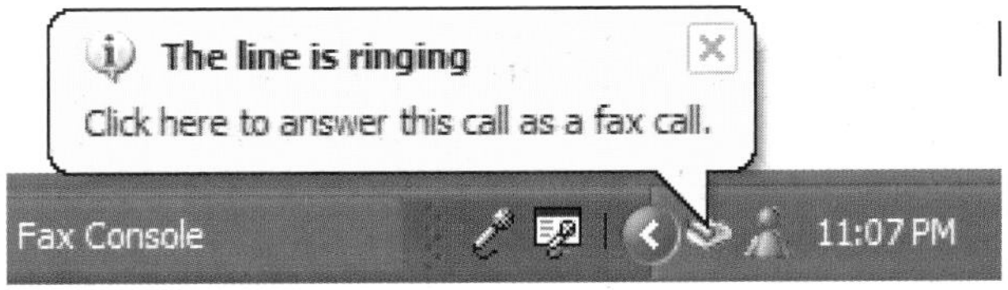

7. If you chose Automatic Answer Mode in the Fax Configuration Wizard, any fax calls to that line will be automatically answered.

   In all cases of receiving a fax, the Fax Monitor will handle the call. Given that there is a fax machine (or a computer impersonating one) on the other end, a fax will be received and the Fax Monitor will display the progress, as you can see in Figure 6-20. When the call is complete, the Fax Monitor will hang up and the received message will appear in the Inbox of the Fax Console. Also, a balloon message saying you received a fax will pop out of the notification area.

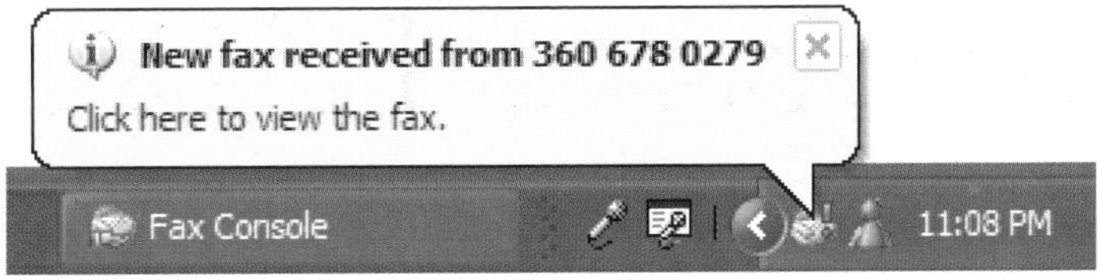

8. Double-click the fax in the Inbox to view it in the Windows Pictures And Fax Viewer. Right-click the fax and choose to View, Delete, Save As (it is already saved in the Inbox), Mail To (attaches to an e-mail message you address), or Print (see "Print Pictures" earlier in this chapter for printing alternatives).

9. Close the Fax Console.

Annotate a Fax

A received fax can be viewed in the Windows Picture And Fax Viewer, which has a set of annotation tools you can use to mark up a fax before sending it back, as shown in Figure 6-21.

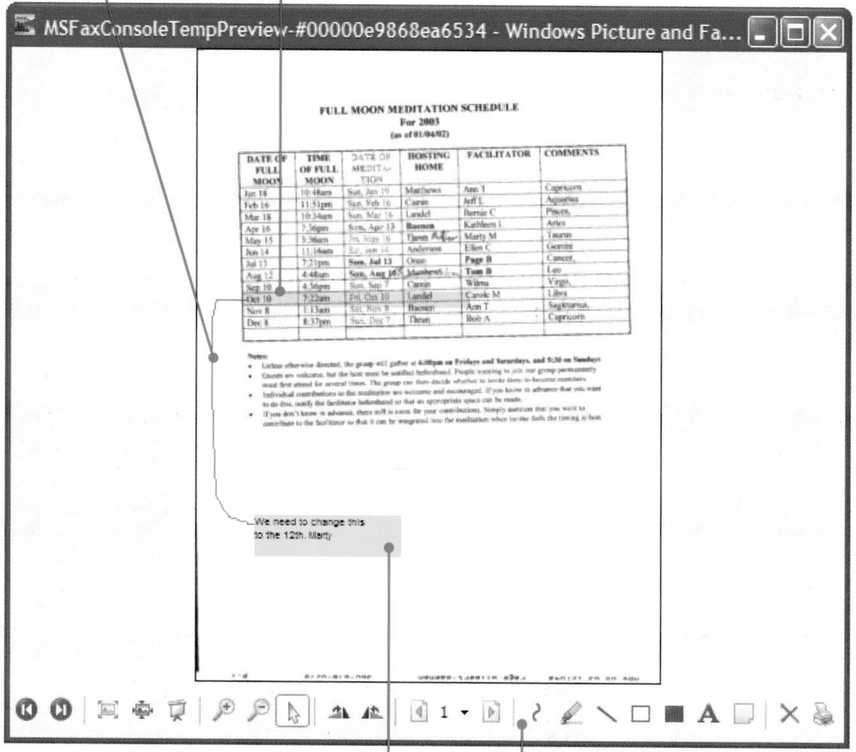

Figure 6-21: A fax in the Windows Picture And Fax Viewer can be marked up and returned

1. In the Fax Console, double-click the fax you want to view and annotate. It will open in the Windows Picture and Fax Viewer.
2. Use the following tools to mark up the fax:
   - **Freehand Annotation**, to draw a line of any shape
   - **Highlight Annotation**, to highlight any part of the fax
   - **Straight Line Annotation**, to draw straight lines
   - **Frame Annotation**, to draw a box around anything in the fax
   - **Solid Rectangle Annotation**, to cover over an area of the fax
   - **Text Annotation**, to enter text on the fax
   - **Attached Note Annotation**, to enter text on the fax with a yellow background behind the text
3. When you have the annotation the way you want it, click **Save** (the ScreenTip says "Copy To"), select the path and folder, enter a name, and click **Save**. 
4. If you want to return the fax to its sender, click **Print**, which opens the Photo Printing Wizard. Select the appropriate settings, including choosing Fax as the printer, and follow the instructions in "Send a Fax," earlier in this chapter. 
5. Close the Windows Picture And Fax Viewer and, if it is open, close the Fax Console.

Create a Fax Cover Page

Windows XP Fax comes with four cover pages you can use. It also has a Fax Cover Page Editor that you can use to modify an existing cover page:

> **NOTE**
>
> Once you have saved a fax with annotation, you cannot reopen it and change the annotation, although you can add new annotation.

1. Open **Start**, select **All Programs**, and choose **Accessories**. Select **Communications**, choose **Fax**, and click **Fax Console**.

   –Or–

   Double-click the Fax "printer" in the Printers And Faxes window.
2. Open **Tools** and choose **Personal Cover Pages**. Click **Copy,** select one of the four standard cover pages, and click **Open**. Select the cover page and click **Open** (Generic was selected for this illustration). The cover page will open in the Fax Cover Page Editor, as shown in Figure 6-22.
3. Use the following tools on the Drawing toolbar to modify an existing cover page, thereby creating a new one of your own:
   - **Selection tool**, to select parts of a cover page
   - **Text tool**, to enter text
   - **Line tool**, to draw straight lines
   - **Rectangle tool**, to draw rectangles
   - **Rounded Rectangle tool**, to draw rounded rectangles
   - **Polygon tool**, to draw multisided polygons
   - **Oval tool**, to draw ovals and circles
   - **Bring To Front**, to move a selected item to the front of a stack of items
   - **Send To Back**, to move a selected item to the back of a stack of items
   - **Space Across**, to equally space items horizontally
   - **Space Down**, to equally space items vertically
   - **Align Left**, to align text and object on the left margin
   - **Align Right**, to align text and object on the right margin
   - **Align Top**, to align text and object on the top margin
   - **Align Bottom**, to align text and object on the bottom margin

4. When you have your cover page the way you want it, click **Save** to save it with its existing name, or open **File** and click **Save As** to give your cover page a new name. Close both the Fax Cover Page Editor and the Personal Cover Pages dialog box, as well as the Fax Console.

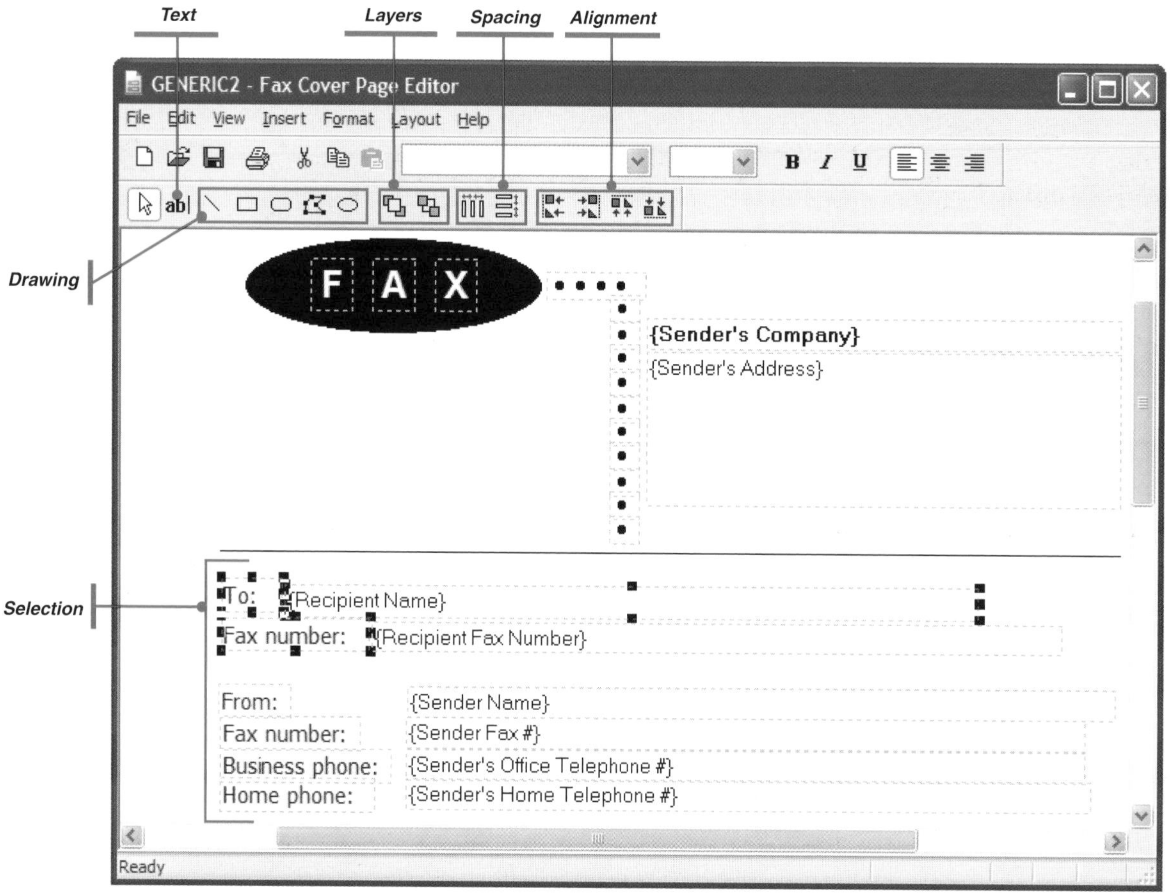

Figure 6-22: Creating your own fax cover page allows you to promote your business or activity

How to...

Chapter 7
Working with Multimedia

Multimedia is the combination of audio and video. Windows XP, as an operating system, has to be able to handle audio and video files and accept their input from a number of different devices. In addition, it has two major programs, Windows Media Player and Windows Movie Maker, that enable you to work with these files and write these files onto CDs. We'll look first at sound by itself, then at video with sound.

Work with Audio

Audio is sound. Windows XP works with and uses sound in several ways, the simplest being to alert you to various events, like an incoming e-mail message or closing down the system. "Change Sound," in Chapter 2, shows you how to customize the use of sounds for these purposes.

The other use of sound is to entertain or inform you—be it listening to music or lectures from CDs, Internet Radio, or another Internet site. It is this use of sound that is the subject of this section.

Play CDs

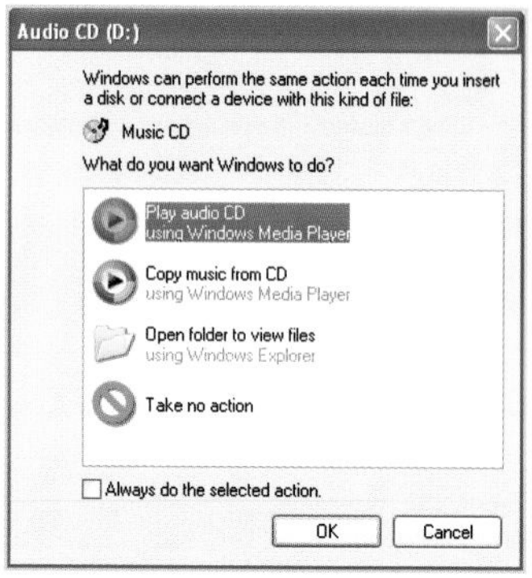

Playing a CD is as easy as inserting a disk in the drive. When you do that, you will be asked if you want Windows Media Player to play the disk. If you click **OK**, Media Player will open and begin playing the disk, as shown in Figure 7-1. The Media Player window has five sets of controls that enable you to determine how Media Player functions and looks:

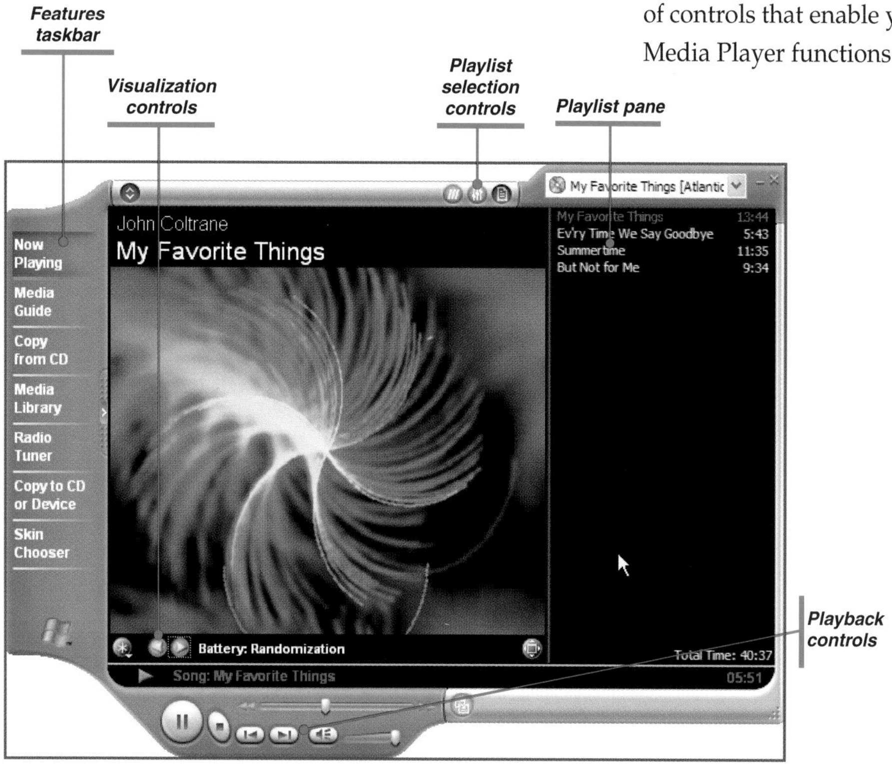

Figure 7-1: Windows Media Player playing a music CD

- **Features taskbar** allows selection of many tools and features.
- **Now Playing** shows visualizations of audio or the display of video.
- **Media Guide** connects to WindowsMedia.com's links to Internet media sites.
- **Copy From CD** plays or copies to the Media Library.
- **Media Library** displays the set of folders used to organize media and Internet links.
- **Radio Tuner** connects to WindowsMedia.com's Internet radio page and links to stations.
- **Copy To CD Or Device** copies music tracks in the Media Library to a writable CD.
- **Skin Chooser** changes the look, or *skin*, of Windows Media Player.

- **Visualization controls** change the visualization displayed in Media Player or the full screen.

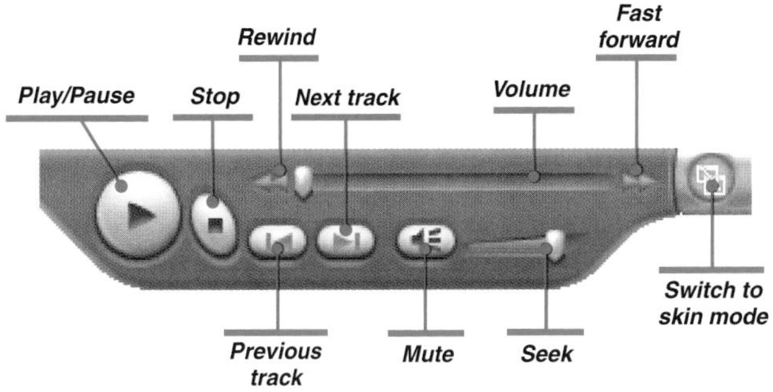

- **Playback controls** provide tape deck–like controls to play/pause, stop, go to previous, go to next, adjust volume, rewind, seek, and fast forward.
- **Playlist pane** lists the current pieces being played.
- **Playlist controls** select what to play, how to play it, and the displays desired.

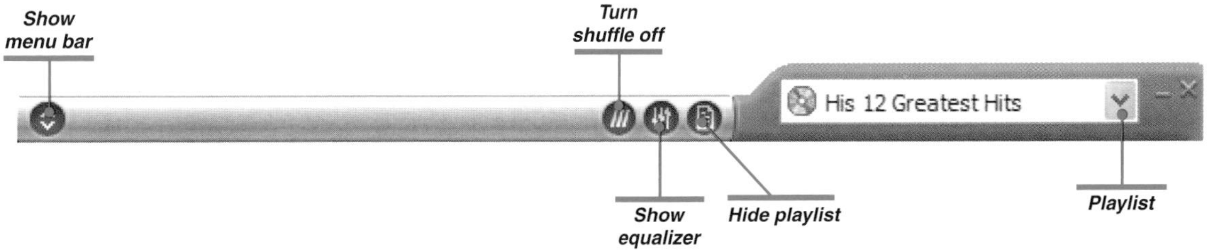

1 2 3 4 5 6 7 8 9 10

1 2 3 4 5 6 7 8 9 10

The playlist controls allow you to display or not the normal Windows title, menu bars, and border as well as the Now Playing tools pane, which can contain several different sets of controls, including a graphic equalizer.

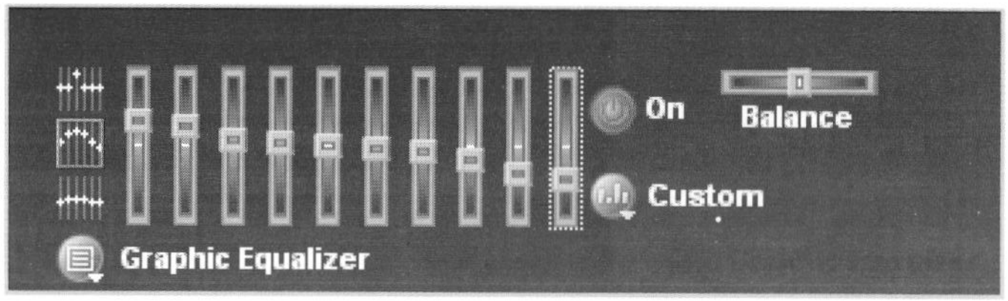

TIP

If you don't see the Volume icon, open **Start** and select **Control Panel**. In Classic view, double-click **Sounds And Audio Devices**, and in the Volume tab, select **Place Volume Icon In The Taskbar**. Close the Sounds And Audio Devices dialog box and the Control Panel.

Control the Volume

You can control your computer's audio volume from several places, including the physical volume control on your speakers or on your laptop computer, the volume control on the bottom right of the playback controls of the Media Player, and the volume icon in the notification area on the right of the taskbar.

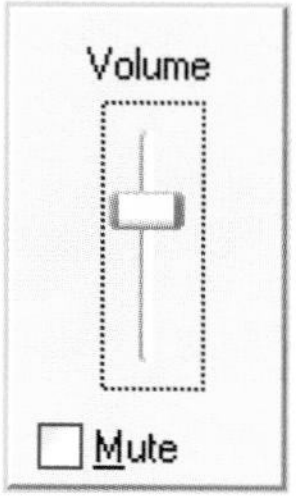

Clicking the notification area **Volume** icon opens a small Volume slider that you can drag for louder or softer sound, or you can click **Mute** to do just that. Click anywhere on the desktop to close the Volume slider.

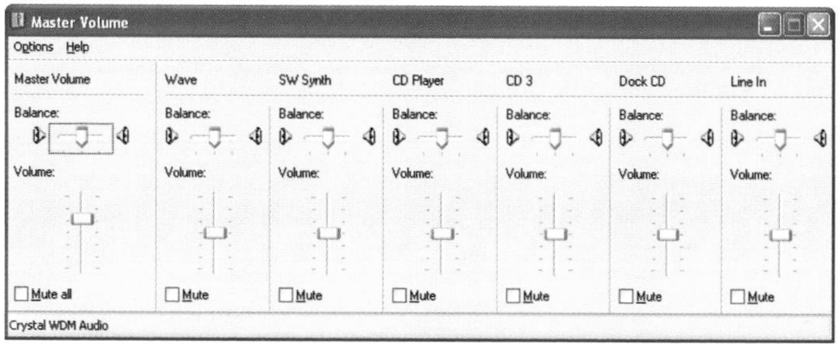

Figure 7-2: Windows XP volume mixer allows the mixing of various sound sources

If you double-click the notification area volume icon, a volume mixer dialog box opens (this is called by several names), as you can see in Figure 7-2. This allows you to control volume of the various sound-producing components on the computer.

Listen to Radio Stations

If you have a broadband Internet connection (as described in Chapter 4) of at least 128 Kbps and sound capability, you can listen to radio stations around the world that have added an Internet connection. Windows Media Player gives you access to these stations through the Radio Tuner feature, which you can see in Figure 7-3. Radio Tuner gives you several ways of finding and playing a particular station:

Figure 7-3: Media Player's Radio Tuner allows you to listen to Internet radio stations

- Choosing from a featured set of stations or an editor's picks of the day
- Selecting a type of music, or genre, for which to search or using your keyword to search for a station's call letters, for instance, or the ZIP code where it is located
- Choosing a station you have recently played or that you have added to a list of your favorite stations

To bring up the radio tuner, locate a station, and add that station to My Stations:

1. Open **Start**, select **All Programs**, click **Windows Media Player**, and then click **Radio Tuner**.
2. In the Search text box, drag over **Search Keyword**, type the call letters of a radio station, and either press **ENTER** or click the **Search** arrow. The Search Results will appear.

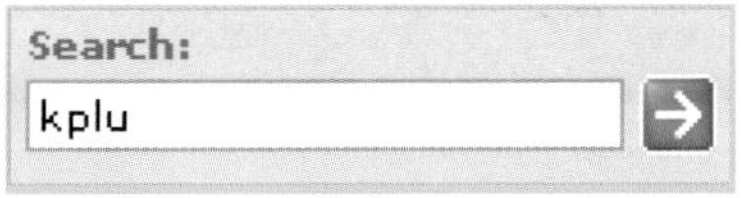

3. Select your choice within the Search Results, and click **Add To My Stations**. You may also follow the instructions to listen to or "play" the station.

TIP

The next time you want to listen to the station you saved in My Stations, after opening **Radio Tuner**, click **My Stations** and click the station.

1 2 3 4 5 6 7 8 9 10

Locate Music on the Internet

There are many other sources of music on the Internet in addition to radio stations. The Media Guide in the Media Player provides links to many of these sites. Like the Radio Tuner, the Media Guide offers links you can follow to featured sites and categories of sites. You can additionally search for a site—the site of a particular artist, for example.

1. Open **Start**, select **All Programs**, click **Windows Media Player**, and then, if it isn't already selected, click **Media Guide**.
2. In the **Search** text box, type the name of an artist for whom you would like to locate sites. Click **Search**. The search results will appear, as shown in Figure 7-4.
3. Click the link you want.

NOTE

In the All Media Results page, the little pair of notes designates music, and the little strip of film designates a music video.

TIP

If you find a piece that you like after searching in the Media Guide, you can save it in your media library by clicking **Media Library** and then clicking **Add To Library**. 

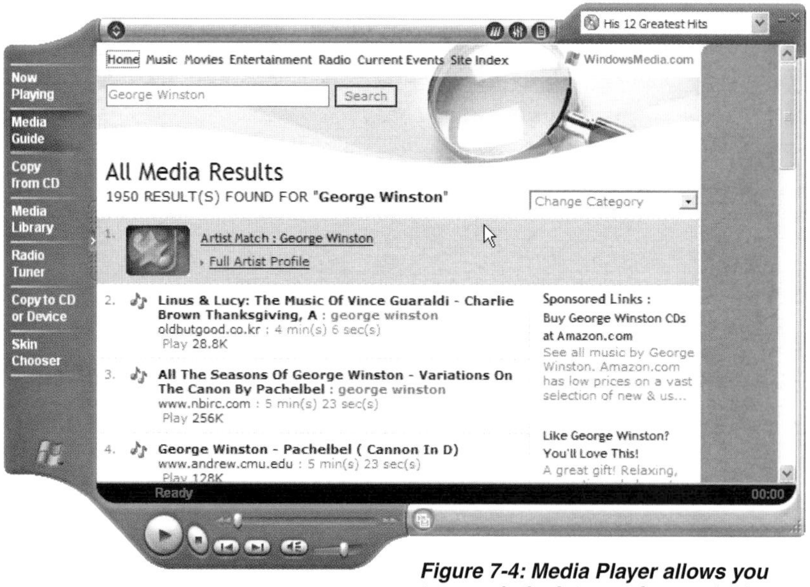

Figure 7-4: Media Player allows you to search the Internet for music that you like

NOTE

Copying a music track from a CD to a digital file on your hard disk is time consuming, even on a relatively fast computer. It also produces large files. To see the copying progress, look at the Copy Status column in the top pane of the Copy From CD window, as shown here:

Copy CDs to Your Computer

Media Player gives you the ability to copy CD tracks that you like to your hard disk, to build and manage a library of your favorite music, and to copy this material to a recordable CD. To copy from a CD (see Figure 7-5):

Figure 7-5: Media Player can be used to build a music library from your CDs

1. Insert the CD from which you want to copy tracks. Click **OK** to open Windows Media Player, then click **Copy From CD** in the Windows Media features taskbar.
2. Select the tracks you want to copy to your hard disk by selecting the check boxes on the left of each track. Click **Play** in the playback controls to listen to the track and to make sure your choices are correct.
3. When you are satisfied that you have selected the correct tracks, click **Copy Music**. A message box will open asking if the copy on your disk should be copy protected so that it cannot be played on other computers and reminding you that you are responsible for respecting copyright laws.
4. Make the copy protection choice that is correct for you, and click **OK**. The selected tracks will be copied to your hard disk. When you are ready, close Media Player.

NOTE

The material on most CDs and DVDs is owned and copyrighted by some combination of the composer, the artist, the producer, and/or the publisher. The copyright law prohibits using the copyrighted material in ways that are not beneficial to the owners, including giving or selling the content without giving or selling the original CD or DVD itself. To back that up, most CDs and DVDs are protected to make copying difficult. Media Player provides the ability to copy copyrighted material to your hard disk and then to a recordable CD or a solid-state device with the understanding that the copy is solely for your own personal use and you will not sell or give away copies. This is both a great gift and a responsibility. As one who makes his living on copyrighted material, I urge you not to abuse it.

Organize Music

Once you have copied several CDs and have downloaded other music to you hard disk, you will want them organized. This is the function of Media Player's Media Library, shown in Figure 7-6. When music and videos are copied to the library, the contents are automatically indexed alphabetically by album, artist, and genre. You can also combine them into a playlist that allows you to play pieces from several albums. To build a new playlist:

> **TIP**
>
> When playing a playlist, you can randomize the order in which the pieces will play by clicking **Turn Shuffle On** in the Playlist selection controls, third button from the right. 

Figure 7-6: Media Library provides a way to manage the media you store on your computer

1. Click **Media Library** in the features taskbar, and then click **New Playlist** in the toolbar. Enter the name you want for the new playlist and click **OK**.
2. Open an album, artist, or genre, and select a piece you want in the new playlist. Either drag the piece to the playlist or click **Add To Playlist** in the toolbar and select the playlist.
3. When you have added all the pieces that you initially want (you can always add more later), listen to the pieces by selecting the playlist and clicking **Play** in the playback controls.

Make a Music CD

Once you have created a playlist (see "Organize Music" earlier in this chapter) you can write it to a writable or rewritable CD or to a solid-state music device, such as an MP3 player, using Media Player's Copy To CD Or Device feature, shown in Figure 7-7.

Figure 7-7: Copying a playlist to a writable CD

1. Put a blank recordable disk in the CD-R or CD-RW drive or connect your solid-state music device to the computer. (If the CD Drive dialog box opens, click **Take No Action,** and then click **OK**.)
2. While still in the Media Library, making sure your new playlist is selected, click **Copy To CD Or Device** in the features taskbar.
3. Make any corrections to the list of pieces that will be copied to the CD or solid-state device by selecting or deselecting the check boxes. You can also change the playlist by opening the playlist drop-down list (in Figure 7-7, this says "John Denver").
4. When you are sure you have the list of pieces you want to copy, click **Copy Music**. The digital files will first be converted to analog music files and then written to a CD or device. The Status column will show you the progress (it is not very fast!).

The resulting CD should be playable in most music CD players.

1 2 3 4 5 6 7 8 9 10

QUICKSTEPS

CHANGING THE LOOK OF MEDIA PLAYER

Media Player has two areas in which you can change its visual appearance: the visualizations in Now Playing and the outer frame or "skin" of the player.

CHANGE THE VISUALIZATION

In Media Player's Now Playing pane there is by default a graphic visualization of the music that is playing, as shown earlier in Figure 7-1. The Visualization controls described in "Play CDs" allow you to select one of the over 70 visualizations that come with Media Player in one of three ways:

- Click **Next Visualization** in the Visualization controls to cycle through each of the visualizations.
- Click **Select Visualization** in the Visualization controls to choose a category of visualization.
- Right-click the **Visualization** control bar, and select first a category and then a visualization, as shown in Figure 7-8.

CHANGE THE "SKIN" OF MEDIA PLAYER

You can change how Media Player looks by clicking **Skin Chooser** in the features taskbar, choosing one of the 20 skins, and clicking **Apply Skin**. If you don't like any of the 20 skins, click **More Skins**. If you are online or can be automatically connected, you will be connected to the WindowsMedia.com Skins page, where there are many more skins to choose from.

Some of the skins are very inventive and take a bit of figuring out, as shown by the Half Life 2 skin in Figure 7-9. Those that are quite small have an anchor window that that can be hidden but gives you some important controls, including switching back to full mode (the default look in all the previous figures), which you can also do by pressing CTRL+1.

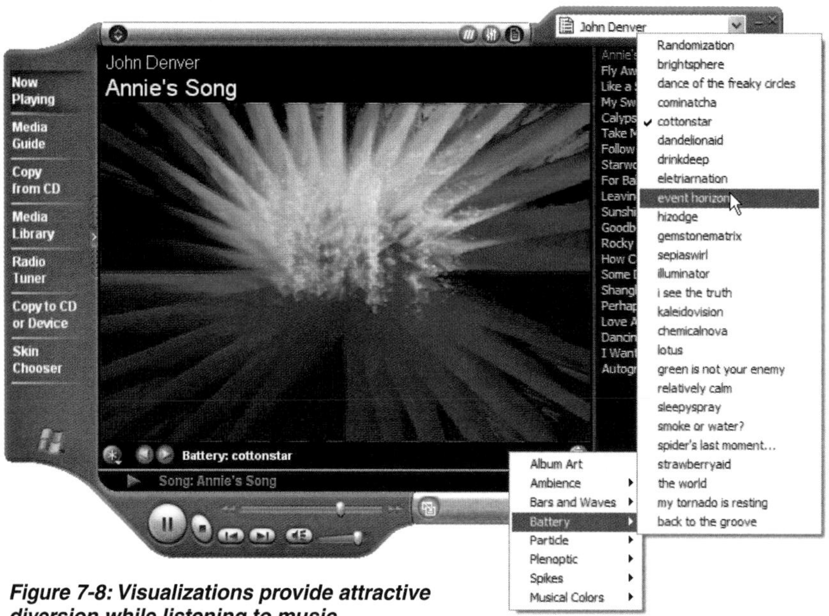

Figure 7-8: Visualizations provide attractive diversion while listening to music

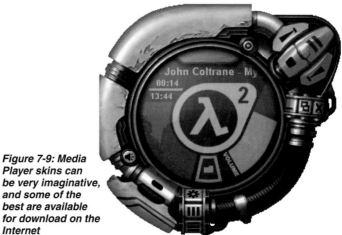

Figure 7-9: Media Player skins can be very imaginative, and some of the best are available for download on the Internet

NOTE

One major drawback with Windows Movie Maker is that you can save your video files only in the Windows Media Video file format, which can be played only with Windows Movie Maker on Windows Me, 2000, and XP systems.

TIP

If you are using Movie Maker to record an analog signal coming from a video capture card and are having problems–which is common–don't fight it. Use the software that comes with the video capture card to create a file on your hard disk, then import that file into Movie Maker (see "Import Files").

NOTE

There can be some copyright issues using music from professionally recorded CDs and tapes. If you are making a movie solely for your own use and are not going to put it on the Internet, sell it, or otherwise distribute it, then there are no issues. If you are going to use your movie in any of the prohibited ways and it contains someone else's copyrighted material (either audio or video), you need to get permission from the copyright holder.

Work with Video

Windows XP lets you play videos from a DVD using Media Player. It also allows you to capture and edit videos or slide shows from a camcorder or imported material using Movie Maker.

Play DVDs

Playing DVDs is as easy as playing CDs: simply insert a DVD into its drive. When you do that, you will be asked if you want Windows Media Player to play the disk. If you click **OK**, Media Player will open and play the disk. The Media Player controls are the same for DVDs as they are for CDs, except there are no visualization controls and the View Full Screen option enlarges the movie or video you are watching to fit the full screen.

Record Video

Recording video directly from your camcorder to your hard disk through Movie Maker is simple and often gives the best results. You start the process in one of two ways: plug your camera into a FireWire port where Windows XP will detect it, or start Windows Movie Maker and direct it to record.

PLUG INTO FIREWIRE

When you plug in to an OHCI-compliant FireWire port and turn on your camcorder, Windows XP will detect it, install the necessary software, and ask you if you want to start Windows Movie Maker.

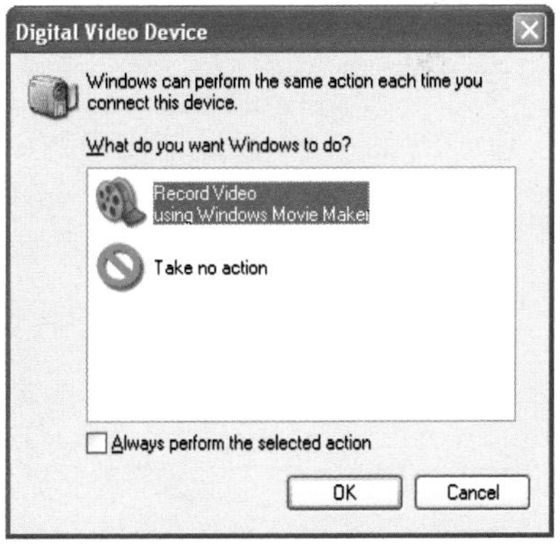

Accept the default, **Record Video,** and click **OK**. Movie Maker will start and open the Record dialog box.

QUICKSTEPS

PREPARING TO MAKE A MOVIE

Movie making with a computer takes more hardware than any other task. The faster your CPU, the more memory it has, and the larger your disk, the more smoothly the task will go. The beauty is that today's new computers have most of what you need.

DETERMINE REQUIREMENTS

The minimum and recommended hardware requirements for movie making are shown next.

Component	Microsoft Minimum	My Recommended
CPU	300 MHz Pentium III	1 GHz Pentium III
RAM memory	64 MB	256 MB
Hard drive free space	2 GB	20 GB
Video recording from DV camcorders	IEEE 1394 FireWire card, OHCI-compliant	
Video capture from analog VCR /Camera	Windows XP–compatible Video Capture card	
Audio capture from microphone, tape	Windows XP–compatible Audio card	

NOTES ON REQUIREMENTS

- Memory is most important. The more, the better.
- With a digital video (DV) camcorder and an IEEE 1394 FireWire interface, get an OHCI-compliant FireWire interface card for your computer.
- A video capture card can bring in an analog video signal from a TV, a VCR, an analog camcorder, and (in most cases) a DV camcorder; however, the result is not as good as a digital recording.
- To add narration and music to the sound track, you will need a sound card, a microphone, and a CD player or tape deck.

START MOVIE MAKER

If plugging in your camera didn't start Movie Maker, or if you are recording from a video capture card, then you need to manually start Movie Maker by opening **Start**, selecting **All Programs**, choosing **Accessories**, and clicking **Windows Movie Maker**. When Movie Maker completes loading, click **Record** in the toolbar. The Record dialog box will open. 

PREPARE FOR THE RECORDING

The Record dialog box, shown in Figure 7-10, has several settings to consider before recording:

- **Video Device**, in the upper-left, should show the device from which you are recording; if not, you need to change it.
- **Record Time Limit** is set to prevent you from running out of disk space (see the bottom-left of the dialog box).
- **Create Clips**, by breaking where the original taping was discontinued, gives you more manageable pieces to edit and is recommended.
- **Disable Preview While Recording** is helpful if you have limited hardware, but you will want to keep close track of the time, using notes you have made ahead of time.
- **Setting** adjusts the quality of the recording, which is dependent upon its intended use and the available disk space.

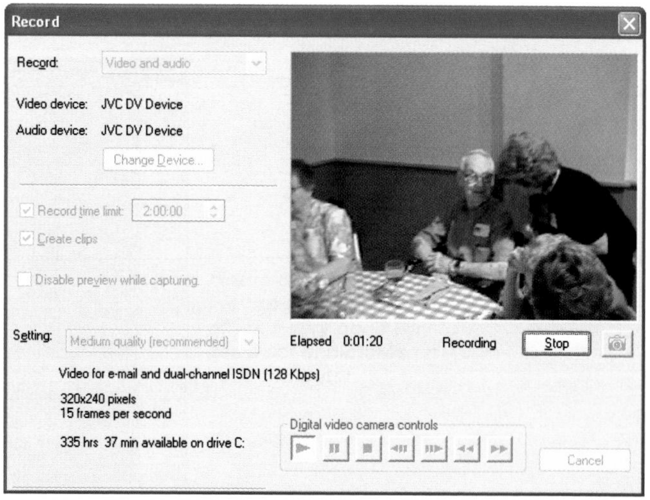

Figure 7-10: With a digital video (DV) camcorder you can directly record the contents of a tape onto your hard disk

1 2 3 4 5 6 7 8 9 10

RECORD

In the Record dialog box, you play the tape and record what you want of it. You can start recording immediately to record the entire tape, or you can record only portions of the tape.

With a DV device through a FireWire port, you can use the controls at the bottom of the Record dialog box to start, stop, advance, and rewind the tape in the camera. Otherwise, you must control the camera or VCR using their own controls.

To record the entire tape, click **Record,** and then start the camera or VCR. To record just segments of the tape, start the camera or VCR, and when you reach the first segment you wish to record, click **Record**.

When you are done recording, click **Stop**. The Record dialog box closes, and you are returned to the Movie Maker window, which will show your newly recorded video and begin the creation of clips from your video.

TIP

When recording several segments of a tape, you may want to stop and back up the tape just a bit, start recording, and then restart the tape.

Import Files

Windows Movie Maker can import a number of file formats, including video, audio, and still pictures (as shown in Table 7-1). These files can be used alone or in combination with recorded clips.

TABLE 7-1: FORMATS FOR MOVIEMAKER IMPORTATION

Type of File	File Formats
Audio	AFC, AIF, AIFC, AIFF, AU, MP3, SND, WAV, WMA
Still Images	BMP, DIB, GIF, JFIF, JPE, JPEG, JPG
Video	ASF, AVI, M1V, MP2, MPA, MPE, MPEG, MPG, WM, WMV

1. If it isn't already open, start Windows Movie Maker by opening **Start**, selecting **All Programs**, choosing **Accessories**, and clicking **Windows Movie Maker**.
2. In Movie Maker, open **File,** and choose **Import**. The Select The File To Import dialog box will open.
3. Select the file you want to import, make sure **Create Clips For Video Files** is checked, and click **Open**. If you are importing a video file, it will be divided into clips. If you are importing either a still image or audio, it will simply go into Movie Maker.

In all cases, the material you imported will appear in the center area of Movie Maker for use in editing and assembling a movie.

Use Movie Maker

Creating a movie out of the captured and imported material involves selecting and editing the available material and then assembling it into the finished product. The window for doing this has three main sections (shown in Figure 7-11):

- **Collections**, on the left of the window, has two panes—a folders pane on the left and a clips pane on the right. If you want more room for the clips pane, you can drag the border between the panes or turn off the folders pane by clicking **Close** in the upper right of the pane.
- **Monitor**, on the right of the window, displays or plays the current clip or the entire movie and displays still images.
- **Workspace**, on bottom of the window, has two views:
- **Storyboard view** (shown in Figure 7-11) is the default view and allows you to easily sequence your clips and rearrange them by dragging.
- **Timeline view** gives you a precise time measurement of your clips and allows you to trim them, adjust the transitions between clips, and add music and narration.

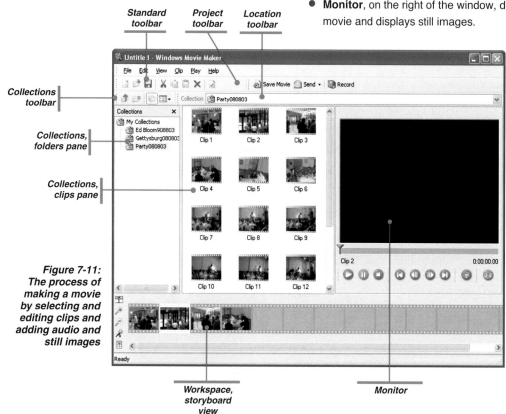

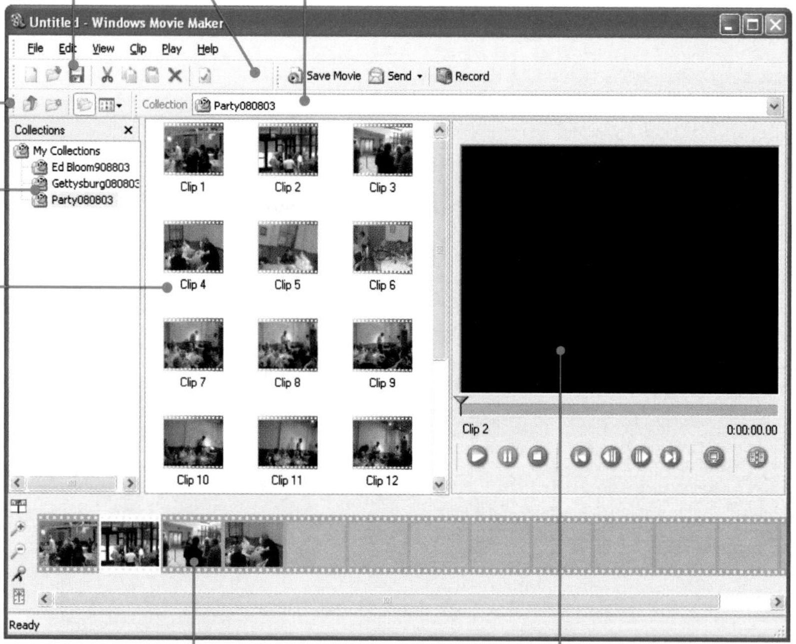

Figure 7-11: The process of making a movie by selecting and editing clips and adding audio and still images

1 2 3 4 5 6 7 8 9 10

NOTE

In Movie Maker terminology, what you record is called a *collection* of clips. Think of a collection as a folder. A clip is a small segment of video, generally one episode of turning the camera on and then off. A *clip* is made up of a series of frames, where each *frame* is a still image that when viewed in rapid succession creates the illusion of motion. As you build a movie, during the in-process stages, it is called and saved as a *project*. Only when you are done and satisfied with the finished project do you save it as a *movie*.

NOTE

Deleting a clip in the workspace does not delete it from the collection; you can re-insert it at a later time, if desired.

The Movie Maker window holds many tools to help you convert video clips, sound, and still images into a movie. In addition to a complete set of menus, four toolbars can be displayed.

- **Standard toolbar**: create a new project, open one, or save one; cut, copy, paste, and delete clips; and open clip properties
- **Project toolbar**: save a movie, send a movie to a web site or e-mail it, and record video
- **Location toolbar**: move up one-level, start a new collection, toggle the Collections list, and change the view
- **Collections toolbar**: select a collection

In the workspace, especially in timeline view, there are also a number of tools that are discussed in the QuickSteps, "Editing Video Clips."

Select Video Clips

Selecting and organizing of clips is a very laborious phase, but it provides the foundation for your project and determines what you have to work with in the editing phase. The process of selecting which parts of which video clips to use has four steps:

1. Double-click the first clip to play it. Decide if you want to use it, if it needs to be trimmed and where, and make appropriate notes.
2. If you want to use the clip, drag it to the workspace, dropping it where you want it in the string of existing clips.
3. Periodically right-click the workspace and choose **Play Entire Storyboard/Timeline** to see how the selection and organization is coming along in the series of clips.
4. If desired, rearrange the clips by dragging them to a different location in the string and/or by deleting a clip you no longer want in the project/movie.

While working in this phase, the storyboard view of the workspace is probably the best view to use, offering the easiest means to see the progression of clips and to drag the clips around the storyboard.

QUICKSTEPS

EDITING VIDEO CLIPS

Editing consists of combining, splitting, and trimming clips to get what you want and then adjusting the transitions between clips to produce the effects you want. When editing clips, the timeline view is probably the best (except for combining). In timeline view, shown in Figure 7-12, clips are shown in proportion to the amount of time they take, and there are a number of tools for project editing.

COMBINE CLIPS

Movie Maker creates clips on a "best guess" basis, breaking a clip where the camera was paused. To combine two or more clips:

1. In the workspace storyboard view, click a short clip that you want to handle with its adjacent clip.
2. Hold down **SHIFT** and click the adjacent clip. If you want to combine additional adjacent clips, continue to hold **SHIFT** and click them.
3. When the clips you want to combine have been selected, right-click them and choose **Combine** from the context menu. The selected clips will become one clip. Press **SPACEBAR** to play the combined clip.

SPLIT A CLIP

To remove frames from the middle of a clip, you need to split them.

1. In timeline view, click a clip that you want to split. Press **SPACEBAR** to start playing the clip. When it nearly reaches the point where you want to split it, press **SPACEBAR** again to pause the play.
2. Use the play controls under the monitor (shown in Figure 7-13) to go forward or backward until you have found the precise spot in the clip where you want it split.
3. Click **Split Clip** on the right of the play controls.

TRIM CLIPS

You can remove unwanted frames by *trimming,* or deleting, frames from the beginning or end of a clip:

Continued…

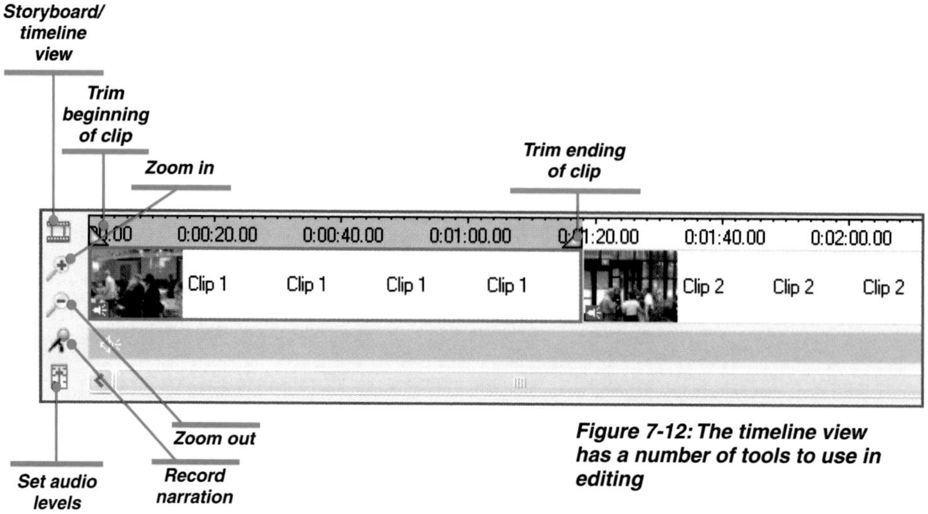

Figure 7-12: The timeline view has a number of tools to use in editing

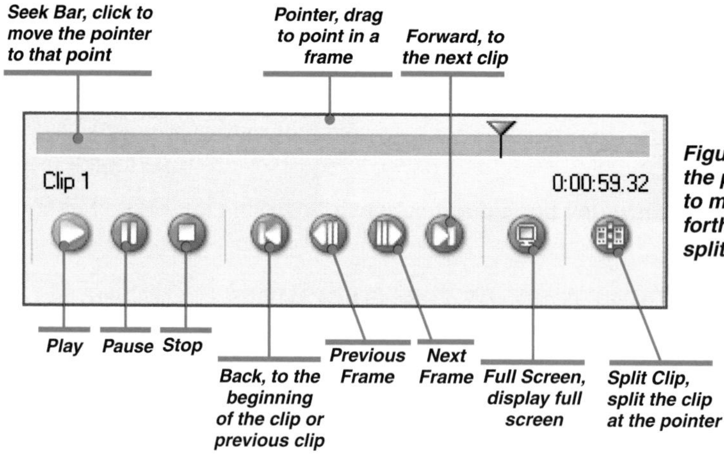

Figure 7-13: Use the play controls to move back and forth and to select a split point in a clip

EDITING VIDEO CLIPS *(Continued)*

1. Select timeline view, if it isn't already selected, and click the clip you want to trim. It will appear with *trimming handles,* which are the small triangles in the corners of the beginning and end of the clip's timeline.

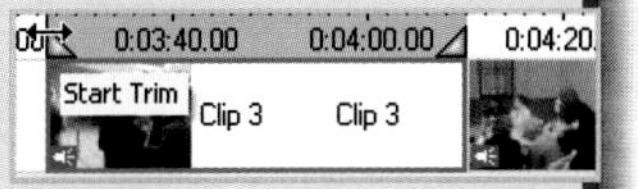

2. Click **Zoom In** to increase the level of detail displayed and to give you greater accuracy in trimming.
3. To trim the beginning of the clip, drag the left trimming handle the desired amount to the right. After an initial trim, play the clip and see the result. If you don't like it, you can adjust the trim.
4. To trim the end of the clip, drag the right trimming handle to the left as you did with the beginning.

ADJUST TRANSITIONS

When you drag a clip to the workspace, it simply abuts the preceding clip. The last frame of the preceding clip plays, and then the first frame of the new clip plays. Movie Maker allows you to partially overlap one clip with another, simultaneously creating a fade out/fade in transition between the two clips. You do this in the timeline by dragging the right-most clip of a pair to the left, over the other clip. You can do this for as much of the clip as you want, but the recommended time is about half a second.

TIP

Zoom in and zoom out in the timeline view of the workspace are time oriented, not visual. In other words, when you zoom in, each timeline division uses a smaller increment of time and each clip takes more space. This is useful for trimming a clip, as you'll see in a moment.

Add Sound to a Movie

Sound is added to a project by either inserting an audio clip or recording narration. The audio clip is an audio file that has been imported into Movie Maker. It can be of any length and in any of the formats identified earlier. Once you have imported it into the parent collection's folder, you can drag it to the workspace in timeline view. (If you try to add an audio clip in storyboard view, you'll get a message that the view needs to change. If you click **OK**, it will be.) To record narrative:

1. Make sure your microphone is connected to your computer and working properly, then click **Record Narration** on the left of the timeline view of the workspace. The Record Narration Track dialog box will open.
2. Talk into your microphone and adjust the Record Level so the bar fills about half of the column.
3. Click **Record**, record the narration you want to add, and when you are finished, click **Stop**. Enter a file name for the audio file that was created from the recorded narration, and click **Save**. The recorded sound clip will appear both on the timeline and in the clips pane.

NOTE

Because there is no way to delete individual frames from the middle of a clip, you need to split a clip if you need to delete frames from its middle.

NOTE

At any time while you are working in the project—even after saving, closing, and reopening it—you can adjust the trim backward or forward, recovering the part you trimmed away.

NOTE

Once a sound clip is in the workspace, it can be selected and trimmed, dragged anywhere in the timeline, and overlapped in the same ways a video clip can be.

After adding a sound clip, either an imported file or a narrated one, you have two sound tracks, one that was on the original recorded tape and one that you have added. By default, the volume level of both tracks is the same unless you click Mute Video Soundtrack in the Record Narration Track dialog box. You can adjust the relative level between the two sound tracks by clicking Set Audio Levels at the bottom left of the workspace in timeline view. The Audio Levels dialog box will open, as you can see next. Dragging the slider one way or the other sets the relative level between the two tracks for the entire project.

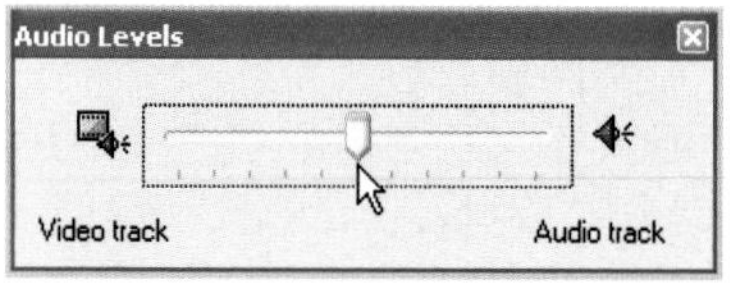

Add Titles and Still Pictures to a Movie

Titles and still images are discussed together because Movie Maker does not have its own titling capability. To make titles, you must create them in some other program—such as Paint, Adobe Illustrator, or Microsoft PowerPoint—then save the title page in one of the still image formats that can be imported into Movie Maker. To make a title or a graphic, import it into Movie Maker, and drag it to a project:

1. Open a graphics program, create the title or graphic, and save it in a format that can be imported into Movie Maker (see Table 7-1).
2. In Movie Maker, open **File,** and choose **Import**. Locate and select the title or graphic file to be imported, and click **Open**. The title image will be imported.
3. Drag the image to the workspace at the point where you want it.

By default, the title slide is played for five seconds, but you can drag the right trim handle to the right to lengthen its play time as long as you wish. This will overlap the clip to the right, but if you don't want that, you can drag that clip to the right and all the clips to the right will move with it.

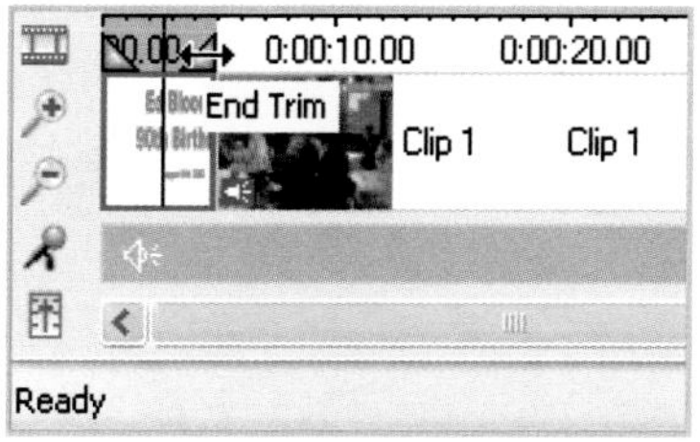

TIP

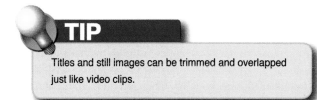

Titles and still images can be trimmed and overlapped just like video clips.

NOTE

Opening a *project* opens the media in Movie Maker, where it can be edited. Opening a *movie* sets it up for playback in Media Player.

Save a Movie

The final step in making a movie is to save it as a Windows video file that can be played by Windows Media Player. When you are happy with your project:

1. Click **Save Movie** in the project toolbar. The Save Movie dialog box will open, as shown in Figure 7-14.
2. Select the quality you want, enter a name and any other information you want, and then click **OK**.
3. Enter the file name and click **Save**. The saving process will take a bit of time, depending on the speed of your computer and the amount of memory.
4. Click **OK** if you want to play the movie. You can also double-click the resulting file, which is stored by default in the My Videos folder, and Media Player will play the movie. Be sure to save the project one last time by following the prompts when you close Movie Maker.

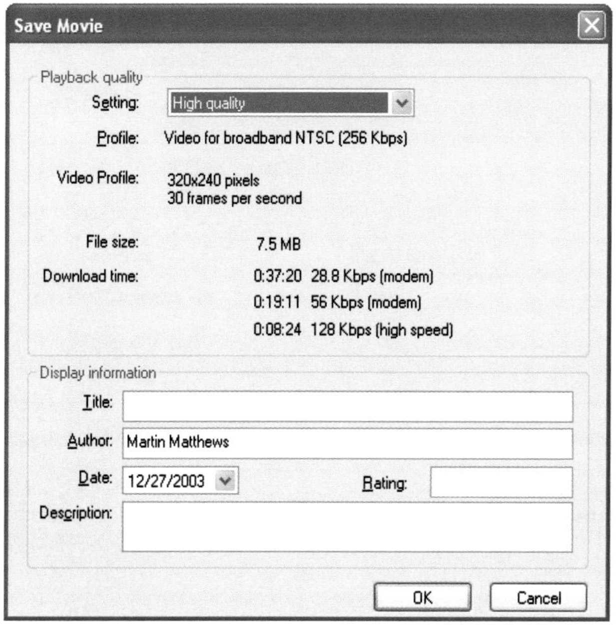

Figure 7-14: Saving a movie is equivalent to printing a document: you still have the original content to rebuild the movie, but the movie itself can't be edited

How to...

- *Set Up a User*
- *Setting Passwords*
- *Reset a Password*
- *Replace Passwords*
- *Customize a User Account*
- *Change Log On Procedure*
- *Switch Among Users*
- *Manage Multiple Users*
- *Set File Sharing*
- *Use and Add Groups*
- *Set Permissions*
- *Protecting Files and Folders*
- *Use Encrypted Files and Folders*
- *Lock a Computer*
- *Set Up an Internet Firewall*

Chapter 8
Controlling Security

Controlling computer security is a complex subject because of the many different aspects that need protection. In this chapter you'll see how to control who uses a computer, control what a user does, protect data stored in the computer, and protect the computer from Internet attack.

Control Who Is a User

Controlling who is a user of a computer means to identify the users to the computer, giving users a secure way of signing on to the computer, while preventing others from using it. This is the process of adding and managing users and passwords.

Set Up a User

If you have multiple people using a single computer, the best protection is to set up separate user accounts that require each user to sign on. To set up a user account:

1 2 3 4 5 6 7 8 9 10

> **NOTE**
>
> This book talks about setting up *local* user accounts, which are set up on and use a local computer and a local area network (LAN). If you and your computer are part of a domain, it is important to use domain user accounts set up on a domain controller. See Chapter 9 for a discussion of domains.

> **NOTE**
>
> Most sets of steps in this chapter require that you be logged on as an administrator. You'll know if you are an administrator by opening the User Accounts window with the steps under "Set Up a User" and seeing whether your account is labeled "Computer Administrator" or "Limited Account."

> **NOTE**
>
> Normally, the first user of a computer is the Computer Administrator and the remaining users have either administrator or limited accounts. The administrator can change passwords and install programs. Limited accounts can change only their own passwords and may or may not be able to install software, depending on the program.

1. While logged on as an administrator, open **Start**, and choose **Control Panel**. While in Classic view, double-click **User Accounts**. The User Accounts window opens.
2. Click **Create A New Account** and enter a name of up to 20 characters. Note that it cannot contain just periods, spaces, or the @ symbol; it cannot contain " / \ [ ] : ; | = ,+ * ? < >; and leading spaces or periods are dropped. Click **Next**.
3. Choose either **Computer Administrator** or **Limited** as the account type. The default is Computer Administrator and its privileges are shown. If you move the mouse over **Limited** (you don't have to click), you can see the privileges there.
4. Click **Create Account**. You are returned to the main User Accounts window. Move the mouse pointer over the new account to see the items you can change in the account, as shown in Figure 8-1 and described in later sections of this chapter.

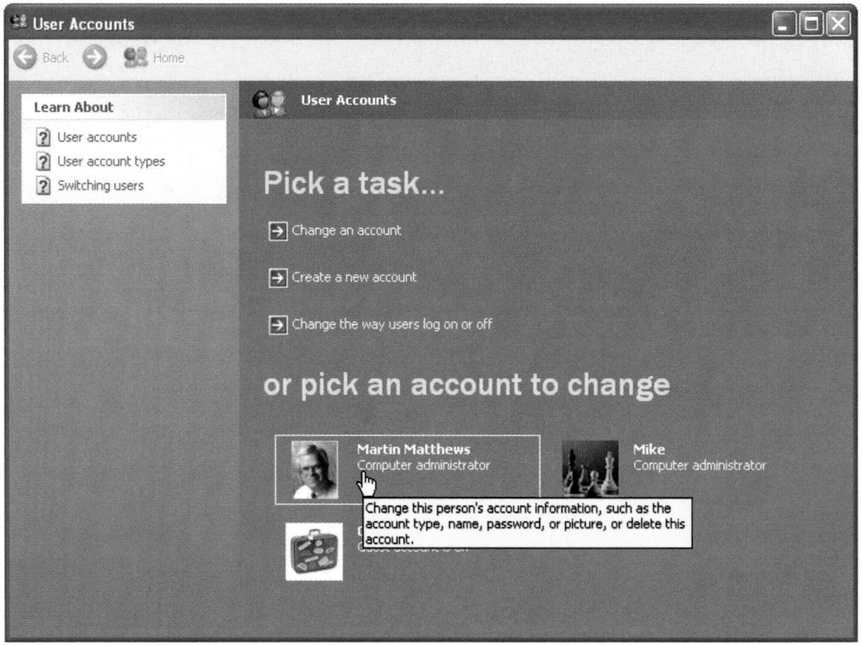

Figure 8-1: Setting up users provides a way of protecting each user from the others and from unauthorized use

QUICKSTEPS

SETTING PASSWORDS

Passwords are the primary keys used to allow some to use a computer and to keep others away. While there are recent alternatives to passwords, see "Replace Passwords" in this chapter, most computer protection depends on them.

CREATE A PASSWORD

After setting up a new user account, add a password that will then be required to use that account.

1. While logged on as an administrator, open **Start** and choose **Control Panel**. While in Classic view, double-click **User Accounts**.
2. Click the account to which you want to add a password. The individual user window opens, as shown in Figure 8-2. Click **Create A Password**.
3. Type the new password, press **TAB**, type the new password again to confirm it, press **TAB** twice, type a non-obvious hint to help you remember the password, and click **Create Password**.
4. If you want to make your files private (keep people with limited accounts from opening your files), click **Yes, Make Private** (this may take a few minutes); otherwise, click **No**. Close User Accounts and the Control Panel.

CHANGE A PASSWORD

If a password has been compromised or if for some other reason it needs to change, you can do so.

1. While logged on as an administrator, open **Start** and choose **Control Panel**. While in Classic view, double-click **User Accounts**. The User Accounts window opens.
2. Click the account for which you want to change the password, and click **Change My/The Password**.
3. Type the current password, press **TAB**, type a new password, press **TAB**, and type the new password

Continued...

Reset a Password

Windows XP has a new feature that allows you to reset a password you have forgotten if you have previously created a reset disk.

CREATE A RESET DISK

1. Insert a floppy disk (either an unused disk or one whose contents can be erased) in its drive. Open **Start**, select **My Computer**, right-click the floppy drive, and choose **Format**. Click **Start** and click **OK** to acknowledge that all data will be erased. When the formatting is finished, click **OK**, close the Format 3½ Floppy dialog box, and close My Computer.

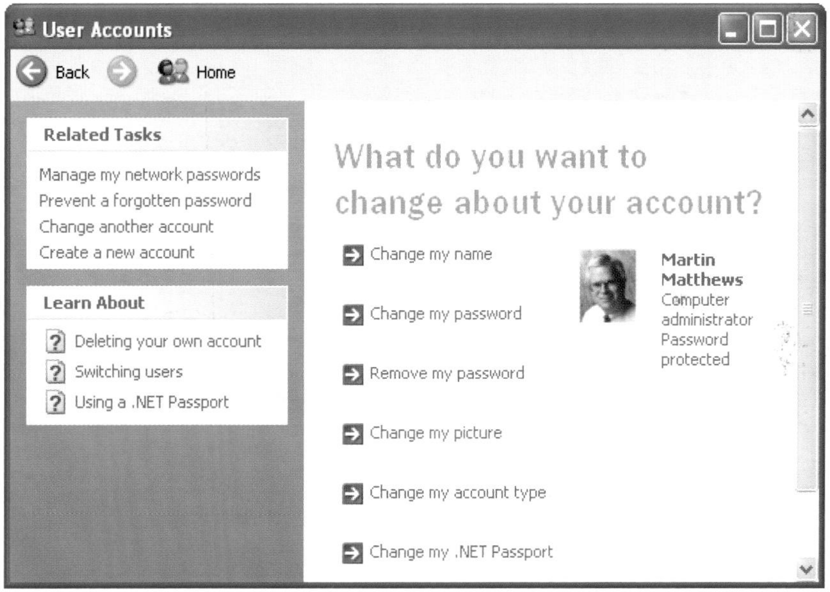

Figure 8-2: User Accounts provides password and user account management

SETTING PASSWORDS *(Continued)*

again to confirm it. Press **TAB** twice, type a non-obvious hint to help you remember the password, and click **Change Password**.

4. Close User Accounts and the Control Panel.

REMOVE A PASSWORD

If you want to remove a password, you can do so.

1. While logged on as an administrator, open **Start** and choose **Control Panel**. While in Classic view, double-click **User Accounts**. The User Accounts window opens.
2. Click the account for which you want to remove the password, click **Remove The/My Password**. If you are removing your own, type your current password. In any case, click **Remove Password**.
3. Close User Accounts and the Control Panel.

TIP

A strong password must have over six characters, use both upper- and lowercase letters, and use a mixture of letters, numbers, and symbols.

NOTE

If your password is over 14 characters, you will not be able to log on to a network from a Windows 95/98/Me computer.

CAUTION

Creating a new password wipes out any other passwords and other security elements for that user, including logon password, passwords for web sites, personal certificates, and encrypted files.

2. Open **Start** and choose **Control Panel**. While in Classic view, double-click **User Accounts**. The User Accounts window opens. If you have a Limited Account, click **Prevent A Forgotten Password** in Related Tasks in the tasks pane.
3. If you have an administrator's account, click your account to open it, and click **Prevent A Forgotten Password** in Related Tasks in the tasks pane.
4. The Forgotten Password Wizard opens. Click **Next**. If you haven't already, insert a blank, formatted floppy disk into its drive. Click **Next** again.
5. Enter the current user account password, and again click **Next**. The disk will be created. When it is done, click **Next**. Then click **Finish**. Remove and label the disk and store it in a safe place.
6. Close User Accounts and the Control Panel.

USE A RESET DISK

If you have forgotten your password and there isn't another person with administrator permissions on your computer who can reset your password, then you can use a reset disk you have previously created.

1. Start your computer. When you reach the Welcome screen, click your name. If you have forgotten your password, click the question mark and look at your hint.

2. If the hint isn't of any help, click the green arrow. In the balloon message that opens, click **Use Your Password Reset Disk**. The Password Reset Wizard opens.
3. Click **Next**. Insert your password reset disk, and again click **Next**. Type a new password, confirm it, type a password hint, click **Next**, and click **Finish**.
4. Once more, click your name, enter your new password, and press **ENTER**.

NOTE

An administrator can also reset a password.

CAUTION

With a reset disk, anyone can reset a password. Therefore, it is very important to store the reset disk in a safe place.

CAUTION

When you reset a password, either through an administrator or with a reset disk, all passwords and encrypted files tied to the original password are no longer accessible with the new password.

Replace Passwords

The weakest link in the Windows XP security scheme is the use of passwords. Users give their passwords to others or forget them, and passwords are stolen or just "found." There is nothing to tie a password to an individual. Two potential means of replacing passwords are smart cards and biometric devices.

SMART CARDS

Smart cards are credit card–sized pieces of plastic that have a tamper-resistant electronic circuit embedded in them that permanently stores an ID, a password, and other information. Smart cards require a personal identification number (PIN), so they add a second layer (smart card plus PIN in place of a password) that is needed to log on to a system.

Windows XP detects and supports smart cards and lets them be used to log on to a computer or network, as well as used for other authentication needs.

Smart cards require a reader attached to the computer through either a USB (universal serial bus) port or a PCMCIA (Personal Computer Memory Card International Association) slot. With a smart card reader, users only need to insert their card at the logon screen, at which point they are prompted for their PIN. With a valid card and PIN, users are authenticated and allowed on the system in the same way as they would be by entering a valid user name and password.

Windows XP lists a number of smart card readers that Microsoft has tested with Windows XP. The drivers for these devices either are included with or are available for Windows XP, and installing them is not difficult; you need only follow the instructions that come with them.

1 2 3 4 5 6 7 8 9 10

1

2

3

4

5

6

7

8

9

10

> **NOTE**
>
> In case you wondered, the PIN is encrypted and placed on the smart card when it is made. The PIN is not stored on the computer.

With a smart card reader installed, set up new accounts (as described under "Set Up a User") and then, for both new and old accounts, open each user's Create Password page and click **Smart Card Is Required For Interactive Logon**, which will appear when a smart card is present. You do not have to enter a password.

BIOMETRIC DEVICES

Smart cards do provide an added degree of security over passwords, but if someone obtains both the card and the PIN, she's home free. The only way to be totally sure that the computer is actually talking to the authorized person is to require some physical identification of the person.

This is the purpose of *biometric devices,* which identify people by physical traits, such as voice, handprint, fingerprint, face, or eyes. Often, these devices are used with a smart card to replace the PIN. Biometric devices are just moving into the mass production stage, and nothing is built into Windows XP specifically to handle them. Devices and custom installations are available from around $100 for a fingerprint scanner to several thousand dollars for a face scanner. In the next few years, these devices will be everywhere. Depending on your needs, you may want to keep them in mind.

Customize a User Account

Each user account can be unique, with his or her Start menu, desktop, color scheme, and screen saver. When programs are installed, you can choose whether they are for just the current user or all users. When you set up a new user, it is as though you are setting up a new computer. The previous chapters of this book talk about how to do that.

As you saw in Figure 8-2, a number of elements of the account itself can be changed, including the name, password, picture, and account type. You can change the name and password in a manner almost identical to what you used to create them, as described in "Set Up a User" and "Setting Passwords" earlier in this chapter.

CHANGE PICTURE

When an account is first established, a clip art image is assigned to the user. If you wish to change it:

1. Open **Start** and choose **Control Panel**. While in Classic view, double-click **User Accounts**. The User Accounts window opens.
2. Click the account for which you want to change the picture, and click **Change The/My Picture**. The window shown in Figure 8-3 opens.
3. Select one of the pieces of clip art or click **Browse For More Pictures**. Locate and select the picture, and click **Open**.
4. Close User Accounts and the Control Panel.

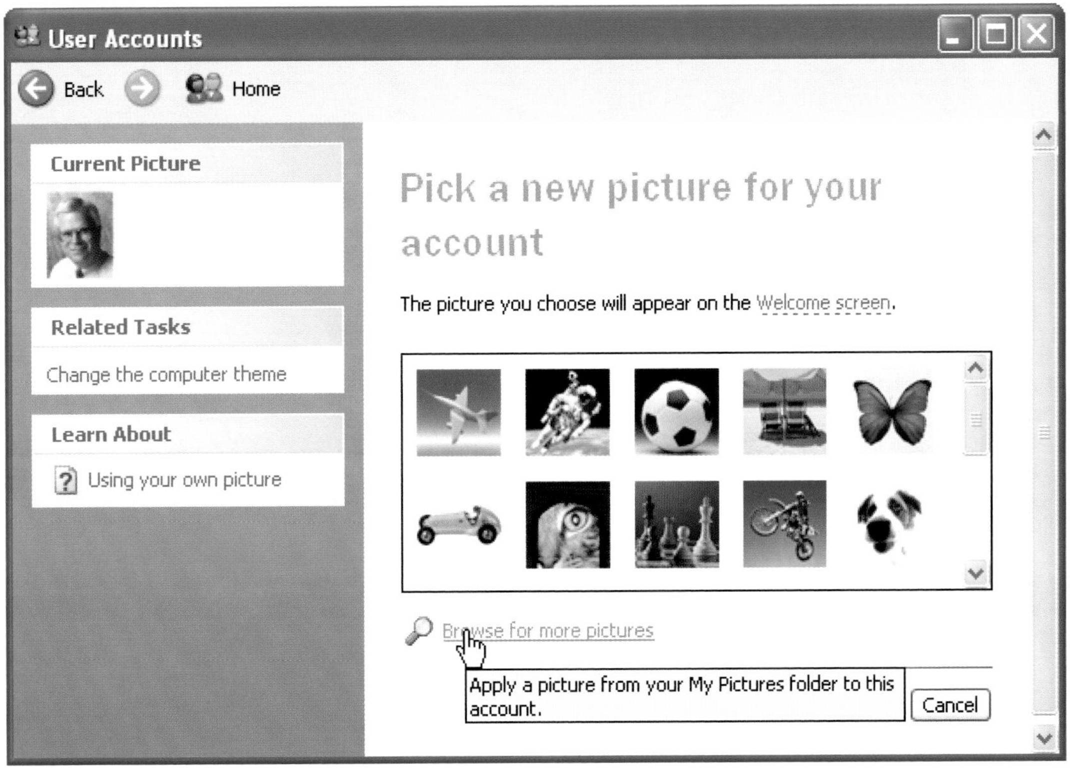

Figure 8-3: You can use one of your own pictures for the user account picture

CHANGE ACCOUNT TYPE

There are two types of user accounts. To switch between them:

1. Open **Start** and choose **Control Panel**. While in Classic view, double-click **User Accounts**. The User Accounts window opens.
2. Click the account you want to change, and click **Change The/My Account Type**.
3. Select one of the following account types:
   - **Computer Administrator** allows installation of all programs, access to all files, and the ability to make system-wide changes and to create and change accounts.
   - **Limited** allows only viewing shared files or files created by the user, and changing only the user's personal account picture and password.
4. Click **Change Account Type** and close User Accounts and the Control Panel.

Change Log On Procedure

The default log on procedure utilizes the "Welcome screen" that you saw in Chapter 1 and in the illustration earlier in this chapter. It is one of two ways to log on. The other method is to use the classic log on prompt in which you enter your user name and password. To change to the log on prompt method:

Figure 8-4: If you switch to the log on prompt, you must give up Fast User Switching that allows you to switch users without shutting down your programs

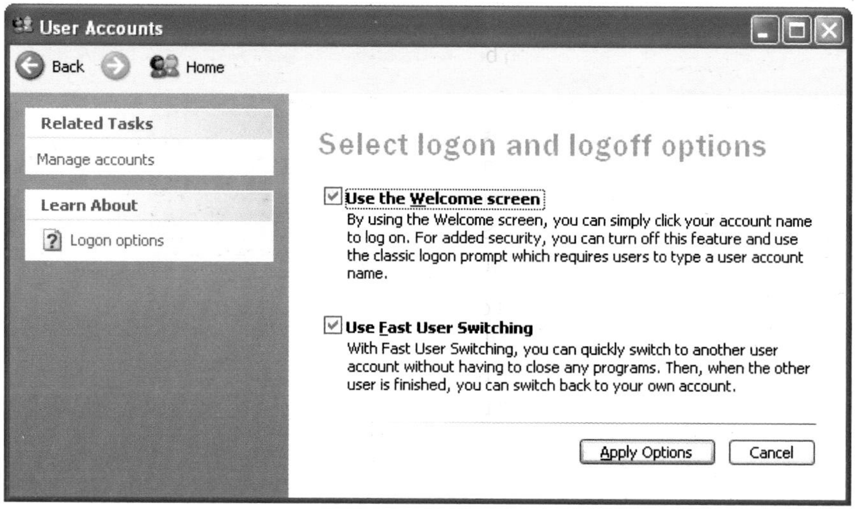

1. Open **Start** and choose **Control Panel**. While in Classic view, double-click **User Accounts**. The User Accounts window opens.
2. Click **Change The Way Users Log On Or Off**. The window changes to that shown in Figure 8-4.
3. Deselect **Use The Welcome Screen**, note that you can no longer use Fast User Switching, and click **Apply Options**. Close User Accounts and the Control Panel.
4. Log off your system. After a couple of moments in which Windows shuts down, the Log On To Windows dialog box appears in which your user name is filled in, leaving you to enter your password.
5. Enter your password and click **OK**. You're back in your system. Repeat steps 1 through 3 to switch back to the Welcome Screen.

Switch among Users

When you have multiple users on a computer, one can obviously log off and another log on; however, if you are using the Welcome screen, you can use Fast User Switching (see Figure 8-4). This allows you to keep programs running and files open when you temporarily switch to another user. Use the steps under "Change Logon Procedure" to turn Fast User Switching on or off. To use Fast User Switching:

1. Open **Start** and click **Log Off**. Click **Switch User**. The Welcome screen will appear. Let the other person log on.
2. When the other person has finished and has logged off, you can log on normally. When you do, you will see all your programs exactly as you left them.

Figure 8-5: The User Accounts dialog box allows to you to see and change user names, reset passwords, and force entry of ctrl+alt+delete to log on

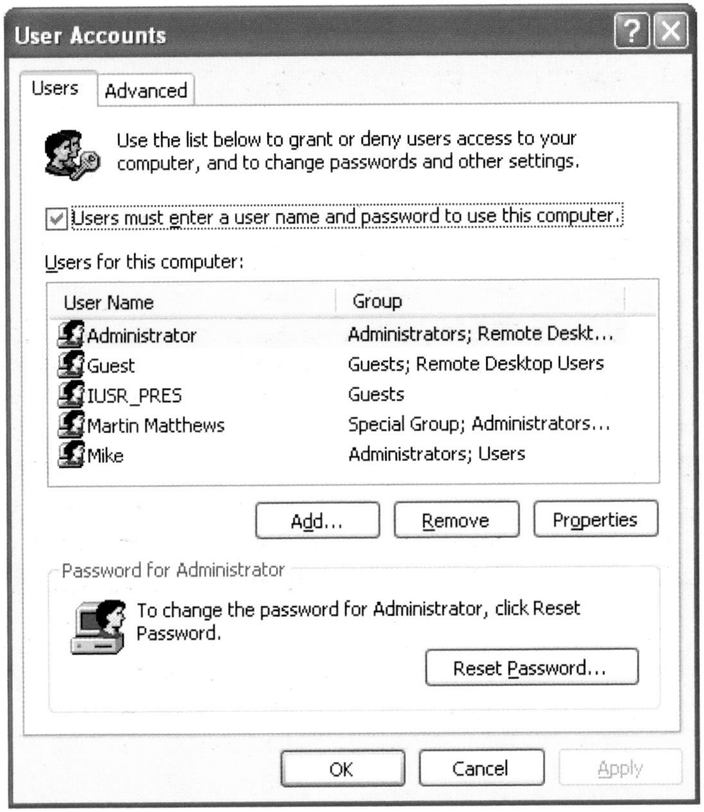

Manage Multiple Users

You can manage multiple users as has been described in the previous sections, yet there is a more detailed User Accounts management dialog box you can use, shown in Figure 8-5. Although it is well hidden, you can open it.

1. Open **Start**, click **Run**, and type control userpasswords2. The User Accounts dialog box will open with the Users tab displayed (see Figure 8-5).
2. Double-click a user name. Here, in the General tab, you can change the user name, the full name, and description. In the Group Membership tab, you can determine what groups the user belongs to (see "Set User Permissions" later in this chapter). Close the user's Properties dialog box.
3. In the upper part of the User Accounts dialog box Users tab, you can determine if the users have to log on with a user name and password. In the bottom part, if you logged on as an administrator, you can reset all user passwords but your own.

1 2 3 4 5 6 7 8 9 10

> **NOTE**
>
> The reason that it is a good idea to use **CTRL+ALT+DELETE** is that this stops every program in the system except the one controlling the entry of **CTRL+ALT+DELETE**, so no other program can pick up your user name and password.

> **NOTE**
>
> Simple File Sharing is permanently turned on in Windows XP Home Edition and can be turned off only in Windows XP Professional.

4. Click the **Advanced** tab. Here you can manage passwords and open the Local Users and Groups window. In the bottom of the Advanced tab to you can specify that all users have to press **CTRL+ALT+DELETE** in order to sign in.
5. When you are done looking at these user management functions, click **OK** to close the User Accounts dialog.
6. If you made any changes to your account, you will be asked if you want to log off and back on again for the changes to take effect. Click **Yes**.

Control What a User Does

User accounts identify people and allow them to log on. What they can then do depends on the permissions they have. Windows XP with the NT File System (NTFS) allows the assignment of permissions for an object. You cannot do this with the FAT or FAT32 file system.

When you install Windows XP, the default is to use *Simple File Sharing,* where most objects give permission for local users to do almost anything, but withhold permission for everyone not a local user. With Windows XP Professional you can turn off Simple File Sharing and change the initial settings using *inheritance* where all files, subfolders, and files in subfolders automatically inherit (take on) the permissions of their parent folder. Every object in Windows XP NTFS, though, has its own set of *security descriptors* that are attached to it when it is created, and with the proper permission, these security descriptors can be individually changed.

NOTE

The first two lines at the top Properties Sharing tab imply that the folder is not shared on the local computer by default and that you must drag it to the Shared Documents folder to be shared. That is *not* correct. All files and folders are shared by default among all users on the computer unless you change that status.

NOTE

When you share or make a folder private, all folders and files within it are given the same sharing status due to inheritance. If that is not what you want for a particular folder, you must individually change its sharing status.

NOTE

You only get the Network Setup Wizard the first time you attempt to do network file sharing.

Set File Sharing

With Simple File Sharing, folders are shared by the creator or owner of an object or by an administrator. Folders are shared, both locally and over the network, through the object's Properties dialog box. Files are shared by being in a shared folder.

1. Open **Start** and choose **My Computer**. Click **Folders** on the toolbar.
2. In the left pane, open the disk and folders necessary to see in the right pane the folder you want to share.
3. Right-click the folder and choose **Properties**. In the Properties dialog box, click the **Sharing** tab, which will open as shown in Figure 8-6. In the Sharing tab, you can reverse the defaults and make the folder private to the local computer users and you can share it on the network.
4. To share the folder over the network, in the lower box under Network Sharing And Security, click **Network Setup Wizard** (the link at the end of the first paragraph), which will then open. (See Chapter 9 on setting up a network.)
5. Click **Next** twice. Select the type of Internet connection you have and click **Next**. Enter the computer description, click **Next**, enter the workgroup name, and click **Next** twice. Select whether you want a network setup disk for other computers, click **Next** again, and click **Finish**.
6. Back in the folder Properties dialog box, you can choose to share the folder, give it a share name, and determine if you want to allow network users to change it. When you are finished, click **OK**, and then close Windows Explorer.

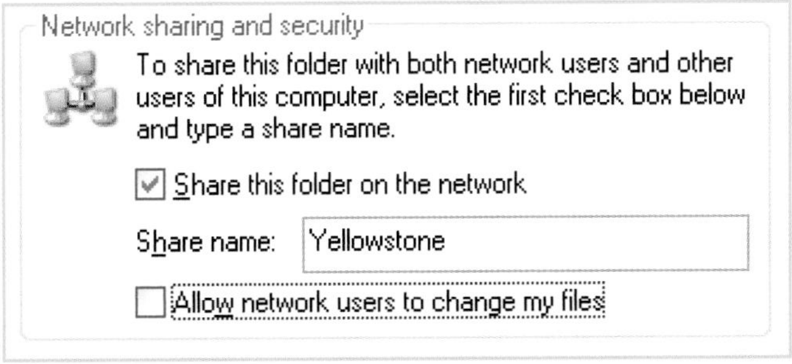

Use and Add Groups

NOTE

Windows XP Home Edition offers limited security and permissions and doesn't support groups.

Groups, or *group accounts*, are collections of user accounts that can have permissions, such as file sharing, granted to them. Most permissions are granted to groups, not individuals, and then individuals are made members of the groups. (See the next section on permissions.) You need a set of groups that handles both the mix of people and the mix of permissions that you want to establish. A number of standard groups with preassigned permissions are built into Windows XP Professional, but you can create your own groups, and you can assign users to any of these.

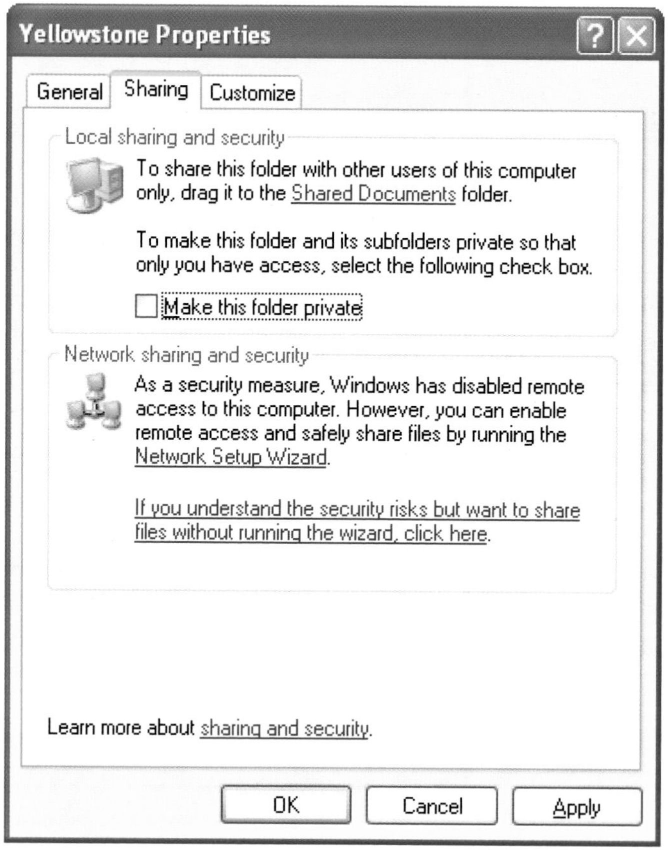

Figure 8-6: The first step in sharing a folder is to run the Network Setup Wizard

OPEN EXISTING GROUPS

To open the groups in Windows XP Professional and see what permissions they contain:

1. Open **Start** and choose **Control Panel**. While in Classic view, double-click **Administrative Tools**, and then double-click **Computer Management**.
2. In the pane on the left, open **System Tools**, open **Local Users And Groups**, and click **Groups**. The list of built-in groups is displayed, as shown in Figure 8-7.
3. Double-click a few groups to open the Properties dialog box for each and see the members of that group.

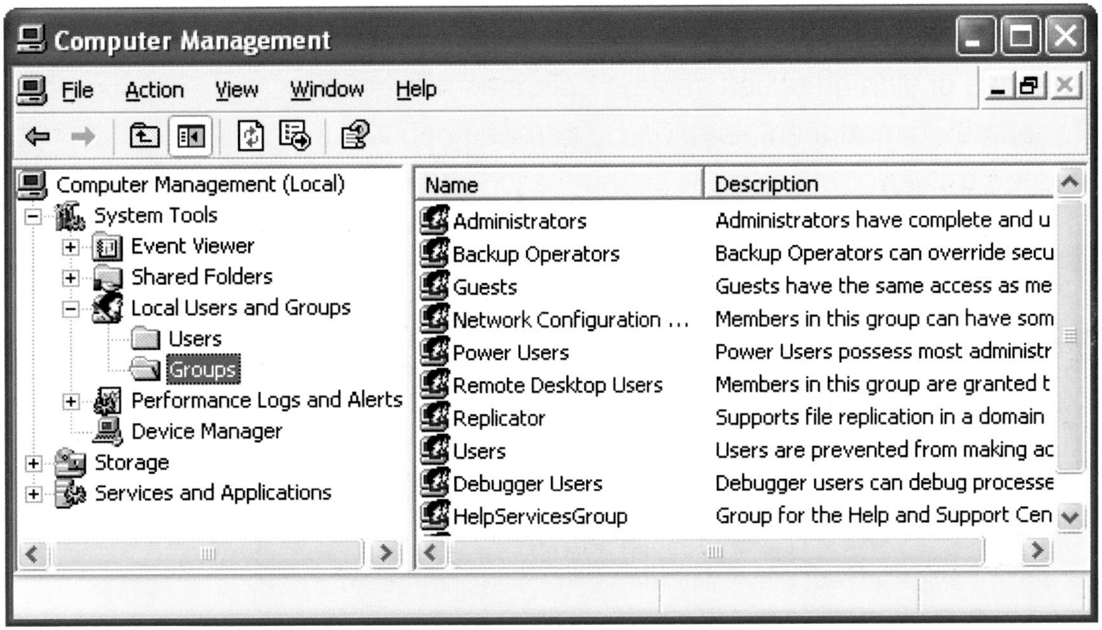

Figure 8-7: Built-in groups in a stand-alone computer to which users can be assigned

ADD USERS TO GROUPS

1. Right-click a group to which you want to add a user, and click **Add To Group**. Click **Add**. The Select Users dialog box will open.
2. Either type a name in the text box and click **Check Names** or click **Advanced** and then click **Find Now**. A list of users on that computer will be displayed. Select the user that you want to add (hold down **CTRL** to select several), and click **OK**.
3. When you are done, click **OK** twice.

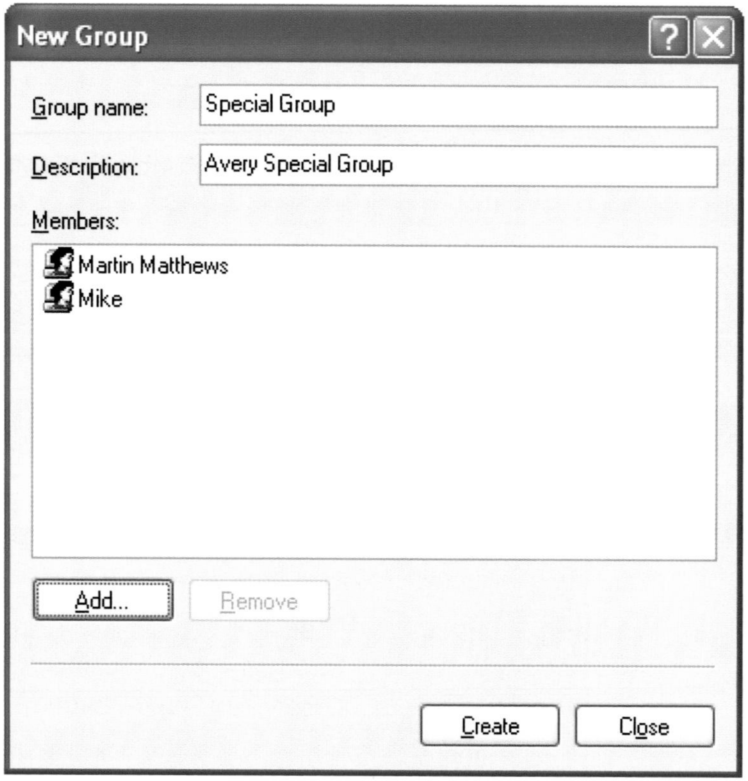

Figure 8-8: Creating your own group lets you give it your own characteristics

ADD A GROUP

1. In the Computer Management window, in the list of groups in the right pane, click in a white area so no group is selected, and then open **Action**, and choose **New Group**. The New Group dialog box opens.
2. Enter a group name of up to 60 characters (Windows XP lets you enter more, but if you ever want to use the group in Windows 2000 or NT systems, it will not work). It cannot contain just numbers, periods, or spaces; it can't contain " / \ [ ] : ; | = ,+ * ? < >; and leading spaces or periods are dropped. Enter the description of what the group can uniquely do, and click **Add**. Then follow the instructions in "Add Users to Groups" except for the final OK.
3. When your group is the way you want it, similar to Figure 8-8, click **Create** and then click **Close**. The new group will appear in the list on the right of the Computer Management window. Close the Computer Management window.

Set Permissions

> **NOTE**
>
> You cannot turn off Simple File Sharing in Windows XP Home Edition.

Permissions authorize a user or a group to perform some function on an object, such as files, folders, disks, and printers. Objects have sets of permissions associated with them that can be assigned to users and groups. The specific permissions depend on the object, but all objects have at least two permissions: Read, and either Modify or Change. Permissions are initially set in one of three ways:

- The application or process that creates an object can set its permissions upon creation.
- If the object allows the inheritance of permissions and they were not set upon creation, a parent object can propagate permissions to the object. For example, a parent folder can propagate its permissions to a subfolder it contains.
- If neither the creator nor the parent sets the permissions for an object, then the Windows XP system defaults will do it.

Once an object is created, its permissions can be changed by its owner, by an administrator, and by anyone else who has been given the permission to change permissions. The following sections look at the default permissions for both folders and files and at how those defaults are changed. In order to see, set, and change permissions, you must first turn off Simple File Sharing.

TURN OFF SIMPLE FILE SHARING

Simple File Sharing is meant to make life easier in an uncomplicated environment, but it takes away a large amount of your security control. In order to work with permissions, you must first turn it off.

1. In Windows XP Professional, open **Start** and choose **My Computer**. Open **Tools** and choose **Folders Options**.
2. Click the **View** tab, scroll to the bottom of the Advanced Settings, and deselect **Use Simple File Sharing** to turn it off.
3. Click **OK** to close the Folder Options dialog box, and then close My Computer.

With Simple File Sharing turned off, an additional Security tab appears, as you can see for a folder in Figure 8-9.

Figure 8-9: By turning off Simple File Sharing, a much more detailed level of control becomes available, as shown here for a folder

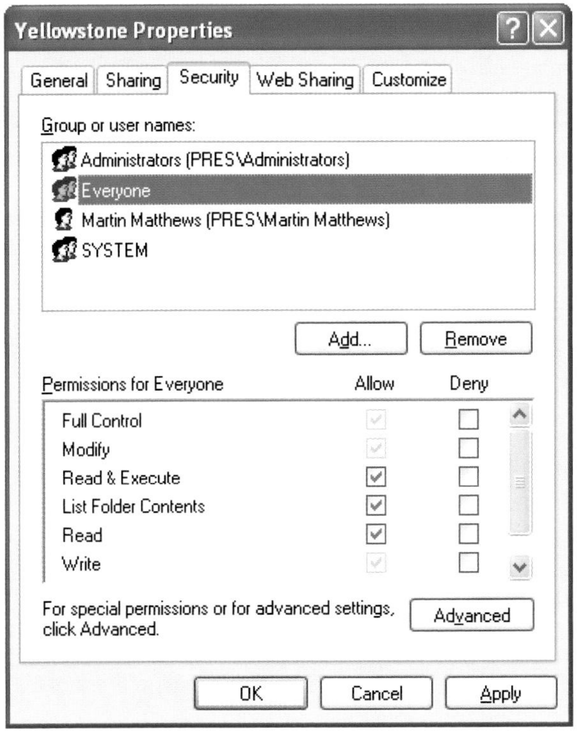

Use File and Folder Permissions

File and Folder permissions are set in the Security tab of the Properties dialog box, which, for a folder, is shown in Figure 8-9 (there are slight differences between file and folder dialog boxes). To open this tab and change the permissions:

1. Open **Start**, choose **My Computer**, and click **Folders** on the toolbar.
2. In the Folders pane on the left, open the drives and folders necessary to see the file or folder for which you want to set permissions.
3. Right-click that file or folder and choose **Properties**. In the Properties dialog box, click the **Security** tab. You can see the default permissions that have been granted, as in Figure 8-9. You can change some these, and you can add new users and groups. Some of the assignments are inherited from the parent folder.
4. To turn off inheritance, click **Advanced** to open the Advanced Security Settings dialog box, shown in Figure 8-10. Deselect the check box in the lower left that begins **Inherit From Parent...** You are warned that you will prevent any inheritable permissions.
5. Select **Copy** to copy the parent's permissions to this object.

   –Or–

   Select **Remove** to remove all of the parents permissions from this object.

   –Or–

   Click **Cancel** to not turn off inheritance.
6. Click **OK** to close the Advanced Security Settings dialog box and return to the folder's Properties dialog box. Click **Add** and use the steps under "Add Users to Groups" to add one or more new users.
7. Select one of the users or groups that you just added and click **Allow** for the permissions that you want that entity to have, or click **Deny** to specifically exclude a permission. Table 8-1 shows the tasks that can be performed with each permission for both files and folders.
8. After selecting the permissions that you want to use, click **OK** to close the file or folder Properties dialog box and then close Windows Explorer.

Figure 8-10: Detailed permission information is available in Advanced Security Settings

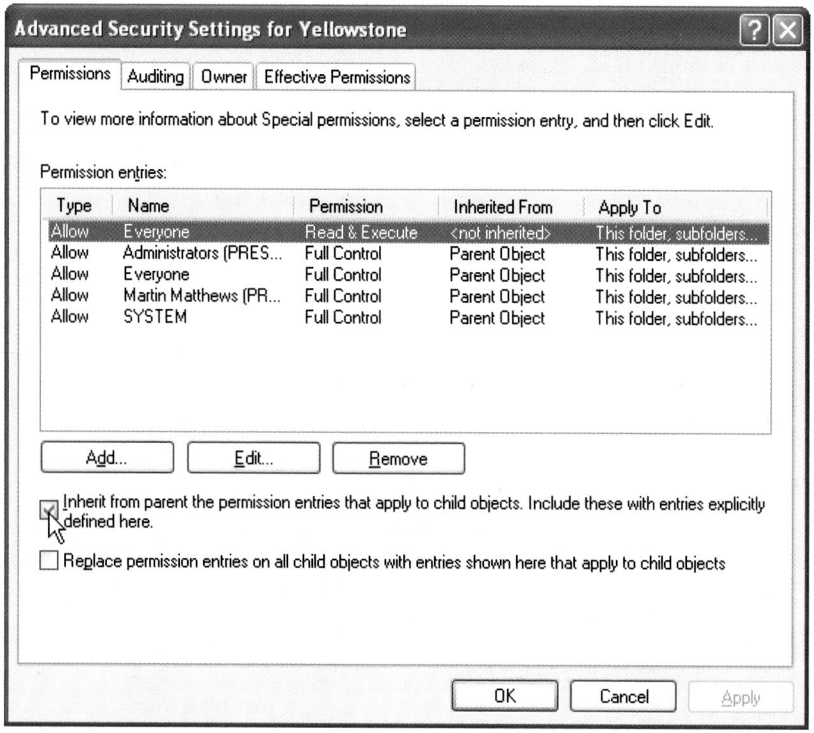

Protect Stored Data

Protecting stored data is a third layer of protection, with user authentication being the first layer, like an outer door, and controlling access being the second layer, or an inside door. Protecting stored data works to make unusable whatever is found by someone who breaks through the first two layers.

TABLE 8-1: TASKS THAT CAN BE PERFORMED WITH EACH PERMISSION

Permission	File	Folder	Tasks That Can Be Performed
Full Control	□	□	The sum of all other permissions, plus delete subfolders, change permissions, and take ownership
Modify	□	□	The sum of the Read & Execute and Write permissions, plus permission to delete the file or folder
Read & Execute	□	□	The same as List Folder Contents, but inherited by both folders and files
List Folder Contents		□	Read permission, plus view the list of subfolders and files in a folder as well as execute files and move through folders to reach other files and folders (inherited only by folders)
Read	□	□	View the contents of subfolders and files in the folder as well as view the folder's attributes (Archive, Hidden, Read-only), ownership, and permissions
Write	□	□	Make subfolders and files inside the folder, plus view the ownership and permissions for the folder and change its attributes
Special Permission	□		Allow unique activities that are related to a particular type of file

1 2 3 4 5 6 7 8 9 10

QUICKSTEPS

PROTECTING FILES AND FOLDERS

There are two things that you can do to protect files and folders from someone who might gain access to them: password protect them and, with Windows XP Professional, encrypt them. Start by opening the file or folder Properties dialog box.

1. Open **Start**, click **My Computer**, and click **Folders**. In the Folders pane, open the disks and folder necessary to locate in the right pane the file or folder you want to protect.
2. Right-click the file or folder you want to protect, and choose **Properties**. The Properties dialog box will open, as shown for a folder in Figure 8-11 (there are slight differences between file and folder dialog boxes).

PASSWORD PROTECT FILES AND FOLDERS

Windows XP gives you two forms of file and folder compression, as discussed in Chapter 3. The newer "zipped" form of folder compression that is enabled when a folder is created or a file or folder is sent to it can be password protected, and you will not be able to open the contents without first entering a password. This gives you a way of encrypting in Windows XP Home, and of encrypting compressed files and folders.

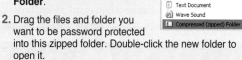

1. In Windows Explorer, in the disk or folder that will contain the new compressed folder, right-click a blank area, choose **New**, and click **Compressed (Zipped) Folder**.
2. Drag the files and folder you want to be password protected into this zipped folder. Double-click the new folder to open it.
3. In the open folder window, open **File** and click **Add A Password**. In the Add Password dialog box, enter and confirm the password you want and click **OK**.

Continued...

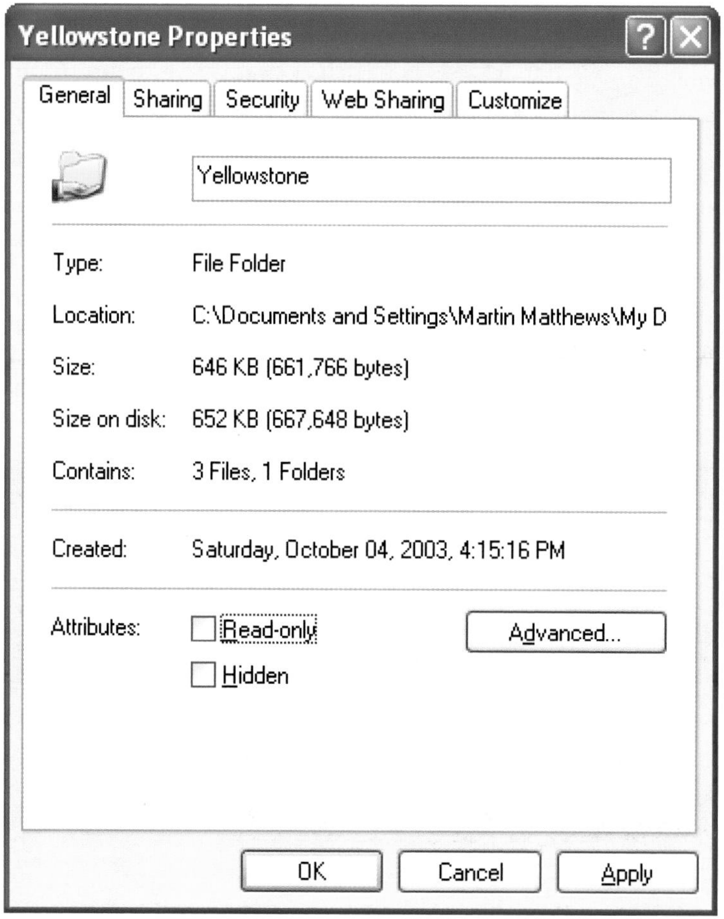

***Figure 8-11:** Protecting files and folders is accomplished from the files and folders Properties dialog box*

PROTECTING FILES AND FOLDERS

(Continued)

When you attempt to open one of the files within the compressed folder, you will get a Password Needed dialog box, making the compressed file also encrypted.

ENCRYPT FILES AND FOLDERS

File and folder encryption, called the *Encrypting File System (EFS),* is built into Windows XP Professional (but not Home Edition) using NTFS. Once EFS is turned on for a file or a folder, only the person who encrypted the file or folder will be able to read it, with the exception that a specially appointed administrator can have a recovery key to access the file or folder. For the person who encrypted the file, accessing it requires no additional steps, and the file is re-encrypted every time it is saved.

To encrypt a file from Windows Explorer:

1. From the file or folder Properties dialog box General tab, click **Advanced**. The Advanced Attributes dialog box opens.
2. Click **Encrypt Contents To Secure Data**.
3. Click **OK** twice. If you are encrypting a file, you get an Encryption Warning that the file is not in an encrypted folder, which means that when you edit the file, temporary or backup files might be created that are not encrypted. Choose whether to encrypt only the file, and then click **OK**.

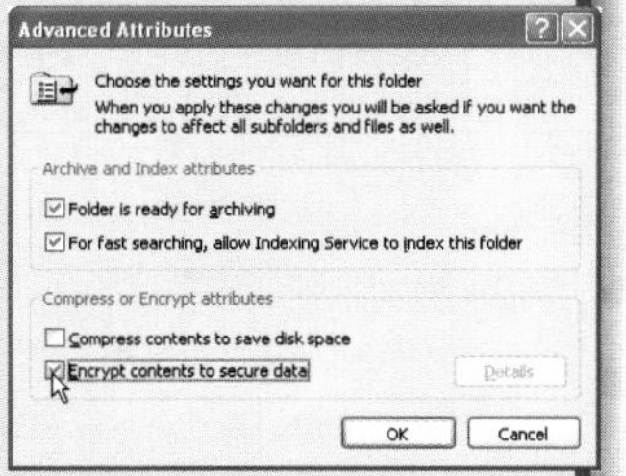

Continued...

Use Encrypted Files and Folders

If you are the person who encrypted a file or folder and you log on as yourself, you can use the file or folder in the exact same way as you would if it hadn't been encrypted. The only way you know the files or folders are encrypted is that Windows Explorer shows them in green, as shown in Figure 8-12. If you log on as someone else or someone else logs on as anyone other than you, they will not be able to use the files or folders. Copying and moving encrypted files and folders, though, has a special set of rules:

Figure 8-12: Windows Explorer shows the information for encrypted files and folders in green

PROTECTING FILES AND FOLDERS

(Continued)

4. If you are encrypting a folder, the Confirm Attribute Changes dialog box opens asking if you want to apply the encryption to this folder only or to both the **Only**, *existing* files and folders in the folder will *not* be encrypted, while files and folders later created in or copied to the encrypted folder will be. If you choose **This Folder, Subfolders, and Files**, all files and folders will be encrypted. Choose the setting that is correct for you, and click **OK**.
5. Log off as the current user and log on as another user. Open **My Computer** and open the drive and folders necessary to display on the right the file or folder you encrypted. You can see that the file exists, but when you try to open it, edit it, print it, or move it, you will get a message that access is denied.

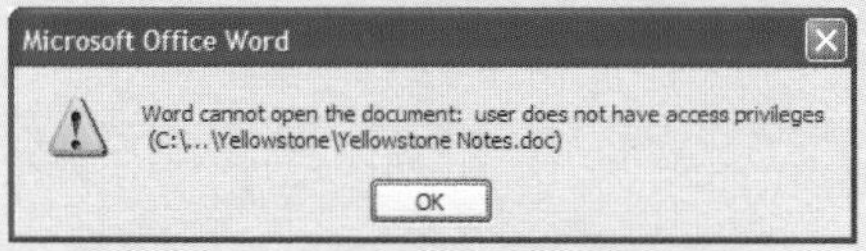

6. To decrypt a file or folder, log on as yourself, reopen the file or folder Properties dialog box, click Advanced, and deselect **Encrypt Contents To Secure Data**.

- If you copy or move a file or folder to an encrypted folder, the item copied or moved will be encrypted.
- If you copy or move a file or folder to an unencrypted folder, the item moved remains as it was prior to being moved. If it was unencrypted, it remains so. If it was encrypted, it is still encrypted after moving.
- Someone other than the owner who tries to copy or move encrypted files or folders to a different computer gets an error message that access is denied.
- If the owner copies or moves an encrypted file or folder to another file system, such as Windows NT 4 NTFS or Windows 98 FAT32, the encryption is removed, but a warning message is generated before the copy or move is complete.
- Backing up encrypted files or folders with Windows XP Backup leaves the items encrypted.

Lock a Computer

By default, when your screen saver comes on and you return to use your system, you must go through the Welcome screen. If you have to enter a password to get back into your system, this provides a lock to prevent entry to a running computer. If you don't want to wait for your screen saver to come on, you can press □ (Windows logo key)+L to immediately bring up the Welcome screen, from which your screen saver will open at the appropriate time.

Depending on your environment, having to go through the Welcome screen every time you come out of the screen saver may or may not be beneficial. To turn off or to turn back on the screen saver protection:

1. Right-click the desktop and choose **Properties**. Click the **Screen Saver** tab.
2. Select or deselect, depending on whether or not you want to display the Welcome screen on returning to your system. (See Figure 8-13.)
3. Click **OK** to close the Display Properties dialog box.

TIP

Because many applications save temporary and secondary files during normal execution, it is recommended that folders rather than files be the encrypting container. If an application is then told to store all files in that folder where all files are automatically encrypted upon saving, security is improved.

CAUTION

If you encrypt a shared folder and specify the encryption for This Folder, Subfolders, and Files, any files or subfolders belonging to others will be encrypted with your key, and the owners will not be able to use their property.

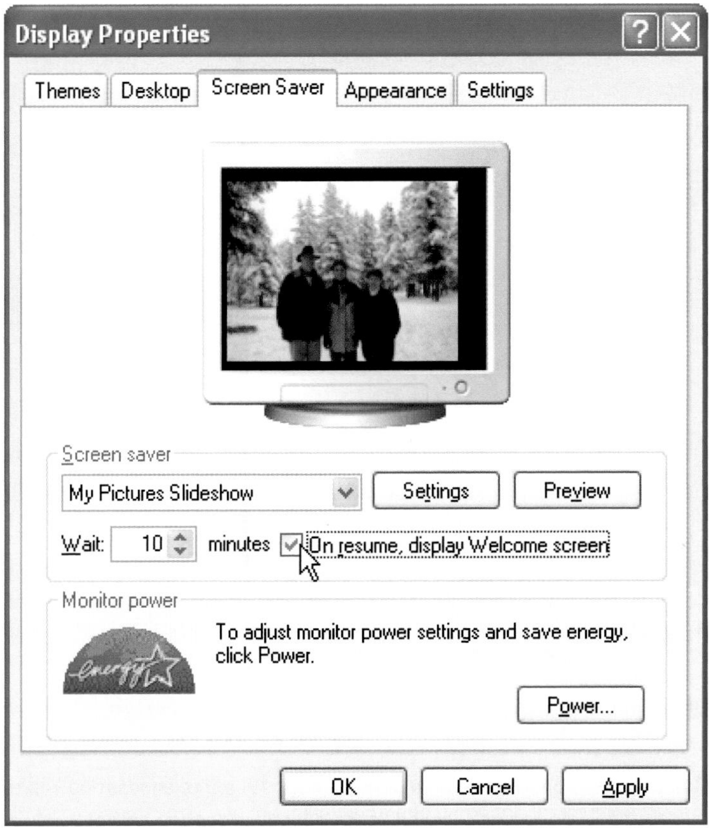

Figure 8-13: You can password protect your system when you leave it unattended by having the Welcome screen appear when you return after using the screen saver

TIP

The ICF is generally worthwhile, but it can get in your way both in a local network and with Internet traffic. If, after enabling the firewall, you are having network problems either locally or on the Internet, try changing the settings or turning the IFC off.

Set Up an Internet Firewall

Windows XP comes with an Internet Connection Firewall (ICF) whose objective is to slow down hackers trying to get into you computer while you are online. Your IFC may be turned on by default. Check to see if it is; if it isn't, turn it on.

1. Open **Start** and click **Control Panel**. While in Classic view, double-click **Network Connections**, right-click the connection you use to connect to the Internet, and click **Properties**.
2. Click the **Advanced** tab. If it isn't already, select **Protect My Computer And Network…**
3. Click **Settings**. In the Advanced Settings dialog box, shown in Figure 8-14, select each of the services running on your computer that you want to allow people to come in from the Internet and use.
4. For each service you select, a Service Settings dialog box will open allowing you to confirm the correct settings. Click **OK** to close Service Settings. When you are ready, click **OK** twice more. Close Network Connections.

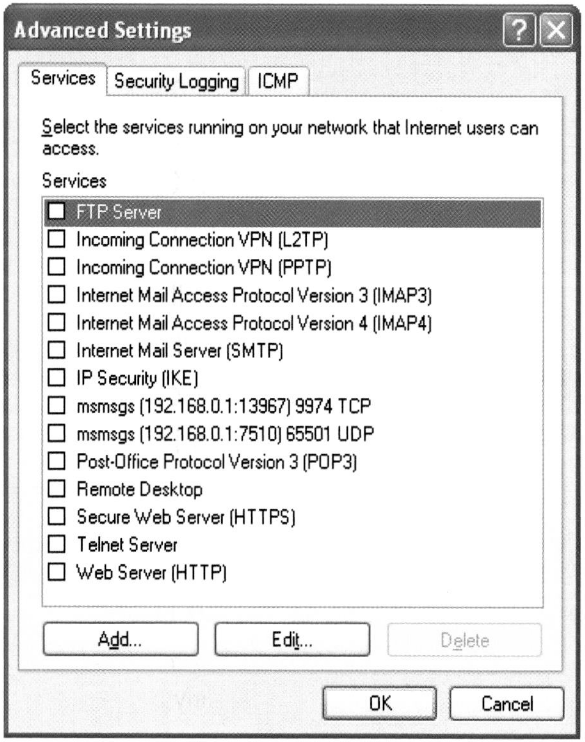

***Figure 8-14:** The Windows XP firewall can be configured to allow certain users into the system*

How to...

Chapter 9 Setting Up Networking

Networking is the sharing of resources and information between two or more connected computers–at home, within an organization, or around the world. Connection to the Internet (discussed in Chapter 4) is a form of networking. It is a wide area network, or WAN.

In this chapter, you will see how to connect to a local area network, or LAN, which is generally confined to a single residence, a building, or, perhaps, just a section of a building. You'll see what comprises a LAN, how to set it up, and how to use it.

Plan a Network

Windows XP is a *network operating system* and allows the interconnection of multiple computers for many purposes:

- **Exchanging information**, such as sending a file from one computer to another
- **Communicating**, for example, sending e-mail among network users
- **Sharing information** by having common files accessed by network users
- **Sharing network resources**, such as printers and Internet connections

Networking is a system that includes the connection between computers that facilitates the transfer of information, as well as the scheme for controlling that transfer. The scheme makes sure that the information is transferred correctly and accurately. This is the function of the networking hardware and software in your computer and the protocols, or standards, they use.

Select a Type of Network

Today the majority of LANs use the *Ethernet* standard, which determines the type of network hardware and software needed by the network, and *TCP/IP* (Transmission Control Protocol/Internet Protocol), which determines how information is exchanged over the network. With this foundation, you can then choose between using a peer-to-peer LAN or a client-server LAN.

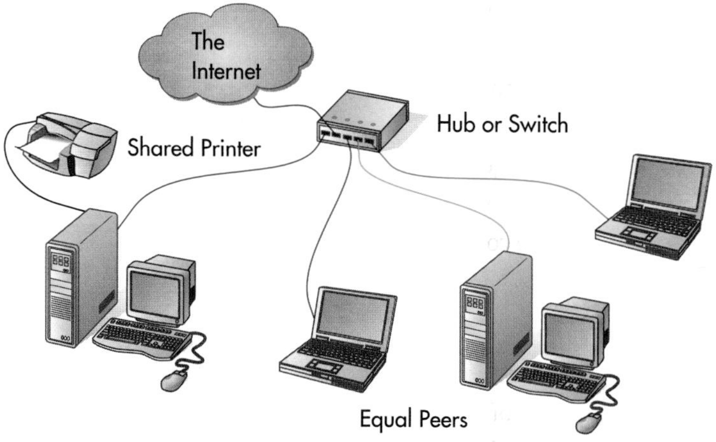

Figure 9-1: In a peer-to-peer LAN all computers are both servers and clients

PEER-TO-PEER LANS

All computers in a *peer-to-peer LAN* are both servers and clients and, therefore, share in both providing and using resources. Any computer in the network may store information and provide resources, such as a printer, for the use of any other computer in the network. Peer-to-peer networking is an easy first step to networking, accomplished simply by joining computers together, as shown in Figure 9-1. It does not require the purchase of new computers or significant changes to the way an organization is using computers, yet resources can be shared (as is the printer in Figure 9-1), files and communications can be transferred, and common information can be accessed by all.

Peer-to-peer LANs tend to be used in smaller organizations that do not need to share a large central resource, such as a database, or to have a high degree of security or central control. Each computer in a peer-to-peer LAN is autonomous and is often networked with other computers simply to transfer files and share expensive equipment. Putting together a peer-to-peer LAN with existing computers is fairly easy and can be inexpensive (less than $50 per station).

CLIENT/SERVER LANS

The computers in a *client/server LAN* perform one of two functions: they are either servers or clients. *Servers* manage the network, centrally store information to be shared on the network, and provide the shared resources to the network. *Clients*, or *workstations*, are the users of the network and are normally desktop or laptop computers. To create a network, the clients and server(s) are connected together, possibly with additional stand-alone network resources, such as printers, as shown in Figure 9-2.

Figure 9-2: In a client/server LAN, one or more computers are servers and the rest are clients

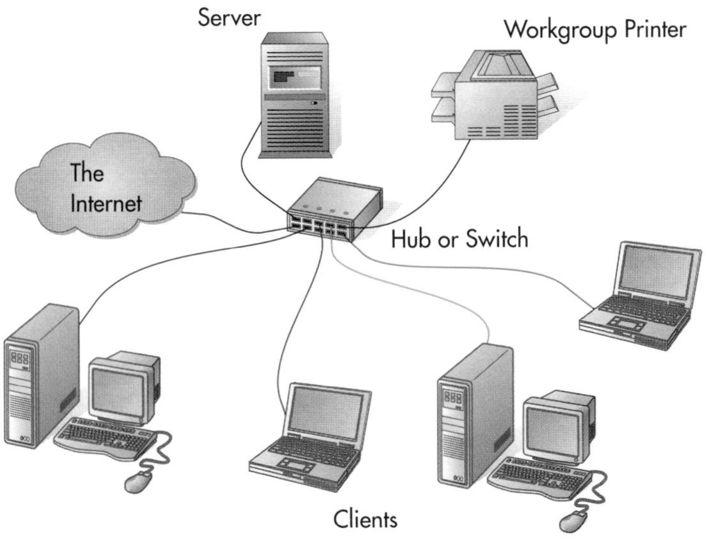

The management functions provided by the server include network security, managing the permissions needed to implement security, communications among network users, and management of shared files on the network. Servers generally are more capable than clients in terms of having more memory, faster (and possibly more) processors, larger (and maybe more) disk drives, and more special peripherals, such as large, high-speed tape drives. Servers, generally, are dedicated to their function and are infrequently used for mundane computer tasks, such as word processing.

Clients are generally less capable than servers and, infrequently, may not even have a disk. Clients usually are normal desktop and laptop computers that perform the typical functions of those types of machines, in addition to being part of a network. Clients can also be "mini-servers" by sharing some or all of their disk drives or other resources. The principal difference between peer-to-peer networks and client/server networks is the presence of a dedicated server.

Windows XP and either Windows Server 2003 or Windows 2000 Server work together to form a client/server network operating environment, with the Windows server performing its function and Windows XP Professional being the client. Several Windows XP Professional workstations or Windows XP Home Edition computers can operate in a peer-to-peer network.

There are simple client/server networks, and there are client/server networks where one or more servers are set up as *domain controllers* and the entire network is considered a *domain*. In a large organization, a domain provides many benefits–most importantly, a central registry for all users so that one registration provides access to all the computers and resources in the domain. Domains, however, are very complex and require significant expertise to set up and manage. This book, therefore, focuses on setting up and using a peer-to-peer network and on connecting to a client/server network.

Select a Network Standard

Windows XP supports the two predominant networking standards: wired Ethernet and Wireless. These, in turn, determine the type of hardware you need.

USE WIRED ETHERNET

The wired Ethernet standard comes in several forms based on speed and cable type. The most common, called 10/100BaseT, provides a network that operates at either the regular Ethernet speed of 10 Mbps (megabit, or a million bits, per second) or at the newer Fast Ethernet speed of 100 Mbps.

NOTE

In the name for the Ethernet standard, 10/100BaseT, the "10/100" indicates the alternative operating speeds in Mbps; the "Base" is for baseband, a type of transmission; and the "T" stands for the type of cabling (twisted-pair).

1 2 3 4 5 6 7 8 9 10

A wired Ethernet 10/100BaseT system, shown in Figure 9-3, has three major components:

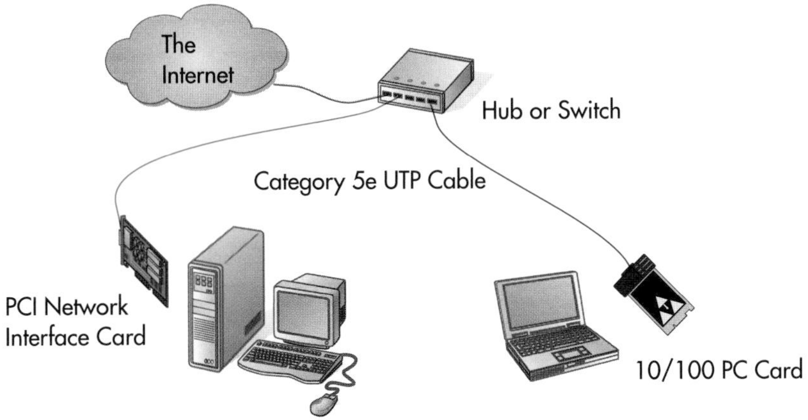

Figure 9-3: A wired Ethernet network consists of a card in your computer, a hub or switch into which other computers are connected, and a cable connecting the two

- The **network interface card (NIC)** plugs into your computer and connects it to the network.
- A **hub**, **switch**, or **router** joins several computers together to form the network.
  - A **hub**, the simplest and cheapest device, is where all computers are on the equivalent of a telephone party line (everybody can hear everybody else).
  - A **switch** is more expensive than a hub, but all computers are on the equivalent of a private telephone line.
  - A **router** joins two different networks, for example, the Internet to a local area network. Often a router is combined with a hub or a switch, either in one device or in two devices, to join the Internet to several computers.
- An **unshielded twisted-pair (UTP)** telephone-like cable with a very simple RJ-45 telephone-like connector joins the NIC to the hub, switch, or router. This cable is called Category 5 or enhanced Category 5 ("Cat 5" or "Cat 5e").

Ethernet networks are very easy to set up (see "Set Up a Network" later in this chapter), have become pervasive throughout organizations, and have an average cost for all components of less than $50 per computer on the network.

WIRELESS LANS

Wireless LANs (WLANs) replace the cable used in a wired network with small radio transceivers (combined transmitter and receiver) at the computer and at the hub or switch. There are several wireless standards, but the most common is 802.11b, which provides data transfer of up to 11 Mbps using a secure transmission scheme. A newer standard, 802.11g, is quickly gaining popularity because it is five-times faster than 802.11b (54 Mbps), is compatible with 802.11b, and is not that much more expensive.

1 2 3 4 5 6 7 8 9 10

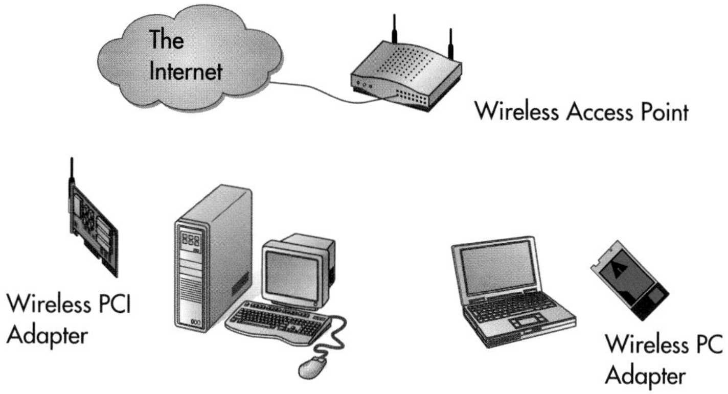

Figure 9-4: A wireless network consists of a card in your computer and an access point that is connected to a wired network, the Internet, or both

A WLAN has two components (see Figure 9-4):

- An **access point** is connected to the wired Ethernet network via a hub, a switch, or a router. It uses a transceiver to communicate wirelessly with cards that are added to computers using the WLAN.
- An **adapter** plugs into your computer and has a transceiver built in to communicate wirelessly to an access point within its range. There are PC adapters for use in notebook computers and PCI (Peripheral Component Interconnect) adapters for use in desktop computers.

If the access point is plugged into a hub or switch on a wired network, the wireless computers within the range of the access point operate on the network in exactly the same way, except for being a little slower, as they would with a cable connection. A WLAN has some significant benefits over a normal wired LAN:

- You do not have the expense of cabling and the even higher expense of installing and maintaining cabling.
- Adding and removing users from the network is extremely easy.
- Users can move easily from office to office.
- Users can roam within an area, say, carrying their laptops to a meeting.
- Visitors can easily get on the network.

The downside is cost and speed, but both of these are improving rapidly. The cost per computer of a wired network, as noted above, is less than $50 per computer; the cost per computer of a wireless network is generally above $50, but the two prices are getting very close. The speed difference is more significant, not just because of the difference between an 11 or 54 Mbps access point and a 100 Mbps network, but because of the net rate of dividing the 11 or 54 Mbps access point by the number of people trying to use it. Despite these drawbacks, there is a great amount of interest in WLANs, and a number of systems are being sold for both offices and homes.

NOTE

In addition to the WLAN standard, the WIFI (wireless fidelity) standard makes sure that hardware from different manufacturers is compatible. Thus, you can walk into any office, airport, or other building with a WIFI standard wireless system and be able to connect to the WLAN if you have the appropriate permissions. In many airports, hotels, and coffee shops, you see signs for "WIFI Hotspots," meaning that you can use a wireless connection.

NOTE

Lessened security is also a potential downside with wireless if it isn't set up properly. For example, if you don't turn on encryption and the use of passwords, your neighbor might be able to get on your network or look at your network traffic.

QUICKSTEPS

SELECTING WIRED ETHERNET HARDWARE

Hardware used in a wired Ethernet network includes a NIC, a hub or switch, and cabling. I recommend using name-brand products from companies who stand behind what you buy. Respected brands include 3Com, D-Link, Linksys (division of Cisco Systems), and Netgear.

SELECT A NETWORK INTERFACE CARD (NIC)

Many new computers come with a built-in 10/100 Ethernet NIC, so you may not need to add this. If your computer has two telephone-style jacks, one slightly larger, then you have a NIC connected to the larger jack. The other jack is for the modem.

If you don't have a NIC, you can add one to your computer. For a desktop computer, you will need to open the computer case and plug in the card. Most computer stores will do that for little more than the cost of the card ($25 to $50). You need to carry in only the computer itself, not the monitor, keyboard, or mouse. You want a 10/100 NIC for the PCI bus in your computer.

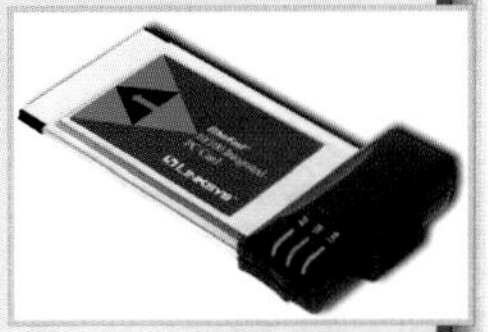

A laptop computer NIC simply plugs into a *PC Card* slot on the outside of the computer. You want a 10/100 PC Card NIC.

Continued...

Set Up a Network

When you installed Windows XP, a basic set of networking services was installed and configured using your input and system defaults. This setup may, but doesn't always, provide an operable networking system. Look at these two areas to set up *basic networking*, which means that your computer can communicate with other computers in the network:

- Be sure the network interface card (NIC) is properly set up.
- Install the networking functions that you want to perform.

Set Up Network Interface Cards

If the computer you are setting up has a NIC that is both certified for Windows XP and is fully Plug and Play-compatible, then your NIC was installed by Setup without incident, and you don't need to read this section. Otherwise, use this section to look at how the NIC was installed and what you need to do to make it fully operational.

Assuming that a NIC *is* properly plugged into the computer, any of these three things could be causing it to not operate:

- The NIC driver is either missing or not properly installed.
- The required resources are not available.
- The NIC is not functioning properly.

Look at each of these possibilities in turn.

SELECTING WIRED ETHERNET HARDWARE *(Continued)*

SELECT CONNECTING DEVICES

There are two common connecting devices: hubs, which are like a party-line telephone system; and switches, which are like a private-line telephone system. Switches currently cost almost the same as hubs and run from under $50, for a 4- or 5-port one, to under $150 for a 24-port switch. You need a port for each user, but you can stack (plug one into another) switches. You want an Ethernet 10/100 switch with the number of ports to meet your needs.

SELECT CABLING

For 10/100 Ethernet networking, you need Category 5e (for enhanced, called "Cat 5e") cabling with RJ-45 male connectors on each end. Such cables come in various colors and in lengths up to 100 feet with the ends molded on, or in lengths up to 1000 feet without the ends, which can be added with the help of a crimping tool.

Photos courtesy of Linksys, a Division of Cisco Sytems, Inc.

NOTE

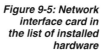

If you want to network only two computers, you can do so without a hub or a switch, using a crossover cable whose connections are reversed on each end. Most computer stores carry these.

CHECK THE NIC DRIVER

Check whether you have a driver installed, and if you don't, install one:

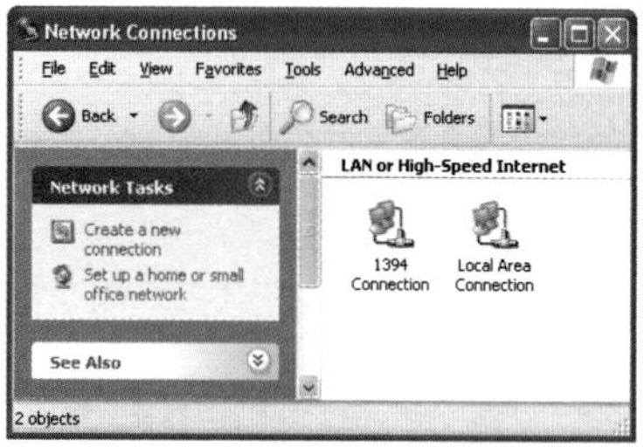

1. Open **Start**, choose **Control Panel**, and while in Classic view, double-click **Network Connections**. The Network Connections window opens. If you have an icon in the window labeled Local Area Connection, as shown here, you have the NIC driver properly installed and you can go on to the next major section, "Install Networking Functions."
2. If you do not have a Local Area Connection icon, you cannot create one by clicking New Connection Wizard. You must first install the NIC using the Add Hardware control panel.

   At this point, it is highly likely that you will need a Windows XP driver for the NIC. It is best to get one before proceeding. If one did not come with the NIC, you need to use another computer attached to the Internet, bring up the manufacturer's web site, locate and download the driver (you need to know the make and model of the NIC) for Windows XP, copy it onto a disk, and then go back to the original computer.
3. Again, open **Start**, click **Control Panel**, and double-click **Add Hardware** in Classic view. The Add Hardware Wizard opens.
4. Click **Next**. When asked if the hardware is connected, click **Yes** (given that the NIC is already in its slot), and click **Next**. A list of installed hardware will appear. You may or may not see your NIC on the list, as shown in Figure 9-5.

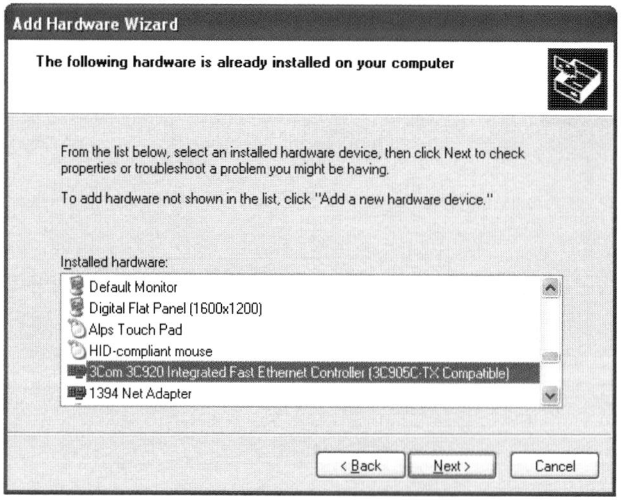

Figure 9-5: Network interface card in the list of installed hardware

TIP

You can change the name, Local Area Connection, that appears in the Network Connections window. For example, if you install two NIC cards, you can give each of them a descriptive name.

NOTE

I went through the process of downloading a driver for an older 3Com card and found it painless. The hard part is figuring out what type of card you have, because often it is not written on the card. You may need to locate purchase records or documentation—if you know which records go with the card.

If you see your NIC and it doesn't have a problem icon (an exclamation point), then Windows thinks that the NIC is installed and running properly. If you double-click the device, you should get a message saying, "This device is working properly." If so, you can click **Finish** to close the Add Hardware Wizard. Your problem may be in software.

5. If you don't see your NIC, click **Add A New Hardware Device** at the end of the list of Installed Hardware. Click **Next**. Choose **Install The Hardware That I Manually Select From A List**—you don't want Windows to search for new hardware; if it was going to find it, it would have—and click **Next**. Skip to Step 7.
6. If you see your NIC with a problem icon, double-click the NIC. You will most likely get a Device Status message telling you that a driver was not installed. Click **Finish** to close the Add Hardware Wizard. The Upgrade Device Driver Wizard opens. Click **Next**. Choose **Display A List of Known Drivers**, and click **Next**.
7. Whether or not you saw your NIC, double-click **Network Adapters** in the list of Common Hardware Types. A list of network adapters appears. If your NIC had been on the list, Setup would have found it, so you need to insert and use the disk you made prior to Step 3 or a disk that came with the NIC.
8. Click **Have Disk**. Accept the default of the A drive (assuming you want to use a floppy), and click **OK**. When it is displayed, select the driver for your adapter, and click **Next**. When told that the device will be installed, click **Next** again.
9. You may get a message stating that the driver you are about to install does not have a Microsoft digital signature. Click **Yes** to go ahead and install it anyway. The driver and its necessary supporting software will be installed.
10. Click **Finish**. The Network Connections window should now show the Local Area Connection icon. If you see the Local Area Connection icon, go to the next major section, "Install Networking Functions."

If you still do not have a Local Area Connection or if some other problem occurred in the preceding process that does not point to an obvious solution, continue through the next two sections to see if a solution is presented.

1 2 3 4 5 6 7 8 9 10

QUICKSTEPS

SELECTING WIRELESS HARDWARE

Hardware for a wireless network includes a wireless adapter and a wireless access point.

SELECT A WIRELESS SPEED

For a new wireless network, choose between 11 Mbps and 54 Mbps speeds, or between the 802.11b and 802.11g standards. The 54 Mbps hardware costs 25 to 50 percent more and provides 500 percent improvement in speed. If you want to use WiFi networks in airports and coffee shops, 11 Mbps is adequate. If you are building a multi-user network, you probably want 54 Mbps.

SELECT A WIRELESS ADAPTER

Some laptops come with a built-in wireless adapter. For a desktop computer, you need a PCI wireless adapter, and you will need to open up the computer to plug it in or have a store install it. For a laptop computer, you need a PC Card wireless adapter, which you can easily plug in.

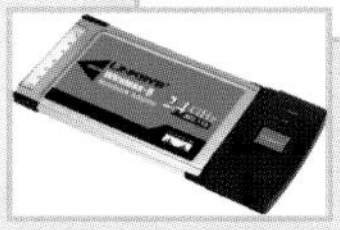

SELECT A WIRELESS ACCESS POINT

Wireless access points come in simple versions that plug into a wired Ethernet network and more sophisticated versions, called "wireless broadband routers," that terminate a DSL or cable Internet connection. You have that choice and a choice of speeds when you choose a wireless access point.

Photos courtesy of Linksys, a Division of Cisco Sytems, Inc.

CHECK NIC RESOURCES

Most interface, or adapter, cards in a PC require resources in order to operate. The resources include interrupt request (IRQ) lines, I/O ports, and direct memory access (DMA) lines. Generally, two devices cannot share the same resources, except that PCI devices can share IRQs. Therefore, if two devices are assigned the same resource, a conflict occurs and the devices will not operate properly. This will cause a NIC to not function and the Local Area Connection icon to not appear in the Network Connections window. Check and correct the resources used by the NIC with these steps:

1. Open **Start**, click **Control Panel**, and in Classic view, double-click **System**. The System Properties dialog box opens.
2. Click the **Hardware** tab, and then click **Device Manager** on the right of the middle section. The Device Manager window opens, as shown in Figure 9-6. If you see a problem icon (an exclamation point) on your network adapter, there may be a problem with the resource allocation.

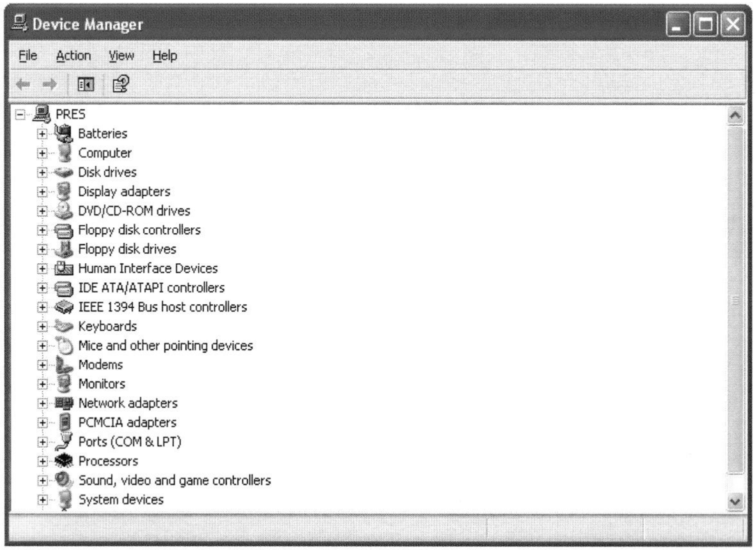

***Figure 9-6:** The Device Manager shows all of the devices in a computer and identifies those with a problem by putting an exclamation mark on their icons*

3. Open the **Network Adapters** category, and double-click the particular network adapter that you are researching. The Properties dialog box for that device will open and give you a device status. If there is a resource problem, it should show up here.

RESOLVE CONFLICTS

1. Click the **Resources** tab. In the Conflicting Device List at the bottom of the dialog box, you will see the specifics of any resource conflicts.
2. If you have a conflict, deselect **Use Automatic Settings**. Then, go through each of the configurations in the **Setting Based On** drop-down list to see if any of them cure the problem.
3. If none of the canned configurations cures the problem, click the problem resource, deselect **Automatic Settings**, and click **Change Setting**. Click the up or down arrow to change the setting, and then click **OK** to see if that fixes the problem. Try several settings.
4. If you are having a hard time finding a solution, go back to the Device Manager (you can leave the NIC Properties dialog box open), open **View**, and choose **Resources By Type**. Here, you can see all of the assignments for a given resource, as shown in Figure 9-7 for interrupt request lines, and find an empty resource to assign to the NIC, like 3 and 7 in Figure 9-7.

NOTE

If you need more than four levels of hubs (hubs plugged into hubs) in a 10BaseT network or more than two levels in a 100BaseT one (or a mixed 10/100BaseT network), you need to use a switch to add more levels.

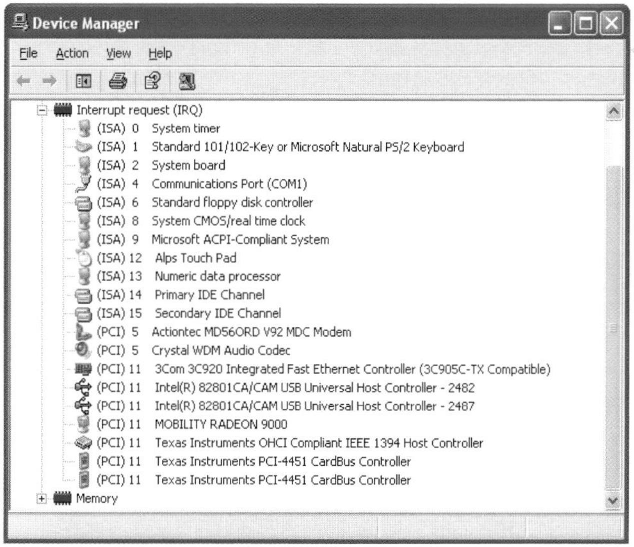

Figure 9-7: You can find an unused resource in the Device Manager's Resources By Type list

Figure 9-8: Windows XP has an extensive hardware troubleshooter for solving problems with your equipment

5. If you find an unassigned resource, go back to the NIC Properties dialog box and assign it to the NIC. If you cannot find an unassigned resource, you may have to make a tough choice between the NIC and a conflicting device. Networking is an important service, and if it is conflicting with a sound card, for example, you may need to remove the sound card to get networking. If both of the cards are ISA (Industry Standard Architecture) cards and you have PCI slots available, you can probably get a new PCI card (which is faster than ISA) and remove the conflict. (New PCI NICs cost from $25 to $50.)
6. If none of the previous suggestions works, return to the NIC Properties dialog box, click the **General** tab, and then click **Troubleshoot**, as you can see in Figure 9-8. Windows XP Help will open and lead you through a series of steps to try to resolve the problem.
7. When you have solved the resource problem as best you can, close Help, if it is still open, close the NIC Properties dialog box, close the Device Manager, and finally close the System Properties dialog box. If you made changes in the resources, you may be told that you need to restart your computer and asked whether you want to do it now. Click **Yes**, and the computer will restart.
8. If you successfully made a change to the resources, you should now see a Local Area Connection icon in the Network Connections window (if necessary, reopen it by opening **Start**, clicking **Control Panel** and double-clicking **Network Connections**). If you see the icon, go to the next major section, "Install Networking Functions." If you don't see a Local Area Connection icon, continue with the following section.

DETERMINE IF A NIC IS FUNCTIONING

If neither installing a NIC driver nor changing its resource allocation caused the Local Area Connection icon to appear, it is very likely that the NIC itself is not functioning properly. The easiest way to test that is to replace the NIC with a known good one, ideally one that is both Windows XP certified and Plug and Play–compatible. It is wise to have a spare NIC; they are not terribly expensive, and switching out a suspected bad one can quickly solve problems.

Install Networking Functions

Networking functions provide the software for a computer to access other computers, and, separately, for other computers to access the computer you are working on. In other words, the two primary functions allow the computer to be a client (it accesses other computers) and to be a server (other computers access it). Make sure that these two services are installed by following these steps:

1. In the Network Connections window (if necessary, reopen it by opening **Start**, clicking **Control Panel**, and double-clicking **Network Connections**), double-click **Local Area Connection**. The Local Area Connection Status dialog box opens, as shown next. In the case shown here, the computer thinks it is connected to the network and it is sending and receiving information.

2. Click **Properties**. The Local Area Connection Properties dialog box, shown in Figure 9-9, opens and displays the services and protocols that have automatically been installed. Under the default circumstances, this includes two services—Client for Microsoft Networks and File and Printer Sharing for Microsoft Networks—and one protocol, Internet Protocol (TCP/IP). If you have the two services installed, you have achieved the objective of this section, but in any case, continue and explore the alternatives.
3. Click **Install**. The Select Network Component Type dialog box opens, in which you can add clients, services, and protocols.

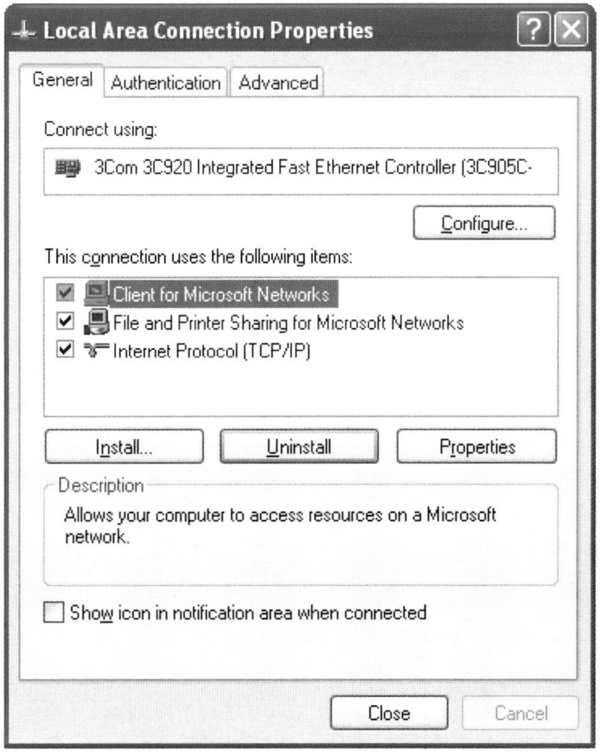

Figure 9-9: At a minimum, networking requires the services and protocol shown here

INSTALL A CLIENT

1. Double-click **Client**. If you already have Client For Microsoft Networks installed, you

will have only Client Service For NetWare in the list.

2. If **Client For Microsoft Networks** is not installed, select it and click **OK**. If you also need to access a NetWare server, select **Client Service For NetWare** and click **OK**.

INSTALL A SERVICE

1. In the Select Network Component Type dialog box, double-click **Service**. If you already have File And Printer Sharing For Microsoft Networks installed, you may have QoS (quality of service) Packet Scheduler available for installation. QoS helps balance a network and alleviate bottlenecks when one part of the network is fast and another part is slow.
2. If **File And Printer Sharing For Microsoft Networks** is not installed, select it and click **OK**. If you need **QoS Packet Scheduler**, select it and click **OK**.

This should ensure that you have the two primary services installed.

Configure a Networking Protocol

Networking protocols are sets of standards used to package and transmit information over a network. The protocol determines how the information is divided into packets, how it is addressed, and what is done to ensure it is reliably transferred. The protocol is, therefore, very important to the success of networking, and its choice is a major one. Windows XP offers two protocols:

- **Internetwork Packet Exchange/Sequenced Packet Exchange (IPX/SPX)**, for use with networks running Novell NetWare
- **TCP/IP**, for use with the Internet and most newer systems

If the computer you are working on is or will be connected to the Internet, it will require TCP/IP. TCP/IP is a very robust protocol, suitable for a demanding environment (like the Internet) and accepted worldwide. Because of this, Microsoft recommends that TCP/IP be installed as your protocol of choice for both your LAN and the Internet. If you also need IPX/SPX to connect to a Novell system, you can additionally install that protocol.

TIP

Each protocol that you install uses CPU, memory, and disk resources and slows startup, so it is important to install only the protocols that are truly needed.

CHECK AND CHANGE PROTOCOLS

Check on and, if needed, change the protocols that have been installed and the settings that are being used:

1. If the Select Network Component Type dialog box is not still open, reopen it by opening **Start**, clicking **Control Panel,** double-clicking **Network Connections**, double-clicking **Local Area Connection**, clicking **Properties**, and then clicking **Install**.

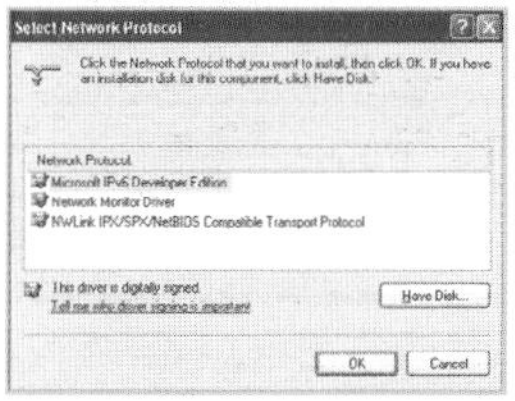

2. From the Select Network Component Type dialog box, double-click **Protocol**. The Select Network Protocol dialog box opens. This lists the available protocols.
3. If you see **Internet Protocol (TCP/IP)**, double-click it. If you want to install another protocol, do so now by double-clicking that protocol. Otherwise, click **Cancel** to close the Select Network Protocol dialog box.
4. Select the **Internet Protocol (TCP/IP)** protocol in the Local Area Connection Properties dialog box, and click **Properties**. The Internet Protocol (TCP/IP) Properties dialog box opens, shown in Figure 9-10. Here you can choose whether to use a dynamic IP (Internet Protocol) address automatically assigned by a server, a DSL router, or to enter a static IP address.

   If you have a server or a DSL router that automatically assigns IP addresses, you need to leave the default **Obtain An IP Address Automatically**.

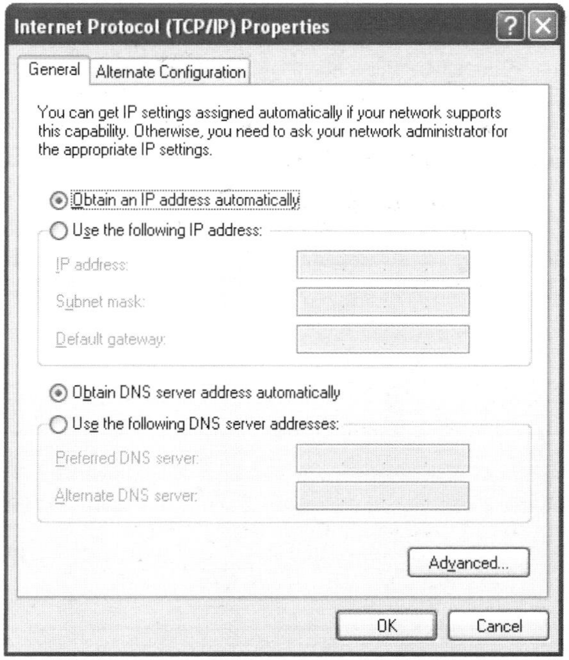

Figure 9-9: You can use dynamic IP addresses that are automatically assigned, or you can enter a fixed IP address that has been assigned to you

NOTE

In the Local Area Connection Properties dialog box, you should see at least one protocol installed, as shown previously in Figure 9-9. In most cases, TCP/IP should already be installed.

TIP

If the server is down or nonexistent, Automatic Private IP Addressing (APIPA) assigns an IP address. APIPA is limited insofar as a computer using APIPA can talk only to other computers in the same range of numbers. If all computers in a small network are using Windows 98/Me or Windows 2000/XP and have Obtain An IP Address Automatically selected, without a DHCP server, they will all automatically use the 169.254.0.0 through 169.254.255.255 range of IP numbers.

> **TIP**
>
> If your organization is small and doesn't plan to access an outside network, then the static IP address can be from the block of APIPA numbers or from several other blocks of private IP addresses. (See the QuickSteps "Getting a Block of IP Addresses.")

> **TIP**
>
> The "Folder" in the Search Results – Computers dialog box is either the domain or the workgroup that the computer is in.

ENTER YOUR OWN IP ADDRESS

1. If you are working on a computer that you know you must assign a static IP address to, then do so by clicking **Use The Following IP Address** and entering an IP address. The IP address you use should be from the block of IP addresses that an Internet service provider (ISP) or other authority has assigned your organization.
2. If you entered a static IP address, you must also enter a subnet mask. This mask tells the IP which part of an IP address to consider a network address and which part to consider a computer, or *host,* address. If your organization was assigned a block of IP numbers, it was also given a subnet mask. If you used the APIPA range of addresses, then use 255.255.0.0 as the subnet mask.

OBTAIN AN IP ADDRESS AUTOMATICALLY

1. If you don't have a specific reason to use a static IP address, click **Obtain An IP Address Automatically** and use the addresses from either a server or DSL router on the network or APIPA.
2. Click **OK** to close the Internet Protocol (TCP/IP) Properties dialog box, click **Close** to close the Local Area Connection Properties dialog box, click **Close** to close the Local Area Connection Status dialog box, and click the **Close** button to close the Network Connections window.
3. Open **Start**, choose **Turn Off Computer**, and select **Restart** from the dialog box that appears.

VERIFY YOUR CONNECTION

1. After the computer has restarted, reopen the Network Connections window (open **Start**, click **Control Panel**, and double-click **Network Connections**). Double-click **Local Area Connection** to open the Local Area Connection Status dialog box. You should see activity on both the Sent and Received sides.
2. If you do not see both sent and receive activity, open **Start**, click **My Computer**, and click **Search** in the toolbar. In the Search pane on the left, click **Computers Or People**, click **A Computer On The Network**, enter a computer name in your same subnet, and then click **Search**. You should see the computer appear with its location on the right. If it does appear, then the computer is networking. If this doesn't work, then you have a problem.

QUICKSTEPS

GETTING A BLOCK OF IP ADDRESSES

The block of IP addresses you use with the Internet Protocol depends on whether the computers to be assigned the addresses will be private or public.

GET PRIVATE IP ADDRESSES

If the computers will be operating only on an internal network, where they are separated from the public network by a router, bridge, or firewall, they are *private* and need only organizational uniqueness. Four blocks of IP addresses have been set aside and can be used by any organization for its private, internal needs without any coordination with any other organization, but these blocks should not be used for directly connecting to the Internet. These private-use blocks of IP addresses are:

- 10.0.0.0 through 10.255.255.255
- 169.254.0.0 through 169.254.255.255 (the APIPA range)
- 172.16.0.0 through 172.31.255.255
- 192.168.0.0 through 192.168.255.255

GET PUBLIC IP ADDRESSES

Computers interfacing directly with the Internet are *public* and thus need a globally unique IP number. If you want a block of public IP addresses, you must request it from one of several organizations, depending on the size of the block that you want. At the local level, a moderate-sized block of IP addresses, can be assigned by your local ISP. For a larger block, a regional ISP may be able to handle the request. If not, you have to go to one of three regional Internet registries:

Continued...

3. If you think you have a problem, double-check all the possible settings previously described.
   - If you are using APIPA, make sure that the computer you are trying to contact is also using that range of numbers either as a static assigned address or with automatic assignment.
   - If all the settings are correct, then check the cabling by making a simple connection to just a couple computers.
   - If you do a direct connection between two computers, remember that you need a special *crossover* cable with the transmit and receive wires reversed.
   - If all else fails, replace the NIC. With a good NIC, good cabling, and the correct settings, you'll be able to network.

Test a Network Setup and Connection

You can use several command-line utilities to test a TCP/IP installation. The more useful of these commands are the following:

- **Ipconfig** is used to determine if a network configuration has been initialized and an IP address assigned. If an IP address and valid subnet mask are returned, then the configuration is initialized and there are no duplicates for the IP address. If a subnet mask of 0.0.0.0 is returned, then the IP address is a duplicate.
- **Hostname** is used to determine the computer name of the local computer.
- **Ping** is used to query either the local computer or another computer on the network to see whether it responds. If the local computer responds, you know that TCP/IP is bound to the local NIC and that both are operating correctly. If the other computer responds, you know that TCP/IP and the NICs in both computers are operating correctly and that the connection between the computers is operable. Figure 9-11 shows the testing results on my system:

1 2 3 4 5 6 7 8 9 10

1 2 3 4 5 6 7 8 9 10

GETTING A BLOCK OF IP ADDRESSES *(Continued)*

- American Registry for Internet Numbers (ARIN), at http://www.arin.net/, which covers North and South America, the Caribbean, and sub-Saharan Africa
- Réseaux IP Européens (RIPE), at http://www.ripe.net/, which covers Europe, the Middle East, and northern Africa
- Asia Pacific Network Information Centre (APNIC), at http://www.apnic.net/, which covers Asia and the Pacific

CAUTION

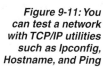

Remember that private ranges work only with computers within their own subnets and with IP addresses from the same range. You can tell what the subnet is from the subnet mask. For example, with a subnet mask of 255.255.255.0, all computers in the network must have IP addresses with the same first three numbers, verying only in the last number. For example, computers with the numbers 192.168.104.001 and 192.168.104.002 are in the same subnet.

NOTE

The 127.0.0.1 IP address is a special address set aside to refer to the computer on which it is entered.

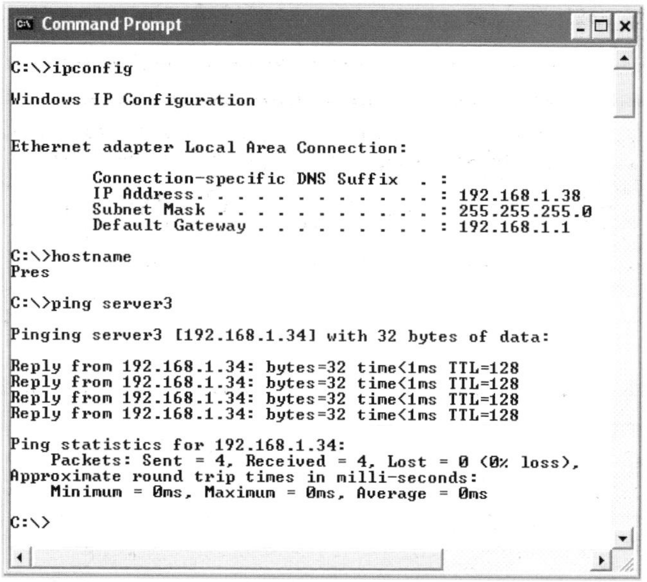

Figure 9-11: You can test a network with TCP/IP utilities such as Ipconfig, Hostname, and Ping

1. Open **Start**, select **All Programs**, choose **Accessories**, and click **Command Prompt**. The Command Prompt window opens.
2. Type ipconfig and press **ENTER**. The IP address and subnet mask of the current computer should be returned. If this did not happen, there is a problem with the current configuration.
3. Type hostname and press **ENTER**. The computer name of the local computer should be returned.
4. Type ping, a computer name, (where computer name is the name of another computer on your network) and press **ENTER**. You should get four replies from the other computer.
5. If Ping did not work with a remote computer, try it on the current computer by typing ping 127.0.0.1 and pressing **ENTER**. Again, you should get four replies, this time from the current computer. If you didn't get a reply here, then you have a problem with either the network setup or the NIC. If you did get a reply here, but not in Step 4, then there is a problem either in the other computer or in the connecting line.
6. Type exit and press **ENTER** to close the Command Prompt.

If you do find a problem here, review earlier sections on setting up network hardware, functions, and protocols to isolate and fix the problem.

How to...

- *Explore a Network*
- *Permanently Connect to a Network Drive*
- *Using Network Addresses*
- *Connect Outside Your Workgroup or Domain*
- *Copy Network Files and Information*
- *Print on Network Printers*
- *Access a Network Internet Connection*
- *Finding a Network Printer*
- *Share Your Files*
- *Share Your Folders and Disks*
- *Share Your Printers*
- *Share an Internet Connection*
- *Set Up a Remote Desktop Connection*
- *Use a Remote Desktop Connection*
- *Set Up Remote Access Service*
- *Use Remote Access Service*
- *Set Up Virtual Private Networking*
- *Choosing VPN and RAS*

Chapter 10
Using Networking

Networking brings a vastly enlarged world of computing to your computer, giving you access to all the computers, printers, and other devices to which you are connected and have permission to access. Using a network and its resources is no more difficult than accessing the hard disk, printer, or Internet connection that are directly connected to your computer. Your network connection can be either wired or wireless and, you'll notice no difference, except for the hardware and the possibility that wireless is slower.

In this chapter, you'll see how to access other computers and printers over a local area network (LAN), how to let others access your computer and resources, and how to access your computer remotely—across a LAN, through a telephone connection, or over the Internet.

1 2 3 4 5 6 7 8 9 10

1 2 3 4 5 6 7 8 9 10

Access Network Resources

Begin to explore networking by looking at the network available to you through your computer. Then, access a disk and retrieve files and folders from another computer, use a network printer, and access the Internet over the network.

Explore a Network

Whether you have just installed a small home network or have just plugged into a large company network, the first thing you'll probably want to do is explore—see what you can see. You can do that from My Network Places or from My Computer, both of which use Windows Explorer.

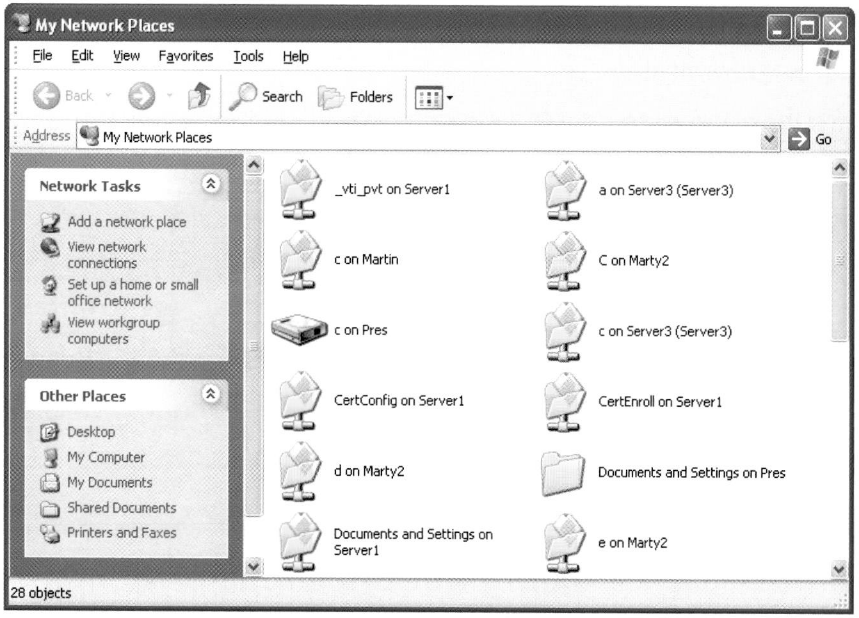

Figure 10-1: Shares are resources on other computers that you can use

EXPLORE USING MY NETWORK PLACES

1. Open **Start**, and click **My Network Places**. The My Network Places window opens, as shown in Figure 10-1. On the right of My Network Places are *shares*, folders or disks on other computers that have been shared and are available to you.
2. Double-click one of the shares. It will open to display the files and folders that are there for you to use.
3. Click **Back**. (If you don't have Back available, click the original My Network Places window.) Click **View Workgroup Computers** (if you are on a domain, this will be View Domain Computers). The computers in your workgroup or domain will be displayed.
4. Double-click one of the computers. It will open and display the shares, printers, and other resources (such as tape drives and removable disks) on that computer, as you can see in Figure 10-2.
5. Click **Back** and click **Close** to close My Network Places.

Figure 10-2: The computers on your network contain the shares and other resources that are available to you

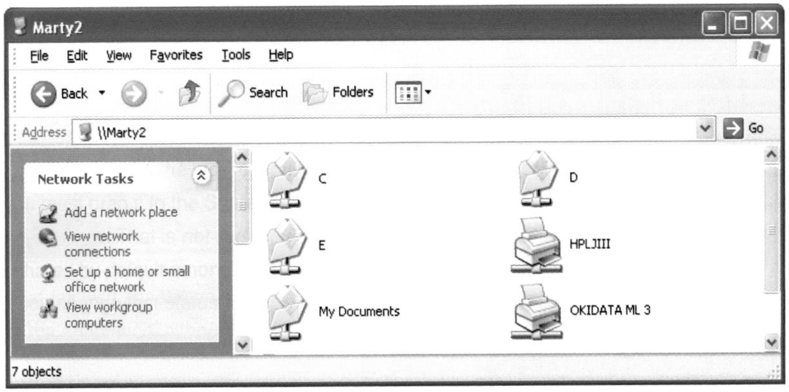

EXPLORE USING MY COMPUTER

My Network Places is just a particular view of Windows Explorer. In most instances, you go out to a network share more directly through My Computer (also a particular view of Windows Explorer).

1. Open **Start**, select **My Computer**, and click **Folders** on the toolbar.
2. In the Folders pane, click **My Network Places** to open it. The network shares will be displayed below My Network Places.
3. Click **Entire Network**, click **Microsoft Windows Network**, click your workgroup or domain, click one of the computers in the workgroup to open it, and, finally, click one of the drives on that computer to open it. You will see the shares on that drive in the right pane.

4. Close My Computer.

NOTE

If you don't see My Network Places on the Start menu, you need to determine whether you are you connected to a network. If you are not sure, refer to Chapter 9 to determine if you are. If you find you are not connected to a network, there are instructions in Chapter 9 for setting it up. After making certain that a network has been set up, if you still do not see My Network Places, use "Explore Using My Computer," later found on this page. After doing that, you should see My Network Places in the Start menu.

TIP

The shares (shared folders, disks, and other resources) that appear when you open My Network Places are the result of your computer having searched your workgroup (or domain) for shares and other resources. When you first set up networking you won't see any shares until they have been shared by other computers and your computer has had time to find them.

Permanently Connect to a Network Share

If you use a specific network share a lot, you may want to connect to it permanently, so you can use it as if it were a drive on your computer. The "share" can be either a folder or a disk drive, and a permanent connection to it is called a "Map Network Drive." Note that it is only "permanent" until you decide to disconnect from the share. See "Disconnect a Mapped Drive" next in this chapter.

1. Open **Start**, select **My Computer**, and click **Folders** on the toolbar.
2. In the Folders pane, click **My Network Places**, click **Entire Network**, click **Microsoft Windows Network**, click your workgroup or domain, and click the computer that contains the share you want to connect to permanently. You should see the share in the right pane.

1 2 3 4 5 6 7 8 9 10

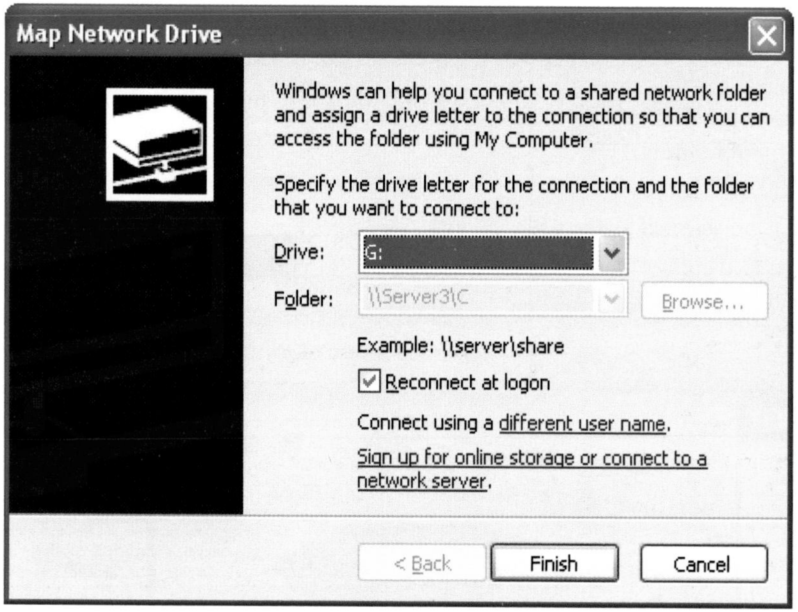

Figure 10-3: Mapping a network drive or share gives you a permanent connection to that device

3. Right-click the share in the right pane, and click **Map Network Drive**. The Map Network Drive dialog box will open (see Figure 10-3).

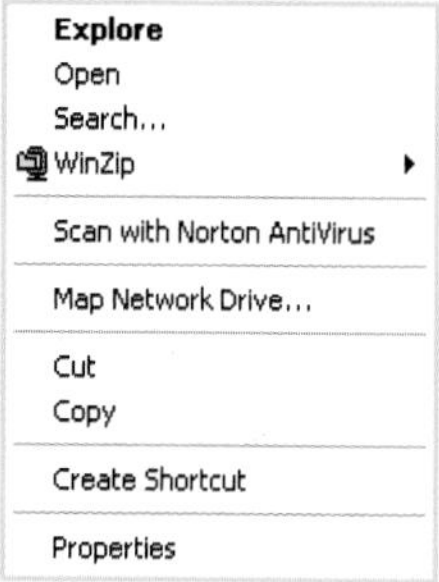

4. Select the drive letter you want to use for the share—the specific folder, if that is applicable—and choose whether you want to reconnect to the share every time you log on to your computer.
5. Click **Finish**. The share will open in a separate window. Close that window.
6. In the Folders pane of the original Windows Explorer window, click the minus sign to the left of **My Network Places** to close it. Then click **My Computer** to open it. Both in the Folders pane and in the detail pane, you should see the new network drive, as shown in Figure 10-4.
7. Close My Computer.

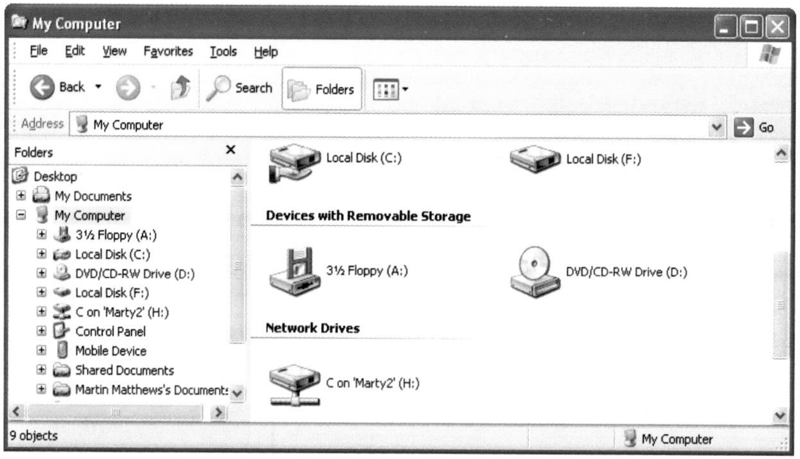

Figure 10-4: A network drive or share in My Computer gives you the same immediate access as any drive on your computer

QUICKSTEPS

USING NETWORK ADDRESSES

Network addressing uses the *Uniform Naming Convention*, or UNC, to identify files, folders, and other resources on any computer on the network.

IDENTIFYING A NETWORK SHARE

A network share, which is a folder or disk on a computer on the network, is identified by: \\computername\pathname\folder or disk nameFor example, on a computer named "Server1" a share named "2005 Budgets" in the Budgeting folder would have the full network address of: \\Server1\Budgeting\2005 Budgets

In most cases it would also work to write: \\Server1\2005 Budgets.

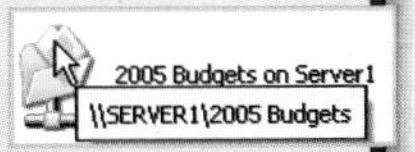

IDENTIFYING A NETWORK PRINTER

Identifying a network printer is very similar to identifying a share. It takes the form of:

\\computername\printername

For example, a printer named HP4500 on Server 1 would have the UNC of: \\Server1\HP4500

NOTE

Once you are on a computer in another workgroup or domain, you can view all the computers in the workgroup or domain by clicking **View Workgroup Computers** in the tasks pane of an Explorer window.

DISCONNECT A MAPPED DRIVE

1. Open **Start**, select **My Computer**, and click **Folders** on the toolbar.
2. In the Folders pane, click **My Computer**, right-click the mapped network share, and click **Disconnect**. The share or drive will disappear from the folder pane.

Connect Outside Your Workgroup Or Domain

If you want to connect to another computer or share outside of your workgroup or domain, you will not see that computer or share when you open My Network Places, and you must use a different procedure to connect to it.

1. Open **Start**, and click **My Network Places**. The My Network Places window opens, as you saw in Figure 10-1.
2. Click **Add A Network Place** in the tasks pane (if needed, click **Folders** on the toolbar to view the tasks pane). The **Add Network Place Wizard** will open.
3. Click **Next**. Click **Choose Another Network Location** and again click **Next**.
4. Enter the network address of the other computer or share (see the QuickSteps "Using Network Addresses") and click **Next**.
5. If requested, enter a user name and a password and click **OK**. Enter a name for the network and click **Next**. Click **Finish**. By default, the computer in the other workgroup will open in Windows Explorer.
6. Close the Explorer.

Copy Network Files and Information

Once you have opened a network share, it is very easy to copy information from the share to your local hard disk:

1. Open **Start**, click **My Computer**, and click **Folders** on the toolbar.
2. In the Folders pane, click **My Network Places** to open it. Then **open Entire Network**, **Microsoft Windows Network**, the workgroup or domain, the computer, drive, and folder(s) in order to see the files that you want to copy.

TIP

You can see the UNC for all the shares on your computer by displaying the shares, as shown in Figure 10-1, and then pausing the mouse pointer on the share.

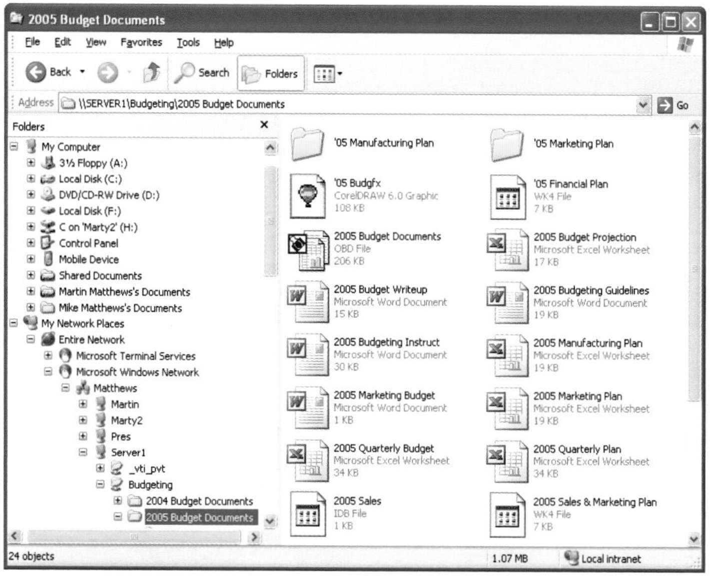

Figure 10-5: You can locate and copy files and folders across the network

3. In the right or pane of Explorer, display the files that you need, as shown in Figure 10-5. In the left pane, open (click the plus (+) sign, do not click the icon to open) your hard disk and the folder(s) you want to hold the information from the network.
4. Click the first file or folder you want to copy, then press and hold **CTRL** clicking the remaining files and/or folders you want. When all are selected, drag them to the folder on the left in which you want them.
5. Close Windows Explorer.

Print on Network Printers

Using a network printer is very little different than using a local printer. With approximately a day on the network, Windows XP should search out and locate most of the shared printers. If you are in a hurry to use a printer, or if for some reason the search did not find the printer you want, you can do your own search for it. See the QuickSteps, "Finding a Network Printer."

To use a network printer that has been found previously, either automatically or manually—from Microsoft Word, for example:

1. Open **File** and click **Print**.
2. Open the **Printer Name** drop-down list and choose the network printer you want to use.
3. Make any other needed adjustments to the printer settings and click **OK** to complete the printing.

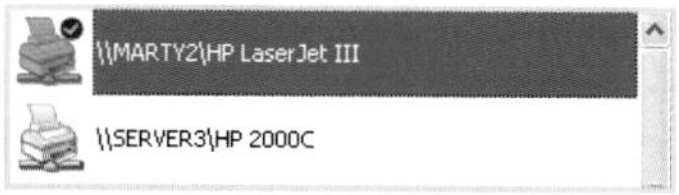

Access a Network Internet Connection

If the network you are on has an Internet connection, you are automatically connected to it and can use it directly unless it requires a user name and password. In most instances, you simply have to open your browser (click **Internet** on the Start menu) or your e-mail program (click **E-Mail**), and you are on and using the Internet. See Chapter 4 for more information.

QUICKSTEPS

FINDING A NETWORK PRINTER

There are two ways to find a network printer: by using Find Printer in some Print dialog boxes and in the Search Companion, and by using Add A Printer in the Printers And Faxes dialog box.

USE FIND PRINTER

Recent versions of Microsoft Office products and other applications have included a Find Printer button to search for and locate network printers. This is the same as the Search Companion's printer search capability, which uses the Windows domain's Active Directory service. To use this you must be in a domain and not in a workgroup.

1. In an Office application, open **File**, click **Print**, and click **Find Printer**.

   –Or–

   Open **Start**, select **Search**, choose **Printers, Computers, or People**, and click **A Printer On The Network**.

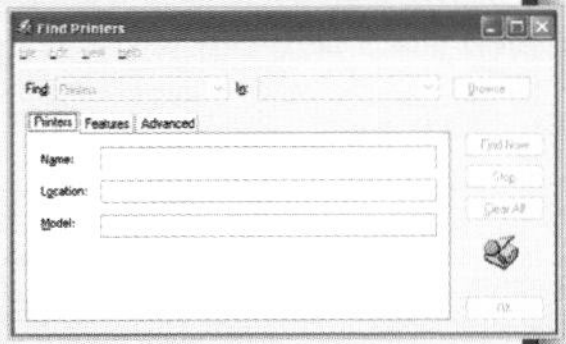

The Find Printers dialog box will open allowing you to search on any of several criteria in three tabs.

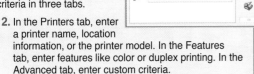

2. In the Printers tab, enter a printer name, location information, or the printer model. In the Features tab, enter features like color or duplex printing. In the Advanced tab, enter custom criteria.
3. Click **Find Now** to search Active Directory for printers. A list of printers will be displayed.
4. Open **View** and click **Details**. This gives you column headings for the list of printers. Click a column heading to sort the list on that column.
5. When you have located the printer you want, right-click that printer and choose **Connect**.

Continued...

Let Others Access Your Resources

The other side of the networking equation is sharing the resources on your computer to allow others to use them. This includes sharing your files, folders, and disks, as well as sharing your printers and other resources, such as a dial-up Internet connection.

Share Your Files

You can share your files by putting them in a shared folder. By default, your computer has one shared folder called Shared Documents (see "Share Your Folders and Disks" to create more shared folders).

1. Open **Start**, choose **My Computer**, and open the disk and folder(s) needed to locate the files you want to share in the right pane.
2. Drag the files you want to share from the right pane to Shared Documents in the tasks pane, as shown in Figure 10-6.
3. Close My Computer.

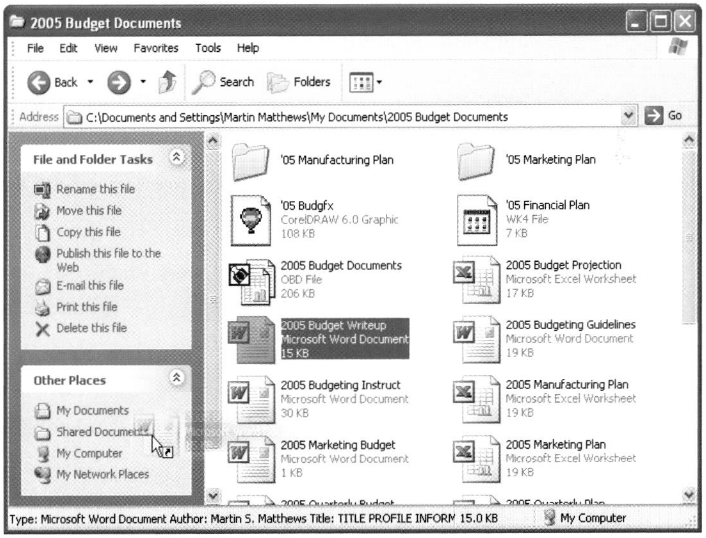

Figure 10-6: You can share a file by putting it in the Shared Documents folder

FINDING A NETWORK PRINTER

(Continued)

6. Close Search Results.

USE ADD A PRINTER

Add A Printer is the most common way to locate a network printer and is available to both workgroup and domain users.

1. Open **Start**, choose **Printers And Faxes**, and click **Add A Printer** in the tasks pane. The Add Printer Wizard opens. Click **Next**.
2. Click **A Network Printer** and click **Next**. Accept the default **Browse For A Printer**, and click **Next**.
3. Click the shared printer you want to use and click **Next**. Click **Yes** or **No** to whether you can to continue and accept the possibility of a virus in the print driver. Click **Yes** or **No** on using this printer as your default printer, click **Next**, and then click **Finish**.
4. Close Printers And Faxes.

NOTE

To share a folder effectively, you may need to open the Security tab of the folder's properties dialog box and set the appropriate permissions for the people who will be accessing the folder. See Chapter 8.

Share Your Folders and Disks

A folder can be shared by creating it within the default shared folder, Shared Documents. In addition, any folder can be shared by changing its properties.

1. Open **Start**, choose **My Computer**, click **Folders**, and open the disk and folder(s) needed to locate the folder you want to share in the right pane.
2. Right-click the folder and choose **Properties**. Click the **Sharing** tab, and click **Share This Folder**, as shown in Figure 10-7.
3. Click **OK**, and close My Computer.

Share Your Printers

The printer(s) directly attached to your computer can be shared with others if you wish.

1. Open **Start**, select **Printers And Faxes**, right-click the printer you want to share, and click **Sharing**.
2. Click **Share This Printer**, and click **OK**.
3. Close Printers And Faxes.

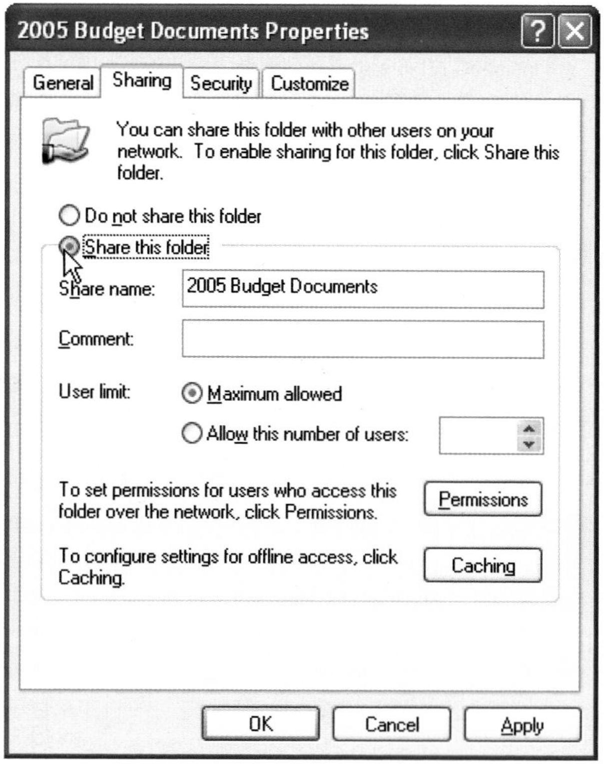

Figure 10-7: Sharing a folder gives people access to it, but they also may need the appropriate permission to do anything with the folder contents

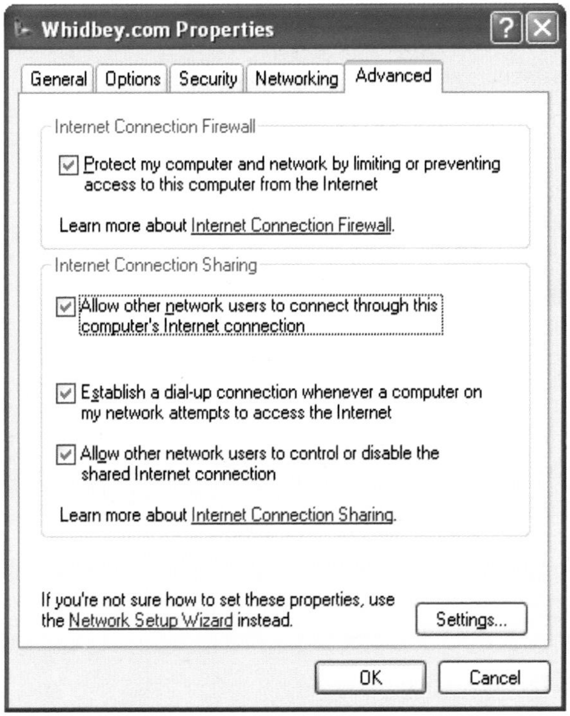

Figure 10-8: With a shared Internet connection, you have even more reason to turn on the firewall

Share an Internet Connection

Chapter 4 describes how to set up a modem and a dial-up Internet connection. Once such a connection is made, it can be shared with other computers on the network. This is called Internet Connection Sharing, or ICS. The computer with the modem is the "host computer" and the other computers are "clients." Both the host and the clients need to be set up independently.

SET UP AN ICS HOST

The ICS host should have its Internet dial-up connection set up and tested, as described in Chapter 4, before you attempt to set up ICS. After that is completed and proven:

1. On the ICS host open **Start**, click **Control Panel**, and double-click **Network Connections** (in Classic view). The Network Connections dialog box opens.

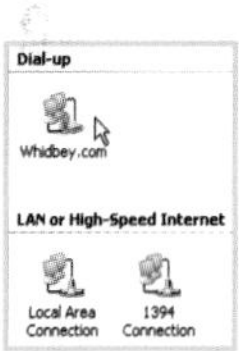

2. Right-click the dial-up Internet connection and choose **Properties**. The connections properties dialog box will open.
3. Click the **Advanced** tab to open it, as shown in Figure 10-8.
4. Turn on both Internet Connect Firewall and Internet Connection Sharing as well as Establish A Dial-Up Connection Whenever A Computer… Whether you allow network users to control the connection is up to you and your computer.
5. Click **OK** and close Network Connections.

SET UP AN ICS CLIENT

The easiest approach to setting up an ICS client is to run Network Setup Wizard.

1. On the ICS client, open **Start**, click **Control Panel**, and double-click **Network Connections** (in Classic view). The Network Connections dialog box opens.
2. Click **Set Up A Home Or Small Office Network** and click **Next** twice.
3. Select **This Computer Connects To The Internet Through Another Computer On My Network…**, and click **Next**.
4. Select **Determine The Appropriate Connections For Me** and click **Next**.
5. Enter a description and name for the computer and click **Next**. Enter a workgroup name.

6. Click **Next**. You'll see a settings summary similar to that shown in Figure 10-9. If it is not correct, click **Back** and correct the problem; otherwise, click **Next**.
7. You are asked if you want to create a Network Setup Disk to use on other computers on the network. Select **Create A Network Setup Disk** and click **Next**.
8. Select the drive, and insert a disk, clicking **Next** after each of those steps. Remove the disk, note the instructions on how to use it, and click **Next**. Click **Finish**.

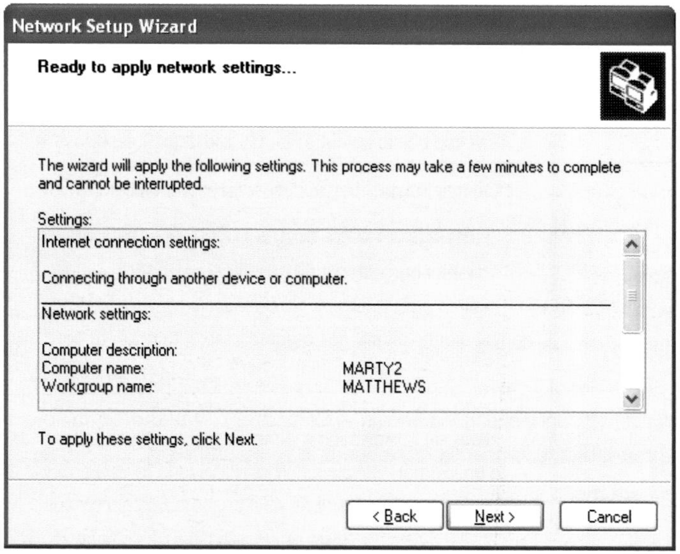

Figure 10-9: The Network Setup Wizard can set up your computer to be an ICS client

TEST ICS CLIENT

Test the Internet connection from the client by opening first your browser and then your e-mail program.

1. Open **Start** and click **Internet**. Your browser will open and cause your ICS host to dial the Internet. After a minute, your browser should display your selected home page. (See Chapter 4 for setting up the Internet Explorer browser and selecting a home page.)
2. Open **Start** and click **E-Mail**. Your e-mail program will open and, if it isn't already connected, your ICS host will dial the Internet. If it's not automatic, select to send and receive your mail. (See Chapter 4 for setting up Outlook Express mail program.)
3. When you are ready, close your browser and mail program. If desired, right-click the Internet connection in the notification area on the host and click **Disconnect**.

Work Remotely

Windows XP has several ways for you to work remotely—remotely from another computer to your own office computer (Remote Desktop connection), remotely from a home computer or laptop to an office server (Remote Access Service or RAS), and remotely from a laptop over the Internet to an office server (virtual private networking or VPN). The objective in all cases is to transfer information and utilize resources from a distance, not necessarily using a local area network (LAN) connection. All three services—Remote Desktop, RAS, and VPN—require a Remote Desktop host.

Set Up a Remote Desktop Connection

Remote Desktop enables you to literally take control of another computer and do everything you could do if you were sitting in front of that computer. Remote Desktop can be run over a LAN, a dial-up connection, or the Internet. In Remote Desktop, there is the computer you are sitting at—the *client*—and the computer you are accessing—the *host*. To set up the host, you must first establish user accounts and then enable both a LAN-based host and a web-based host.

NOTE

Windows XP Home Edition cannot be a Remote Desktop host, but it can be a Remote Desktop client.

SET UP REMOTE DESKTOP ACCOUNTS

To use Remote Desktop, the host must have user accounts established for that purpose, and the user account must have a password. Therefore, the first step in setting up the account is to set up one or more of such accounts.

1. Open **Start**, click **Control Panel**, and double-click **User Accounts** (in Classic view).
2. Click **Create A New Account**, enter the name for the account (I'm using "Remote"), click **Next**, select the type of account you want, and click **Create Account**.
3. Click the new account, click **Create A Password**, enter the password, press **TAB**, type the password again, press **TAB** twice, enter a hint if you wish (anyone can see the hint), and press **ENTER**. Close the User Accounts window.

Figure 10-10: User accounts must be members of the Remote Desktop Users group in order to use remote connectivity

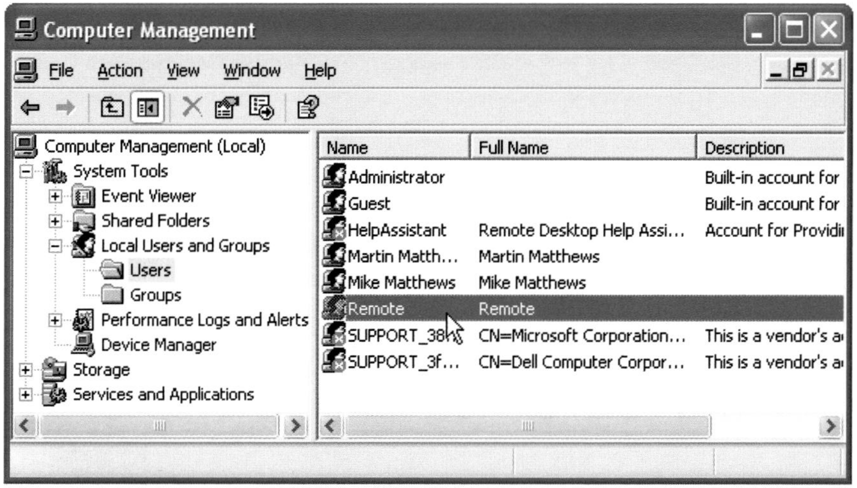

4. In the Control Panel, double-click **Administrative Tools** (in Classic view), and double-click **Computer Management**.
5. In the left pane, open **Computer Management**, **System Tools**, **Local Users and Groups**, and click **Users**. In the detail or right pane, double-click the new user you just created, as shown in Figure 10-10.
6. Click the **Member Of** tab and click **Add**. In the Select Groups dialog box, click **Advanced** and then click **Find Now** to search for groups. Select **Remote Desktop Users**, click **OK** three times, and close both the Computer Management and Administrative Tools windows.

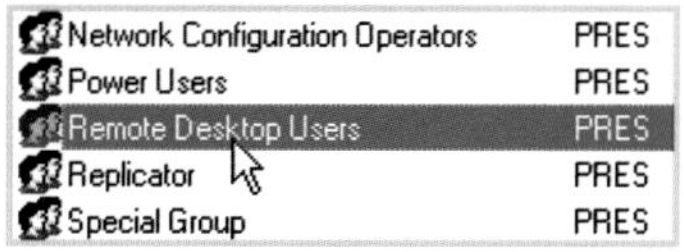

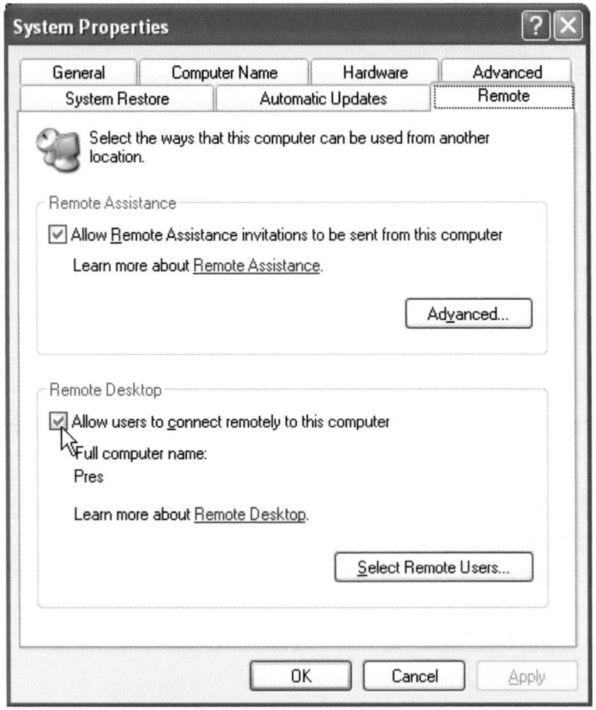

Figure 10-11: Remote Desktop is not turned on by default

NOTE

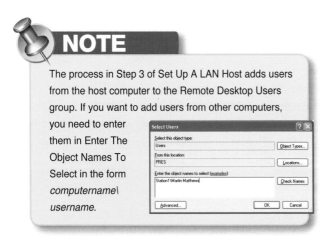

The process in Step 3 of Set Up A LAN Host adds users from the host computer to the Remote Desktop Users group. If you want to add users from other computers, you need to enter them in Enter The Object Names To Select in the form *computername\ username.*

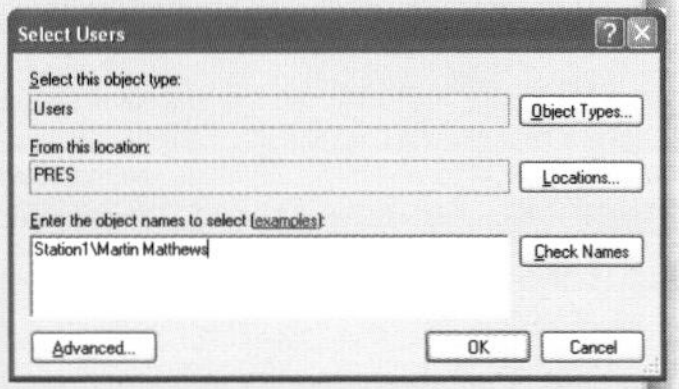

SET UP A LAN-BASED HOST

Set up the host for using Remote Desktop within a LAN:

1. Open **Start**, click **Control Panel**, and double-click **System** (in Classic view). Click the **Remote** tab. In the bottom Remote Desktop panel, click **Allow Users To Connect Remotely To This Computer**, as shown in Figure 10-11.
2. If you are reminded that accounts to access Remote Desktop need passwords, click **OK**. Click **Select Remote Users**. Users that you added to the Remote Desktop Users group are displayed.
3. If you want to add more users to the Remote Desktop Users group, click **Add**, click **Advanced**, and click **Find Now**. Select the users to include by pressing and holding **CTRL** while clicking the users, and then click **OK** four times to close all open dialog boxes. Close the Control Panel.

SET UP A WEB-BASED HOST

The Web-based host requires that Windows XP Professional's Internet Information Services (IIS) be installed (IIS is not available on Windows XP Home Edition), followed by the Web-based Remote Desktop host:

1. Open **Start**, click **Control Panel**, double-click **Add Or Remove Programs**, and select **Add/Remove Windows Components**.
2. Click **Internet Information Services**, click **Details**, select **World Wide Web Service**, and again click **Details**. If it isn't already selected, click **Remote Desktop Web Connection**, leave the Printers Virtual Directory and World Wide Web Service selected, as shown in Figure 10-12, click **OK** twice, and click **Next**.
3. Insert your Windows XP Professional CD when requested, click **OK**, and close the Setup Welcome window. When IIS installation is complete, click **Finish**, close Add Or Remove Programs, close the Control Panel, and remove the CD.

SET UP A REMOTE DESKTOP CLIENT

The Remote Desktop Connection client is probably already installed on the computer you will be using for the client, since it is a part of the default Windows XP installation. Check on it and, if it is not installed, do so.

1. Open **Start**, select **All Programs**, choose **Accessories**, and click **Communications**. You should see Remote Desktop Connection.
2. If you see Remote Desktop Connection, you need to do nothing further here.

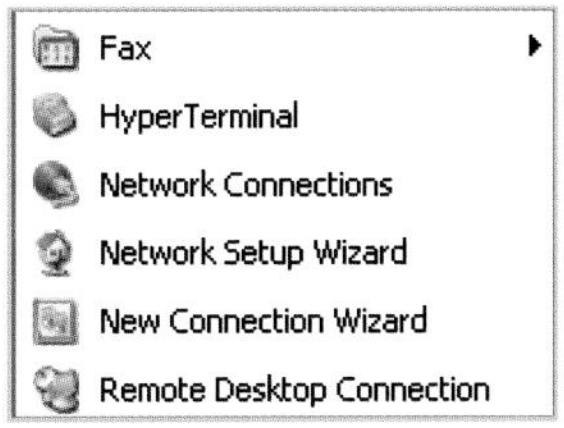

3. If you do not see Remote Desktop Connection, insert the Windows XP installation CD in its drive. In the Welcome window, click **Perform Additional Tasks**, and then click **Set Up Remote Desktop Connection**. The Remote Desktop Connection – InstallShield Wizard opens.
4. Click **Next**, click **I Accept The Terms In The License Agreement**, and click **Next**. The current User Name and Organization are displayed, as is the default Anyone Who Uses This Computer Can Use Remote Desktop Connection. Accept or change these as needed, click **Next**, and then click **Install**
5. When the installation is complete, click **Finish**, close Setup's Welcome window, and remove the CD.

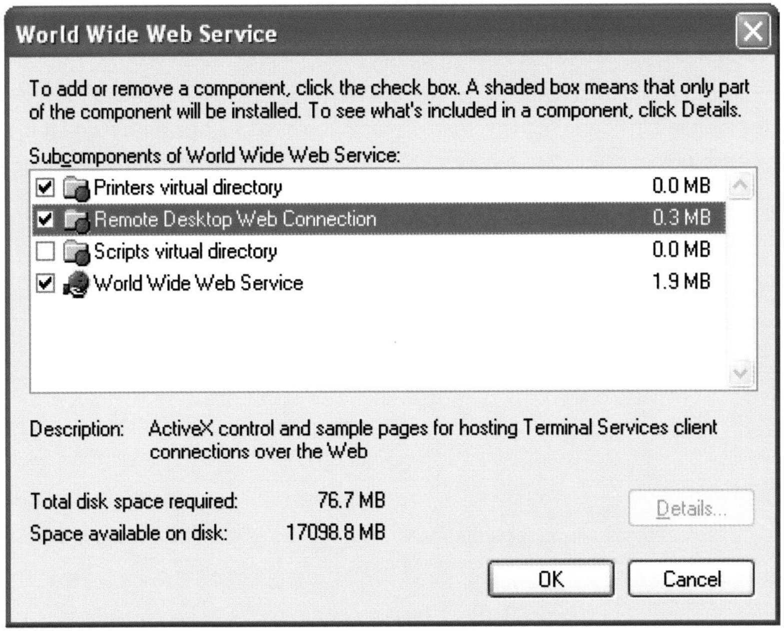

Figure 10-12: Remote Desktop Web Connection requires that you install Internet Information Services

CONNECT TO A REMOTE DESKTOP OVER A LAN

When you are sitting at the client computer and are connected to the host with a LAN, connect to Remote Desktop host:

1. Open **Start**, select **All Programs**, choose **Accessories**, and click **Communications**.
2. Click **Remote Desktop Connection**. The Remote Desktop Connection dialog box opens.

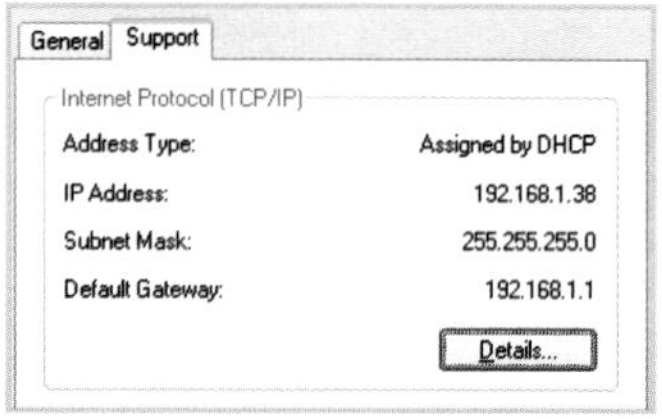

3. Enter the name or IP address of the computer to which you want to connect. If you are not sure of the computer name, click **Browse For More** in the Computer drop-down list box, which will display a list of the computers in your immediate domain or workgroup.
4. After you have entered the computer name, click **Connect**. The Remote Desktop toolbar appears in the top center of the screen. Enter the user name and password for the Remote Desktop host computer, and click **OK**. If you get the message that someone is currently logged on to the remote host, decide if you can disconnect them and click the appropriate choice. (See "Use a Remote Desktop.")

Figure 10-13: A remote desktop Web connection begins in a browser, but it can be set to go to full screen so that the browser window isn't displayed

1 2 3 4 5 6 7 8 9 10

CONNECT TO A REMOTE DESKTOP OVER THE WEB

The use of a Web connection can be across a local intranet within an organization or across the Internet. The steps are the same; the only difference is the security. For an Internet connection, you will probably want to use VPN, which is discussed later in this chapter. Here is a simpler and less secure approach to be used with an intranet:

1. Open **Start**, click **Internet**, and enter the Uniform Resource Locator (URL) for the host computer followed by Tsweb. For example, *http://hostname/tsweb*. Press **ENTER**. The Remote Desktop Web Connection page will open, as shown in Figure 10-13.
2. Enter the remote host's computer name or IP address (Internet Protocol, see Note on this page), select the screen size to use, and click **Connect**. Enter your User Name and Password and click **OK**. If you get the message that someone is currently logged on to the remote host, decide if you can disconnect them and click the appropriate choice. You will be logged on as you were in the LAN-based technique.

NOTE

The Internet Protocol (IP) address is assigned, either temporarily or permanently, to every computer on the Internet and every computer on a LAN that uses the TCP/IP protocol. It is, of course, simpler just to enter the computer name, but when you are outside of your network—at home, for example—you will probably have to use the computer's IP address. You can find out a computer's IP address by opening **Start**, clicking **Control Panel**, and double-clicking **Network Connections** (in Classic view). Right-click the connection you use to connect to your intranet or the Internet, and choose **Status**. In the LAN Status dialog box, click the **Support** tab. You will see the IP address of the computer you are on.

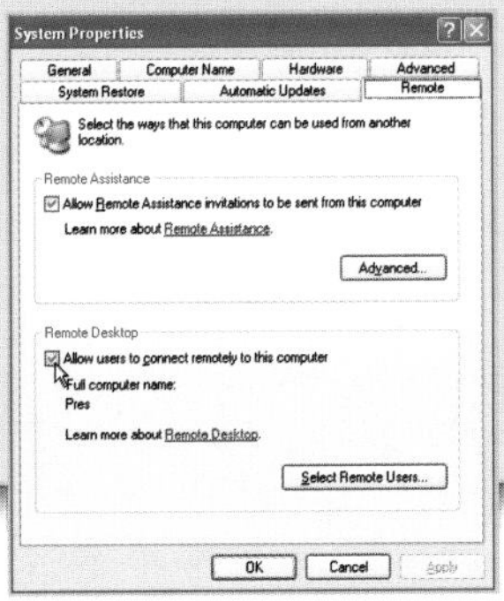

Use a Remote Desktop Connection

Once you are connected to the host computer, you can do much of what you could do if you were sitting in front of that computer. You can run programs, access data, and perform most other functions you could perform at that computer. In addition, the Remote Desktop toolbar, called the "Connection Bar," allows you to close the Remote Desktop window without logging out, so your programs will keep running; to minimize the window, so you can see the computer you are sitting at; and to maximize the window. Additionally, there is a pushpin icon that determines whether the Connection Bar is always on the desktop or if it is only there when you move the mouse to the top of the screen.

The Remote Desktop also gives you the capability of transferring information between the host computer and the client computer you are using. This means that you can:

TIP

If your LAN has particularly heavy traffic and is slow, you might want to reduce the screen size and number of colons.

- Print to a local printer connected to the client—the default
- Work with files on both the remote host and the client in the same window—not the default
- Cut and paste between both computers and documents on either one—not the default

The local client resources that are available in a Remote Desktop session are controlled by the Remote Desktop Connection dialog box options.

1. Open **Start**, select **All Programs**, choose **Accessories**, select **Communications**, and click **Remote Desktop Connection**. The Remote Desktop Connection dialog box opens. Click **Options**, and the box expands to give you a number of controls for Remote Desktop.
2. Click the **Display** tab. The default for a LAN is to use Full Screen and up to True Color (24 bit), if your computer can handle it, as well as to display the Connection Bar.
3. Click the **Local Resources** tab. As you can see in Figure 10-14, you can determine if you want sound brought to the client and if you want the ability to use shortcut keys. If you want to transfer information—even cut and paste—between the two computers, select Disk Drives. If you want to print on the printer attached to the local client, keep the default Printers selection. If you intend to use a modem or other serial device on the local client, choose Serial Ports.
4. If you want to start a program when you open the Remote Desktop Connection, open the **Programs** tab, click the check box, and enter the path and file name of the program and the starting folder to use.
5. Click the **Experience** tab and select the connection speed you are using. This will determine which of the items below the drop-down list box are checked. You can change the individual items if you want.
6. Click the **General** tab. If you will use several settings, save the ones you just made by clicking **Save As**, entering a name, and clicking **Save**.
7. Finally, enter your password and click **Connect**.

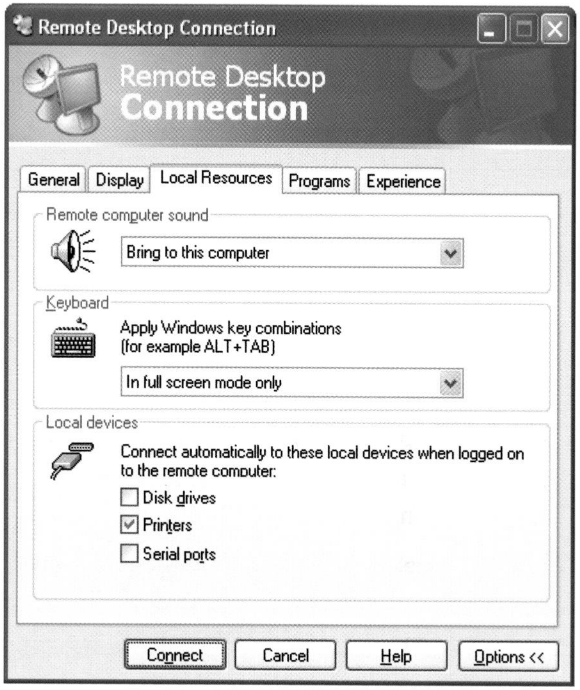

Figure 10-14: You can control what client devices are available with Remote Desktop

8. When you are done using Remote Desktop, you may leave it in any of three ways:

- Click **Close** on the Connection Bar. This leaves you logged on, and any programs you have will remain running. If you restart Remote Desktop Connection with the host computer and no one else has logged on locally, you will return to the same session you left.
- Open **Start** and click **Log Off**. This terminates your Remote Desktop session, and all programs are stopped. If you restart Remote Desktop Connection with the host computer and no one else has logged on locally, you will begin a new session.
- Open **Start** and click **Disconnect**. This is the same as clicking the Close button in the Connection Bar.

> **NOTE**
>
> To cut or copy and paste, you must have the local client's disk drives available. They must therefore be selected in the Remote Desktop Connection dialog box Local Resources tab.

Set Up Remote Access Service

Remote Access Service, or *RAS* (pronounced "razz"), allows a computer to use a dial-up phone line to connect directly to another computer without using the Internet. The receiving computer, or host, can allow the calling computer, or client, to utilize the network to which the host is connected and to use Remote Desktop.

> **TIP**
>
> RAS is a foundation service behind VPN, and making sure that RAS is operating properly will significantly help you set up VPN. I therefore recommend that you set up RAS before attempting VPN.

SET UP RAS ON THE HOST

Setting up RAS and using the host's connection to the network assumes that the correct networking hardware has been installed and is operating properly with the correct drivers. It also assumes that Windows XP has been configured appropriately. See Chapter 9 to assure yourself of this.

RAS is installed by default as a part of installing Windows XP Professional, but it is not enabled. Therefore, setting up RAS is simply enabling and configuring it. To do this, you must have administrative privileges.

> **NOTE**
>
> For RAS and especially for VPN, you need to have a static IP address assigned by an ISP. In other words, you need an IP address that is acceptable across the Internet, not one, such as 10.0.0.2, that you assigned yourself.

1. Open **Start**, select **Control Panel**, and double-click **Network Connections** (in Classic view).
2. Click **Create A New Connection**. The New Connection Wizard will open. Click **Next**.

NOTE

RAS can be configured to call back a person who is trying to connect through a dial-up connection. You may want to do this as a security measure if the callback number is fixed, or you may want to allow the caller to identify a callback when the cost of the outbound call from the host is cheaper than the inbound call from the client. You can set this on a user-by-user basis in the User Permissions page of the New Connection Wizard by clicking a user, clicking **Properties**, and opening the **Callback** tab.

Figure 10-15: RAS allows a remote computer to connect to the network through a modem

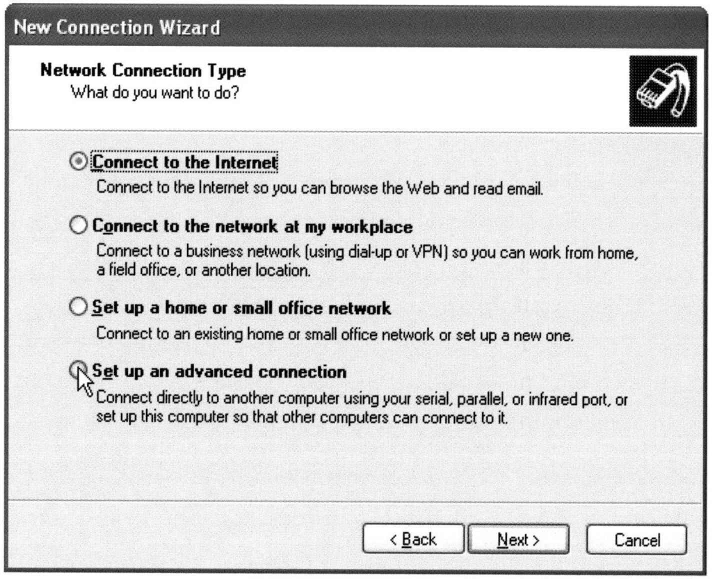

3. Click the bottom option, **Set Up An Advanced Connection**, which, as you can see in Figure 10-15, includes setting "up this computer so that other computers can connect to it." Click **Next**.
4. Accept the default of **Accept Incoming Connections** and click **Next**. Select the modem as the connection device and click **Next**.
5. Click **Allow Virtual Private Connections**, since you will be doing that eventually, and click **Next**.
6. Select the users you want to be able to come into the RAS connection. After you complete selecting and entering the desired user information (see the Note about calling back), click **Next**.
7. Select the networking software you want active (which is probably already selected) and click **Next**, and then click **Finish**. A new Incoming Connections icon will appear in the Network Connections windows.

SET UP A DIAL-UP CONNECTION IN THE CLIENT

To use RAS, you must have a dial-up connection in the client. It is assumed that the client is also running Windows XP, either Home or Professional, and that you are using a modem connection that is already installed and running (Chapter 4 has instructions for installing a modem).

1. On the client computer, open **Start**, select **Control Panel**, and double-click **Network Connections** (in Classic view). In the Network Connections dialog box that opens, click **Create A New Connection** to open the New Connection Wizard. Click **Next**.
2. Click **Connect To The Network At My Workplace** and then click **Next**. Select **Dial-Up Connection** and click **Next**. Enter a name for the connection and once more click **Next**.
3. Enter the phone number of the server (including, if necessary, "1" and the area code), then click **Next**. Depending on how the client is set up, you may be asked if you want the connection for Anyone's Use or for My Use Only. Respond and click **Next**.
4. If you want a shortcut to this connection on the desktop, select that option and then click **Finish**. A new connection will appear in the Network Connections window and, if you chose it, on the desktop.

Use Remote Access Service

With a dial-up connection set up on the client and a remote access server set up and enabled on the server, you can use RAS with these steps:

1. Log on to the dial-up client with a user name and password that can be authenticated by the RAS. Then, on the client, open **Start**, choose **Connect To**, and select the dial-up connection you want to use. The Connect dialog box opens, as you can see in Figure 10-16.
2. Enter the appropriate user name and password, and click **Dial**. You will see messages stating that the number you entered is being dialed, that the user name and password are being checked, that the computer is being registered on the network, and that the connection is complete. The connection icon will appear in the notification area on the right of the taskbar.
3. Test the connection in the client by opening **My Network Places** and looking at the network for remote shares. If you can see these shares, the remote access connection is working.
4. Test the connection in the host by opening **Start**, selecting **Connect To**, clicking **Show All Connections**. In the Network Connections window, you should see 1 Client Connected.
5. Use the connection and try Remote Desktop on it. When you are done testing the RAS connection, you can terminate it by clicking the connection icon in the notification area on the right of the task-bar of the client and then clicking **Disconnect** in the dialog box that opens.

With RAS fully accessible from a remote dial-up client, you know that all but the unique VPN components of the two tested computers are entirely operational. If your dial-up to RAS connection did not work, look back at Chapters 4 and 9, which discuss communications and networking in more detail.

TIP

Be sure to test RAS with the two computers near each other so that you can make any necessary adjustments to the settings before trying this at a distance. You will need two phone lines, and be sure to disconnect the client from the network.

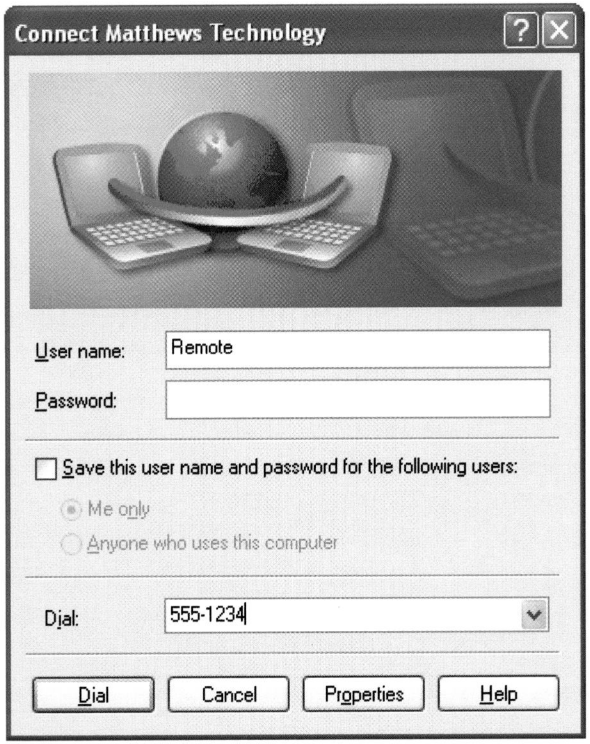

Figure 10-16: Connecting to a RAS host requires a modem in both the client and the host with a phone line between them

Set Up Virtual Private Networking

Virtual private networking (VPN) uses an insecure public network to handle secure private networking. Most commonly, VPN means using the Internet to connect to a LAN. You can think of VPN as a secure pipe through the Internet connecting computers on either end. VPN replaces both leased lines between facilities and the need for long-distance dial-up connections with RAS. In both cases, significant cost savings are achieved.

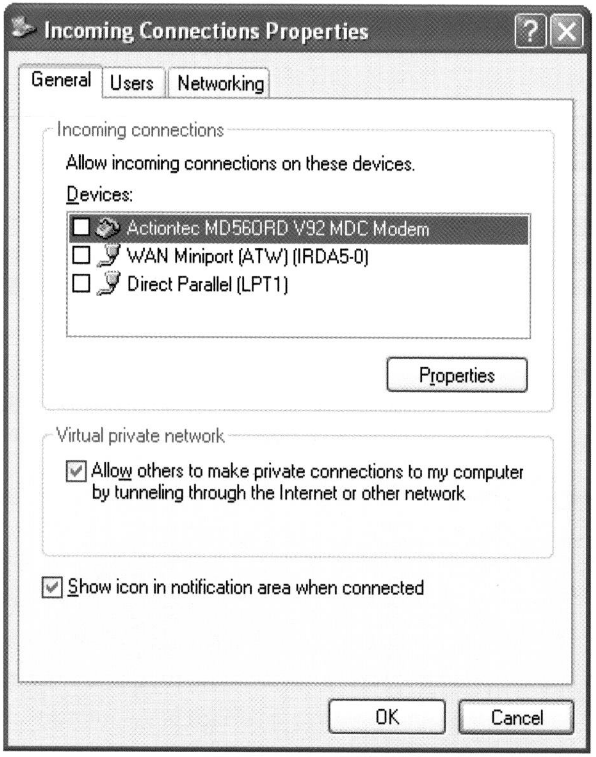

Figure 10-17: VPN comes into the host over the Internet

SET UP A VPN HOST

To set up VPN, you need to have both networking and Remote Access Service (RAS) set up and running. VPN requires that you have an incoming connection (RAS) configured for VPN, which, if you followed the earlier instructions for RAS, you have already done. Check to make sure RAS is properly configured in the host for VPN:

1. Open **Start**, select **Control Panel**, and double-click **Network Connections** (in Classic view). If you don't have Incoming Connections, see "Set Up RAS on the Host" earlier in this chapter.
2. Double-click the **Incoming Connections** icon. Uncheck the devices that are checked, and make sure the Virtual Private Network Allow Others To Make Private Connections… box is checked, as shown in Figure 10-17.
3. Make one final check of the Users tab to assure yourself that the users you want have the appropriate permission, and then click **OK**.

QUICKSTEPS

CHOOSING VPN OR RAS

If you have a choice between a VPN/Internet connection and a direct dial-up RAS connection, consider the pros and cons of each choice.

CHOOSE RAS

Factors that would lead you to choose RAS, given that RAS is over a public phone line and uses a 56 Kbps modem on both ends:

- An RAS connection is simpler to set up.
- An RAS connection may be easier to use.

CHOOSE VPN

Factors that would lead you to choose VPN, assuming that it is over a high-speed Internet connection on both ends:

- A VPN connection is faster with the assumptions here.
- A VPN connection is probably more secure.
- A VPN connection is possibly cheaper if the RAS connection requires a long distance toll.

NOTE

It is very important that you know RAS is operating correctly before setting up VPN. Too often, a problem in RAS is the cause for VPN to operate incorrectly.

SET UP A VPN CLIENT

A VPN client requires a connection to the Internet, possibly a dial-up connection, and then an Internet connection between the client and the VPN host. In Windows XP, there is an integrated and automated approach to these two tasks, but it is still done in two steps: connecting to the Internet and connecting to the VPN host.

Setting up a dial-up connection is described above in "Set Up a Dial-Up Connection in the Client," and setting up a LAN connection is described in Chapters 4 and 9. The VPN connection is just another network connection:

1. Open **Start**, select **Control Panel**, and double-click **Network Connections** (in Classic view). In the Network Connections window, click **Create A New Connection** to start the New Connection Wizard. Click **Next**.
2. Select **Connect To The Network At My Workplace** and click **Next**. Choose **Virtual Private Network Connection**, as shown in Figure 10-18, and click **Next**.
3. Enter the name of the company or connection, click **Next**, choose whether to automatically dial a connection or use an existing connection, (if you have a direct broadband connection to the Internet and not a dial-up, click Do Not Dial The Initial Connection), and click **Next**.

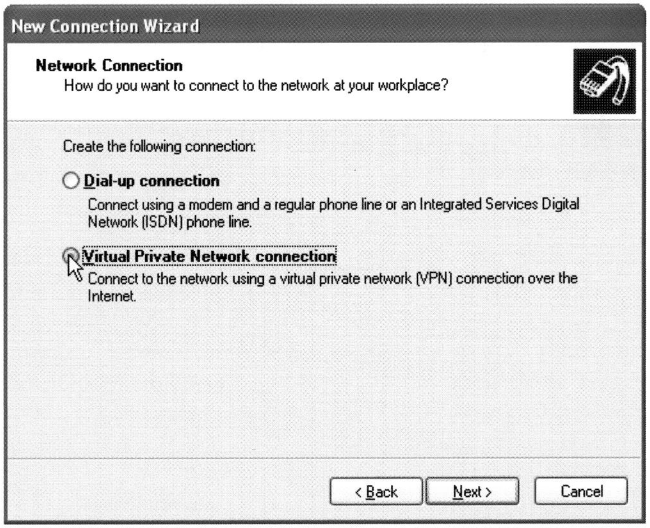
New Connection Wizard
Network Connection
How do you want to connect to the network at your workplace?
Create the following connection:
Dial-up connection
Connect using a modem and a regular phone line or an Integrated Services Digital Network (ISDN) phone line.
Virtual Private Network connection
Connect to the network using a virtual private network (VPN) connection over the Internet.
< Back
Next >
Cancel

Figure 10-18: The client needs both an Internet connection and VPN connection to make VPN work

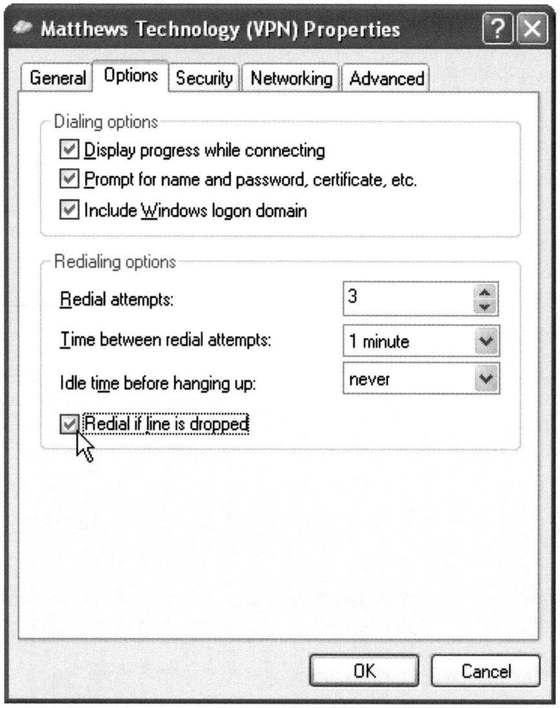

Figure 10-19: The biggest problem with VPN is getting all the settings correct

4. Enter a registered host name (such as osborne.com) or an IP address, like 123.10.78.100, and click **Next**. If you get the Connection Availability dialog box again, determine if you want the connection for Anyone's Use or for My Use Only, click **Next**, and click **Finish**. The Connect dialog box will open.
5. Click **Dial**, or click **Connect** if you have a direct connection, to establish the Internet connection. After the Internet connection is established, enter the user name and password required by the VPN host, choose whether to save the user name and password for you personally or for anyone using this computer, and click **Properties**.
6. Click the **Options** tab. If your client computer is on a domain, select **Include Windows Logon Domain**; if you are using a dial-up connection, select **Redial If Line Is Dropped**, as shown in Figure 10-19. In the Security tab, use **Typical** settings and check **Automatically Use My Windows Logon Name And Password**.
7. Click the **Networking** tab, select **PPTP VPN** as the Type Of VPN, clear **File And Printer Sharing For Microsoft Networks**, and click **OK**. You should be connected to the VPN server and be able to browse the portions of the network for which you have permission. A balloon should confirm the connection, and two connection icons should appear in the notification area on the right of the taskbar.

If you did not connect, take heart; I didn't connect the first time, either. There are a number of reasons for this to happen. If RAS works, many of the potential reasons are eliminated. First, look at whether the firewall is enabled on the host (it shouldn't be) by right-clicking the Internet connection, selecting **Properties**, clicking the **Advanced** tab, and making sure the check box is unchecked. Then look at the permissions that have been established for the VPN user in the host by opening **Control Panel**, double-clicking **Administrative Tools**, double-clicking **Computer Management**, and opening **System Tools**, **Local Users and Groups**, **Users**. Then double-click the user name, open the **Member Of** tab, and look at the groups assigned to the user. Finally, carefully go over all the preceding steps looking for what you did differently.

Index

Q

R

S

T

U

V

W

Z

International Contact Information

AUSTRALIA
McGraw-Hill Book Company Australia Pty. Ltd.
TEL +61-2-9900-1800
FAX +61-2-9878-8881
http://www.mcgraw-hill.com.au
books-it_sydney@mcgraw-hill.com

CANADA
McGraw-Hill Ryerson Ltd.
TEL +905-430-5000
FAX +905-430-5020
http://www.mcgraw-hill.ca

GREECE, MIDDLE EAST, & AFRICA
(Excluding South Africa)
McGraw-Hill Hellas
TEL +30-210-6560-990
TEL +30-210-6560-993
TEL +30-210-6560-994
FAX +30-210-6545-525

MEXICO (Also serving Latin America)
McGraw-Hill Interamericana Editores S.A. de C.V.
TEL +525-1500-5108
FAX +525-117-1589
http://www.mcgraw-hill.com.mx
carlos_ruiz@mcgraw-hill.com

SINGAPORE (Serving Asia)
McGraw-Hill Book Company
TEL +65-6863-1580
FAX +65-6862-3354
http://www.mcgraw-hill.com.sg
mghasia@mcgraw-hill.com

SOUTH AFRICA
McGraw-Hill South Africa
TEL +27-11-622-7512
FAX +27-11-622-9045
robyn_swanepoel@mcgraw-hill.com

SPAIN
McGraw-Hill/Interamericana de España, S.A.U.
TEL +34-91-180-3000
FAX +34-91-372-8513
http://www.mcgraw-hill.es
professional@mcgraw-hill.es

UNITED KINGDOM, NORTHERN,
EASTERN, & CENTRAL EUROPE
McGraw-Hill Education Europe
TEL +44-1-628-502500
FAX +44-1-628-770224
http://www.mcgraw-hill.co.uk
emea_queries@mcgraw-hill.com

ALL OTHER INQUIRIES Contact:
McGraw-Hill/Osborne
TEL +1-510-420-7700
FAX +1-510-420-7703
http://www.osborne.com
omg_international@mcgraw-hill.com